D1797384

Teacher's Book

¡Así!

1

BARBARA BROWN, NIOBE O'CONNOR AND AMANDA RAINGER
SERIES AUTHORS: MICHAEL CALVERT AND HELENA GONZÁLEZ-FLORIDO

Published in 2004 by:
Nelson Thornes Ltd
Delta Place
27 Bath Road
CHELTENHAM
GL53 7TH
United Kingdom

04 05 06 07 08 / 10 9 8 7 6 5 4 3 2 1

A catalogue record for this book is available from the British Library

ISBN 0 7487 7812 8

Page make-up by TechSet Ltd., Gateshead

Printed in Great Britain by Antony Rowe

Contents

Introduction

Welcome to *¡Así!*, a three-stage course designed to guide and motivate your students as they learn Spanish and develop their skills as language learners.

¡Así! 1 addresses all the major recent initiatives for raising standards seamlessly in one course:

- it fulfils the requirements of the **National Curriculum** for England and Wales
- it is underpinned by the **QCA Scheme of Work**
- it is specially written to support the **MFL KS3 Framework** (final published version)
- it is also appropriate for the **5–14 Curriculum** in Scotland.

Components

Student's Book: designed to help students learn

- The Student's Book has 12 short units.
- The units are composed of four self-contained sections, which begin with clearly defined objectives so goals are quickly achievable.
- Exercises marked i**extra**! provide a challenge for more able students.
- Bilingual vocabulary lists at the end of each unit provide a clear reference and support.
- Each unit has two pages of additional practice in the *¡Ahora tú!* section at the back of the Student's Book. These provide differentiated self-access exercises for each of the unit sections, and are ideal for homework, cover lessons or quiet work in class.
- After every two units, a revision page with exercises covering all four skill areas prepares students for the assessment.
- Every second unit also has a page of extended reading, with accompanying exercises.

Resource and Assessment File

- Each unit is supported by nine worksheets:

Visuals	pictures and labels for practising key language, which can be copied onto acetate for the OHP or onto paper. They can be cut up and used in guessing or matching games (see list on page 10).
Resumen:	bilingual reference lists which can be pasted into students' exercise books.
Escuchar:	additional listening practice.
Hablar:	pairwork or group exercises.
Leer:	further reading practice.
Escribir:	writing practice of key language.
Skills:	a focus on developing language-learning skills.
Gramática:	further practice of key grammar.
i**extra**!	challenging exercises to stretch the more able.

- The file also contains a 30-page assessment section.

Workbooks

- Differentiated workbooks provide further practice of the key language: reinforcement at a simple level in Workbook A and more challenging exercises in Workbook B.
- For ease of use in the classroom, the two levels contain parallel exercises.

Audio CD pack

- The four audio CDs may be copied for use within your school or for students' individual work at home.
- Transcripts are provided in the Teacher's Book, within the notes for each section.

Flashcards and OHTs CD-Rom

- The CD-ROM provides 105 flashcards and 37 pages which can be printed onto OHTs, laminated or displayed using a data projector or electronic whiteboard (see page 10 for a list).

Just Click CD-ROM

- The teacher's resource is both a planning tool and a bank of resources, consisting of editable schemes of work and lesson plans, interactive exercises and a bank of images, videos, animations etc. for use on an interactive whiteboard or with a projector and screen for whole-class teaching, ready-made lesson sequences and a tool to create your own lessons.
- The student's resource contains interactive exercises for students to use on individual PCs, games and readers.

Teacher's Book

- The Teacher's Book provides detailed teaching notes and suggestions, answers and audio transcripts for the students' exercises, plus ideas for starters and plenaries.
- The National Curriculum levels and KS3 Framework Objectives are given for each exercise.
- An overview grid at the beginning of each unit will help you plan your work.
- The Framework section on page 12 provides you with detailed information and guidance in implementing the Framework objectives in your lessons.

Learning new language

- *¡Así! 1* is underpinned by a sound methodology: after new language is presented, students practise it thoroughly in guided exercises before they go on to use it productively.
- Key language is outlined in boxes within each section so that students know exactly what they are practising.
- Bilingual vocabulary lists at the end of each unit provide a clear reference and support, and include a particular focus on high-frequency words. They are also reproduced on worksheets, so that they can be pasted into students' exercise books.
- Tips on how to learn new language help students to memorise what they have been practising.
- Key language is revised and recycled throughout the course for additional reinforcement.

Grammar

- *Gramática* boxes appear in each section at the point of need and use various approaches: simple presentation of grammar points, as well as inviting and guiding students to work out patterns where appropriate.
- The boxes are followed by specific practice exercises, so that grammar points are practised in a focused way before being used in more open-ended work.
- Each unit has a worksheet dedicated to grammar practice.
- An overview of the grammar covered is provided in a separate reference section, on page 142 of the Student's Book.

Skills

- Active work on skills development in *¡Así! 1* helps to ensure students' success as language learners. The aim is to motivate by demystifying language learning and give students a greater sense of ownership and purpose.
- In addition to standard practice of listening, speaking, reading and writing, specially designed exercises and *¡Así se hace!* (skills) features give specific tips, guidance and practice to help students develop transferable skills in learning and using language.

- One worksheet per unit focuses specifically on skills development.
- Particular attention is paid to pronunciation. Specific sound/spelling patterns are highlighted and practised.

Differentiation

- *¡extra!* exercises in the Student's Book and on the worksheets provide a greater challenge. Encourage students to tackle them whenever they can. Differentiation is achieved in a variety of ways, as appropriate to an exercise: by input, support, complexity of task, length of task and outcome.
- Each unit has an *¡extra!* worksheet, pitched at a higher level.
- Workbooks are at two levels: Workbook A provides easier exercises, while Workbook B has more difficult ones.
- Transcripts of listening exercises can be used as support.
- Further suggestions for extra support and differentiation are given in the Teacher's Book.

Assessment

- There are opportunities for formative assessment throughout the course: certain exercises lend themselves well to demonstrating students' strengths and showing where any weaknesses lie. These exercises have been highlighted in the unit teaching notes and are preceded by a tick symbol.
- Specific summative assessment exercises are provided in the Resource and Assessment File, for assessments after units 2, 4, 6, 8, 10 and 12. There is also a full end-of-year assessment.

See **The MFL Framework** (page 12) for notes on assessment for learning.

Cross-curricular links

- *¡Así! 1* has a number of cross-curricular links, e.g. English (comparison between Spanish and English structures, development of skills such as reading for gist); ICT (use of specific ICT exercises, as well as key terminology); geography (focus on towns and areas in Spain) and numeracy (time and prices).

Approximate rate of progress through **iAsí!**: *(actual progress will depend on when holidays fall)*

Y7 starters

	Year 7	Year 8	Year 9
Term 1	iAsí! 1 Units 1–3	iAsí! 1 Units 9–11	iAsí! 2 Units 5–7
Term 2	iAsí! 1 Units 4–6	iAsí! 1 Unit 12 iAsí! 2 Units 1–2	iAsí! 2 Units 8–10
Term 3	iAsí! 1 Units 7–8	iAsí! 2 Units 3–4	iAsí! 2 Units 11–12

Y8 starters*

	Year 8	Year 9
Term 1	iAsí!1 Units 1–5	iAsí!2 Units 1–5
Term 2	iAsí!1 Units 6–9	iAsí!2 Units 6–9
Term 3	iAsí!1 Units 10–12	iAsí!2 Units 10–12

Y9 starters*

	Year 9
Term 1	iAsí!1 Units 1–9
Term 2	iAsí!1 Units 10–12 iAsí!2 Units 1–5
Term 3	iAsí!2 Units 6–12

*Fast tracking
A more detailed fast-tracking table is available at www.nelsonthornes.com.

Instructions   page 3

Words and phrases used in instructions are explained for you here

Welcome to iAsí!   page 6

- Spanish-speaking countries
- introduce yourself
- greetings
- introductions
- names of some Spanish-speaking countries
- -o and -a endings

Unidad 1 En clase   *In class*   page 8

- meet people and say how you are
- classroom instructions
- the alphabet
- school items
- numbers 1–10
- classroom language

- **tú** and **usted**
- **el, la, los, las** – the
- **un, una** – a and **unos, unas** – some
- plural of nouns

- practising dialogues
- pronunciation: vowels
- punctuation rules (i! ¿?)
- learning words and gender together

Unidad 2 ¿Quién eres?   *Who are you?*   page 16

- age and birthday
- months of the year
- numbers 11–39
- where you live
- nationalities
- what languages you speak

- the verbs **tener** and **vivir**
- the verb **ser**
- masculine/feminine adjectives
- the verb **hablar**

- spotting patterns
- pronunciation: e, I
- pronunciation: c
- the negative no

Revision (Units 1–2) and reading page   **page 24**

Unidad 3 Mi familia   *My family*   page 26

- brothers/sisters
- numbers 40–100
- what you look like
- what other people look like
- pets

- the verb **llamarse**
- position and ending of adjectives
- **yo, tú, usted, él, ella**
- **mi/mis, tu/tus, su/sus**
- plural nouns

- pronunciation: h, j
- linking sentences with y and pero
- asking how to say something in Spanish

Unidad 4 En el pueblo   *In town*   page 34

- what there is/isn't in town
- describing your town/village
- what you can do in town
- what you like/don't like

- **hay** – there is, **no hay** – there isn't
- the verbs **ser** and **estar**
- **se puede** – you can
- **a + el/la/los/las** – to the
- the verb **gustar**

- pronunciation: v, b
- learning vocabulary
- identifying nouns, adjectives and modifiers
- using a dictionary

Revision (Units 3–4) and reading page   **page 42**

Unidad 5 En casa   *At home*   page 44

- your house
- distances
- rooms
- furniture
- what is good/bad about a place

- **está a** – it is … away
- **de + el/la/los/las** – from the
- **de** – of
- prepositions + **de**
- **lo malo/bueno es que**
- the verbs **ser** and **estar** (revision)

- working out the meaning of new words
- learning new vocabulary
- pronunciation: z

1 Acquiring knowledge and understanding of the target language Students should be taught:	¡Así! 1: examples of coverage
a the principles and interrelationship of sounds and writing in the target language	Pronunciation boxes and exercises
b the grammar of the target language and how to apply it	Grammar boxes, exs and worksheets
c how to express themselves using a range of vocabulary and structures	All language practice exs

2 Developing language skills Students should be taught:	¡Así! 1: examples of coverage
a how to listen carefully for gist and detail	p.44 ex1b, p.94 ex2, WS3
b correct pronunciation and intonation	Pronunciation boxes and exercises
c how to ask and answer questions	p.17 ex3b, p.53 ex5a
d how to initiate and develop conversations	p.59 ex4
e how to vary the target language to suit context, audience and purpose	pp.8–14 classroom lang, p.91 ex2b, WS47
f how to adapt language they already know for different contexts	p.57 ex4a, pp.86–87, WS52
g strategies for dealing with the unpredictable	Asking the teacher for help; using the glossary, reading and listening skills (throughout)
h techniques for skimming and for scanning written texts for information, including those from ICT-based sources	p.47 ex3a, p.94 ex1, reading pages (see teaching notes)
i how to summarise and report the main points of spoken or written texts, using notes where appropriate	p.44 ex1b, p.50 ex1, p.53 ex5c, p59 ex3a, WS1
j how to redraft their writing to improve its accuracy and presentation, including the use of ICT	p.45 ex4, p.57 ex4c, p.85 ex3c, (revision pages)

3 Developing language – learning skills Students should be taught:	¡Así! 1: examples of coverage
a techniques for memorising words, phrases and short extracts	p.9 ex4, p.48 ex1a, p.91 ex1b
b how to use context and other clues to interpret meaning	p.47 ex3a, p.88 ex3, WS18, WS33
c to use their knowledge of English or another language when learning the target language	p.17 ex4a, p.52 ex1a
d how to use dictionaries and other reference materials appropriately and effectively	p.47 ex3a, p.94 ex1 + 3, WS94, notes at beginning of glossary
e how to develop their independence in learning and using the target language.	General ¡Así se hace! training throughout; ¡Ahora tú! self-access pages for each unit (pp.118–141); reading pages

4 Developing cultural awareness Students should be taught about different countries and cultures by:	¡Así! 1: examples of coverage
a working with authentic materials in the target language, including some from ICT-based sources	Unit 10 ICT suggestions in Teacher's Book
b communicating with native speakers	Unit 10 Suggestions in Teacher's Book for contact with tourist offices
c considering their own culture and comparing it with the cultures of the countries and communities where the target language is spoken	Unit 5, Spanish houses, Unit 9, Spanish schools
d considering the experiences and perspectives of people in these countries and communities	

5 Breadth of study	¡Así! 1: examples of coverage
During KS3 and 4, students should be taught the knowledge, skills and understanding through:	
a communicating in the target language in pairs and groups, and with their teacher	Pairwork exs marked ✎, shared reading 📖 and writing ✐ exercises
b using everyday classroom events as an opportunity for spontaneous speech	Asking teacher for help (e.g. ¿Cómo se dice?) shared reading and group work
c expressing and discussing personal feelings and opinions	p.53 ex5b, p.88 ex1c, WS16, WS32
d producing and responding to different types of spoken and written language, including texts produced using ICT	p.87 ex3, p.91 ex2a (revision pages), reading pages
e using a range of resources, including ICT, for accessing and communicating information	Suggestions in Teacher's Book for contact using email; Website www.nelsonthornes.com
f using the target language creatively and imaginatively	WS5, WS15
g listening, reading or viewing for personal interest and enjoyment, as well as for information	Reading pages, as well as reading texts within sections
h using the target language for real purposes	Asking for help in class, reading for interest, enjoyment and information
i working in a variety of contexts, including everyday activities, personal and social life, the world around us, the world of work and the international world	The course covers the full range of contexts

Covering the QCA Scheme of Work

¡Así! 1 takes into account the QCA Scheme of Work for Key Stage 3, covering all the language content and contexts for learning, although not in exactly the same order. The course echoes the principles that underpin the Scheme of Work: progression, differentiation, a firm grammatical base and the development of language and language-learning skills as well as cultural awareness.

You can find a QCA correlation document on www.nelsonthornes.com.

Covering the Scottish Modern Languages 5–14 Guidelines

¡Así! 1 aims to develop communicative competence, learner autonomy and learning and thinking skills, all aims of the 5–14 Guidelines, through the design and sequencing of the exercises and the specific guidance given as ¡Así se hace! . The cultural strand and many of the topics and exercises contribute to the development of personal and social skills, while the content and structure of the course echo the Guidelines' planning principles of breadth, balance, coherence, continuity and progression.

You can find a correlation document on www.nelsonthornes.com showing coverage in ¡Así! 1 of each strand of the four attainment outcomes.

Flashcards (105)

Unit 1
1 un lápiz
2 un bolígrafo
3 una pluma
4 un cuaderno
5 un libro
6 una goma
7 una regla
8 un estuche
9 una mochila

Unit 3
10 tres peces de colores
11 una serpiente
12 una cobaya
13 dos pájaros
14 un perro
15 un hámster
16 un ratón
17 dos gatos
18 un caballo
19 una tortuga
20 no tengo animales

Unit 4
21 me gusta
22 me gusta mucho
23 me encanta
24 no me gusta
25 no me gusta nada
26 odio
27 prefiero

Unit 6
28 jugar al fútbol
29 jugar al tenis
30 practicar la natación
31 escuchar música
32 salir con amigos
33 ver la tele
34 salir de compras
35 ir al cine
36 tocar el piano
37 navegar por internet
38 hacer los deberes
39 ir al centro
40 en primavera
41 en verano
42 en otoño
43 en invierno

Unit 7
44 una Coca-Cola
45 una Fanta de limón
46 un granizado de limón
47 un té sólo
48 un té con leche
49 un café sólo
50 un batido de chocolate
51 un batido de fresa
52 un agua mineral con gas
53 un agua mineral sin gas
54 un chocolate caliente
55 un zumo de naranja
56 una hamburguesa
57 un perrito caliente
58 un bocadillo de jamón
59 un bocadillo de queso
60 un bocadillo de atún
61 una ensalada
62 una tortilla española
63 unas patatas fritas
64 unos calamares
65 unas aceitunas
66 unas patatas bravas
67 una pizza

Unit 8
68 la carne
69 el pescado
70 la verdura
71 la pasta
72 la fruta
73 el pollo
74 las galletas
75 el pastel
76 el yogur
77 los cereales
78 el bacón con huevos fritos
79 (barras de) chocolate
80 (bolsas de) patatas fritas
81 las tostadas
82 el pan con aceite
83 llueve
84 nieva
85 hay tormenta
86 hace sol
87 hace frío
88 hace buen tiempo
89 hace mal tiempo
90 hace calor
91 hiela

Unit 11
92 unas botas marrones
93 unos pantalones azules
94 unos vaqueros negros
95 unas zapatillas de deporte rojas
96 unos zapatos blancos
97 una falda gris
98 un abrigo verde
99 unos calcetines naranja
100 una chaqueta lila
101 una camiseta blanca
102 un vestido amarillo
103 una camisa azul
104 unas medias negras
105 un jersey rosa

OHTs (21)

Unit 1
1A SB p.6–7: world map reproduced
1B overlay for 1A with text for countries
2A SB p.8–9: photos of people greeting each other reproduced
2B overlay for 2A with speech bubbles
3 alphabet
4A classroom instructions
4B overlay for 4A with speech bubbles

Unit 2
5 Spanish calendar

Unit 3
6 family members
7A family tree
7B overlay for 7A with speech bubbles

Unit 4
8 locations (e.g. town, village, etc.)
9 places in town

Unit 5
10A types of housing
10B overlay with speech bubbles
11 transport: on foot, by car etc.
12A conversations about where people live
12B overlay with speech bubbles for 12A

Unit 6
13 conversations about going out

Unit 7
14 conversations in café

Unit 9
15A school plan
15B labels for 15A

Unit 10
16A tourist office conversations
16B overlay with speech bubbles for 16A
17 directions

Unit 11
18 patterns/types of clothes
19A conversations in clothes shop
19B overlay with speech bubbles for 19A

Unit 12
20 part-time jobs
21 teenage activities

Visuals in (R&A File)

Unit 1
WS 1 classroom objects

Unit 2
WS 10 map of Europe with labels

Unit 3
WS 19 hair and eyes
WS 20 physical/personality traits

Unit 4
WS 29 map of Mallorca with labels + place descriptions, e.g. quiet

Unit 5
WS 38 rooms in the house
WS 39 furniture items

Unit 6
WS 48 free time activities

Unit 7
WS 57 food and drink, money
WS 58 disjunctive pronouns

Unit 8
WS 67 daily routine

Unit 9
WS 76 school subjects

Unit 10
WS 85 directions
WS 86 what I did yesterday

Unit 11
WS 95 clothes

Unit 12
WS 104 things I spend my pocket money on

SB = *Student's Book*
WS = *Worksheet*

Using the flashcards

Here are some ideas for using the flashcards:

'Flash' the card quickly: students have to identify it correctly (this could be a team game).

Show a flashcard and say a word/phrase. Students repeat only if the word matches the card.

Verb phrases: show the flashcard and say the phrase. Students repeat the phrase and mime the activity.

Place a flashcard at the top of the pile: students guess which one it is. If there are eight cards in the pile, they score a point if they can guess the card in four guesses or less. After a while, students who guess correctly come to the front and choose the next card to lay on the top of the pile.

Students guess which flashcard you are holding. If they guess correctly, they keep the card. Once all the cards are distributed, students say a word and the name of the student they think has the matching card. If correct, the student has to hand the card over.

Place the flashcards at different places in the classroom. When you say a word, students have to point towards the appropriate flashcard. You can make this a *Simon dice* game: students point at the flashcards only if you have said *Simon dice...*

Having practised new nouns with flashcards, put down the cards and challenge your students to recall all the words they have practised. Write them on the board or OHP as your students say them. Can volunteers now come to the board and add the correct article, *el* or *la*?

Using the visual worksheets

The pictures from the visual worksheets in each unit can be photocopied onto OHT and used to present and revise vocabulary. Here are some suggestions:

- Display the pictures and practise the pronunciation of the words. Then say one of the words: students tell you the number of the appropriate picture.

- Reverse the above game: you say a number, students say the word.

- Students match each caption with the appropriate picture.

- Students call out words and you lay the pictures on the OHP as they are mentioned. Can students remember them all?

- Point to a picture and say a word. Students repeat the word only if it matches the picture.

- Display a number of pictures for a few seconds. Darken the screen with card, and remove two pictures. Remove the card: your students tell you which pictures are missing.

- Superimpose three pictures. Can your students tell you what they are?

- Kim's game: display a number of pictures on the OHP for 30 seconds, then switch off the OHP. Your students write down or tell you as many words/phrases as they can remember.

The words/phrases can also be copied onto paper or card: students work in pairs or individually and match the captions with the pictures. If working in pairs, this could be done collaboratively using one set, or as a race with two sets.

The MFL Framework

What is the MFL Framework?

The Framework for teaching modern foreign languages is part of a more general initiative: the Key Stage 3 National Strategy, which aims to improve standards in schools. The strategy covers several subjects: English, maths, science, ICT, and Foundation Subjects including modern foreign languages.

The MFL Framework sets out a structured set of teaching objectives for each year in KS3 (based on the National Curriculum Programme of Study), along with guidance to teachers.

Teaching thinking

Teaching thinking, a key feature of the Framework, is addressed in ¡Así! 1 in a variety of ways. In many places, students are encouraged to work out the meaning of new language, using strategies such as applying their knowledge of Spanish, looking for cognates and considering the context. Where appropriate, the grammar boxes guide students in working out the patterns for themselves, and students regularly apply their grammatical knowledge to concrete situations. The ¡Así se hace! tips guide students in developing their skills as independent and competent language learners and users, and these skills are transferred where possible to new areas. Students are also encouraged to reflect on the progress of their own learning, using plenary sessions to check their learning against objectives.

Key thinking skills exercises are marked 💡 in the teaching notes.

Assessment for learning

Assessment for learning is formative assessment: it provides feedback on what has been achieved and also on which areas need further work, and can be used to inform your lesson planning.

Draw students' attention to the objectives listed at the beginning of each section, so that they are aware of the nature and purpose of the work they will be doing. As they work through each section, certain exercises (particularly those marked ☑ in the teaching notes) give students the opportunity to assess their progress against these aims, as does the whole-class plenary session at the end of each lesson. Teacher assessment, self-assessment and peer assessment are all possible ways of checking progress.

Another key point for assessment for learning is the *Repaso* page at the end of every second unit, which acts as preparation for the summative assessment sheets (found in the Resource and Assessment File).

The cultural strand

Culture is one of the five Framework strands. In *¡Así! 1*, geographical and cultural information is presented both in reading texts and through maps. Social and linguistic conventions of Spanish (such as greetings and forms of address) are met through the topics and linguistic content of the course.

Lesson planning

Framework lessons have a three-part format: starter, teaching sequence, plenary.

Starters

These should be brief and focused, with the aim of settling students, engaging their attention (e.g. by intriguing or challenging them) and helping them to switch from their last class into a 'learning Spanish' mindset. Here are some suggestions:

- Students revise vocabulary from the last lesson by brainstorming as many items as they can in pairs or groups. Which group can remember the most?

- Write on the board or OHP sets of four/five key words: students identify the odd one out in each set. Take words from a range of topics, not just the current one. There may be more than one correct answer (e.g. based on gender or initial letter as well as meaning) – students justify their answer.

- Use flashcards or OHT visuals to revise key language. For example, hold a flashcard so it is facing you. Students have to guess what it is. The person who gets it right comes out to the front of the class and continues the game.

- Speak some simple addition and subtraction calculations in Spanish. Students write down their answers as numbers – on mini whiteboards if you have them.

- Display a flashcard or OHT visual and say or write up two alternative words, one correct and one incorrect: "A (+ word)" or "B (+ word)"? Students hold up pieces of paper with A or B. This way, all students are involved in answering.

- Designate the wall on the students' left as the 'masculine' wall, the opposite one as the 'feminine' wall. For each flashcard you display, students point to the wall you should stick it on. Include flashcards from previous topics as well as the current one.

Teaching sequence

The teaching sequence is described in detail on pp. 29–180.

Plenaries

Plenaries help students to draw together and take stock of what they have learnt, not only the content but also the skills. They also give you an opportunity to assess ' progress, and so they inform your lesson planning. Some suggestions:

- Students look back to the objectives at the beginning of the section and discuss in pairs what they have learnt for each one.

- In teams, students jot down as many new words as they can remember in one minute.

- Recap on the aims of the lesson and ask students how confident they feel about each one. They each show one of three coloured cards: green (very confident), orange (quite confident) and red (not confident).

- In pairs, students explain the skill or grammar point they have just learnt as if teaching it to someone who missed the lesson.

- Students work in pairs, and for each letter of the alphabet they try to think of *one* word featured in the section. (There won't be one for every letter, but the winners are the students who find words for most letters.)

- At the end of a unit, students reconstruct the areas of language they have learnt, displaying the information in the form of a word web.

Year 8 Framework references

8W1	Adding abstract words	Unit 8B WS75
8W2	Connectives	Unit 9A p82 ¡Así se hace! & ex1b, WS73
8W4	Word endings	Unit 11A p101 Gram., Unit 7D WS63, WS65
8W5	Verb tenses	Unit 6E p60 ex1a & Gram., Unit 10D p96
8W8	Non-literal meanings	Unit 7A p64 ex1 (Stage 2)
8S1	Word, phrase and clause sequencing	Unit 5B p47 Gram., Unit 8D p78 ex2
8S2	Connectives in extended sentences	Unit 6B p55 ex3, WS53
8S3	Modal verbs	Stage 2
8S5	Negative forms and words	Unit 11A p100 ex2
8S6	Substituting and adding	Unit 8A p73 ex2b, Unit 8C p 77 ex4c, Unit 8D p78 ex4b, Unit 11A p101 ex5b
8S7	Present, past and future	Unit 10D p96, Unit 12D p114 ex4, WS87, WS93
8T	Meanings in context	Unit 7A WS60
8T2	Expression in text	Unit 8C p77 Gram.
8T4	Dictionary use	Unit 4C WS35
8T5	Writing continuous text	Unit 11A p100 ex3, Unit 12D p114 ex4
8T6	Text as model and source	Unit 6A p53 ex4b, Unit 11B p102 ex1b
8L1	Listening for subtleties	Unit 11B p102 exs1a&c, Unit 7C WS64
8L3	Relaying gist and detail	Unit 6C p57 ex4c
8L4	Extending sentences	Unit 9D p88 ex2, Unit 11A p101 ex5a
8L5	Unscripted speech	Unit 7A p64 ex2c
8L6	Expression in speech	Unit 8C p77
8C1	Historical facts	Unit 10C p94 ex1

Framework strand coverage

The following grids show examples of coverage in *¡Así!* 1 of the Framework objectives for each of the five strands.

		Unit 1	Unit 2	Unit 3
7W1	Everyday words	p.8, WS2	p16 ex1, p17 ex4b, WS11	p26 ex1a, p28 ex1a, p30 ex1a, p32 ex1, WS23 WS24
7W2	High-frequency words	pp.12–13	pp16–17	p30 Gram.. p31 Gram.
7W3	Classroom words	pp.10–14		p30 Gram.. WK24, WS27
7W4	Gender and plural	p11 ex4, p12 ex2, p13 ex4a, WS8	p20 ex1 & Gram.	p26 ex1a, p28 ex2, p29 Gram. & ex4, p30 ex1a, p32 ex1, WS27
7W5	Verbs present (+ past)		p18 Gram., p20 ex2, WS17	
7W6	Letters and sounds	p10 ex3, p11 exs6a&b, p14 ex1a, WS3	p19 Pron.	p26 Pron.
7W7	Learning about words	p12 *¡Así se hace!*	p17 *¡Así se hace!*	p30 ex1b, p30 ex2. WS27, WS28
7W8	Finding meanings	WS9	p18 ex2	p29 ex5
7S1	Typical word order	WS7	WS18	p28 Gram.&ex2
7S2	Sentence gist			WK24, p32 ex1
7S3	Adapting sentences	p8 ex3a, p11 ex5, p13 ex4, p14 ex1b	p17 ex5c, p18 ex1b, p21 ex6, WS14, WS17	p31 ex5b, p32 ex4
7S4	Basic questions	p14	p16 *¡Así se hace!*	
7S5	Basic negatives	WS7		
7S6	Compound sentences			WS25
7S7	Time and tenses			
7S8	Punctuation and orthographic features	p6 ex1, p14 ex2& *¡Así se hace!*		
7S9	Using simple sentences	WS4	WS13	
7T1	Reading using cues	p10 ex1, p13 ex5b, WS5	p16 ex3a, p20 exs1b–3, WS14	p31 ex5a, WS24, WS26
7T2	Reading aloud	p8 ex1b, p14 ex3	p17 ex3b, ex5c	WS26
7T3	Checking before reading			
7T4	Using resources	WS6	p25 Reading	
7T5	Assembling text		p19 ex4, p22 exs1a&b, WS15, WS16	p29 ex6
7T6	Texts as prompts for writing	p14 ex1b		p29 ex6, p31 ex5b, WS24
7T7	Improving written work			
7L1	Sound patterns	p8 ex1a, p10 ex2, p14 ex2	p21 Pron.	p32 Gram.. WS22, WS26
7L2	Following speech		p24 ex2	p26 ex1a, p30 ex1a, WS22
7L3	Gist and detail	p6–7, p9 ex5, p12 exs1a&b, p14 ex1a	p16 ex2, p17 exs5a&b, p18 ex1a, p22 exs1a–2	p26 ex1b, p28 ex3, p30 ex3. WS22
7L4	Classroom talk	pp.10–14		p32 ex1
7L5	Spontaneous talk	p9		
7L6	Improving speech	WS4		p26 ex1c, p29 ex 5b, WS23
7C1	Geographical facts	p7	p18 ex2	
7C2	Everyday culture		OHT5	
7C3	Contact with native speakers		p22 ex1a	p27 ex4b
7C4	Stories and songs	p11, p13 songs		
7C5	Social conventions	p8 ex1a		

		Unit 4	Unit 5	Unit 6
7W1	Everyday words	p34 ex1a, p35 ex2a, p36 ex1, p38 ex1, p40 ex2, WS34, WS35	p48 ex1a, WS38, WS39, WS40	p57 ¡Así se hace!. WS48, WS49
7W2	High-frequency words	p35 ex2a, p36 ex1, p39 ex4, p40 ex2, WS35	p44 Gram.	
7W3	Classroom words	WS37		
7W4	Gender and plural	p36 ex1, p39 ex4, p40 Gram.&ex5, WS37	WS46	p52 Gram., p60 Gram., WS55
7W5	Verbs present (+ past)	p37 Gram., p40 Gram.&ex2		p59 Pron.. ex 4b
7W6	Letters and sounds	WS35	WS45	WS54
7W7	Learning about words	p38 ex2. WS35, WS37	p46 ex1. p48 ¡Así se hace!	p53 ex4a, p55 ¡Así se hace!. p58 ex1
7W8	Finding meanings		p49 ex3a. WS47	p53 ex4a. p55 ex3
7S1	Typical word order		p45 ex3c, p49 ex3b. WS46	
7S2	Sentence gist			p53 ex5c
7S3	Adapting sentences	p39 ex4. p40 ex5. WS32. WS34	p49 ex5. WS44	p53 ex5a
7S4	Basic questions	WS36		p54 ex2b
7S5	Basic negatives	p35 ex3a		
7S6	Compound sentences			
7S7	Time and tenses	WS36	p44 Gram.	p56 ex1c, p59 ex3b. p60 ex1a&b
7S8	Punctuation and orthographic features			
7S9	Using simple sentences		OHT10A&B, p48 ex2	p55 ex4b. p58 ex1. p60 exs1b–3. WS51
7T1	Reading using cues	p34 ex1c, p36 ex1. WS37	p44 exs1a&2a, p46 ex2a, p50 ex1. WS43	p52 ex1. p54 ex1. p56 ex1a. p58 ex1
7T2	Reading aloud	p34 ex1a	WS43	p52 ¡Así se hace!. WS52
7T3	Checking before reading	p34 ex1c, p36 ex1. WS37, p40 ex4	WS47	p53 ex4a
7T4	Using resources	p35 ex2a, p37 ex3a, p39 ex6		p53 ex4a. WS56
7T5	Assembling text	p37 ex3		p53 ex4b
7T6	Texts as prompts for writing	p35 ex3b, p40 ex5. WS34		p59 ex3b. WS53
7T7	Improving written work	p35 ex3b. WS37		
7L1	Sound patterns	p34 ex1b. WS31	WS45	p52 ex1a, p53 ex5a. WS54
7L2	Following speech	p34 ex1a, p38 ex3. WS31	p44 ex1a. WS41	
7L3	Gist and detail	p40 ex1. p 40 ex3. WS31	p44 exs1b&2, p48 ex1b, p49 ex4, p50 exs2a&b	p52 ex2a, p54 exs2a&b, p56 ex1a–2b. p58 exs2a&b. p60 ex1a. WS50
7L4	Classroom talk		WS42	p53 ex3
7L5	Spontaneous talk		p50 ex3	p53 ex5b, p55 ex3, p59 ex4, p60 ex2, WS51
7L6	Improving speech	p35 ex2b, p39 ex5. WS32	p50 ex3	p59 Pron.
7C1	Geographical facts			
7C2	Everyday culture		pp.44&45	
7C3	Contact with native speakers		p46 ex1	
7C4	Stories and songs			p63 Reading
7C5	Social conventions			

Framework strand coverage

	Unit 7	Unit 8	Unit 9
7W1 Everyday words	p64 ex1, p66 exs1&2a	p72 ex1, p74 ex1a	p85 Gram.&¡Así se hace! · p88 ex2, WS76, WS77
7W2 High-frequency words	p64 ex1, p66 ex1, p67 Gram., p70 ex1a	p72 ex1, p75 Gram., WS75, p77 Gram., p78 ex 3, WK73	p83 Gram., ¡Así se hace! &2b
7W3 Classroom words	WS63	WS75	
7W4 Gender and plural			
7W5 Verbs present (+ past)	p64 Gram., p67 Gram., WS65	p72 ex1, p73 exs2a&b, WS74	p88 Gram., WS80
7W6 Letters and sounds	p69 Pron.		p84 ex1a
7W7 Learning about words	p64 ex1		
7W8 Finding meanings	p66 ex1		
7S1 Typical word order	p67 ex2b		p83 ex4
7S2 Sentence gist	WS61, WS63		
7S3 Adapting sentences	p64 ex2b		p82 ex1b, p85 ex3a, p86 ex1c, p88 ex1c
7S4 Basic questions		p73 exs2a&b, WS70	
7S5 Basic negatives			p88 ex2
7S6 Compound sentences	p70 ex3		p82 ¡Así se hace!
7S7 Time and tenses		p73 ex3a	p85 ¡Así se hace!
7S8 Punctuation and orthographic features			
7S9 Using simple sentences	p64 ex2a, p69 ex2, p70 exs1a&b, WS62		
7T1 Reading using cues	p64 ex2a, p66 ex2a, p68 ex1a, p70 ex1a	p73 ex3b, p74 ex1a, p77 ex1, WS71	p82 ex1a, p83 ex3b, p86 exs1a&b, p88 ex1b
7T2 Reading aloud	p70 ex1b	p73 ex3a, p77 ex1	
7T3 Checking before reading	p69 ex1c	p73 ex3a.	
7T4 Using resources	p67 ex3b, p70 ex3		
7T5 Assembling text		p77 ex4a, p78 ex4b, WS72	p85 ex3b
7T6 Texts as prompts for writing		p77 ex4a, WS72	p85 ex2b, WS81
7T7 Improving written work		p78 ex3	WS81
7L1 Sound patterns	p69 Pron., WS64		WS82
7L2 Following speech	p64 ex2a	p77 ex 1, WS69, WS75	p82 ex1a, p88 ex1a, WS78
7L3 Gist and detail	WS60, p67 ex3a, p69 ex3, p70 ex2	p78 ex1	p82 ex1c, p84 exs1a&b, p86 exs1a&b, WS78
7L4 Classroom talk		p77 ex2, WS75	p84 ex1c
7L5 Spontaneous talk		WS75	p84 ex1c
7L6 Improving speech	p67 ex3b, WS61, WS64	p77 exs4b&c, p78 ex4a, WS75	p85 Gram.&ex3a, p88 ex1c
7C1 Geographical facts			
7C2 Everyday culture	p66 ex1, p68 ex1a	p72 ex1, p73 ex3a, p77 ex1	pp.86–87
7C3 Contact with native speakers		p73 ex3b	
7C4 Stories and songs	p68 ex1a		
7C5 Social conventions	p64 ex2c		

Framework strand coverage

	Unit 10	Unit 11	Unit 12
7W1 Everyday words	WS85, WS86	p103 ex4	
7W2 High-frequency words	WS91, WS92	p100 ex2, p102 ex1c, WS102, WS103	p112 Gram., WS108, WS112
7W3 Classroom words		p101 ex4a	
7W4 Gender and plural		WS102, WS103	
7W5 Verbs present (+ past)	p90 Gram., p92 Gram.	p103 Gram., p103 ex4	p108 ex1d, WS111
7W6 Letters and sounds	p95 Pron.	p106 Pron.	
7W7 Learning about words			
7W8 Finding meanings		p103 ex2, p106 ex1	
7S1 Typical word order		WS100	
7S2 Sentence gist	p99	p102 ex1c, p104 ex1b	p110 ex1a, p112 ex2, p114 ex2
7S3 Adapting sentences	p91 exs1c&2b	p100 ex3, p102 ex1d, p103 ex4, WS98, WS100	p110 ex2, WS107, WS109
7S4 Basic questions			
7S5 Basic negatives			
7S6 Compound sentences	p96 exs1a–2a, WS87, WS93	p100 ex3, p103 ex4	WS112
7S7 Time and tenses		p102 ex1c, WS99	
7S8 Punctuation and orthographic features			
7S9 Using simple sentences	p98 ex2		
7T1 Reading using cues	p90 ex1a, p94 ex1, p96 ex1a, WS89	p100 ex1, p104 ex1a	p110 ex1a, p112 ex1, WS110
7T2 Reading aloud	p90 ex1a	p102 exs1a&c	
7T3 Checking before reading	p98 ex3	p102 ex1b, p104 ex1a	p108 ex1c, p114 ex4
7T4 Using resources		p102 ex1b, p106 ex1	p109 ex4
7T5 Assembling text	p91 ex1c, p93 ex5a	p100 ex3, p103 ex4, WS100	p113 ex4, WS109
7T6 Texts as prompts for writing	p98 ex4, WS90	p103 ex4	p112 ex1
7T7 Improving written work			p113 ex5
7L1 Sound patterns		p106 Pron.	
7L2 Following speech	p90 ex1a	p102 ex1a, WS97	
7L3 Gist and detail	p92 exs1&2, p94 ex1, p96 ex1b	p105 ex3, p105 *¡Así se hace!*, WS101	p108 exs1a&b, p110 exs1b&c, p113 ex3
7L4 Classroom talk			
7L5 Spontaneous talk			
7L6 Improving speech	WS88	p103 ex4, WS98	p109 ex2, p110 ex2, WS107
7C1 Geographical facts	p94 ex1		
7C2 Everyday culture		p106 ex1	p110 ex1
7C3 Contact with native speakers	p91 ex2a		
7C4 Stories and songs			
7C5 Social conventions	p90 Gram., p92 Gram.		

Sample lesson plans
Lesson plan • Unit 1, lesson 1/Unit 1C

Framework objectives			Teaching and learning
SB ex 1a, 1b	7L3	Identify gist in continuous spoken passages	Recognise and produce names of classroom objects
SB ex 2, Gramática section, WS8	7W4	Gender and plural patterns in nouns and how other words may be affected	Extrapolate rules and exceptions for applying gender
SB ex 3, Canción	7C4	Meet songs in the target language	Listen to and sing the number song
	7L1	Engage with the sound patterns of the spoken language	

Note: for more detail on all activities listed below, see TB p32.

Lesson objectives for students:

Main objective:
- Name things you use in school.

Related objectives:
- Recognise masculine and feminine nouns.
- Learn numbers 1–10.
- Homework WS8

Lesson starter (precedes preliminary exercise and SB, ex 1):

- Use the alphabet OHT3 for quick alphabet practice. Then ask an individual to choose a classmate without saying who it is and to spell out his or her name. The other members of the class write down the letters that they hear. The first person to guess correctly takes over.

Teaching sequence:

1 *Presentation and practice of classroom vocabulary items*
- Use flashcards 1–9 to present and practise the nine new classroom objects with *un/una* and then with *tengo un/una…*
- Look at the pictures in the book. Say an item and ask an individual to spell it.
- **SB ex1a** Listen and write the letter of the object mentioned each time.
- **SB ex1b** Listen and write the letters of the objects mentioned each time.
Resources: Flashcards 1–9, CD1, tracks 10 & 11

2 *Extrapolate rules and exceptions for applying gender*
- Read and discuss the Gramática and ¡Así se hace! notes.
- **SB ex 2** Sort the new words into masculine and feminine.
Resources: WS8

3 *Presentation and practice of numbers*
- Present the numbers on OHT or board.
- Play the song.
- Get students to sing along with and then without the CD.
Resources: CD1, track 12

Plenary (follows Canción):

In pairs, students explain the general rule for *un/una*, as if teaching it to someone who missed the lesson.

Note: SB = Student's Book, TB = Teacher's Book, WS = Worksheet, WB A & B = Workbooks

Framework objectives			Teaching and learning
SB ex 1a	7L3	Listening for gist	Understand and use classroom language
SB ex 1b	7S3	Adapting a simple sentence to communicate basic information	
SB Gramática	7W6	The alphabet and other characters	Identifying and using question and exclamation marks
SB ex 2	7S4	Formulating a basic question	
	7L1	Engaging with the sound patterns of the language	
SB ex 3	7T2	Working out the gist of sentences	

Note: for more detail on all activities listed below, see TB p36.

Lesson objectives for students:

Main objective:

● Say things you need in the Spanish class.

Related objectives:

● Understand when to use ¡...! and ¿...?
● Homework WS7

Lesson starter (precedes SB, ex 1):

● Recap on definite and indefinite articles and plurals. Have some known nouns written on board. Point to a word, students call out *un/una* + word.
● Then write some numbers on the board. Point to a number and a word. Students call out e.g. *tres mochilas*.
● Finally ask how you say 'the' for all those things.

Teaching sequence:

1 *Presentation and production of classroom language*
   • **SB ex 1a** Look at the seven pictures. Discuss with the class what they think each represents.
   • Can they recognise any words in the accompanying sentences (*pizarra, Venezuela,* 'pen')? Does that help in matching pictures to text?
   • Play the CD. Students identify the sentences and match them to the pictures.
   • Discuss possible gestures to accompany these sentences, e.g. a shrug for don't understand, legs crossed for *baño*.
   • **SB ex 1b** Discuss which of the words or phrases given best fits each new sentence as an alternative.
   • Students work in pairs to produce alternative sentences.
   • Practise all the combinations orally.
   Resources: CD 1, track 13

2 *Identifying and using question and exclamation marks*
   • Read the **¡Así se hace!** section together. Are there examples of question sentences on the page? Where have they met sentences with exclamations? Which types of sentences might be written with exclamation marks? (The commands in Section B).
   • **SB ex 2** Students listen and indicate whether each sentence that they hear is a statement or a question.
   • Play the CD again. Where appropriate invite the class to produce statement versions of questions and vice versa.
   • **SB ex 3** Students work in pairs or groups to produce pairs of statements/questions.
   • Pairs of students read out their statements/questions.
   Resources: CD 1, track 14, WS7

Plenary (follows SB, ex 3):

Ask the class to look at the Resumen. Go through it with students section by section. Have they grasped all these points? Ask them to indicate whether they are happy and have grasped something (*Sí, muy bien*), or unhappy and have not understood (*No comprendo*) about each section.

Note: SB = Student's Book, TB = Teacher's Book, WS = Worksheet, WB A & B = Workbook

Framework objectives			Teaching and learning
SB ex 1	7W1	Build a stock of everyday words	Say your age
SB ex 2	7L3	Listen for gist	
SB ex 3a, 3b	7T2	Read aloud a simple text	
SB ex 4a	7W1	Build a stock of everyday words	Learn the months of the year
SB ex 4b		Engage with the sound patterns of the spoken language	

Note: for more detail on all activities listed below, see TB p43.

Lesson objectives for students:

Main objective:

⦿ Say your age.

Related objectives:

⦿ Learn the months of the year.
⦿ Homework: Use WS11 Resumen to learn spellings of 11–20 and months.

Lesson starter (precedes SB, ex 1):

⦿ Revise numbers 1–10 by using the number song from Unit 1.

Teaching sequence:

1 *Presentation of new numbers 11–20.*
   • Introduce the numbers aurally first, using OHT, board or number chart.
   • Students repeat the numbers after the CD, (track 22).
   • Point to random numbers and ask students to say what they are.
   • Individuals read aloud the list of numbers in the book.
   • Students work in pairs: A points to a figure on the picture, B points to the corresponding written number.
   • Introduce the question *¿Cuántos años tienes?*
   • **SB ex 2** Students note the people's ages and discuss the different forms of answer used.
   • Read the *¡Así se hace!* section together.
   • **SB exs 3a, 3b** Students work in pairs to practise the dialogues, pairs of students read out a dialogue each.
   Resources: CD 1, tracks 22 & 23, OHT, board or number chart for numbers, WS11 Resumen

2 *Presentation of the months of the year*
   • Read *¡Así se hace!*, discuss spelling features.
   • **SB ex 4a** Arrange and/or copy the months in order.
   • **SB ex 4b** Listen to and repeat the months.
   Resources: CD1, track 24, WS11, Resumen

Plenary (follows SB ex 4b):

Students look at spellings of numbers 1–20 and discuss patterns.
Elicit the facts that 11–15 end in -ce, 16–20 have *diez(diec)* + unit.
Why does the *seis* in *dieciséis* need an accent?

Note: SB = Student's Book, TB = Teacher's Book, WS = Worksheet, WB A & B = Workbook

Framework objectives			Teaching and learning
SB ex 1a	7L3	Listening for detail	Presentation of names of European countries
WS10 (Visuals)	7W1	Build stock of everyday words	
SB ex 1b	7S3	Adapt a simple sentence to communicate personal information	Recognise and use parts of *vivir*
	7T1	Read and understand texts	
Gramática	7W5	Present tense forms of high frequency verbs	
SB ex 2	7S1	Recognise and apply typical word order	Recognise and use names for compass points
	7T1	Read and understand texts	
	7C1	Learn some basic geographical facts	

Note: for more detail on all activities listed below, see TB p45.

Lesson objectives for students:

Main objective:
- Say where you live.

Related objectives:
- Use the present tense of *vivir*.
- Learn the names of some countries.
- Homework: Learn the names of the new countries using WS10.

Lesson starter (precedes preliminary exercise and SB, ex 1):
- Use OHT3 or a board alphabet chart to practise the Spanish alphabet.

Teaching sequence:

1 *Presentation of names of European countries*
   - **SB ex 1a** Students first listen out for country mentioned and find it on map, then note letter.
   - Use **WS10** to match names to countries and to practise pronunciation and spelling.
   Resources: CD1, track 26, Wall or OHT map of Europe, WS10

2 *Recognise and practise parts of vivir*
   - **Gramática** Look at singular paradigm of *vivir*, and question and answer example on page.
   - Practise Q & A orally with class members.
   - **SB ex 1b** Students work in pairs to ask and answer the question: *Vivo en* (town) *en* (country).

3 *Recognise and use names for compass points*
   - Present and discuss these via **SB ex 2**.

4 *Extension:* Students form sentences about themselves using compass point language.
   Resources: Wall/OHT maps of Spain and Britain

Plenary (follows SB ex2):

How many things can students now say about themselves? (name/age/birthday/where they live...).

Note: SB = Student's Book, TB = Teacher's Book, WS = Worksheet, WB A & B = Workbook

Framework objectives			Teaching and learning
SB ex 1	7W4	Gender patterns	Presentation of adjectives of nationality and gender markers
	7T1	Recognise and apply typical word order	
SB ex2, Grámatica	7W5	Present tense forms of high frequency verbs	Recycling and extension of *ser*
SB ex 3	7W4	Gender patterns	Recognition and application of gender markers in adjectives of nationality

Note: for more detail on all activities listed below, see TB p46.

Lesson objectives for students:

Main objective:

⬤ Say what nationality you are.

Related objectives:

⬤ Use the present tense singular of *ser*.
⬤ Recognise masculine and feminine forms of nationalities.
⬤ Homework: Learn adjectives of nationality on *Resumen*.

Lesson starter (precedes preliminary exercise and SB, ex 1):

⬤ Everyone thinks of one thing to say about themselves in Spanish. Encourage use of *Soy...*

Teaching sequence:

1 *Listening presentation of nationalities with* ser
- **SB ex 1** Elicit recognition of m and f forms of adjectives of nationality.
- Ask *¿Cuál es tu nacionalidad?* Elicit reply e.g. *Soy (inglés/galesa).*
  Resources: CD1, track 28, Wall/OHT map of British Isles

2 *Consolidation of parts of ser*
- Read through Gramática section together.
- Make and elicit examples referring to yourself and class members: *Kelly, eres inglesa. Kelly y Joanne son inglesas. Soy inglés.*
- **SB ex 2** Speaking practice. Students interview each other using the captions in exercise 1 as prompts.

3 *Recognition of gender markers in adjectives of nationality*
- **SB ex 3** Read through the first ones together and give answer: *Un chico/una chica.* Do the rest individually or in pairs.
- Check answers and discuss the patterns for forming adjectives that emerge.

4 *Extension:* Students use dictionaries to find out and form other relevant adjectives of nationality.

Plenary (follows SB ex 3):

Students look back on the adjectival forms they have met and try to establish rules about formation and agreement.

Note: SB = Student's Book, TB = Teacher's Book, WS = Worksheet, WB A & B = Workbook

Framework objectives			Teaching and learning
SB ex 1a	7W1	Build a stock of words relating to everyday contexts and settings	Say if they have any brothers and sisters, ask and understand others
	7W4	Recognise clues to gender	
	7L2	Write heard words, hold up for checking	
SB ex 1b	7L3	Listen for detail	
SB ex 1c	7L6	Use new language in speaking activity	
SB Gramática	7W5	Present tense form of high-frequency verb	Understand and use *él/ella/usted* and *ellos/as* forms of *llamarse*
SB Pronunciación	7W6	Sound patterns	Pronunciation of letter *h*
SB inuevo!	7W1	Build a stock of words relating to everyday contexts and settings	Learn and understand numbers 40–100

Note: for more detail on all activities listed below, see TB p56.

Lesson objectives for students:

Main objectives:
- Say if you have any brothers and sisters, ask and understand others.
- Say what your brothers and sisters are called.

Related objectives:
- Say words containing the letter *h*.
- Understand and say the numbers 40–100.
- Homework: write two brief paragraphs, one for each of two characters from a book or soap opera, explaining how many brothers and sisters they have and what they're called.

Lesson starter (precedes SB, ex 1a):

- Revise known information about gender (*un/a*) and endings of words: -*o*/-*a*. Teacher calls out words for family members ending in -*o*/-*a* and students call out *masculino* or *feminino*, or hold up a card M or F.

Teaching sequence:

1 *Introduction*
Explain that in this lesson, students are going to learn how to talk about their brothers and sisters, giving their names, and learn the numbers from 40–100.

2 *Presentation of the new language*
- **SB ex 1a** Present and practise the new language for brothers and sisters, using OHT6 and the pictures in **ex 1a**.
- Consolidate by calling out sentences like: *Tengo un hermano (que se llama) Tomás*. Students write down Ho. for *herman(astro)*, and Ha. for *herman(astra)*.
Resources: CD1, track 37

3 *Focus on listening*
- **SB ex 1b** Listening practice: students note numbers of brothers and sisters.
Resources: CD1, track 38

4 *Grammar*
- Discuss grammar point, highlight *se llama* for one person (he, she) and *se llaman* for more than one (they).

5 *Productive use of the new language*
- **SB ex 1c** Oral pairwork.

6 *Pronunciation of the letter h*
- Work through the examples given. Students write down other words for practice which you read out.
Resources: CD1, track 39

7 *Presentation of numbers 40–100*
- Revise numbers 1–39 using counting games. Present numbers 40–100, and practise using number and guessing games.

Plenary (follows SB ex 2 and presentation of numbers):

See Alternative plenary (p57) whole-class work on similarities and differences in numbers.

Note: SB = Student's Book, TB = Teacher's Book, WS = Worksheet, WB A & B = Workbook

Framework objectives			Teaching and learning
Starter	7W7	Use knowledge of letter strings to pronounce new words	How to reapply previous learnt rules
SB ex 1	7W1	Build a stock of words relating to everyday contexts and settings	Say what colour of eyes and hair they have and understand others
SB ex 2	7W4	Understand singular and plural gender patterns for adjectives	Understand the position of adjectives in a sentence
	7S1	Recognise and apply typical word order	
SB ex 3	7L3	Identify gist and some detail	Practice in recognising the new language
SB ex 4	7W4	Understand and apply adjectival endings	Practice in forming adjectives of colour and using agreement

Note: for more detail on all activities listed below, see TB p58

Lesson objectives for students:

Main objective:

- Say what somebody looks like.

Related objectives:

- Learn how to use adjectives.
- Homework: students write a list of the contents of their pencil case or school bag, using adjectives of colour and making them agree in number and gender.

Lesson starter (precedes SB, ex 1):

- Write up new words *verde, azul, gris, negro, rubio, rojo, castaño, marrón, el pelo, el pelo, los ojos* with their English equivalents, and ask students to work out how to pronounce these.

Teaching sequence:

1 *Presentation*
- Use Visual 19 for presentation: have colour adjectives written up under the headings for hair and eyes, and allow students to suggest to you what colour to shade in the eyes and hair of each young person.
- Consolidate with **SB ex1**: students read aloud for practice, then work in pairs on an oral *¡Verdad/Mentira!* exercise.
Resources: CD1, track 41

2 *Grammar*
- Read through the **Gramática** section, eliciting the difference in word order between Spanish and English. Highlight also the singular noun *el pelo* and adjective, and the plural noun *los ojos* and adjective.
- **SB ex 2** students rewrite sentences in the correct order. Show students how the adjectival agreement gives them a vital clue in doing this.

3 *Listening practice*
- **SB ex 3** Students listen to the recordings and choose the correct face for each.
Resources: CD1, track 42

4 *Writing practice*
- **Gramática** Read through with students and consolidate the rule met earlier.
Point out the absence of an accent on *marrón* in the plural.
- **SB ex 4** Students rewrite the sentences, adding the correct colour adjective in the correct form.

Plenary (follows SB ex 4):

(see Alternative plenary on page 59). Use a thought-shower activity to help students think of other topic areas in which they might need adjectives of colour. Use the previously met classroom items (e.g. *un boli, un libro*) to provide practice in using colour adjectives with other singular and plural nouns.

Note: SB = Student's Book, TB = Teacher's Book, WS = Worksheet, WB A & B = Workbook

Framework objectives			Teaching and learning
Starter	7W1	Apply a stock of words relating to everyday contexts and settings	Revision of vocabulary
	7W3	Accumulate and apply words for use in language learning	Learn and use words for simple grammatical terms
SB 1b	7W1	Build and apply words relating to everyday contexts and settings	Use and understand adjectives about size and personality
	7W4	Gender and plural patterns	Further practice with adjectives
	7S1	Typical word order	Learn about position of adjectives after verbs
	7T1	Follow the written version of a text	
	7L4	Use classroom routine expressions	
SB Gramática	7W2	Learn high-frequency words	Learn subject pronouns
	7W3	Learn words for use in language learning	
	7W5	Present tense of high-frequency verbs	Revision of parts of *llamarse*
SB 2	7W7	Memorise the meaning and main attributes of words	Understand new adjectives and their opposites
SB 3	7L3	Listen for gist and detail	Listening practice
WS24 Leer	7W1	Build and apply a stock of words relating to everyday contexts and settings	Spotting cognates (*los cognados*)
	7W3	Learn words for use in language learning	
	7S2	Work out the gist of a sentence	Deciphering meaning
	7T1	Learn about cognates	Reusing part of the question in the answer
	7T6	Answer questions in the target language	

Note: for more detail on all activities listed below, see TB p59.

Lesson objectives for students:

Main objective:

● Describe height and size and personality.

Related objectives:

● Find out more about the endings of adjectives.
● Decipher meaning using cognates for help.
● Homework: **WS 24** Leer **ex 3**: answer questions in the target language.

Lesson starter (precedes SB, ex 1a):

● Use *Pilla al intruso* activity, and encourage use of Spanish for grammatical terms when feeding back answers.

Teaching sequence:

1 *Presentation*
   • Use Visual 20 to present the new language.
   • **SB ex 1a** Students listen, follow and read aloud. Highlight the postion of the adjective after the verb, as in English (contrast with position of Spanish adjective).
   Resources: CD1, track 44

2 *Writing practice*
   • **SB 1b** Students copy the correct adjective for each person.

3 *Grammar*
   • Read through the **Gramática** section on subject pronouns. Check students understand which one to use with names (e.g. *Felipe = él*). Write these up alongside the relevant parts of *llamarse* (met on page 26) or *ser*.

4 *Reading and Oral Practice*
   • **SB ex2** Students match up opposites, using the glossary if necessary.
   • Remind students of classroom routine language *¿Cómo se dice... en español/inglés?* Students work in pairs, focusing on the new adjectives.

5 *Listening practice*
   • **SB ex3** Students choose the correct person for each picture. The pictures can be used for speaking practice afterwards.
   Resources: CD1, track 45

6 *Reading skills*
   • **WS24 Leer exs 1 & 2** Practice in spotting and guessing the meaning of cognates, using these to get the gist of a sentence.

Plenary (see Alternative plenary on page 61):

Ask students to formulate the rule for the feminine of the adjectival forms met in the unit so far. They can then invent and translate new sentences containing these adjectives, or give feminine equivalents of masculine nouns + adjectives (e.g. *Mi padre es hablador/Mi madre es habladora también*), and vice versa.

Note: SB = Student's Book, TB = Teacher's Book, WS = Worksheet, WB A & B = Workbook

Framework objectives			Teaching and learning
SB ex 1	7W1	Build a stock of words relating to everyday contexts and settings	New language for pets
SB Gramática	7W4	Plural nouns	Further plurals
SB ex 2a	7S1 7T1 7L1	Word order for adjectives Using cues to aid understanding Reading aloud	Position of *mucho/a/os/as* Grammatical markers help with meaning Practising pronunciation
WS25 Escribir	7S6	Connectives	Using *y, pero, que*

Note: for more detail on all activities listed below, see TB p62.

Lesson objectives for students:

Main objective:

- ⚫ Say what pets you have and understand others.

Related objectives:

- ⚫ Learn how to use connectives.
- ⚫ Homework: students complete exercises 3 and 4 on **WS25** Escribir

Lesson starter (precedes SB, ex 1):

- ⚫ Students work in pairs within a time limit to write down four each of: numbers, colours, adjectives of height, size or character, as well as the Spanish for 'I have' and 'have you got...?'.

Teaching sequence:

1 *Presentation*
- • Use flashcards and games to present and practise the language for pets.
- • **SB ex1** Students listen and follow the text, and repeat for pronunciation practice.

Resources: flashcards 10–20, CD1, track 46

2 *Grammar: plurals of nouns*
- • **Gramática** Read through this section with students. Give them further words to put into the plural, using the rules met in this section.

3 *Reading skills*
- • **SB ex 2a** Reading aloud practice and memory game.
- • Focus on the adjectives: where do they come in relation to a noun/a verb? Highlight the position of *muchos* before the noun.
- • Focus on the incomplete first halves of the sentences 1–6. What type(s) of words might students anticipate coming next: noun, adjective, number, verb? Match up sentence halves.
- • **WS25** Escribir **ex 1, 2** Connectives.

Plenary (follows SB ex 2a):

(see Alternative plenary page 63) Flashcard consolidation games, and oral pairwork games using the pictures in exercise 1.

Note: SB = Student's Book, TB = Teacher's Book, WS = Worksheet, WB A & B = Workbook

Framework objectives			Teaching and learning
Starter	7W8	Working out the meaning of unfamiliar words, cognates	Find meanings and recognise cognates in the new vocabulary
SB 1a	7W1	Build a stock of words relating to everyday contexts and settings	Understand and pronounce the new language
	7T3	Scan text for difficulty	Pronunciation, intonation practice
	7T2	Read aloud a simple text	Practice in recognising new language
	7L2	Improve their capacity to follow speech	
SB 1b	7L3	Listen for gist and detail	
SB 1c	7T1	Read and understand simple texts	Developing reading skills
SB Gramática	7W2	High-frequency words	Absence of *un/a* after *no hay*
SB 2a	7W1	Using and reapplying stock of words	Using known vocabulary
	7W2	Using high-frequency words	to describe their own town
	7T4	Developing dictionary skills	Looking up compound words

Note: for more detail on all activities listed below, see TB p68.

Lesson objectives for students:

Main objective:

- Say where you live and what facilities there are.

Related objectives:

- Use *hay/no hay*.
- Homework: **SB ex 2a** Students write two lists, one of places there are in their town, one explaining what there isn't (using dictionary, if liked).

Lesson starter (precedes SB, ex 1a):

- Give students the English equivalents of some of the key vocabulary (cognates), which they look up in the glossary, noting whether each noun is *m* or *f*, and therefore *un* or *una*. Fast-finishers work out plurals.

Teaching sequence:

1 *Scanning for difficulty*
- **SB ex 1a** ask pupils to glance through the text and decide on its level of difficulty: *muy difícil, bastante difícil, está bien, fácil, muy fácil*. Discuss what makes it so (quantity of text, number of unknown words etc.).
- Ask students to scan text with a partner – how many cognates can they find?

2 *Presentation*
- Use **OHT8/9** for presentation: OHT8 covers the language in the first paragraph in each section of **SB ex 1a**, and OHT9 the second paragraph.
- Students listen and read **ex 1a** silently, then aloud in sections. Turn the recording down for a few seconds, then up again – are students in the same place? Stop the recording at intervals – students have to chorus the next word.
  Resources: CD1, track 55

3 *Listening practice*
- **SB ex 1b** Students listen to the shorter sentence and identify who is speaking.
  Resources: CD1, track 56

4 *Speaking practice*
- Use the pictures in **ex 1a** for pairwork. Modelling their utterances on the recording they've just heard, students take it in turns to make a statement (e.g. *Vivo en la costa*) and their partner points to the relevant part of the picture.

5 *Reading practice*
- **SB ex1c** students read the statements 1–7, and decide if they are true or false.

6 *Grammar*
- **Gramática**: read through the section on *hay/no hay* with students, and check their understanding.

7 *Dictionary practice*
- Show students how to look up compound words in the dictionary, e.g. railway station, shopping centre, giving them further examples for practice.

Plenary:

Use the new language box to the right of **ex 2b** to highlight and give practice pronouncing and recognising aurally the letter *c*: the soft and hard sounds, and the double *cc*. Use the suggested additional words for aural and written or pronunciation practice.

Unidad 1 • Overview

Welcome to Así

(pp. 6–7)

Objectives
- learn about Spanish-speaking countries
- learn how to introduce yourself

Topic/Language/Culture

Greetings: *buenos días, buenas tardes, hola, ¿qué tal?*

Introductions: *me llamo, soy, soy de*

Names of some countries where Spanish is spoken: *Argentina, Chile, Colombia, Cuba, Estados Unidos, Méjico, Perú, Venezuela*

Culture Spanish as a world language

Grammar and skills

Grammar
soy de + place
Use of inverted exclamation and questions marks

Skills
Receptive strategies for understanding the spoken word 7L3
Recognising cognates and near cognates 7L3

Pronunciation
-o and *-a* endings

National criteria

Attainment AT 1.Level 1, AT 3 Levels 1–2
Framework objectives 7W1, 7S2, 7S8, 7L3 7C1
Programmes of Study 4c
QCA Scheme of Work Language content: Unit 1
Context: Unit 1, Unit 7
Assessment for learning Objectives, p.6, Plenary

Unidad 1 En clase

1A ¡Pasad!
(pp. 8–9)

Objectives
- meet people and say how you are
- learn how to say 'you'
- learn how to practise speaking in Spanish

Topic/Language/Culture

Greetings (relaunch)
More greetings: *cómo está(s). señor/señora/señorita, fatal/mal/muy bien/regular, ¿y tú/usted?, adiós, hasta luego*
introductions (relaunch)
introductions: *¿cómo te llamas?*
answering the register: *voy a pasar lista, ausente, presente, sí, no, no está*

Culture Using appropriate formal/informal language

Grammar and skills

Grammar
tú/usted

Skills
Memorising dialogues 7L6 7T2
Practising speaking skills 7L6

National criteria

Attainment AT Levels 1–3, AT Levels 2–3, AT 3 Levels 1–2, AT Level 4.1
Framework objectives 7W1, 7S3, 7S9, 7L1, 7L3, 7L6, 7T2, 7C5
Programmes of Study 2a, 3a
QCA Scheme of Work Language: Unit 1. Context: Unit 1
Assessment for learning Objectives, p.8 Ex 2, Plenary

1B Mirad la pizarra, por favor
(pp. 10–11)

Objectives
- understand classroom instructions
- learn how to pronounce vowels
- use 'the' and the Spanish alphabet

Topic/Language/Culture

classroom instructions:
mirad el libro/la pizarra, escuchad, abrid/cerrad la puerta/las ventanas, levantaos, sentaos, sacad los libros/los cuadernos, recoged las cosas, ¡silencio!
la mesa
por favor

Grammar and skills

Grammar
Definite articles, indefinite articles, commands

Skills
Notion and patterns of noun gender and number

Pronunciation
Vowel sounds, alphabet

National criteria

Attainment AT1 Level 1, AT 2 Level 1, AT3. Level 1–2, AT4 Level 1
Framework 7W1, 7W3, 7W4, 7W5, 7W6, 7S3, 7L1, 7T1
Programmes of Study 1a, 1b, 2a, 2b
QCA Scheme of work Language: Unit 1
Context: Unit 1
Assessment for learning Objectives, p.11 Ex 5, Plenary

1C ¿Tienes?
(pp. 12–13)

Objectives
- name things you use at school
- learn how to say 'a' and 'some'; learn how to make nouns plural
- learn numbers 1–10

Topic/Language/Culture

Classroom equipment:
¿tienes?/tengo un bolígrafo/cuaderno/estuche/lápiz/ libro, una goma/pluma/mochila/regla
cross-topic words: *en, y, mi/tu*
numbers 1–10

Grammar and skills

Grammar
Indefinite articles, relaunch: plurals

Skills
Learning new nouns with an appropriate article

National criteria

Attainment AT1 Levels 1–2, AT 2 Levels 1–3
AT 3 Levels 1–3, AT 4 Levels 1–3
Framework objectives 7W1, 7W4, 7W6, 7W7, 7S3, 7S6, 7L3, 7T1, 7T5, 7C4
Programmes of study 1b, 2e
QCA Scheme of work Language: Unit 1. Context: Unit 1
Assessment for learning Objectives, p.13 Ex 4, p.13 Ex 5c, Plenary

---

1D ¿Puedo?
(pp. 14–15)

Objectives
- say things you need in the Spanish class
- understand when to use *i...!* and *¿...?*

Topic/Language/Culture

asking for help or permission: *¿cómo se escribe/se dice?, ¿qué significa?, ¿puedo ir (al baño, al patio, a la cantina)?, no sé, ¿puede repetir?*
relaunch: classroom equipment

Grammar and skills

Grammar
Use of *¿...?* and *i...!*

Skills
Distinguishing questions in speech and writing

Pronunciation
Intonation for questions

National criteria

Attainment AT 1 Level 2, AT 3 Levels 1–3, AT 4 Levels 1–4
Framework objectives 7W1, 7W4, 7S1, 7S3, 7S4, 7S5, 7L1, 7L3, 7T1, 7T2
Programmes of study 1a, 2b
QCA Scheme of work Language: Unit 1. Context: Unit 1
Assessment for learning Objectives, p.14 Ex 2, Plenary

Welcome to ¡Así!

Aquí se habla español pp. 6–7

> **Objectives:**
> - learn about Spanish-speaking countries
> - learn how to introduce yourself
>
> **Key Language:** see p.28 for full list
> - greetings
> - introductions
> - names of some Spanish-speaking countries
>
> **Grammar:**
> - *soy de* + place
> - use of inverted exclamation and questions marks
>
> **Skills:**
> - receptive strategies for understanding the spoken word
> - recognising cognates and near cognates
>
> **Pronunciation:** -o and -a endings
>
> **Resources:** OHTs 1A and 1B (reproduction of world map and overlay) ; CD 1; Worksheet 2 (Resumen)

This spread presents simple greetings in the context of Hispanophone countries.

Introduction

Greet class using *Buenos días/Buenas tardes* as appropriate: *Buenos días/Buenas tardes, clase*. Go round and greet individuals as appropriate: *Buenos días, Sam/Buenas tardes, Charlotte*.

Ask the class what they think you were saying. Point out that just as they understood this, they will find they can understand a lot of Spanish. Establish conventions to distinguish parts of the lesson where Spanish or English is to be spoken. For example, depending on the language, point to a Spanish or British flag which can either be in the form of a flashcard or on the wall at either side of the board. Tell students that if they do not understand something, they must let you know. Again establish a linguistic or kinaesthetic convention for this (e.g. *por favor*/hand up). Aim to have concentrated periods of time where Spanish is spoken.

As a pre-listening activity, show the class OHT 1A: Say, for example: *Aquí tengo un mapa, un mapa del mundo. Aquí hay España. Aquí hay América del Sur y aquí los Estados Unidos.*

Say the names of the countries that feature on the CD, point to them on the map and ask students to repeat.

1 💿 Escucha (1–8) y mira el mapa. Escribe el número y la letra. AT1.1, AT3.2; 7L3, 7S8

Ask the students to turn to pp. 6–7 and to look at the map. You can use OHT 1A to point out the countries.

Explain that they are going to hear the young people in the photos saying who they are and where they come from. Discuss what details they think they need to listen out for (names and countries). Go through the example with them. The students match the person with the country. This activity could be used for assessment.

When correcting the answers, introduce the students to the letters a–h receptively.

Play the CD again and ask the students to spot the greetings in each one. Ask them if they can work out what they mean and what the difference is between the formal/polite and informal sets of greetings. Say different greetings (including *Buenas noches*) and ask them to indicate whether this is formal or informal. Focus on the difference between *Buenos días* and *buenas tardes* when they are pronouncing them.

Underline the interchangeability of *Me llamo…* and *Soy…* by saying e.g.: **Me llamo** *Señorita Black…* **Soy** *Señorita Black*. Ask confident students to introduce themselves using one or other of these structures.

Ask the students whether they notice anything unusual about the punctuation. Elicit the fact that interrogatives have ¿…? and exclamation marks are written ¡…! This feature is dealt with more fully in section 1D.

Pronunciation

Ask the students to identify all the words that have 'a' in them. Pronounce them as they say them and stress that an 'a' is always pronounced in the same way. Contrast this with English where 'apt' and 'April' are very different whereas '*apto*' and '*abril*' are not. Give them the following tongue-twister: *Alberto Alonso abre la apertura con alegría.*

Do likewise with 'o'. Ask them to compare the two 'o's in 'October' and '*ocho*'. Explain that English has long and short vowels, whereas in Spanish vowels have equal value. Ask them to say: *Ochenta y ocho olivos olorosos.*

Gramática 7S2

Students have met and practised *Soy…* Now the focus is on *Soy de* to say where one is from. Ask students to find examples of this phrase, on the page. Then ask them to find examples of *Soy…* In fact, the two forms mirror their English equivalents.

El español es importante 7C1

A series of facts to demonstrate that Spanish is a world language. The language used is English.
Students may like to know some of the following facts:
- Spanish is the third most widely spoken language in the world (after Mandarin Chinese and English).
- There are currently 400 million Spanish speakers.
- Spanish is spoken throughout Spain and its territories, Ecuatorial Guinea and the Sahara, the Philippines and Central and South America except Brazil (where Portuguese is spoken), the Guyanas and the United States.

- In the US there are 30 million Spanish speakers.
- In the year 2020 probably one in five US citizens will be Hispanic.
- Two thirds of Spanish-speakers are Mexican. The remainder come from Central and South America (15%), Puerto Rico (9%), Cuba (4%), with 6% from other Spanish-speaking countries.
- The USA took over 5 states that were previously under Mexican control, hence all the place names in Spanish.
- Hispanics of Mexican origin represent 56% of the population of the American West Coast – a very high percentage.
- Hispanics represent the youngest ethnic group (35% under 18), this points to the continued growth of the Hispanic community.

¡extra! Questions for more confident students to follow up in the library or on the internet. Some pointers are given above.

If they are researching on the internet, key words such as 'Conquistadors', 'El Dorado', 'Aztecs' and 'Incas' might provide useful starting points. Students might also be asked to find out why Portuguese is spoken in Brazil.

Plenary

Ask students what they have learnt about Spanish and the Spanish-speaking world. Ask what they have found surprising or different about Spanish. Ask if they have noticed any similarities (e.g. between the names of the countries in both languages).

1 En clase

Note:

 = Exercises which practise Thinking Skills (see page 12)

 = Assessment for learning exercises (see page 12)

1A ¡Pasad! pp. 8–9

Objectives:
- meet people and say how you are
- learn how to say 'you'
- learn how to practise speaking in Spanish

Key Language: see p.28 for full list
- more greetings: *adiós, … señor/señora/señorita*
- more introductions: *¿y tú?, ¿cómo te llamas?*
- answering the register: *voy a pasar lista, ausente, presente, sí, no, no está*

Grammar: *Tú/usted*

Skills:
- memorising dialogues
- practising speaking skills

Resources OHTs 2A and 2B (greetings plus overlay); CD1; Worksheets 2 (Resumen), 4 (Hablar – practising dialogues); Workbooks A & B p.3; Prop clock; *Just Click* CD-Rom.

On these two pages greetings are revised and further meeting and greeting formulae are introduced. Students also learn to answer the register.

Introduction

Revise *¡Hola!, Buenos días/Buenas tardes* by greeting individuals as themselves: *Hola, Mary*, or in a more formal way: *Buenos días, señor*.

Make the formal greetings sound more formal. Recap by asking when to use *Buenos días* (more formal morning), *Buenas tardes* (more formal afternoon) and *¡Hola!* (informal all day). Give students two minutes to greet the people around them informally and more formally.

1a ⏺ Escucha y lee. AT1.1, AT3.2; 7L1, 7CS

Students listen to and read four short exchanges involving greetings. The exchanges use both the *tú* and *usted* forms. The following language items are new: *¿Cómo está(s)?, fatal, mal/muy bien/regular, hasta luego, adiós.*

Use OHTs 2A and 2B to present this exercise. Ask students to shut their books and to listen carefully. Ask them to put their pens down and to concentrate. Show just OHT 2A. Play the CD several times. Play each exchange separately and ask the class what they think the people are saying. Ask them to listen to/look carefully at the first two exchanges. What is the difference in the form of *¿Cómo está(s)?* Now put on overlay 2B. On the board/OHT build up a table of greetings. Put the informal form on one side and its formal equivalent on the other.

¡hola!	buenos días/buenas tardes (señor/señora/señorita)
¿cómo estás?	¿cómo está?
¿qué tal? ¿y tú?	¿qué tal? ¿y usted?
fatal/mal/muy bien/regular	fatal/mal/muy bien/regular
adiós, hasta luego	adiós, hasta luego

Practise the exchanges with choral repetition. Say a sentence and ask them to say which picture it refers to: 1, 2, 3 or 4. To increase the challenge, ask them to cover their books.

CD1, track 02

- ¡Hola! Susana. ¿Cómo estás?
- Muy bien. ¿Y tú?
- Buenos días Jaime. ¿Cómo estás?
- Regular. ¿Y usted?
- Buenas tardes, señorita. ¿Qué tal?
- ¡Fenomenal!
- ¿Qué tal, Conchita?
- ¡Fatal! Adiós.

1b 💬 Practica los diálogos con tu pareja. AT2.2; 7T2

Ask the students to practise the dialogues from 1a in pairs and to take turns to play each role. From the start, insist on the students speaking in Spanish during pairwork.

Work with the class to set out some ground rules, for example:
- Don't raise your voice.
- Always speak in Spanish (unless you need help).
- Put your hand up if you need help.
- Make sure you've practised the dialogue and are confident before asking the teacher/assistant to listen.

Give the students a strict time limit and a challenge. How many exchanges can you do in two minutes? Can you sound just like the people on tape? Then ask for volunteers to 'act out' the short exchanges. The rest of the class can be given a task while the pair are speaking. For example, which picture is it?

Gramática: *Tú* and *usted* – you 7C5

An initial alert to the grammatical difference in register. This will be dealt with more fully in Unit 10.

2 ☑ ⏺ Escucha (1–6). Escribe a–d AT1.1, AT3.1; 7L3

Six short dialogues. Students listen and identify the greeting used each time.

Explain that you will play the CD several times. Ask the students to listen to all the extracts with their pens down before doing the exercise for real. This avoids the students being too busy writing to listen carefully. Tell them to listen to the 'plot' or 'geography' of what they are going to hear. How long, fast, complicated is it? Where is the information that I want to find? What predictions can I make as to possible answers? What words am I likely to hear?

To make listening more of a fun activity and as a pre-listening exercise, give each student/pair/row an expression and ask them to stand up each time they hear it. This active participation keeps them literally on their toes and is a technique that can be used to identify a variety of language.

When checking on the answers, try to focus on how well they did and on any problems they encountered rather than crude scores. It is important that they realise from the beginning that understanding why you got something wrong is more important than the mark.

This exercise could be used for assessment.

TRANSCRIPT
CD1, track 03

1 – Buenos días.
 – Buenos días.
 – ¿Cómo te llamas?
 – Me llamo Ángel.
2 – ¡Hola! Marisol.
 – ¡Hola! ¿Qué tal?
3 – Buenas tardes, señorita.
 – Buenas tardes, Fede.
4 – ¡Hola! ¿Qué tal?
 – ¡Hola! ¿Cómo te llamas?
 – Me llamo Maite. ¿Y tú?
 – Sara.
5 – Buenos días, señora.
 – Buenos días.
6 – Buenas tardes, señor.
 – Buenas tardes. ¿Qué tal?
 – Bien.

Answers

1 b 2 a 3 c 4 a 5 b 6 c

3 Escucha (1–7). ¿Cómo están? AT1.3, AT4.1; 7L3

Students identify how people say they are. The exchanges provide a pattern for pairwork. Encourage students to be suitably dramatic so as to differentiate between e.g. *fatal* and *mal*.

TRANSCRIPT
CD1, track 04

1 – ¡Hola **Isabel**! ¿Qué tal?
 – **Muy bien**.
2 – ¡Hola! ¿Cómo te llamas?
 – Me llamo **Bea**.
 – ¿Cómo estás?
 – **¡Fatal!**
3 – Buenos días, me llamo **Antonio**. ¿Cómo estás?
 – **Regular**. ¿Y tú?
4 – ¡Hola!, **Mariluz**. ¿Qué tal?
 – **¡Fenomenal!**
5 – ¡Buenas tardes! Me llamo **Alfonso**.
 – ¡Buenas tardes! ¿Cómo estás?
 – **Muy bien**, gracias.
6 – ¡Buenos días! Me llamo **Nuria**.
 – ¡Buenos días! ¿Cómo estás?
 – **Regular**. ¿Y usted?
7 – ¡Hola! **Paca**. Qué tal?
 – **¡Fatal!** ¿Y tú?

Answers

1 b 2 d 3 c 4 a 5 b 6 c 7 d

¡extra! Escucha otra vez y escribe el nombre de las personas. AT1.3; 7L3

Students listen again to the CD extract and note each of the forenames that they hear. All the names appear on the page. Before they start, ask them to suggest strategies for keeping up with the CD, for example, just writing the first one or two letters of each name as they hear it, then listening again to check and to fill in the rest of the name.

Answers

1 Isabel 2 Bea 3 Antonio 4 Mariluz 5 Alfonso 6 Nuria
7 Paca

4 Habla con tu pareja. AT2.3; 7S3

Some students may find it helpful to copy out the dialogue, filling it in with their own and their partner's names. However, encourage them to memorise the dialogues and not to rely on the written form.

WS 4 (Hablar) offers a simple gapped proforma that can be completed by students working in pairs, as a preliminary to oral practice.

¡Así se hace! 7L6

A reminder of the disadvantages of reading, rather than saying a dialogue.

Ask students to think of other disadvantages (head down – inaudible with some students; no eye contact with person you are speaking to; no premium on memory or need to learn; lack of intonation and fluency).

5 Escucha (1–6). Escribe ✓ (presente) o ✗ (no está). AT1.1; 7L3

Go through the responses with the class and explain that this is how you are going to begin each lesson. Practise saying the names of class members who are present or absent. You could include some celebrities to liven up the activity. As extension vocabulary, introduce *Está enfermo/a, Está con el señor X*.

The students could hear this twice. The first time they only have to mark present or absent. The second time they have to write exactly what was said. Alternatively, you can differentiate by asking those who can to write what was said and those who can only identify ✓ and ✗ to do so.

TRANSCRIPT
CD1, track 05

1 – Voy a pasar lista... Pablo
 – ¡Presente!
2 – Julia.
 – No está.
3 – Rafa.
 – Sí, señor.
4 – Ángel.
 – ¡Presente!
5 – Nuria.
 – Sí, señor.
6 – Paca.
 – Ausente.

A final exercise could involve asking selected pairs of students to re-enact the dialogues they prepared and practised for exercise 2b.

Extension

Other groups could prepare and act out a short exchange between a teacher and a group of students.

Plenary

☑ Ask students to look at the objectives at the top of the section and to tell you in pairs what they think they have learnt.

1B Mirad la pizarra, por favor pp. 10–11

Objectives:
• understand classroom instructions
• use 'the' and the Spanish alphabet
• learn how to pronounce vowels
Key Language: see p.28 for full list
Grammar:
• *Tú/Usted*
• definite articles
• indefinite articles
• commands
Skills: spotting language patterns (gender and number)
Pronunciation: vowel sounds
Resources: OHT 3 (alphabet); CD1;
Worksheet 2 (Resumen); Workbooks A and B p.4;
Just Click CD-Rom.

On these two pages students meet some simple classroom instructions, the definite article and the Spanish alphabet.

Lesson starter

Take the class register out of order. Ask everyone to call out 'Presente' for people that are here and 'Ausente' or 'No está' for absentees.

Alternative lesson starter (for lessons starting part-way through the section)

Call out different instructions (e.g. Sacad los libros/Escuchad). Everyone must mime the appropriate action. Watch out for any problems and do that one again later.

1 Escucha (1–10). Une las frases y los dibujos. AT1.1, AT3.2; 7W5, 7T1

Listening and reading presentation of ten classroom instructions. The instructions all use a plural imperative verb. Students listen, then match each spoken and written instruction to the correct picture. You may already be using some or all of these instructions. Otherwise, before you start, go through the pictures with the class and establish what is happening in each picture. Ask them if they can identify a written instruction for any of the pictures. This should eliminate *Silencio* and perhaps *Repetid*. To help comprehension you may like to pause the CD at each instruction while you mime to it.

TRANSCRIPT   CD1, track 06

1 Mirad la pizarra.	6 Sentaos.
2 Escuchad.	7 Sacad los libros.
3 Abrid las ventanas.	8 Recoged las cosas.
4 Repetid.	9 Cerrad la puerta.
5 Levantaos.	10 ¡Silencio!

Answers

1 b 2 a 3 d 4 e 5 f 6 g 7 h 8 c 9 j 10 i

Once the instructions have been presented, try to use them regularly in class.

2 Trabaja con tu pareja. A escucha a B y hace la acción. AT1.1, AT2.1; 7L1

Students take it in turns to say an instruction chosen from the list in 1a, and their partner acts it out. To introduce a measure of challenge, students can be given five lives and lose a life if they are unable to carry out the action.

3 Rellena los espacios. AT4.1; 7W6

A series of familiar gapped words and phrases for students to copy and complete. Fast-finishers can write four more sentences with gaps for their partners.

Answers

1 Abrid la puerta. 2 Levantaos, por favor. 3 Sentaos.
4 Repetid. 5 Cerrad la puerta. 6 Recoged los libros.

Pronunciación: a, e, i, o, u 7W6, 7L1, 7L6

Explains the fact that in Spanish vowel sounds are constant, unlike English with its long and short vowels.

Ask the class and then individuals to practise the sample sentences. You could ask people to practise these for homework.

TRANSCRIPT   CD1, track 07

Alfonso habla alemán.
Emilio y Enrique escriben en el estuche.

Use OHT 3 for a final pronunciation session. Point in turn to all the letters that contain the same vowel sound: b, c, d etc./q, u/i, i griega etc. and get the class to chant them.

¡Así se hace! 7W3

Help with how to ask what something means.

Gramática: the – el, la, los, las 7W4

A first lesson on gender and number. As a starter, you could put a number of familiar singular words ending in -o and -a on the board (e.g. *libro, puerta, señor, señora*) and ask students to work out the two categories and invite them to say what the difference might be. Those who have already studied French will be familiar with the use of gender. Once you have made two groups of singular nouns, ask students to read the Grammar section and to tell you whether they take *el* or *la*. Then ask how you would talk about more than one of each of the nouns and what article you would need to use.

NB *Día* is an exception to the rule, as are some other words they will meet later in this book: *mapa, problema, idioma, turista* (m&f).

4 Put the correct form of 'the' in front of the following words and translate them. AT4.1; 7W4

A set of singular and plural nouns to which students add the correct definite article before translating them.

Answers

1 el libro 2 las pizarras 3 la puerta 4 la mesa 5 el diálogo
6 las ventanas 7 la cosa 8 los cuadernos

5 ✓ Escribe frases en 5 minutos. AT4.1; 7S3

Students compose and write as many command phrases as possible, mixing and matching from the grid given. They can repeat any word. Some combinations will be unusual but acceptable (*Mirad las cosas*) others will not (*Sentaos la ventana*). This exercise could be used for assessment.

Give students two minutes to make up sentence combinations as suggested in exercise 5. Read out a command and ask students to call out the ending(s) they have put. Ask the class to translate any potentially odd combinations into English.

6a Escucha y repite el rap del alfabeto. 7W6

Listening and reading presentation of the Spanish alphabet. Use OHT 3 to point to the letters as they are pronounced. Ask students what they notice that is different from the way the English alphabet is set out (ñ as a separate letter). The alphabet has been recorded twice: students can first listen to the letters being recited, then hear it being sung (accompanied by music) as a rap. After students have repeated the alphabet rap, do more oral practice in class, e.g.

- display the letters on the OHP. Cover a few up: which have disappeared?
- say a sequence of three letters: which letter comes next?
- say a letter, which letter precedes it in the alphabet?
- say a Spanish word: what is its first letter?

A, B, C   D, E, F   G, H, I   J, K, L   M, N, Ñ   O, P, Q
R, S, T   U, V   W, X   Y, Z

6b ⬤ Di las letras de tu nombre. AT2.1; 7W6

Students are invited to spell their own names in Spanish. Ask individuals: *Deletrea tu nombre.* Then ask them to work in pairs. After they have practised spelling their own names they could choose someone in the class and spell that person's name to their partner. The partner must guess who it is as quickly as possible and before the spelling is completed.

Extension

Divide the class into two teams. Choose one person in each team to keep the score. Point to a letter at random and to a member of one team. They must try to pronounce it correctly. If they don't succeed, ask an individual in the other team.

Plenary

✓ Display a list of the instructions introduced in the lesson. As you read out each, students put both hands up (understand), one hand up (think I understand) or no hands up (don't understand). You might also provide pieces of different coloured card for students to hold up on this and subsequent occasions (e.g. red = understand, orange = think I understand, yellow = don't understand).

1C ¿Tienes...? pp. 12–13

Objectives:
- name things you use at school
- learn how to say 'a' and 'some'; learn how to make nouns plural
- learn numbers 1–10

Key Language: see p.28 for full list

Grammar:
- indefinite articles
- plural nouns

Skills: learning new nouns with an appropriate article

Resources: Flashcards 1–9 (classroom equipment); Visual 1, CD1; Worksheets 1 (visuals, classroom equipment), 2 (Resumen), 3 (Escuchar – classroom equipment), 6 (Escribir – cartoon story), 8 (Gramática – gender); Visual 1, Workbooks A and B p.5; OHT or wall chart for numbers; *Just Click* CD-Rom.

In this section students meet words for classroom equipment, the indefinite article and numbers 1–10.

Lesson starter

Use the alphabet OHT 3 for more quick class alphabet practice. You spell out the name of a person in the class or a famous personality. Class members shout out as soon as they have identified the name.

Alternative lesson starters *(for lessons starting part-way through the section)*

Choose from a selection of number games:

- Bingo: Students write down any four numbers between 1 and 10. Call out numbers in random order: students ring the numbers which you call. The first student with all four numbers ringed is the winner. In time, students can split into groups, with one of the group calling the numbers. Remind the callers to write down the numbers they choose as they call them, for checking in case of disputes.

- Memory game: display any six numbers on an OHT for 10 seconds, then switch the OHT off. Students, working in pairs, try to recall and write down the numbers which they saw. Elicit the numbers, orally, from different groups. The winners are the students who give you the correct eight numbers.

You can make this exercise more challenging by:
  - writing the numbers as words instead of figures on the OHT
  - increasing the number of words from six to eight.

- **más, menos:** Think of a number between 1 and 10. Half the class has to try and guess the number: students call any number, and you say *más* or *menos* until they get it. Keep a tally of the number of guesses. Now the other half of the class has a go, and tries to guess your number with fewer guesses than the first group.
The reverse of this game would work equally well. A student decides on a number and writes it down on a miniboard/paper and shows it to the rest of the class; you must not see it. You then try to guess and the students call out *más, menos*.

- Divide your class into two groups. Give each member of each group a card with a number between *uno* and *diez* written on it. Students have to line up in numerical order by looking at each other's cards (they are not allowed to speak). The first group to line up correctly wins.

- **español, inglés:** Students call out numbers, in order, alternately in Spanish and English, e.g.

student A	**uno**
student B	two
student C	**tres**
student D	four
etc.	

The aim is to get to 10 without tripping up.

In time, you can make this game more challenging by selecting the next student at random, so that students cannot prepare their number in advance.

Introduction

Pre-exercise: Reading presentation of nine pieces of classroom equipment.

These classroom items also feature as flashcards and as mini-flashcards on Worksheet 1.

Practise the new vocabulary using flashcards 1–9 or classroom objects.

Hold up one card and say e.g. *un lápiz.* Encourage the class and then individuals to repeat. Introduce several cards in this way, using indirect articles. Then hold up one of them and elicit its name from the class and then individuals. Move on to asking *¿Tienes (una pluma)?* As you ask, give that card to an individual and encourage him/her to reply: *Sí, tengo (una pluma).* Introduce all the cards in this way.

1a 💿 Escucha (1–8). Escribe la letra. AT1.1; 7L3

Students listen and look for the item mentioned in each exchange, and write the letter.

Some of the exchanges use negative forms.

1 – ¿Tienes un libro?
   – Sí, señor. Tengo un libro.
2 – ¿Tienes una goma?
   – No, no tengo goma.
3 – ¿Tienes una regla?
   – Sí, tengo una regla. ▶

4 – ¿Tienes un cuaderno?
– No, no tengo cuaderno.
5 – ¿Tienes un bolígrafo?
– Sí, tengo un bolígrafo.
6 – ¿Tienes una mochila?
– No, no tengo mochila.
7 – ¿Tienes un estuche?
– Sí, tengo un estuche.
8 – ¿Tienes una pluma?
– No, no tengo pluma.

Answers

1 e **2** f **3** g **4** d **5** b **6** i **7** h **8** c

Draw students' attention to the note about the negative form used in 1a.

Demonstrate the negative form by holding up a card and saying *Tengo (una mochila)*. Then hide that card and say: *No tengo mochila*. Give a card to an individual. Ask that person whether they have it: *¿Tienes (una goma)?* Elicit the answer: *Sí, tengo una goma*. Leave the card with that person and ask someone else the same question. Elicit the answer: *No, no tengo goma*.

1b Escucha (1–5). Escribe las letras de las cosas en orden. AT1.1; 7L3

Students hear five exchanges about classroom equipment. For each one they note down the letter that corresponds to the item mentioned. These exchanges contain a mixture of positive and negative forms.

> TRANSCRIPT   **CD1, track 11**
>
> **1** – ¿Tienes un lápiz?
> – Sí, tengo un lápiz.
> **2** – ¿Tienes un bolígrafo?
> – No, no tengo bolígrafo.
> **3** – ¿Tienes una goma?
> – No, no tengo goma.
> **4** – ¿Tienes una regla?
> – Sí, tengo.
> **5** – ¿Tienes una pluma?
> – No, no tengo pluma.

Answers

1 a **2** b **3** f **4** g **5** c

Gramática: 'a' and 'some' 7W4

Identification of singular indefinite article.
Students should be able to tell you that both words mean 'a' but *un* is for masculine words (generally ending in -*o*) while *una* is for feminine words (generally ending in -*a*).

2 Put the following words into two columns: those that take *un* and those that take *una*. AT4.1; 7W4

Students list the new equipment words according to gender. There are two masculine words in the presentation which do not end in -*o* (*lápiz* and *estuche*).

More able students might be able to tell you another exception they have already met (*día*).

Drawing attention to these exceptions will confirm the importance of the advice in the ¡Así se hace! section.

Answers

un bolígrafo/cuaderno/estuche/lápiz/libro;
una goma pluma/mochila/regla

Possible extension

Give some further unknown vocabulary items and ask students to say whether they are *un* or *una*.

¡Así se hace! 7W7

See note for exercise 2.

WS 8 (Gramática) offers more support and practice on gender.

Before the next exercise students will need to be familiar with numbers 1–10, listed at the top of the page. Introduce these using an OHT, or wall chart or by just writing the 10 figures on the board. Start by saying them and asking the class to repeat, move on to chanting them in order. Then point to a number and ask the class to say it. Move on to doing the same thing with individuals.

Once the students have learnt these numbers, encourage them to go home and teach their parents or siblings.

3 Vamos a cantar. AT2.1; 7C4

A song using just the numbers 1–10. Students first practise singing along with it slowly. The text could be shown on OHT with some of the words removed. Delete more words as they progress. On a subsequent rendition you could ask them to close their books.

You could stop the tape at any point and ask the students to continue. Alternatively you could turn down the volume partway through the song. The students have to sing at exactly the right speed so that when the volume is turned up again, they are in the right place. Stress the importance of learning numbers as they occur in so many situations.

> TRANSCRIPT   **CD1, track 12**
>
> | | | | | |
> |---|---|---|---|---|
> | uno | dos | tres | cuatro | |
> | cinco | seis | | | |
> | siete | ocho | nueve | diez | (×6) |
> | | | | | |
> | diez | nueve | ocho | siete | |
> | seis | cinco | | | |
> | cuatro | tres | dos | uno | (×2) |

Once students have mastered the song you could try getting them to sing it faster.

Extension

Confident students might be able to reverse the words and sing them backwards:

4 Habla con tu pareja. AT2.3; 7S3

Using the new numbers and the classroom equipment words, students work in pairs to build up a list of vocabulary along the lines of 'I went to market…'. Challenge them to produce as long a list as possible.

Students must be aware of need to put *y* before the last item in the list like English 'and'.

Extension

More able students might be able to add a *no tengo…* option at the end.

This exercise could be used for assessment.

Gramática: plurals 7W4

Recap on gender and plural.

5a Put the following nouns into the plural: AT 4.1; 7W4

Students now produce the plural forms of a list of known regular singular nouns.

Answers

plumas, diálogos, bolígrafos, cuadernos, mochilas, pizarras, puertas, gomas

5b 📖 Lee las descripciones: a, b, c o d? AT3.3; 7T1

A set of four descriptions. Students must find the one that fits the picture.

Answer

b

Ask students what strategies would be useful for checking this kind of work. For example, look at the first description, it says *dos bolígrafos*. Look at the picture, there is only one biro so it's not description (a) OR descriptions (c) or (d).

5c ☑ ✏ ¿Qué tienes en tu mochila y en tu estuche? Escribe una lista. AT4.3; 7T5

Writing practice. The teacher can have such a list ready or answer questions on demand. Individuals list what they have in their own schoolbags and pencil cases. Students might well ask what felt tips and other implements there are. This could also be a spoken exercise.

Extension

More able students could add what they don't have. This exercise could be used for assessment.

WS 3 (Escuchar) offers practice in distinguishing positive from negative, as well as spelling revision.

Use the mini-flashcards from Worksheet 1 for group work games:

- Students divide up the cards without showing each other which ones they've got. They take it in turns to ask each other ¿*Tienes (una mochila)?* If the person has the thing they must hand it over saying *Sí, tengo (una mochila)*. If they haven't got it they say *No, no tengo (mochila)* and it is then their go. The person with the most cards after five minutes is the winner.
- Students work in pairs, timing each other to see how quickly they can match the pictures to the labels.

WS 6 (Escribir) would fit well as a homework exercise after work on this section has been completed.

Plenary

☑ In pairs students explain the general grammar rule for *un/una*, as if teaching it to someone who missed the lesson.

1D ¿Puedo...? page 14

> **Objectives:**
> - say things you need in the Spanish class
> - understand when to use ¡...! and ¿...?
>
> **Key Language:** see p.28 for full list
> **Grammar:** use of ¡...! and ¿...?
> **Skills:** how to recognise a spoken or written question
> **Pronunciation:** intonation for questions
> **Resources:** OHTs 4A and 4B (classroom scene with students asking for help, plus overlay); CD1; Worksheets 2 (Resumen), 5 (Leer – matching rhyming words, joining sentences), 7 (¡**Así se hace!** – sentence order), 9 (¡**extra!** – reading comprehension); Workbooks A and B p.6; *Just Click* CD-Rom.

This final section presents ways of asking for things in class, highlights the usage of inverted exclamation and question marks and offers a resumé of the whole unit.

Lesson starter

Recap on definite and indefinite articles. On board write e.g. *mochila* and *cuaderno*. How do you say 'a' for each of them? Then look back to section B. What about 'the'? What about more than one?

Alternative lesson starter *(for lessons starting part-way through the section)*

Revise numbers 1–10 by counting together. Then get one half of the class to call out the evens and the other half to call out the odds.

1a 💿 Escucha (1–7) y lee las frases. Escribe el número correcto. AT3.2; 7L3

Presentation and practice of new classroom language. Students read, listen and match the sentences with the pictures.

> **TRANSCRIPT**   CD1, track 13
>
> 1 ¿Cómo se escribe *Venezuela*?
> 2 ¿Cómo se dice 'pen' en español?
> 3 ¿Qué significa *pizarra*?
> 4 ¿Puedo ir al baño, por favor?
> 5 No comprendo.
> 6 No sé.
> 7 ¿Puede repetir, por favor?

Answers

1 d **2** a **3** e **4** c **5** b **6** f **7** g

As with the previous classroom instructions, once this language has been introduced build it into daily classroom routine, encouraging students to use it on all occasions when appropriate.

1b ✏ ¡extra! Cambia las palabras en itálica en 1a con las palabras de abajo. AT4.3; 7S3

Students adapt the key sentences in 1a to include the alternative words and phrases listed. This can be prepared in pairs. Students can also practise all the possible combinations orally.

Possible answers

1 ¿Cómo se escribe estuche/regla/lápiz?
2 ¿Puedo ir al patio/a la cantina, por favor?
3 ¿Qué significa estuche/regla/lápiz?

 ¡Así se hace! i...! or ¿...? 7L6

A note about the use of the inverted exclamation mark and question mark that are peculiar to written Spanish.

2 ☑ 💿 **Listen (1–10) and write ¿...? for questions or ¡...! for exclamations or nothing for normal statements.** AT1.2; 7S4, 7L1

Students listen and decide whether each of the sentences they hear is a statement or a question.

This exercise could be used for assessment.

TRANSCRIPT   CD1, track 14

1 ¡Hola! ¡Hola, Juan!
2 Abrid el libro, por favor.
3 ¿Cómo te llamas?
4 ¿Tienes un bolígrafo?
5 Tengo dos lápices en mi estuche.
6 ¡Fantástico! ¡Estupendo!
7 Me llamo Carlitos.
8 Buenas tardes, señora.
9 ¿Puedo salir, señorita?
10 Voy a pasar lista.

Answers

¿...?: 3, 4, 9   ¡...!: 1, 6.   Nothing: 2, 5, 7, 8, 10

Play the CD again pausing to notice intonation of each sentence. Then you or the class try to change the same sentence to a question/order/statement.

Subsequently, you could say a sentence twice: once as a question and once as a statement. Students indicate which each one was. Or you say a statement/question and students give the alternative intonation (i.e. question – statement; statement to question).

WS 7 (**¡Así se hace!**) offers further work on word order and a reminder on the perils of literal translation.

WS 5 (Leer) combines reading with listening and speaking skills in two exercises focusing on rhyming words.

3 💬 **¡extra! Escribe cinco frases con ¿...? y sin ¿...?. Lee las frases a tu pareja.** AT4.2; 7T2

Further practice of exclamation and interrogation marks.

Resumen (page 15)

This section offers a resumé of all the vocabulary, grammar, skills and tips presented in the unit. Talk students through the page and show them that the new language is split into groups, with English translations. Tell them that they can use these pages as a reference point, e.g. if they want to check the meaning or spelling of a word or phrase. If they miss a lesson, they can check the words they have missed.

Below the vocabulary list, the Gramática points of the unit are summarised, along with the **¡Así se hace!** and

pronunciation skills students have learnt. Cross-topic words are also highlighted, i.e. words which students can learn and re-use in other contexts.

The page is also duplicated as a worksheet, which students can stick into their exercise books.

WS 9 (**¡extra!**) confronts the issue of recognising more words than you have actually learnt. As an end-of-lesson or homework exercise, it would help to convince students of how much they have learnt.

Plenary

☑ Ask the class to look carefully at the Resumen. Go through it together. Does all the vocabulary now look familiar? Have they understood the grammar points? In speaking exercises, have they remembered about equal vowel values? Ask people to indicate whether they are happy (Sí, muy bien) or unhappy (No comprendo) about each section.

¡Ahora, tú! (pp. 118–119)

The exercises in the ¡Ahora, tú! section at the back of the Student's Book contain differentiated self-access exercises to give your students more reading and writing practice with the language from each unit. You can use them as follows:

• as you work through the units, or as revision when working on subsequent units
• with students who finish a classroom exercise before the others
• as homework tasks
• as work to set if you are absent
• for further classroom practice of points which need more work
• as preparation for an assessment.

Page 118

1 📖 **Copy the grid and sort sentences into two groups.**

Answers

Profesor	Alumno
Sentaos	No tengo cuaderno
¿Cómo te llamas?	Buenos días, señor
Sí, tengo un bolígrafo.	¡Presente!
Mirad la pizarra.	¿Puedo ir al baño?
¿Tienes un libro?	No comprendo.
Recoged las cosas	¿Cómo se dice 'lápiz' en inglés?
Levantaos	¡Ausente!
	¿Cómo se escribe 'cuaderno', por favor?
	Buenos días, señorita.
	¿Puede repetir?

2 🖊 **Do the following sums.**

Answers

1 siete 2 diez 3 siete 4 seis 5 nueve
6 siete 7 cinco 8 seis 9 uno 10 cuatro

3  **Match the opposites.**

Answers

1 Abrid la ventana – Cerrad la ventana. **2** Ausente – Presente.
3 Cerrad el libro – Abrid el libro. **4** Levantaos – Sentaos.
5 Comprendo – No comprendo.

4 ✏️ **Write out the dialogue. Choose phrases to replace words in italics.**

Answers

¡Hola! *Buenos días* (<u>Buenas tardes</u>).
   Bueno, mirad la pizarra y sacad *el libro*. (<u>el cuaderno</u>)

Buenos días, señor. (<u>Buenas tardes, señorita</u>)
   ¿Puedo ir al baño?

¡Sentaos! Voy a pasar lista. ¿Ángel Álvarez?
   ¡No! (<u>Sí</u>)

¡Presente! (<u>Ausente</u>)
   ¿Cómo se escribe 'bolígrafo' en español?

¿Ana Botín?
   b-o-l-í-g-r-a-f-o.

¡Presente! (<u>Ausente</u>)
   Gracias.
   Trabaja con tu pareja.

Page 119

1  **Separa las palabras de tres frases diferentes.**

Answers

1 Me llamo Frederico. Tengo un lápiz. ¿Puedo ir al baño?
2 Cerrad la puerta. Voy a pasar lista. Mirad la pizarra.
3 Buenos días señor. Escribe en el cuaderno. Recoged las cosas.

2 **Copia y rellena los espacios.**

Mirad la *pizarra*. Buenos *días*. Me *llamo* Bea. Tengo dos *gomas* en mi estuche. ¿Qué *significa*? Tengo un estuche en mi *mochila*. ¿Cómo se *dice*? Tengo *tres* bolígrafos.

3 **Copia y haz frases lógicas.**

1 Tengo un estuche en mi mochila. **2** Tengo cinco reglas en mi estuche. **3** Tengo una goma en mi estuche. **4** Tengo tres bolígrafos en mi estuche. **5** Tengo dos cuadernos en mi mochila.

Worksheets Unit 1

1 En clase AT3.1; 7W1

Visuals: A set of nine pictures and labels depicting classroom equipment, for use during work on pages 12 and 13. They can be cut up and used either with or without their labels, for card games and matching exercises.

2 Resumen AT3.1; 7W1

A useful worksheet version of the Unit Resumen. It can be used for homework and learning exercises.

3 Escuchar AT1.1, AT1.2, AT4.1; 7L3, 7W6

A set of three listening activities each one focusing on a different listening skill. They all refer to work on pages 12 and 13.

1   Practice in identifying details. Students decide which piece of classroom equipment is being discussed and whether the person has one or not.

Answers:

1	Carlos	✓				
2	Ana		✗			
3	Juan			✓		
4	María					✗
5	Belén	✓				
6	Alfonso		✓		✗	

TRANSCRIPT

CD1, track 15
Ejemplo:
1 – Carlos, ¿tienes una pluma?
   – Sí, tengo una pluma.
2 – Ana, ¿tienes un lápiz?
   – ¿Un lápiz? No, no tengo lápiz.
3 – ¿Tienes una goma, Juan?
   – ¿Una goma? Sí.
4 – ¿No tienes un cuaderno, María?
   – No señor. No tengo cuaderno. ►

5 – ¿Tienes un bolígrafo, Belén?
   – Sí. ¡Tengo tres bolígrafos!
6 – Alfonso, ¿tienes una regla y un lápiz?
   – No tengo regla, pero tengo un lápiz.

2   This exercise practises spellings. Students fill in each person's name and country as they hear them spelt. More able students could be asked to listen again and to note which country each person comes from.

TRANSCRIPT

CD1, track 16
Ejemplo:
1 ¡Hola! Me llamo Emilia: E-M-I-L-I-A. Soy de Italia. ►

2 Me llamo Vicente: V-I-C-E-N-T-E. Soy de Méjico.
3 Buenos días. Soy de Perú. Me llamo Pablo: P-A-B-L-O.
4 Buenos días. Soy de España. Me llamo Enrique: E-N-R-I-Q-U-E.
5 ¡Hola! Soy de Cuba. Me llamo Carolina: C-A-R-O-L-I-N-A.
6 ¡Hola! Soy Consuelo: C-O-N-S-U-E-L-O. Soy de Argentina.

3   This listening exercise practises listening for gist by introducing a few new vocabulary items to otherwise familiar sentences. Students must try to identify what is being said by picking out the words and phrases that they know.

1. Me llamo Gloria
   y soy de Guatemala en América Central.
2. ¡Uf! Tengo calor. ¿Puedo abrir la ventana?
3. Mi nombre... sí, sí. Es Susaeta: se escribe S-U-S-A-E-T-A
4. ¿Me puedes prestar un bolígrafo? Es que hoy no tengo...
5. ...No, no está aquí, señora. Creo que hoy está ausente.
6. Bueno, me voy ahora. Adiós, hasta mañana.

Answers

1 c **2** f **3** a **4** e **5** b **6** d

4 Hablar AT2.2, AT 2.3; 7L6, 7S9

This sheet would be suitable for use during work on pages 8 and 9.

1 The first half of this sheet offers two sample dialogues for students to read aloud or act out with a partner. Students are invited to evaluate their performance. (Framework 7L6, Improving performance.)

2 The second exercise asks them to imagine what the characters depicted might be saying to each other. The context underlines the wider application of the language they have learnt. Some students may like to act out these scenes or others of their own invention. (Framework 7S9 – Using simple sentences.)

Possible suggested answers

1. ¡Hola! ¿Qué tal?
   ¿Te llamas Bea, no?
   Sí. Y tú, ¿eres Juán?
2. Buenos días. ¿Eres nuevo, no?
   Sí, señor. Soy nuevo.
   ¿Cómo te llamas?
   Me llamo Alfonso, señor.
3. Buenas tardes... ¿Cómo te llamas?
4. Buenos días, señor. ¿Qué tal?
   Buenos días, señora.

5 Leer AT3.2, AT3.3; 7T1, 7T1

This sheet would be suitable for use during work on pages 14 and 15 when all this vocabulary will have been introduced.

These two reading exercises both draw on listening and speaking skills too and reading using cues.

1 Students use cues of spelling and pronunciation to match up pairs of familiar words. This exercise might be done as pairwork.

Answers

Argentina/cantina; libros/dos; tres/estuches; Ángel/Isabel; me llamo/como; sacad/cerrad; tú/Perú; doce/no sé; no/uno; instrucción/canción

2a Six questions or commands to match up with their answers. In each case the final word of the question or command rhymes with that of the answer.

Answers

1 e **2** c **3** a **4** f **5** b **6** d

2b Students are invited to make up further pairs of questions and answers using the rhymes offered in the first exercise. (Framework 7T6, Texts as prompts for writing.)

6 Escribir AT4.3, AT4.4; 7T5

Suitable as a classwork or homework exercise during or after work on pages 12 and 13, this writing frame allows students to make certain choices, giving them the opportunity to assemble a short text, using familiar structures and known vocabulary.

There is no one possible answer for this exercise. A suggested text is offered below.

With less able students the exercise can be prepared as a class activity.

Possible answer

Frame 1
Madre: Adiós, Jose. Hasta luego.
José: Adiós. Hasta luego.

Frame 2
Conchi: ¡Mira, Juan! ¿Es nuevo?
Juan: Sí, (es nuevo).

Frame 3
Conchi: ¡Hola!
Juan: ¡Hola! ¿Que tal?
José: ¡Hola!

Frame 4
Conchi: Me llamo Conchi.
Juan: Soy Juan. ¿Y tú?
José: Soy José.

Frame 5
Teacher: ¡Sacad el libro!

Frame 6
Teacher: Saca el libro.
José: (No tengo libro, señor.) ¡Soy nuevo!

More able students can extend the scope of the utterances in some of the balloons.

7 ¡Así se hace! AT4.4; 7S1, 7S5

This sheet focuses on words and on the omission of certain words in negative sentences in Spanish. It would support work on pages 12–15.

1 After an alert about word order, students are asked to rearrange some jumbled sentences.

Answers

1. ¿Puedo ir al baño?
2. No tengo bolígrafo.
3. ¿Qué significa pizarra?
4. Tengo dos bolígrafos en mi mochila.
5. ¿Puede repetir por favor?
6. Escribe el número correcto.

1b Students first translate into English the sentences from exercise 1 before saying in which sentences the order is different from English.

Answers

2, 3 and 6.

2a Focus on the way to form negatives and implications for word order and omission of words. Six sentences to put into the negative.

2b Students again translate into English the sentences they constructed in the previous exercise before considering their word order.

Answers to 2a and 2b

1. No tengo mochila. (omission of 'a')
2. ¿No puedo ir al patio?
3. Pizarra no significa 'pen'.
   (not + means – no word for doesn't)
4. No soy Pepe. (not + am)
5. No es un mapa de España. (not + is)
6. Antonio no practica el diálogo. (not + practises – no word for doesn't)

8 Gramática AT3.1, AT4.1; 7W4

This sheet focuses on the importance of recognising and using gender markers. It supports work on pages 10–13.

1 Students are asked to allocate a series of nouns to the masculine or feminine box and to write each one with one or other of its gender markers.

Answers

Masc (el/un): libro, cuaderno, lápiz, estuche, bolígrafo, alfabeto, nombre, saludo, número, diálogo, señor

Fem (la/una): puerta, cosa, ventana, regla, mochila, instrucción, lista, persona, señora, letra, pizarra, pluma, acción

2 This extra exercise invites students to decide the gender of some unknown words (actually from the next unit). They all end in -o or -a except for *conversación* which could be guessed on the analogy of *instrucción*.

9 ¡extra! AT4.4; 7W8

A reminder that you can often work out the meanings of unfamiliar words from form or context. This sheet can be tackled at any time.

a In the reproduction of the hotel brochure students first underline the words they recognise. In fact many of these words are very similar to English or can be extrapolated from context.

b A set of questions about the brochure.

Answers

1 Yes, you can get a family room.
2 No, you can have a bathroom with a bath, not a shower.
3 Yes, they've got air-conditioning.
4 Yes, there's a terrace.
5 There's a gym and a swimming pool.
6 450€.
7 No, you don't have to book.

Workbook A Unit 1

page 3 (*Section A*)

Answers

ex 1a:

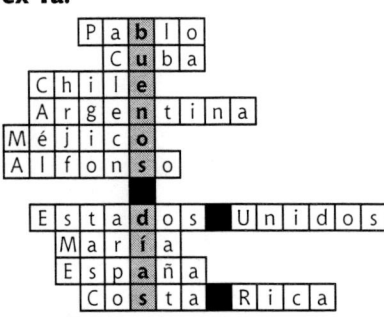

The greeting is *buenos días*.

---

ex 1b:

Countries	People
Argentina	Alfonso
Chile	María
Costa Rica	Pablo
Cuba	
España	
Estados Unidos	
Méjico	

ex 2a:

1 Buenos días, señor.
 Buenos días. Voy a pasar lista. Jaime.
 ¡Presente!
 Hola, Jaime.
2 Buenas tardes, señora.
 Buenas tardes. Voy a pasar lista. Ana.
 ¡Sí, señora!
 Hola, Ana. Conchi.
 ¡Presente!
3 Mariluz.
 Sí, señor.
 Buenos días, Mariluz... ¿Marisol?
 Marisol no está, señor.
4 Voy a pasar lista. Isabel.
 ¡Sí, señorita!
 Hola, Isabel... Pablo.
 Ausente, señorita.
 Pablo no está...

Note: the conversations in 2a are recorded on CD1, track 18, for pronunciation practice.

page 4 (*Section B*)

Answers

ex 1a:
a Escuchad el diálogo.
b Cerrad la puerta.
c Sacad los libros.
d Mirad la pizarra.
e Abrid las ventanas.
f Recoged las cosas.

ex 1b:
1 e 2 d 3 f 4 c 5 a

¡extra! Cerrad la puerta (Close the door)

ex 2:
1 los (plural article, rest are singular)
2 la (singular article, rest are plural)
3 el (singular article, rest are plural)
4 puertas (plural noun, rest are singular)
5 libros (plural noun, rest are singular)

ex 3:
1 los 2 la 3 la 4 libro 5 cosas

---

page 5 (*Section C*)

Answers

ex 1:
1 un 2 un 3 dos 4 una 5 una, dos 6 un

ex 2:
a i b g c l d k e h f j

ex 3a:
b No tengo. c mochila. d tengo goma.
e No. No tengo estuche. f ¿Tienes una regla? No. No tengo regla.

Note: the dialogues in 3a are recorded on CD1, track 20, for pronunciation practice.

page 6 (*Section D*)

Answers

ex 1a:
¿Qué?, ¿Puedo?, ¿Cómo?

ex 1b:
1 ¿Cómo te llamas? 2 ¿Puedo abrir la ventana? 3 ¿Tienes un lápiz?
4 ¿Cómo se dice 'ruler' en español?
5 ¿Qué significa 'puerta'? 6 ¿Cómo se escribe?

ex 1c:
1 c 2 a 3 f 4 d 5 b 6 e

Note: the ¡Así se hace! section on the Resumen page in the workbook (p.7) is recorded on CD1, track 21.

Workbook B Unit 1

page 3 (*Section A*)

Answers

ex 1a:

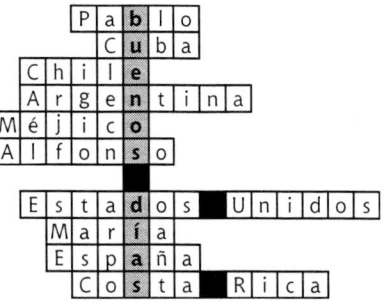

The greeting is *buenos días*.

ex 1b:

Countries	People
Argentina	Alfonso
Chile	María
Costa Rica	Pablo
Cuba	several possible answers
España	
Estados Unidos	
Méjico	
several possible answers	

ex 2:
1 Buenos días, señor.
  Buenos días. Voy a pasar lista. Jaime.
  ¡Presente!
  Hola, Jaime.
2 Buenas tardes, señora.
  Buenas tardes. Voy a pasar lista. Ana.
  ¡Sí, señora!
  Hola, Ana. Conchi.
  ¡Presente!
3 Mariluz.
  Sí, señor.
  Buenos días, Mariluz... ¿Marisol?
  Marisol no está, señor.

Note: the conversations in 2 are recorded on CD1, track 19, for pronunciation practice.

page 4 (*Section B*)

Answers

ex 1a:
Mirad la pizarra; Sacad los libros;
Sentaos; Silencio; Cerrad la puerta;
Escuchad; Repetid; Recoged las cosas;
Levantaos

¡extra! Abrid los cuadernos.

ex 1b:

Singular	Plural
la cosa	las pizarras
el cuaderno	los diálogos
el libro	las puertas
la puerta	los Estados Unidos
el mapa	las letras
el número	las señoras

ex 2 + ¡extra! :
1 los (plural article, rest are singular)
2 abrid (ending in id, rest end in ad)
3 la (singular article, rest are plural)
4 libro (singular noun, rest are plural)
5 libros (noun, rest are verb commands)
6 diálogos (plural, rest are singular)

page 5 (*Section C*)

Answers

ex 1:
1 un 2 dos 3 un 4 una, dos 5 un
6 un 7 dos 8 una

ex 2:
1 siete
2 cero
3 tres
4 cinco
5 nueve

ex 3a:
a ¿Tienes un lápiz? No. No tengo lápiz.
b ¿Tienes un cuaderno? No. No tengo cuaderno.
c ¿Tienes una mochila? No. No tengo mochila.
d ¿Tienes una goma? No. No tengo goma.
e ¿Tienes un estuche? No. No tengo estuche.
f ¿Tienes una regla? No. No tengo regla.

Note: the dialogues in 3a are recorded on CD1, track 20, for pronunciation practice.

page 6 (*Section D*)

Answers

ex 1a:
1 ¿Cómo te llamas? 2 ¿Puedo abrir la ventana? 3 ¿Tienes un lápiz? 4 ¿Cómo se escribe España?
5 ¿Cómo se dice 'ruler' en español?
6 ¿Puedes repetir? 7 ¿Qué significa 'puerta'?

ex 1b:
1 c 2 a 3 e 4 g 5 d 6 f 7 b

¡extra! No. It's too cold!

Note: the ¡Así se hace! section on the Resumen page in the workbook (p.7) is recorded on CD1, track 21.

Unidad 2 • Overview

Unidad 2 ¿Quién eres?	Topic/Language/Culture	Grammar and skills	National criteria
2A ¿Cuántos tienes? (pp. 16–17) **Objectives** • say your age and birthday • learn the months of the year • use numbers 11–39	¿cuántos años tienes? Tengo… años estupendo ¿Cuándo es tu cumpleaños? Mi cumpleaños es el (number) de enero, febrero, marzo, abril, mayo, junio, julio, agosto, septiembre, octubre, noviembre, diciembre Numbers 11–39 **Culture** Spanish calendar, birthdays, saints' days	**Grammar** tener used to express age **Skills** How to avoid repeating questions Acquiring basic high-frequency words 7W2 Recognition of cognates	**Attainment** AT1 Levels 1–3; AT2 Level 3; AT3 Levels 1–3; AT4 Level 1 **Framework objectives** 7W1, 7W8, 7S2, 7S3, 7S4, 7T1, 7T2, 7L1, 7L3, 7C2 **Programmes of study** 2c, 3c **QCA Scheme of work** Language: Unit 1. Contexts: Unit 1 **Assessment for learning** Objectives, p.17 Ex 5c, Plenary
2B ¿Dónde vives? (pp. 18–19) **Objectives** • say where you live • use the present tense singular of tener and vivir • learn how to pronounce e and i	countries: Alemania, América, Escocia, España, Francia, Gales, Inglaterra, Irlanda, Italia, Méjico compass points: en el norte/sur/este/oeste/centro **Culture** towns and geographical locations of Spain	**Grammar** tener, vivir (singular) **Pronunciation** e, i	**Attainment** AT1 Levels 2–3; AT2 Level 2; AT3 Levels 1–2; AT4 Levels 2–3 **Framework objectives** 7W1, 7W5, 7W8, 7S1, 7S3, 7T1, 7T5, 7L3, 7C1 **Programmes of study** 1b, 2a, 3c **QCA Scheme of work** Language: Unit 1, Unit 3. Context: Unit 3 **Assessment for learning** Objectives, p.19 Ex 4, Plenary
2c ¿Cuál es tu nacionalidad? (pp. 20–21) **Objectives** • say your nationality • use the present tense singular of ser • recognise masculine and feminine forms	¿cuál es tu nacionalidad? Soy… alemán/ana, escocés/esa, español/ola, francés/esa, galés/esa, inglés/esa, italiano/a, mejicano/a, portugués/esa **Culture** Hispanophone countries, Latin America	**Grammar** ser (singular) **Skills** Recognise masculine and feminine forms **Pronunciation** ce, ci	**Attainment** AT1 Level 2–3 AT2 Levels 3–4 AT3 Levels 2–4 AT4 Level 1 **Framework objectives** 7W4, 7W5, 7W6, 7S9, 7T1, 7T4, 7T6, 7L1, 7L3 **Programmes of study** 1a, 1b, 3b **QCA Scheme of work** Language: Units 2 and 7. Context: Unit 7 **Assessment for learning** Objectives, p.20 Ex 5, p.21 Ex 6, Plenary
2D ¿Qué idiomas hablas? (pp. 22–25) **Objectives** • learn how to make sentences negative • use the present tense of regular -ar verbs.	¿qué idiomas hablas? Hablo (un poco de) alemán, español, francés, inglés, italiano, portugués y, pero	**Grammar** hablar, negative **Skills** How to make sentences negative	**Attainment** AT1 Levels 3–4; AT2 Levels 3–4; AT3 Levels 3–4; AT4 Levels 3–4 **Framework objectives** 7W1, 7W5, 7S2, 7S3, 7S5, 7S6, 7T1, 7T2, 7T4, 7T5, 7T6, 7L2, 7L3, 7L5, 7L6 **Programmes of study** 3b, 3d **QCA Scheme of work** Language: Units 2 and 7. Context: Unit 7 **Assessment for learning** Objectives, p.22 Ex 2, Plenary, All revision activities p.24

Other resources: ¡Ahora tú! pp 120–21 WS 10–18 OHT 5 WRA & B pp 8–12 Assessment units 1–2 (R & A file pp 116–117) *Just Click* CD-Rom

2 ¿Quién eres?

2A ¿Cuántos años tienes?
pp.16–17

Objectives:
- say your age and birthday
- learn the months of the year
- use numbers 11–39

Key Language: (see p.42 for full list)
Grammar: *tener* used to express age
Skills:
- how to avoid repeating questions
- acquiring basic high-frequency words
- recognition of cognates

Resources: OHT 5 (Spanish calendar); CD1; Worksheet 11 (Resumen); Workbooks A and B p.8; Optional – A large number chart containing numbers 1–39; *Just Click* CD-Rom.

Lesson starter

Revision of numbers 1–10. Everyone sings the number song from Unit 1. Use the CD to start, then turn it down so that the class is singing alone. Move on to getting one half of the class to sing one line and the other half to sing the next line.

Alternative lesson starter *(for lessons starting part-way through the section)*

Using an OHT, board or number chart get the class to chant the numbers 1–20 in order, then point to random numbers and get the class and then individuals to say them or the number that follows. See also number games in Unit 1.

In this section students learn the names of the months and numbers up to 31 so that they can understand and say ages and birthdays.

1 Escucha y lee. AT1.1, AT3.1; 7W1

Students listen to and read the new numbers 11–20. The numbers appear as figures in the illustration but are listed as words in the ¡nuevo! section next to it.

With less able students, you may prefer to introduce numbers aurally first, in which case have the numbers available on OHT, whiteboard or a number chart, then ask the students to close their books and look at the board, and you point to the numbers as they are read.

Play the CD several times, asking students to join in and repeat. Finally point to the numbers on the board in order and then randomly, and ask the class and then individuals to tell you what they are.

Ask individuals to read aloud the written list of numbers. Ask the class to work in pairs. A points to a figure on the picture, B points to the corresponding written number.

TRANSCRIPT CD1, track 22

once	doce	trece	catorce	quince
dieciséis	diecisiete	dieciocho	diecinueve	veinte

Here are some further suggestions for number practice. Using an OHT with numbers jumbled up, cover one up: students put their hands up and say the number that has been covered in Spanish. Progress to covering two or three numbers at the same time. This can be turned into a competition if the class is divided into two teams: if the appointed member of a team does not know which number has been covered, the point goes to the other team. Other ideas could be simple mathematical operations written on the board, e.g. *tres + ocho* = etc., odd numbers, even numbers, counting forwards and backwards in two, threes, etc.

2 Escucha (1–5). Escribe el número y la letra. NT1.3; 7L3

This listening exercise also recalls the number 10, so use a number chart to run through all the numbers 1–20 before you begin.

Before doing the listening exercise, the question *¿Cuántos años tienes?* needs to be introduced. The question could be written on the board in Spanish, and several examples introduced of famous people whose ages the students are likely to know.

Once they have deduced what the question means, the teacher can ask several of the students how old they are, thus providing a pre-listening exercise.

Alternatively ask an individual, e.g. *Sian, ¿tú tienes 13 o 14 años?* Or, introduce the subject by finding out, before the lesson, the ages of several people in the class and saying *Jason tiene doce años, Samantha tiene trece años.*

To avoid confusion, letters instead of numbers are used to identify the dialogues. Ask less confident students to write these five letters down before they start to listen.

TRANSCRIPT CD1, track 23

1
– Hola, ¿cuántos años tienes?
– Tengo **doce** años.
2
– ¿Cuántos años tienes?
– Tengo **diez** años.
3
– ¿Cuántos años tienes?
– **Catorce**.
4
– Y tú, ¿cuántos años tienes?
– Tengo **dieciséis** años.
5
– ¿Cuántos años tienes?
– **Once** años.

Answers

1 h **2** a **3** c **4** b **5** g

¡Así se hace! 7S2

Use of *tener* with ages. For students who have studied French, this is how French expresses age too. If appropriate, point out that it is actually more logical to say 'I have 12 years' as opposed to 'I am 12' (12 what?). It is important to stress that *tener* is only used in a few expressions where English would use 'to have'. It is not a substitute for *ser/estar*.

3a 📖 Lee las conversaciones. ¿Cuántos años tienen? NC3.3; 7T1

This exercise introduces the written version of the question *¿Cuántos años tienes?* Students read a series of conversations using familiar language and structures from this and the previous unit. They must identify the ages mentioned and write them in figures. The question in the title uses the third person plural of the verb. Dialogue 3 brings in 38, though not as the answer. This is a number higher than those learnt and practised so far although 21–31 will be introduced in the following section.

Answers

1 12 **2** 26 **3** 16 **4** 22 **5** 15

3b 💬 Habla con tu pareja. Usa los diálogos en 3a como modelo. NC2.3, 3.3; 7T2

The dialogues in the preceding exercise offer models for students to practise asking and saying their ages.

¡extra! Fast-finishers could give the name of someone else, perhaps a famous person whose age they know.

More confident students could mix and match the dialogues to produce further exchanges of their own. NC2.4; 7T6

The dialogues can also be memorised and acted out.

4a 💡📀 ¡extra! Pon los meses en orden. NC3.1, 4.1; 7W1

More confident students and fast-finishers can now place or write out the months in order. This would be more of a challenge if done with cut-out words on the board or OHT.

¡Así se hace! 7W8

Reading presentation of the months.

As the feature suggests, this is a good opportunity to introduce the concept of cognates. All the names of the months are similar enough to guess in Spanish. Recurring changes between Spanish and English that students might notice include: *-iem-> -em-, -o> -y, -re> -er.*

Ask students if they've noticed any other Spanish words that resemble their English counterparts (*clase, importante, diálogo, letra, número* are just a few).

4b 💡📀 Escucha y repite los meses. NC1.1; 7L1

Students listen to and repeat the names of the months.

TRANSCRIPT CD1, track 24

enero	febrero	marzo
abril	mayo	junio
julio	agosto	septiembre
octubre	noviembre	diciembre

¡extra! ¡Así se hace! 7W8

Introduction to numbers 21–31 and a cue to find out further numbers in the series by extrapolation. See page 34 for ideas on how to practise numbers.

5a 📀 Escucha (1–6) y escribe los cumpleaños. NC1.3, 4.1; 7L3

Students listen to a set of exchanges and write down when each person's birthday is. This exercise also presents the main question and answer used, in written form.

To ensure that students concentrate on listening and don't fall behind while writing the answer, you may like to prepare in advance, perhaps by producing a gapped format for each answer, e.g. ... *de...* . Establish abbreviations of the months, and remind students to jot down only the number and the abbreviation as they listen.

TRANSCRIPT CD1, track 25

1 – ¿Cuándo es tu cumpleaños, Maite?
  – Es el 2 de mayo. Tengo ocho años.
2 – ¿Cuándo es tu cumpleaños, Luis?
  – El 13 de septiembre.
3 – ¿Cuándo es tu cumpleaños, Isabel?
  – Mi cumpleaños es el 22 de agosto. Tengo doce años.
4 – ¿Qué día es tu cumpleaños, Marcelo?
  – El 31 de diciembre y tengo dieciocho años.
5 – ¿Cuándo es tu cumpleaños, Aurora?
  – Es el 15 de marzo.
6 – ¿Cuándo es tu cumpleaños, Inés?
  – El 19 de noviembre, en invierno. Tengo dieciséis años.

Answers

1 2 de mayo **2** 13 de septiembre **3** 22 de agosto **4** 31 de diciembre **5** 15 de marzo **6** 19 de noviembre

5b 📀 ¡extra! Escucha otra vez. Escribe los nombres. ¿Hay información extra? AT1.1, 4.1; 7L3

Students listen again, this time writing the name of each person and age, if stated.

Answers

1 Maite, ocho años.
2 Luís.
3 Isabel, doce años.
4 Marcelo, dieciocho años.
5 Aurora.
6 Inés, dieciséis años.

OHT 5 7C2

OHT 5 will give students an idea of the importance of religious festivals in Spain. Use it to practise dates. Say e.g. *El día de los Reyes* and elicit the answer *el seis de enero.*

Explain that saints' days are also celebrated in Spain, and in some families are more important than birthdays. If appropriate, use a *santoral* to give students the date of their *día del santo*

Cumpleaños feliz. 7C2

Next time it's the birthday of someone in the class teach the class to sing *Cumpleaños feliz.*

5c ☑️ 💬 ¿Y tú? Habla con tu pareja. Cambia las palabras. AT2.3, 3.3; 7S3, 7T2

A sample dialogue that revises introduction and practises ages and birthdays.

Students work in pairs, adapting it to refer to themselves.

More ambitious pairs could work in further language such as asking how the other person is.

This exercise can be used for assessment.

Extension

Now that students have met numbers 11–31, some more ambitious number games can be tried in this or subsequent sessions:

1 Mental arithmetic: divide the class into two teams and ask e.g. *tres más ocho*. Students put their hand up if they know the answer. An answer that is linguistically and mathematically correct gains two points. An answer that is nearly linguistically correct gets one point.

2 Count round the class using odd numbers, then even numbers, or count forwards and backwards in twos, threes etc.

Plenary

☑ Ask the class to look again at the numbers 1–31 and discuss with them what patterns they can see. This is best done using a number chart, perhaps with numbers 1–100, arranged in tens. Elicit the fact that from 16 onwards the pattern is:

after these, join the next number on:	dieci veinti	uno dos (dós)
these are followed by a separate word:	treinta y cuarenta y cincuenta y sesenta y setenta y ochenta y noventa y	tres (trés) cuatro cinco seis (séis) siete ocho nueve

If appropriate, give them a preview of how to say 40 and 50.

2B ¿Dónde vives?

pp. 18–19

Objectives:
- say where you live
- use the present tense singular of *tener* and *vivir*
- learn how to pronounce *e* and *i*

Key Language: see p.42 for full list

Grammar:
- *tener*
- *vivir*

Pronunciation: *e* and *i*

Resources: Visual 10 Map of Europe; CD1; Workbooks A and B p.9; Worksheets 10 (Visuals – countries), 11 (Resumen), 12 (Escuchar – identity cards); optional: OHT/Wall map of Europe, OHT/Wall map of Spain, OHT/Wall map of Britain; *Just Click* CD-Rom.

In this section students learn how to understand and express geographical locations, and to say where they live.

Lesson starter

☑ Display mini-dialogues with language that students have learnt so far, each with numbered gaps. As students come in, hand them a small sheet of paper (you can get 8–12 to an A4 sheet) with all the missing words/phrases on them. In pairs, students note down a word for each gap. The students put numbers against the words on the sheet, according to which gap they fit. Then call a name and ask for the answer to No. 1, and so on. Students tick or change their answers.

As a homework they could be given the dialogue with gaps and asked to use their sheet to fill in the gaps. This way a homework is prepared for the less able, and you can check whether they were right or not.

Alternative lesson starter *(for lessons starting part-way through the spread)* **or preliminary exercise.**

Ask the class to look at the map of Europe on OHT 7. Ask e.g. *¿Cómo se escribe Francia/España etc.?* Go through all the countries on the map, asking the individuals to spell them, while the other students check their spellings, calling out *¡No!* if there is a mistake.

Introduction

As an alternative way to familiarise students with the country names and their locations, Worksheet 10 offers mini-flashcards of these and some other European countries. The small visuals can be matched to the country outlines on a map of Europe.

1a 🔊 Escucha (1–6). ¿Dónde viven? NC1.2; 7L3

A series of short introductions. Each speaker gives his/her name, country, town or region, sometimes adding the geographical location.

On a first playing, ask students just to listen out for the country mentioned and to write down its initial.

Extension

On subsequent playings and/or with more able students, ask them to try to write down the town mentioned and listen out for extra information.

Compass points will be introduced further down the page. However some students may guess what *en el sur/norte/centro* mean.

TRANSCRIPT — CD1, track 26

1 ¡Hola! Soy Víctor. Vivo en Madrid, que está en el centro de España.
2 ¿Qué tal? Me llamo Stephanie. Soy de Berlin, en Alemania.
3 Buenos días. Me llamo Marco, y vivo en Roma, en Italia.
4 ¿Qué tal? Soy Andrew, y vivo en la región de Snowdon, en Gales.
5 ¿Qué tal? Me llamo Françoise. Vivo en Montpellier, en el sur de Francia.
6 Buenas tardes. Soy Rick. Vivo en Newcastle, que está en el norte de Inglaterra.

Answers

1 Víctor: España (Madrid, centro) 2 Stephanie: Alemania (Berlin) 3 Marco: Italia (Rome) 4 Andrew: Gales (Snowdon) 5 Françoise: Francia (Montpellier, sur) 6 Rick: Inglaterra (Newcastle, norte)

1b 💬 ¿Y tú? ¿Dónde vives? Habla con tu pareja. NC2.2, 3.2; 7S3, 7T1

Students now adapt the new language to talk about themselves. A pattern is given on the page. In most classes students will all be answering with the same country name, so to vary the responses they could use the formula used on the CD: *Vivo en (Manchester) en Inglaterra.*

Students could learn their exchanges by heart and act them out to the rest of the class.

Monitor and correct the pronunciation of *v* in *vives/vivo* etc.

2C ¿Quién eres? • **2**

Gramática: the present tense 7W5

Presentation of the singular forms of *tener* and *vivir* and an alert about change of endings. The first and second persons of these verbs have already appeared, as have the third person plurals. To practise all the forms do some oral question and answer using ¿*Dónde vives?* and ¿*Cuántos años tienes?* Then ask of people who have already been questioned ¿*Dónde vive Brian?* and ¿*Cuántos años tiene Rachel?* eliciting third person replies.

2 ✏ ¿Qué dicen? NC3.2, 4.2; 7S1, 7T1, 7C1

A reading introduction to the compass points first mentioned in exercise 1a. Students match each speaker with where they live and then decide which of the compass descriptions in the box best fits the location.

Ask the class to look at the box and to tell you what it signifies. Say each phrase in turn and ask them to repeat. If you have a map of Britain handy say the names of some large towns and ask students to tell you at which point of the compass they are: Edinburgh – *en el norte*, Cardiff – *en el oeste* etc.

Read through the example and allow students time to establish that Santander is in the north then look at the next picture. Ask the class to follow the line to where Inés lives and then collectively to supply the rest of the sentence.

Ask the class to look at the bits of the two sentences that stay the same, then work with them to establish the pattern for all the sentences: ¡*Hola! Soy* (name). *Vivo en* (town) *en el* (compass point) *de España.* Students should now be able to complete the other sentences.

Answers

1 ¡Hola! Soy Pilar. Vivo en Santander, en el norte de España.
2 ¡Hola! Soy María. Vivo en Santiago de Compostela, en el oeste de España.
3 ¡Hola! Soy Inés. Vivo en Sevilla, en el sur de España.
4 ¡Hola! Soy Juan. Vivo en Granada, en el sur de España.
5 ¡Hola! Soy Pedro. Vivo en Barcelona, en el norte de España.
6 ¡Hola! Soy Ricardo. Vivo en Valencia, en el este de España.
7 ¡Hola! Soy Ana. Vivo en Madrid, en el centro de España.

Once the exercise is finished, ask some third person questions: ¿*Dónde vive Ana? Vive en Madrid.*

To familiarise students with the geography of Spain, use the map to ask about the compass locations of other places marked: ¿*Dónde está (la Costa Brava/el Mar Mediterráneo)?* etc.

3 📖 Lee las descripciones. ¿Quién habla? NC3.2; 7W8, 7T1

Seven first person descriptions to match with seven pictures. In some cases the speaker does not live in his or her country of origin. This formula will be useful for those students for whom this is also true.

Tell students to look at all the pictures, then read carefully though all the options and eliminate the answers they are sure of. Most of the language here is familiar but *ahora* is new. Ask what they think *ahora* means.

Answers

1 D 2 B 3 F 4 E 5 C 6 G 7 A

WS 13 💿 offers a set of identity cards to fill in, based on the language of this section.

Pronunciación: *e* and *i* 7L1, 7W6, 7L6

Focus on vowel sounds *e* and *i*. Ask the class what else they have learnt about vowel sounds. (All examples of a vowel sound are constant and have equal value.) Practise saying all the examples in class before asking them to practise in pairs.

TAPESCRIPT CD1, track 27

Escocia	**I**nglaterra	**M**éjico
Gales	**E**spaña	Alemania
Irlanda	**E**stados Un**i**dos	**I**talia

4 ☑ ✏ Escribe unas frases sobre ti: tu nombre y dónde vives. Otras cosas: tu cumpleaños, tu edad. NC4.3; 7T5

Students to assemble the various pieces of personal information they have learnt in this and the previous unit and to write a short piece about themselves.

Students should be taught from the beginning to recognise patterns that they can apply in order to produce original language.

Although some irregular verbs have already appeared, here the teacher should concentrate on the verbs seen so far: *me llamo, tengo, vivo…*

Until the students see the preterite tense, they should learn to identify the ending *-o* in verbs with the first person singular of the present.

This exercise can be used for assessment.

Plenary

☑ In connection with the previous exercise, a chance to reflect on how many different things students have now learnt to say about themselves. Each student says a sentence and the next student changes it slightly or comes up with a new sentence.

More able students should be able to offer alternative wording for some facts (*Me llamo/Soy, Vivo en/Soy de, Vivo en el sur de Inglaterra, en Londres/Vivo en Londres, en el sur de Inglaterra* etc.)

2C: ¿Cuál es tu nacionalidad?
pp. 20–21

Objectives:
• say your nationality
• use the present tense singular of *ser*
• recognise masculine and feminine forms
Key Language: see p.42 for full list
Grammar: *ser* (singular)
Skills: recognise masculine and feminine forms
Resources: CD1; Worksheets 10 (Visuals – countries), 11 (Resumen), 13 (Hablar – identity information gap); Workbooks A and B p.10; optional: OHT/Map of Europe, OHT/Map of world; *Just Click* CD-Rom.

On these pages students learn how to form adjectives of nationality and to make them agree.

Lesson starter

Ask everyone to think of **one** thing to say in Spanish about themselves and to write it down or memorise it but not to tell anyone else. Not counting personal names, the aim is to prepare a sentence that is a bit different from anyone else's in word order or content. Ask an individual to say his/her sentence. Anyone who has got a variation on that puts their hand up and offers their version. Collect all the possible versions of e.g saying where you live, on the board.

Alternative lesson starter *(for lessons starting part-way through the section)*

Offer a list of jumbled nationality adjectives on board or OHT. Point to an adjective. Students must call out *¡chico!* if it applies to a boy and *¡chica!* if it is feminine.

For support with slower students this would work with single cut-out words dropped onto the OHP.

1 Escucha (1–8) y lee. AT1.3, 3.3; 7W4, 7T1

Students listen to and read a series of short personal descriptions. These draw upon familiar language but add *ser* + nationality. Explain that students are going to hear some things they know but also something new.

Play the CD twice, asking students to point to each description as they hear it. Ask the class what they think the new sentences mean. Tell them to look for clues in sentences 1, 3, 4 and 7 (where the adjective of nationality comes after the name for the country). Once you have established the meaning of the new adjectives, ask what they notice about sentences 1 and 5, 2 and 6, and 4 and 7. Ideally, elicit the fact that it's the same adjective but in two different forms depending on the gender of the speaker.

Extension

More alert students may notice that, unlike English, these adjectives don't begin with a capital letter.

TRANSCRIPT   CD1, track 28

1 Hola, me llamo Paul. Soy de Inglaterra. Soy inglés.
2 Buenos días. Soy Verónica. Vivo en Madrid. Soy española.
3 ¿Qué tal? Soy Martin. Vivo en Escocia. Soy escocés.
4 Buenas tardes. Me llamo Peter. Vivo en Bonn. Soy alemán.
5 Hola. Me llamo Mark. Vivo en Gales. Soy galés.
6 Buenos días. Me llamo Kate. Soy inglesa.
7 Hola. ¿Qué tal? Soy Antonio. Soy español.
8 Buenas tardes. Soy Anna y soy de Gales. Soy galesa.

2 Habla con tu pareja. Cambia las palabras AT4.1; 7W5

A gap-filling task based around the captions and photos in exercise 1. Students adapt the model conversation on the page to practise asking about someone's nationality.

3 Lee las frases. Escribe si habla un chico o una chica. AT3.2; 7W4

A set of phrases using *soy* + adj of nationality. Students decide whether each speaker is masculine or feminine according to the form of the adjective. They will have to think carefully about some of the forms used.

Some of the adjectives used here feature in exercise 1 so students will know anyway from the pictures whether these are masculine or feminine.

There are other associations they should make. Also from exercise 1 they should grasp that the pattern *-és/esa* can be applied to other adjectives (e.g. *portugués*). In exercise 1 the adjective *alemán* appeared in the masculine. Here it appears in the feminine as well. The same feminine ending *-ana* appears here in *italiana* and *mejicana*, which should lead students to conclude that *-ano* is a masculine ending.

Answers

chico: 1, 4, 7, 9; chica: 2, 3, 5, 6, 8, 10

4 Escucha (1–10). Escribe en inglés la nacionalidad y el género. AT1.2; 7L3

Students decide which nationality and gender each speaker is. They note these in English.

By way of support, help less confident students by agreeing abbreviations (M/F, Eng, It etc.) before you start. Tell them to note one piece of information at a time and play the CD several times for them to note all the information.

TRANSCRIPT   CD1, track 29

1	Soy española.	6	Soy alemán.
2	Soy mejicano.	7	Soy italiana.
3	Soy inglés.	8	Soy español.
4	Soy galesa.	9	Soy alemana.
5	Soy escocés.	10	Soy portuguesa.

Answers

1 Spanish, girl **2** Mexican, boy **3** English, boy **4** Welsh, girl **5** Scots, boy **6** German, boy **7** Italian, girl **8** Spanish, boy **9** German, girl **10** Portuguese, girl

Gramática: nationalities 7W4

Formalisation of all previous observations about gender (see notes to exercise 3).

5 Copy the table and fill in the gaps.

Students copy the grid and fill in correct masculine and feminine endings to the adjectives.

Answers

(Masc) escocés, francés; (Fem) galesa, alemana, española, italiana, portuguesa, mejicana

Pronunciación: c 7W6, 7L1, 7L6

Explanation and practice of the sound *c + e/i*

TAPESCRIPT   CD1, track 30

francés	nacionalidad	diecinueve
escocesa	centro	doce
Francia	diecisiete	diciembre

Gramática: *ser* – to be 7W5

Presentation of the singular, and third person plural of *ser*. Students will already be familiar with *soy* and *es*. Ask them where they have met these forms, e.g. *Soy Jessica, soy de Inglaterra, mi cumpleaños es...*

6 ☑ ◯ ¡*extra!* **Habla con tu pareja. Cambia las palabras.** AT2.3; 7S3

Students adapt the model conversation on the page to ask and answer about their own and someone else's nationality. Encourage students to think of a friend whose nationality is not the same as their own. If this is not possible a friend of the opposite gender should be selected.

This exercise could also be used for assessment.

WS 14 (Leer) is an information-gap exercise that practises age, birthdays, domicile and nationality. It could be used from this point on.

Plenary

☑ Ask students to look back at the table they produced for exercise 5 and to tell you what they think the *m/f* pattern is. How would they explain it to a classmate who missed the lesson?

2D ¿Qué idiomas hablas?

page 22

> **Objectives:**
> • learn how to make sentences negative
> • use the present tense of regular *-ar* verbs.
> **Key Language:** see p.42 for full list
> **Grammar:**
> • *hablar* (singular and third person plural)
> • negative with *no*
> **Skills:** how to make sentences negative
> **Resources:** CD1; Worksheets 11 (Resumen), 14 (Leer), 15 (Escribir), 16 (¡*Así se hace!*), 17 (Gramática), 18 (¡*extra!*); Workbooks A and B p.11; *Just Click* CD-Rom.

The first of these pages presents names for different European and world languages and introduces the concept of the negative. The Resumen recaps on the language and skills of the whole unit.

Lesson starter

As students come in give them a card bearing either the name of a country or a nationality (language) adjective. (Duplicate these according to the number of students in the class.) Students must go round and find their correct pair. As soon as they have done so they stand together and hold up their cards. Pairs could be:

Alemania alemán	*Inglaterra inglés*
Escocia escocés	*Irlanda irlandés*
España español	*Italia italiano*
Francia francés	*Portugal portugués*
Gales galés	

Alternative lesson starters *(for lessons starting part-way through the section)*

Use Visual 10 with cut-out words for the different languages. Put the cut-outs down the side of the map. As you indicate each one, ask students to call out where it should go. They can do this by telling you the name of the country or by giving you its geographical location within Europe (*en el norte/oeste* etc.). Write a few sentences in the affirmative or negative on an OHT or the board. Ask different students to change them. The rest of the class calls out *sí* if it is correct and *no* if it is not. They could also give the translation in English.

1a 💿 **Escucha y lee. Escribe en inglés los idiomas que se mencionan.** AT1.4, AT3.4; 7S2, 7T1, 7L3

Presentation of the names for some languages. The dialogue also offers examples of the negative and parts of the featured verb *hablar*. First play the CD and ask the class to follow in their books. Ask students what it is about. Elicit the fact that it is about what languages people speak, then ask what they noticed about the names for the languages. Elicit the deduction that the language is the same as the masculine form of the adjective. Now ask students to read and listen again and to note the languages that are mentioned.

Extension

More able students can be asked to write the names of the different people as well as the languages mentioned, and the number of times each language is mentioned. They could also listen with their books closed.

> **TRANSCRIPT**
> CD1, track 31
>
> – Hola, Belén.
> – Hola, Marisa. Dime, ¿qué idiomas hablas?
> – Pues hablo español, claro, inglés y un poco de francés. ¿Y tú?
> – Yo hablo alemán, pero no hablo inglés.
>
> – ¡Hola, Marco! ¿Qué idiomas hablas?
> – Hablo español, italiano e inglés. No hablo alemán.
>
> – ¿Qué tal, Miguel?
> – Muy bien.
> – Miguel, ¿qué idiomas hablas?
> – Hablo español, y un poco de portugués.
> – ¿Hablas inglés?
> – No, no hablo inglés.
> – Bueno, pues tenemos español, inglés, francés, alemán, italiano y portugués. ¡Qué bien!

Answers

Marisa: español, inglés, francés
Belén: alemán
Marco: español, italiano, inglés
Miguel: español, portugués

Students should also have noticed that, like nationalities, languages are not spelt with a capital letter in Spanish.

¡*Así se hace!* 7W5

Students are asked to formulate the rule for forming the negative. The rule is that the word *no* goes before the verb. Although the system for the negative is much simpler in Spanish than in English, the teacher should not assume that the students can distinguish where the verb is (in Spanish or in English!).

Start by eliciting from the students their definition of what a verb is. Then a list could be drawn on the board of the verbs that they know so far in Spanish (*tengo, me llamo, soy, vivo, hablo, es...*).

Extension

Here are some sentences that students could be asked to put into the negative. **AT4.4; 7S5**

1 Tengo doce años.
2 Hablo español.
3 Vivo en Inglaterra.
4 Soy galés.
5 Mi cumpleaños es el 24 de febrero.
6 Me llamo Inés.

Answers

1 No tengo doce años.
2 No hablo español.
3 No vivo en Inglaterra.
4 No soy galés.
5 Mi cumpleaños no es el 24 de febrero.
6 No me llamo Inés.

1b ☍ Mira el texto. Habla con tu pareja.
AT2.4; 7S6, 7L5

A takes the identity of one of the people on the list in the preceding exercise and lists which languages he/she speaks. B guesses which character A is. Ask two confident students to act out the dialogue. The exercise can be repeated, changing the identity of the speaker and with A and B changing places.

Support

Less confident students may only be able to answer *Hablo* + one language.

Extension

Encourage more able students to use *y* and *pero* in their answers.

WS 18 (¡extra!) offers practice and tips about changing from first to third person.

Gramática: regular -ar verbs 7W5

Presentation of part of the paradigm of *hablar*.

2 ☑ ✎ Copia y rellena la carta. AT4.3–4; 7T5

Students complete a short letter using visual cues to help them. This exercise could be used for assessment.

Support

Less able students could simply write the words in the blanks.

Extension

More able ones should be able to copy and complete the whole letter.

Answers

doce; veintisiete de agosto; sur; España; española; español, francés, inglés y alemán; portugués, italiano.

WS 14 (Leer) offers a longer and more complicated letter that uses this and other language.

WS 16 (¡Así se hace!) offers help on adapting a sample text of the kind that is required here.

Plenary

☑ Ask the class to look carefully at the Resumen. Go through it together. Does all the vocabulary now look familiar? Have they understood the grammar points? In speaking exercises, have they remembered about equal vowel values? Ask people to indicate whether they are confident (green card), quite confident (orange card) or not confident (red card). NB: This practice could be used at any point in the book to inform your lesson planning and identify areas that need more work.

Resumen (*page 23*)

This section offers a resumé of all the material in the unit. For use as a homework aid and as a record, the Resumen is reproduced on Worksheet 11.

Repaso (*page 24*)

☑ The revision and assessment section tests work on Units 1 and 2.

There is a Repaso page at the end of every second unit in **¡Así! 1**. When you have finished working through Unit 2, use this page to revise Unit 1; when you have finished working through Unit 3, come back to this page to revise Unit 2. In this way, you will always be revising the unit preceding the one you have just been working on, keeping it alive in students' minds.

Alternatively, work through the Repaso page as preparation for an assessment (Assessments Units 1 and 2: see pages of the Resource and Assessment File.)

1 💿 Escucha (1–6). ¿Qué tienen ✓ y no tienen ✗ en sus mochilas? AT1.4; 7L3

Before embarking on the exercise, revise this vocabulary using real objects or Flashcards 1–9.

A series of exchanges about whether people have or have not got items of school equipment and a reminder about the formation of the negative.

Ask students to start by writing each person's name, leaving a space to note what each person has and has not got.

Explain that you are going to play the CD recording twice so that students will have two chances to hear the answers.

Support

You may prefer to offer a table with the names down the side and words for classroom equipment across the top. Students can then simply tick or cross the items they hear mentioned.

TRANSCRIPT CD1, track 32

1 – ¿Qué tienes en tu mochila, Julián?
  – Tengo un lápiz y dos libros.
  – ¿Tienes goma?
  – No, no tengo goma
2 – ¡Hola, Esperanza! ¿Qué llevas en la mochila?
  – Pues... tres libros, dos cuadernos... no, un cuaderno y tres bolis.
  – ¿Llevas regla y lápices?
  – No llevo regla, pero sí tengo cuatro lápices.
3 – ¿Qué tal Marcos? ¿Qué tienes en tu mochila?
  – Tengo un estuche y tres libros pero no tengo ningún cuaderno.
4 – ¿Qué tienes en tu mochila, Pablo?
  – A ver. Tengo dos libros y un estuche.
  – ¿Tienes bolis y lápices?
  – Tengo un boli y cuatro lápices
5 – ¡Hola, Macarena! ¿Qué tienes en tu mochila?
  – Tengo una goma, un bolígrafo, dos libros y dos cuadernos.
  – ¿No tienes lápices?
  – No, no tengo lápices.
6 – ¿Qué tal, Esteban? ¿Qué llevas en tu mochila?
  – Pues... no mucho. Sólo un libro y un cuaderno.
  – ¿No tienes estuche?
  – No, y no tengo pluma tampoco.

Answers

1 Julián: ✓ lápiz, dos libros; ✗ goma
2 Esperanza: ✓ tres libros, un cuaderno, tres bolis, cuatro lápices; ✗ regla
3 Marcos: ✓ un estuche y tres libros; ✗ cuaderno
4 Pablo: ✓ dos libros, un estuche, un boli, cuatro lápices
5 Macarena: ✓ una goma, un bolígrafo, dos libros, dos cuadernos; ✗ lápices
6 Esteban: ✓ un libro, un cuaderno; ✗ estuche, pluma

2 ◯ Habla con tu pareja. Contesta a las preguntas. AT2 3–4; 7T2, 7L2, 7L6

Students work in pairs, taking it in turns to ask and answer a series of questions about themselves. Once they are familiar with the question forms, students should be encouraged to do this exercise orally, not writing down the answers.

Support

Lower-ability students may need to be given the beginning of each answer in Spanish.

Before enacting the conversation in front of you or the *asistente*, encourage students to practise the dialogue in pairs, to evaluate their efforts and to discuss how to improve them.

3 📖 Une las preguntas y las respuestas. AT3.3; 7T1

A set of questions and answers to be paired up. There is only one set of possible pairings.

Support

Encourage less confident students to check off the pairs that they are sure of first before deciding about the trickier ones.

Extension

More able students who finish early might answer or adapt the questions to apply to themselves.

Answers

1 b 2 f 3 g 4 d 5 h 6 c 7 a 8 e

4 ✏️ Escribe frases para los dibujos. AT4.4; 7T5

Students are given a series of visual cues, for each of which they must produce a sentence. In several cases there is more than one possible answer.

Support

Some students may find this a daunting task. For these students you could give the beginning of each sentence.

WS 15 (Escribir) offers practice in identifying and replying to similar questions to these.

Suggested answers

1 Vivo en el centro de Inglaterra.
2 Hablo francés y español.
3 En mi mochila tengo/hay un cuaderno y un estuche.
4 Tengo/No tengo regla ni goma.
5 Valencia está en el este de España.
6 Tengo diez años.
7 Mirad la pizarra.

Reading (page 25)

AT3.4; 7T1, 7T4

This reading presentation uses a variety of language and structures from Units 1 and 2. The presentation offers a mixture of dialogue and realia-style text. This exercise should be used to help students develop the ability to scan for information, and skip unnecessary or unknown information. Students should be able to guess the information they do not know through the known information and the pictures in the cartoon.

Support

Students could be given a photocopy of the page. They could be asked to underline in one colour the words they know the meaning of, in another one the ones they can guess.
They can look up in a dictionary any words that have not been underlined.

1 What do Quique and María buy? Write a list. AT 3.4; 7T1

Students go through the story and list the items that Quique and María actually buy and the numbers of each.

Answers

Quique: 10 estuches, 15 reglas, 8 cajas de lápices, 3 mochilas, 20 bolis, 15 cuadernos
María: 2 gomas, 2 cuadernos

2 Why does María look so surprised in the last picture? What has she just realised?

Quique is probably selling his wares to other students.

¡Ahora, tú! (pp. 120–121)

Differentiated self-access reading and writing exercises: see page 37 for more information.

page 120

1 📖 Join the speech bubbles to the pictures.

Answers

1 f 2 b 3 h 4 c 5 d 6 a 7 e 8 g

2 ✏️ Copy and complete the names of the months.

Answers

febrero, mayo, junio, septiembre, noviembre, diciembre.

3 ✏️ Copy and fill the gaps.

10	diez	5	cinco
8	ocho	6	seis
23	veintitrés	18	dieciocho
31	treinta y uno	25	veinticinco
15	quince	12	doce

page 121

1 📖 **Read the form. Copy and fill in the gaps in the letter.**

¡Hola! ¿Qué tal? Me llamo *Antonio*. Tengo *36* años y mi *cumpleaños* es el *siete* de marzo. Soy de *Málaga* pero vivo en los *Estados Unidos*. De vacaciones vivo en *Málaga*. Está en el *sur* de España.

Hablo *español* y *inglés* y también un poco de *francés*.

3 ✏️ **Copy and fill in the gaps.**

1 siete + doce = *diecinueve*
2 ocho − dos = *seis*
3 quince + *dos* + tres = veinte
4 cinco × *cinco* + veinticinco
5 nueve + *cinco* − tres = once
6 *veintiuno* + doce − cuatro = veintinueve
7 *treinta* − doce = dieciocho
8 cuatro × tres = *doce*
9 once − *diez* = uno
10 *seis* × cuatro = veinticuatro

Worksheets Unit 2

🔟 Los países de Europa
AT3.1; 7W1

A map of Europe with the featured countries outlined and identified visually, but with blanks for students to stick the correct label. Can be done at any time after work on pages 18–19 has been completed.

1️⃣1️⃣ Resumen AT3.1; 7W1

List of key language from the unit (see p.37 for more information).

1️⃣2️⃣ Escuchar AT1.3; 7L3

a A multiple-choice exercise. Students hear a series of interviews with young people. They choose and ring the details on each person's identity card. The first one is partly filled in.

b Students use the examples to make their own identity cards. Can be done any time after work has been completed on pages 18–19.

TRANSCRIPT

CD1, track 33

1 – Hola, ¿cómo te llamas?
– Me llamo Belén.
– Y ¿cuántos años tienes, Belén?
– Tengo 14 años.
– Catorce… muy bien. Y ¿cuándo es tu cumpleaños?
– Es el 21 de agosto.
– El 21 de agosto…Y finalmente… ¿dónde vives?
– Vivo en España.
– España… muy bien. Gracias, Belén.

2 – Hola, ¿quién eres?
– Soy José.
– José… ¿Cuántos años tienes?
– Tengo 16 años.
– Y ¿tu cumpleaños?
– Es el 6 de enero.
– ¿Y, tú?… ¿dónde vives?
– Vivo en Portugal.
– Gracias, José. ►

3 – ¿Eres María, no?
– No, no, soy Marina.
– Ah, Marina. Y ¿cuántos años tienes?
– Tengo 22 años.
– Y ¿cuándo es tu cumpleaños?
– Es el 15 de marzo
– Y… ¿dónde vives?
– En Italia.
– Gracias.

4 – Hola, ¿quién eres?
– Me llamo Ramón… Tengo 13 años… Mi cumpleaños es el 11 de noviembre y vivo en Méjico.
– ¡Ah! Gracias, Ramón.

1️⃣3️⃣ Hablar AT2.3–4; 7S9

An information-gap pairwork exercise based on pages 16–21.

A starts by asking the questions about his or her gapped identity cards. B starts by replying to A's questions. Then they change round.

1️⃣4️⃣ Leer AT3.3; 7T1, 7S3

Two reading comprehension exercises both based on the same email. The worksheet can be tackled at any time after students have worked on pages 22–23.

1 A gapped email. Students fill in the gaps choosing from the words in the box. There are two distractors.

Answers

¡Hola! **¿Qué** tal? Me llamo Raúl. **Mi** cumpleaños es el 31 de octubre y tengo diéciseis años. **Soy** español. Vivo en Barcelona. Es la capital de Cataluña, en **el** este de España. Hablo **dos** idiomas, español **y** catalán. También hablo un poco de francés, pero no hablo inglés.

Tengo dos mejores amigos: son José y Consuelo. José tiene quince años. Es **mejicano** pero no vive en Méjico. Ahora vive **en** el este de los Estados Unidos, en Nueva York. Habla **español** e inglés.

Mi **amiga** Consuelo tiene dieciséis **años**, como yo. Vive en Bilbao. Está en el País Vasco, en el **norte** de España. Habla vasco y español y un poco de alemán, pero no habla ni francés ni inglés.

2 A true/false exercise

Answers

1 V 2 V 3 M 4 M 5 V 6 M 7 M 8 V

3 An invitation to write a personalised email along similar lines.

1️⃣5️⃣ Escribir AT4.2; 7W1, 7T5

1 This worksheet alerts students to the multivalency of the language they are learning. The situations presented here are not the same as those they have encountered in, for example, a class situation. However, they require the same language. Students must decide which of the questions they have learnt would best fit each answer and situation. This exercise can be done at any time after students have worked on pages 16–23.

Some students might like to think up further situations and illustrate them.

Answers

1 ¿Cómo te llamas?
2 ¿Cuántos años tiene?
3 ¿Cuál es tu nacionalidad?
4 ¿De dónde eres?
5 ¿Dónde vives?
6 ¿Qué idiomas hablas?

2 A suggestion to think up further situations in which the same questions could be used. Students could illustrate the situation, and write an appropriate answer to the question.

16 ¡Así se hace! AT4.4; 7T5

This sheet offers some hints and tips about how to adapt a text to reflect personal circumstances.

Students use the annotated model to write a piece about themselves.

17 Gramática 7W5

This sheet resumes and practises all the verbs presented in this unit.

a A multiple-choice exercise where students must choose the correct verb form in each case.

Answers

1 soy **2** vives **3** tienes **4** habla **5** es **6** tenéis.

b This time students must produce the correct form of each verb.

Answers

1 tiene **2** vivís **3** soy **4** hablamos **5** viven **6** es

18 ¡extra! AT3.4; 7S2, 7S3

1 A more advanced interview based on the work from the unit. The multiple-choice questions are deliberately more tricky, featuring information in a different order or with different wording and including a little new but guessable vocabulary. (*Ecuador – ecuatoriano/a*). Students are advised to read the information and the questions very carefully, especially looking out for negatives.

Answers

1 c **2** a **3** b **4** a **5** b **6** b

2 A set of questions on the interviewee. The answers require manipulation of verb persons, pronouns etc.

1 La chica se llama María Elena.
2 Tiene quince años.
3 Es de Ecuador.
4 En este momento vive en España.
5 Es ecuatoriana.
6 Habla español y un poco de portugués. (Pero no habla ni inglés ni alemán.)

Pruebas Unidades 1 y 2

R and A file pp.116–119

Prueba: Escuchar (*page 116*)
ex 1: AT1.1–2

Answers

Example: **1**V **2**V **3**M **4**V **5**M **6**V **7**V
Corrected phrases: Tengo dos gomas. Tengo una mochila y un estuche.
Mark scheme: 1 mark for each correct answer, excluding example. 1 mark for each phrase correctly modified.
Total: 6. 4 marks or more shows evidence of performance at Level 1 6+ shows evidence of performance at Level 2.

TRANSCRIPT

CD4, track 24

Ejemplo: **1** Tengo un bolígrafo.
2 Tengo un lápiz.
3 Tengo dos gomas.
4 Tengo un libro y un estuche.
5 Tengo una mochila y un estuche.
6 Tengo una regla y una mochila.
7 Tengo dos lápices y un bolígrafo.

ex 2: AT1.1

Answers

Example: **1** = 2nd box **2** = 3rd box **3** = 5th box **4** = 7th box **5** = 6th box **6** = 4th box
Mark scheme: 1 mark for each correct answer.
Total: 6. 4+ shows evidence of performance at Level 1.

TRANSCRIPT

CD4, track 25

Ejemplo: **1** Sacad el libro
2 Levantaos
3 ¡Silencio!
4 Repetid
5 Recoged las cosas
6 Cierra la puerta

ex 3: AT1.1

Answers

Example: **1** 5 May **2** 15 November **3** 4 January **4** 11 March **5** 23 July **6** 30 September **7** 16 June **8** 14 February
Mark scheme: 1 mark for each correct answer. Both number and month must be correct for the mark. No half marks.
Total: 7. 4+ shows evidence of performance at Level 1.

TRANSCRIPT

CD4, track 26

Ejemplo: **1** Mi cumpleaños es el cinco de mayo.
2 Mi cumpleaños es el quince de noviembre.
3 Mi cumpleaños es el cuatro de enero.
4 Mi cumpleaños es el once de marzo. ▶

5 Mi cumpleaños es el veintitrés de julio.
6 Mi cumpleaños es el treinta de septiembre.
7 Mi cumpleaños es el dieciséis de junio.
8 Mi cumpleaños es el catorce de febrero.

ex 4: AT1.1

Answers

Example:
1	Argentina	Spanish
2	France	French
3	Spain	Spanish
4	England	English/German
5	Italy	Italian
6	Peru	Spanish
7	Mexico	Spanish/English

The two extra languages are: English/German, depending on what the student noted as the first language. Spanish/English, depending on what the student noted as the first language.
Mark scheme: 1 mark for each correct answer, both nationality and languages must be correct. No half marks.
Total: 6. 4+ shows evidence of performance at Level 1.

TRANSCRIPT

CD4, track 27

Ejemplo: **1** Soy de Argentina y hablo español.
2 ¡Hola! Soy de Francia y hablo francés.
3 Buenos días. Soy de España y hablo español.
4 Buenas tardes. Soy inglesa y hablo inglés y alemán.
5 ¡Hola! Hablo italiano porque soy de Italia.
6 ¡Hola! Vivo en Perú y hablo español.
7 ¿Qué tal? Soy mejicano y hablo español y un poco de inglés.

Prueba: Hablar (*page 117*)
ex 1: AT2.1

Answers

Hola
Buenos días
Me llamo + name
Soy de + place
(Example) Tengo... años
¡Adiós!
Mark scheme: 1 mark for each statement which would be understood by a sympathetic native speaker.
Total 5: 3+ or more shows evidence of performance at Level 1.

ex 2: AT2.1–2

Answers

Levantaos
Sentaos
Abrid las ventanas
Cerrad la puerta
Sacad el libro/los libros
Mirad la pizarra
Mark scheme: 1 mark for each statement which would be understood by a sympathetic native speaker. 1 mark for each extra correct picture of other instructions.
Total: 6. 4+ shows evidence of performance at Level 1.
6+ shows evidence of performance at Level 2.

ex 3: AT2.1

Answers

Ocho Doce Treinta y uno Veintisiete Dieciséis Diez Quince Veintiuno
Mark scheme: 1 mark for each sentence which would be understood by a sympathetic native speaker.
Total: 8. 4+ shows evidence of performance at Level 1.

ex 4: AT2.2

Answers

Example **1:** Tengo un lápiz **2** Tengo un libro. **3** Tengo dos reglas. **4** Tengo una mochila. **5** Tengo un estuche. **6** Tengo cuatro libros. **7** Tengo tres plumas.
Mark scheme: 1 mark for each sentence which would be understood by a sympathetic native speaker. 1 mark for each correct extra phrase.
Total: 6. 4+ shows evidence of performance at Level 2.

Prueba: Leer (page 118)
ex 1: AT3.2

Answers

Example **1**d: **2**c **3**e **4**g **5**b **6**f **7**a
Mark scheme: 2 marks for each correct answer.
Total: 12. 4+ shows evidence of performance at Level 2.

ex 2: AT3.2

Answers

Example **1**: tal **2** llamas **3** bolígrafo **4** tengo, bolígrafos **5** lápices **6** Puedo
Mark scheme: 1 mark for each correct answer.
Total: 5. 4+ shows evidence of performance at Level 2.

ex 3: AT3.2–3

Answers

1 Spanish **2** Seville/south of Spain. **3** 12 **4** 15th December **5** Spanish/French/English **6** He/she speaks Italian **7** Where are you from? Where do you live? How old are you? When is your birthday?
Mark scheme: 1 mark for each correct answer. 1 mark for extra details added. The details are: The other languages and questions as listed above. She's a new friend. She lives with her family. She says write soon.
Total: 8. 5+ shows evidence of performance at Level 2.
8 marks shows evidence of performance at Level 3.

Prueba: Escribir (page 119)
ex 1: AT4.2

Answers

Example **1**: El dos de agosto **2** El diecinueve de enero. **3** El treinta de septiembre. **4** El nueve de junio. **5** El primero de abril. **6** El cuatro de octubre. **7** El veintidós de marzo.
Mark scheme: 1 mark for each correct answer. Both the number and the month must be correct for the mark (numbers in words, not in digits). No half marks.
Total: 6. 4+ shows evidence of performance at Level 2.

¡extra! 1 mark for each extra correct date given.

ex 2: AT4.1

Answers

1 Puedo **2** dice/escribe **3** se **4** significa **5** No **6** favor
Mark scheme: 1 mark for each correct answer.
Total: 6. 4+ shows evidence of performance at Level 1.

ex 3: AT4.1
The list may include any of the items included in the unit. The words need not necessarily be absolutely correct but should be easily understood by a sympathetic native speaker.
Mark scheme: 1 mark for each correct answer.
Total: 5. 3+ shows evidence of performance at Level 1.

¡extra! 1 mark for each extra correct article listed.

ex 4: AT4.2–3

Answers

Hola Hola
¿Qué tal? Muy bien (Regular, Fenomenal, Fatal)
¿Cómo te llamas? Me llamo + name
¿Dónde vives? Vivo en + place
¿De dónde eres? Soy de + place
¿Cuántos años tienes? Tengo X años
¿Cuándo es tu cumpleaños? (Mi cumpleaños) es + date
Adiós Adiós
Mark scheme: 1 mark for each correct answer.
Total: 8. 4+ shows evidence of performance at Level 2.
7+ shows evidence of performance at Level 3.

¡extra! 1 mark for each extra phrase (question or answer added).

Workbook A Unit 2

page 8 (Section A)

Answers

ex 1:
11 once; 12 doce; 13 trece; 14 catorce; 15 quince; 16 dieciséis; 17 diecisiete; 18 dieciocho; 19 diecinueve; 20 veinte

Note: the numbers 15–20 are recorded on CD1, track 34, for pronunciation practice.

ex 2:
enero; febrero; marzo; mayo; junio; julio; agosto; septiembre; octubre; noviembre; diciembre

¡extra! abril

ex 3:
2 dieciséis, septiembre; **3** veinte, diciembre; **4** diecinueve, enero; **5** quince, junio; **6** once, febrero

page 9 (Section B)

Answers

ex 1: ¡extra!
Irlanda, Paraguay

ex 2a:
vivo — I live
vives — you (one person) live
vive — he or she lives
vivimos — we live
vivís — you (more than one person) live
viven — they live

ex 2b:
1 tengo **2** viven **3** vivo **4** tienes **5** vive **6** tiene

53

page 10 (*Section C*)

Answers

ex 1b:
2 escocés **3** español **4** alemana
5 inglesa

ex 1c:
2 Soy galés **3** Soy italiana **4** Soy inglés
5 Soy alemán

ex 2:
Nationalities ending in a consonant add
-a if it's a girl (and lose the final accent
if they have one).

inglés, español, alemán
become
inglesa, española, alemana

Nationalities ending in -o change the -o
to -a if it's a girl.

chileno, italiano, venezolano
become *chilena, italiana, venezolana*

page 11 (*Section D*)

Answers

ex 1:
alemán German; español Spanish;
francés French; inglés English; italiano
Italian

ex 2:

hablo	I speak
hablas	you (*singular*) speak
habla	he or she speaks
hablamos	we speak
habláis	you (*plural*) speak
hablan	they speak

ex 3:
af; gb; hc; de

Note: the dialogues in ex 3 are
recorded on CD1, track 35, for
pronunciation practice.

Workbook B Unit 2

page 8 (*Section A*)

Answers

ex 1:
11 once **12** doce **13** trece **4** catorce
15 quince **16** dieciséis **17** diecisiete
18 dieciocho **20** veinte **31** treinta y
uno

¡extra! 19 diecinueve

Note: the numbers 15–20 are recorded
on CD1, track 34, for pronunciation
practice.

ex 2:
enero febrero marzo mayo junio
julio agosto septiembre octubre
noviembre diciembre

¡extra! abril (month number 4)

ex 3:
2 Tengo dieciséis años. Mi cumpleaños
es el quince de septiembre. **3** Tengo
veinte años. Mi cumpleaños es el nueve
de diciembre. **4** Tengo dieciocho años.
Mi cumpleaños es el veintitrés de enero.
5 Tengo quince años. Mi cumpleaños es
el treinta de junio. **6** Tengo once años.
Mi cumpleaños es el veintisiete de
febrero.

page 9 (*Section B*)

Answers

ex 1a:

vivir	(to live)
vivo	I live
vives	you (*one person*) live
vive	he or she lives
vivimos	we live
vivís	you (*more than one person*) live
viven	they live
tener	(to have)
tengo	I have
tienes	you (*one person*) have
tiene	he or she has
tenemos	we have
tenéis	you (*more than one person*) have
tienen	they have

ex 1b:
2 tengo **3** viven **4** vivo **5** tienes
6 vive **7** tiene

page 10 (*Section C*)

Answers

ex 1a:
2 de **3** Soy de, Soy **4** de, alemana
5 de, Es inglesa

ex 1b:
Down
1 eres **2** es **3** irlandesa **4** italiana
5 escocés

Across
1 argentino **2** inglesa **3** chilena
4 galés **5** alemana **6** español

ex 1c:
2 Soy galés **3** Es italiana **4** Es inglés
5 Soy alemán

ex 2:
Masculine adjectives of nationality
ending in a consonant add -a to form
the feminine and lose the final accent if
they have one.

español, alemán, inglés, escocés
become
española, alemana, inglesa, escocesa

Masculine adjectives of nationality
ending in -o change the -o to -a to form
the feminine.

*chileno, italiano, mejicano, venezolano,
portorriqueño, dominicano*
become
*chilena, italiana, mejicana, venezolana,
portorriqueña, dominicana*

page 11 (*Section 11*)

Answers

ex 1:
alemán German; español Spanish;
francés French; inglés English; italiano
Italian

ex 2:

I speak we speak	hablo hablamos
you (*singular*) speak you (*plural*) speak	hablas habláis
he or she speaks they speak	habla hablan

ex 3:
b f a e c d

Note: the dialogues in ex 3 are
recorded on CD1, track 36, for
pronunciation practice.

Unidad 3 • Overview

Unidad 3 Mi familia	Topic/Language	Grammar and skills	National criteria
3A ¿Tienes hermanos? (pp. 26–27) **Objectives** • say who is in your family • use numbers 40–100 • use the reflexive verb *llamarse* (to be called) • learn how to pronounce silent *h*	Family members: *¿Tienes hermanos? Tengo un/una hermano/a, hermanastro/a, hijastro/a, dos hermanos/as que se llama(n) … (y) …* *Soy hijo/a único/a* Numbers: 40–100	**Grammar** *llamarse* (7W5 Launch) **Skills** Asking about meanings *¿Cómo se dice … en español?* (7S9 Relaunch) **Pronunciation** Silent *h* (7W6 Launch)	**Attainment** AT1.1, AT2.1, AT3.1–3; AT4.1–4 **Framework objectives** 7W1, 7W4, 7W6, 7T4, 7T6, 7L1, 7L2, 7L3, 7L4, 7L6, 7S3 **Programmes of study** 1abc; 2abfh; 3ab, 5ab, 4i **QCA Scheme of work** Language content: Unit 2: Context: Unit 2 **Assessment for learning** Objectives, p.26 Ex 1c, p.27 Ex 3, 4a+4b, Plenary
3B ¿Cómo eres? (pp. 28–29) **Objectives** • say what somebody looks like • learn how to uses adjectives • learn how to pronounce *j*	Personal characteristics (hair and eyes): *Tengo el pelo negro/liso/rubio/castaño, la piel azules/marrones/grises/verdes, gafas/pecas*	**Grammar** Position and endings of adjectives (7W4 Launch) **Pronunciation** *j* (7W6 Launch) **Skills** Difference in word order between English and Spanish (7S1 Launch)	**Attainment** AT1.1, AT2.1, AT3.1–3; AT4.1–4 **Framework objectives** 7W1, 7W4, 7W7, 7W8, 7S1, 7T6, 7L3, 7L6 **Programmes of study** 1abc; 2abfh; 3ab, 5ab, 4i **QCA Scheme of work** Language content: Unit 2: Context: Unit 2 **Assessment for learning** Objectives, p.29 Ex 6, Plenary
3C ¿Cómo son? (pp. 30–31) **Objectives** • describe other physical aspects and personality • use possessive adjectives • link sentences	Adjectives of height and shape: *Es alto/a, bajo/a, gordito/a, delgado/a* Adjectives of personality: *simpático/a, antipático/a, hablador/a, callado/a.*	**Grammar** Possessive adjectives: *mi/s, tu/s, su/s* Subject pronouns: *yo, tú, él, ella, usted* (7W2 Relaunch) **Skills** Linking sentences with *y* and *pero* (7S6 Launch)	**Attainment** AT1.3, AT2.1–3, AT3.2, AT4.1–4 **Framework objectives** 7W1, 7W2, 7W3, 7W4, 7W7, 7S2, 7T1, 7T2, 7T6, 7L1, 7L2 **Programmes of study** 1abc; 2abcdeh; 3abcd; 5abdf **QCA Scheme of work** Language content: Unit 2: Context: Unit 2 **Assessment for learning** Objectives, p.31 Ex 5b, WS23. Plenary
3D ¿Tienes animales? (pp. 32) **Objectives** • talk about pets • learn more about how to make nouns plural	Pets: *¿Tienes animales? Tengo un caballo, dos gatos, un hámster, tres pájaros, un pero, tres peces de colores, un ratón, una cobaya, una serpiente, una tortuga. No tengo animales.*	**Grammar** Formation plural nouns (7W4 Relaunch) **Skills** WS28: rules for stress (7W6 Launch). WS25: simple compound sentences (7S6 Relaunch)	**Attainment** AT2, 1–4: AT3.3: AT4. 1–4. **Framework objectives** 7W1, 7W4, 7S1, 7S3, 7T1, 7T6, 7L1, 7L2, 7L4 **Programmes of study** 1abc. 2b, 3ac. 5a **QCA Scheme of work** Language content: Unit 2 Context: Unit 2 **Assessment for learning** Objectives, p.32 Ex 2b. WS23. Plenary

Other resources: *¡Ahora tú!* pp.122–123   WS 19–28   OHTs 6–7   WBA & B pp.13–17   Assessment units 3–4 (R & A file pp.120–123)   *Just Click* CD-Rom

3 Mi familia

3A ¿Tienes hermanos?

pp. 26–27

> **Objetives:**
> - say who is in your family
> - use numbers 40–100
> - use the reflexive verb *llamarse* (to be called)
> - learn how to pronounce the silent *h*
>
> **Key language:** (see p.55 for full list)
> **Grammar:** *llamarse*
> **Skills:** use of *¿Cómo se dice...?*
> **Pronunciation:** letter *h*
> **Resources:** OHTs 6 (brothers and sisters), 7A and 7B (family tree and overlay); CD1; Worksheet 22 (Escuchar); *Just Click* CD-Rom

Lesson starter 7W4

Remind students that Spanish nouns ending in *-o* are usually masculine (e.g. *un libro, un bolígrafo*) and those ending in *-a* are feminine (e.g. *una pluma, una regla*). Explain that you are going to call out the Spanish words for members of the family (e.g. brother, sister, aunt) and ask students to reply *masculino* or *feminino* each time. Make sure you include those in exercises 1a and 2. As an alternative, students can write M or F on paper, or hold up a card showing this.

Alternative lesson starter *(for lessons starting part-way through the section)*

Revise numbers 1–40 by having students count up in twos with you on even numbers, and backwards on odd numbers. Students to listen carefully as you call out Spanish for 40, 50 etc. up to 90 and listen for the ending (*-enta*). What is this equivalent in English? (-ty).

Introduction

Focus students' attention on the objectives: say who is in your family, and understand/use the numbers 40–100.

1a 🔘 Escucha y lee. AT1.1, AT3.1; 7W1, 7W4, 7L2

Students listen and read. You might like to use a family which students will recognise (the Simpsons, the Royal Family or one from a current soap opera) to present the language of brothers and sisters for exercise 1a, e.g. *Me llamo Lisa Simpson – tengo un hermano Bart y una hermana Maggie/Soy Bart Simpson – tengo dos hermanas, Lisa y Maggie*. Ask students to work out what *hermanos* might be, explain that *hermanastro* is half-brother/step-brother (what might half-sister/step-sister be?), and do the same with *hijo único/hija única*. The images on OHT 6 and the accompanying labels for OHT 7A will be useful here.

> **TAPESCRIPT** CD1, track 37
>
> Tengo un hermano y una hermana.
> Tengo dos hermanas.
> Soy hijo único.
> Tengo dos hermanos y un hermanastro.

1b 🔘 Escucha (1–5). ¿Tienen hermanos? ¿Cómo se llaman? AT1.1; 7L3

Divide the exercise into stages. On the first hearing, students note the numbers of brothers and sisters. To avoid copying out words, agree a convention of stick drawings for brothers/sisters and write the number of each in front. More able students can be asked to distinguish *hermano/a* from *hermanastro/a*, writing an extra *s* to denote the latter. On second hearing, students write the first letter of the name(s), e.g. N for *Noelia* and AB for *Ana Belén*.

> **TRANSCRIPT** CD1, track 38
>
> **1** – Hola, ¿tienes hermanos?
>   – Sí, tengo un hermano que se llama Antonio. ¿Y tú?
> **2** – Tengo dos hermanas que se llaman Helena y Blanca.
> **3** – ¿Tienes hermanos?
>   – Tengo una hermanastra. Se llama Ana Belén.
> **4** – Tengo una hermanastra también. Se llama Noelia... y tengo un hermano que se llama Miguel Ángel. Y tú, ¿tienes hermanos?
> **5** – Sí, tengo un hermanastro que se llama Sergio.

Answers

1 un hermano, Antonio **2** dos hermanas, Helena y Blanca **3** una hermanastra, Ana Belén **4** una hermanastra, Noelia; un hermano, Miguel Ángel **5** un hermanastro, Sergio

1c ☑ 💬 ¿Y tú? Habla con tu pareja. AT2.1; 7L6

Students ask and give information about brothers and sisters: could be done as a group or class survey. Prepare students by referring them to the supporting language box and highlighting *se llama/se llaman*. This exercise could be assessed for AT2.1, Level 1.

Gramática: *llamarse* – to be called 7W5

Presentation of part of the paradigm of *llamarse*.

Pronunciación: *h* 7W6, 7L1, 7L6

Work through the examples given, as students practise. Other words you might like to give them for practice could include *hablo, hace, hago, hasta, hay, historia, hoja, hora, hospital*.

> **TAPESCRIPT** CD1, track 39
>
> hijo, hija
> hermano, hermana
> hermanastro, hermanastra
> hijastro, hijastra

Presenting Numbers 40–100 7W1

Use the ideas in the alternative starter above. Reinforce passive understanding with number games like Lotto (restrict to any 9 numbers between 10 and 20 plus 20, 30, 40 etc. up to 100). Give active practice using *más/menos* game modelled with whole class first, then in small groups or pairs. For this, A thinks of a number 1–100 and B makes guesses. A gives feedback '*más*' (more) or '*menos*' (less) to help B get increasingly closer to the final number.

Presenting other members of the family 7W1

Use OHT 7A for this, using small pieces of paper to blank out the names and ages. These can be revealed as each new family member is presented. Write up the new Spanish and English word for each relationship on the board as you go (e.g. *madre* – mother) for support. For a more interactive approach, make a copy of OHT 7A with blanks for the names and ages, and either put a list of possible male and female names on the board or give these to students on a sheet of paper. Students can then choose how to build up the family tree by suggesting a name and an age for each person you reveal on the OHT, and this will give them an opportunity for using the third person *se llama* and *tiene*, e.g.

T: *Ésta es la madre* (write '*madre* – mother' on board). *¿Cómo se llama (la madre)?*

S1: *Se llama Amelia.* (T writes '*Amelia*' on OHT).

T: *¿Y cuántos años tiene Amelia?*

S2: *Tiene cuarenta y cinco años.* (T writes '45' on OHT next to '*Amelia*').

2 💿 Escucha (1–9). Escribe las edades. ¡extra! Escribe los nombres. AT1.1; 7L3

Students listen for the ages of each person and their name. Let students know that section 4 of the recording contains two names, and that there are three names which they've met before which are not spelt out (these are María, Blanca and Pedro). In preparation for the listening exercise, play the recording and ask students to raise their hands every time they hear a number.

TRANSCRIPT

CD1, track 40

1 Mi hermana se llama Helena. Se escribe H-E-L-E-N-A. Tiene diecinueve años.

2 Nadina es mi prima. Tiene quince años. Su nombre se escribe N-A-D-I-N-A.

3 Mi primo Manuel tiene dieciocho años. Su nombre se escribe M-A-N-U-E-L.

4 María es mi tía y Juan es mi tío. María tiene treinta y siete y Juan tiene cuarenta y cinco años. Juan se escribe J-U-A-N.

5 Sergio es mi padre. Se escribe S-E-R-G-I-O. Tiene cincuenta y siete años.

6 Mi hermano se llama Miguel. M-I-G-U-E-L. Tiene cinco meses.

7 Blanca es mi abuela. Se escribe B-L-A-N-C-A. Tiene setenta y seis años.

8 Mi madre se llama Ana, A-N-A, y tiene treinta y nueve años.

9 Mi abuelo es estupendo. Se llama Fernando, F-E-R-N-A-N-D-O, como yo, y tiene setenta y ocho años.

Answers

1 19 **2** 15 **3** 18 **4** 37 and 45 **5** 57 **6** 5 meses **7** 76 **8** 39 **9** 78.

¡extra! **1** Helena **2** Nadina **3** Manuel **4** María and Juan **5** Sergio **6** Miguel **7** Blanca **8** Ana **9** Pedro.

Students who need more support can be given the ages in numeric form, and asked to write the number of the section of the recording alongside each.

WS 22 (Escuchar) could be used at this point.

3 ☑ 🖊 ¿Y tú? ¿Cómo es tu familia? Dibuja tu árbol genealógico. Escribe los nombres y las edades. AT4.1; 7L4

Students prepare a simple family tree, writing in the names of their family members and the Spanish for that relationship, e.g. *Jackie, mi madrastra*. This exercise could be assessed for AT4 Level 1.

¡Así se hace! 7W3, 7L4

Prepare students for this exercise by writing up the new phrase *¿Cómo se dice... en español/inglés?* Use the newly met vocabulary in exercise 3 to practise with the whole class and then in pairs, e.g. *¿Cómo se dice 'sister' in español?* Students can then be encouraged to ask you in Spanish for any new vocabulary they need to complete their family tree.

4a ☑ 📖 Lee y escribe si las frases son verdad (V) o mentira (M). AT3.3; 7T4

Students read the letter and decide whether each sentence **1–8** is true or false. They will need dictionaries for the unfamiliar language *aún, mayor, mía* or you may prefer to write these on the board or OHP. For students who need support, provide them with a way in to this longer piece of text. Divide the class in two and, as you read the letter aloud and they follow it, one half listens for any number words and calls out *¡ya!* when they see/hear them, and the other half does the same for relationship words calling *¡sí!* This exercise could be assessed for AT3 Level 3.

Answers

1 V **2** M **3** M **4** V **5** M **6** V **7** M **8** V

4b ☑ 🖊 ¡extra! Contesta a la carta de Cristina. Describe a tu familia. AT4.4; 7S3, 7T6

Students use the letter as a model for writing about their own family. Prepare students for this by reading through the sentences in the first paragraph, and asking them to call out which words could be changed to give a new sentence, e.g. *Soy Cristina y tengo diecisiete años.* Elicit a new sentence, e.g. *Soy Felipe y tengo catorce años.* Ask students to work in pairs to do the same for the second paragraph, identifying possible changes and producing new oral versions. Elicit sample answers and check for any problems before students work at their own pace. This exercise could be assessed for AT4 at a variety of levels, depending on outcome.

Plenary 7W7

☑ Ask students to look back over the vocabulary of the two pages, and highlight or make a note in their vocabulary books or pages of any words they found hard to remember – brainstorm useful strategies for vocabulary learning, e.g. look/cover/check/write, or copy out consonants, then close book and rewrite word from memory with correct vowels in etc. Ask each student to set themselves a homework target for this and write it down.

Alternative plenary *(for lessons ending part-way through the section)* 7W6

☑ Focus on the similarities/differences between numbers which are sometimes confused. Give each pair of students one of the numbers 3–9, and ask them to write down three other numbers which contain it – one from the 11–20 group, and two in the 30–100 range (e.g. 3/13/30/33). What are the Spanish words for these numbers? Which parts of them look and/or sound similar, and which look/sound different? How can you remember them? Model this on the board or OHT with 2/12/20/22 – *dos, doce, veinte, veintidós*. Pairs of students then work with another pair to show and teach them about 'their' numbers.

3B ¿Cómo eres? pp. 28–29

> **Objectives:**
> * say what somebody looks like
> * learn how to use adjectives
> * learn how to pronounce *j*
> **Key language:** see p.55 for full list
> **Grammar:** agreement of singular and plural adjectives
> **Skills:** pronunciation of letter *j*
> **Resources:** Visual 19 (Faces); CD1; *Just Click* CD-Rom.

Lesson starter 7W7

Write up on the board or OHT the new words *verde, azul, gris, negro, rubio, rojo, castaño, marrón, el pelo, los ojos* with their English equivalents. Ask students, in pairs, to work out how to pronounce these, using what they know of the rules of pronunciation already (7W7). Either set a short time limit or reveal the words one at a time, keeping the class working together. Then elicit student replies and have the class repeat the correct pronunciation for each several times.

Alternative lesson starter *(for lessons starting part-way through the section)*

Call out a list of known nouns (from this and the previous unit) and colour adjectives one at a time, e.g. *azules, negros, el pelo, verdes, la hermana, grises, los ojos, castaños, marrón, la madre, rubio, los tíos, pelirrojo*. Students call out either the Spanish singular or plural. Reread the list, with the items in a different order, and students have to call out *adjetivo* or *sustantivo* (7W3). As an alternative they can hold up a piece of paper labelled S or P, Sub or Adj.

Support

Allow students to see the word as you call it out.

Extension

Omit the definite article when calling out items from the list. Students will then have to focus more closely on the meaning.

Introduction

Highlight the first objective 'say what somebody looks like' and ask students to work out from the pictures on the spread which words they might expect to hear/need to learn: Spanish for 'hair', 'eyes', colours etc.

As an alternative to exercise 1, use Visual 19 for presenting the new vocabulary for hair and eyes, beginning with *el pelo* and *los ojos*. Underneath the pictures, or on the board, have the Spanish for the adjectives of colour (*verdes, azules* etc.) as support and involve students by giving them a choice of two colours, and allow them to decide as you colour in the hair or eyes appropriately, e.g. T *¿Tiene los ojos azules o verdes?* S *Azules.* T *Muy bien. Tiene los ojos azules.*

1 🔊 Escucha (1–6) y lee. AT3.2; 7W1

This can initially be used for presentation or consolidation, reading aloud together and checking meaning. As a follow-up, instruct students to work in pairs. Student A reads any sentence 1–6, and B, with his/her hand covering up the sentences, gives the number of the appropriate picture.

Extension

Both students cover up the sentences 1–6 with a piece of paper. They work together to produce an oral description of each picture in turn, sliding the paper down to check their version against the original.

> **TAPESCRIPT** CD1, track 41
>
> **1** Tengo los ojos verdes y el pelo rubio.
> **2** Tengo el pelo negro y los ojos marrones.
> **3** Soy pelirrojo y tengo los ojos azules.
> **4** Tengo el pelo rubio y los ojos marrones.
> **5** Tengo el pelo castaño y los ojos grises.
> **6** Tengo el pelo negro y los ojos verdes.

💡 Gramática: position of adjectives 7S1

Read the sentences with students and elicit the difference (the adjective comes after the noun in Spanish). Point out also how the singular noun *el pelo* is followed by a singular adjective and the plural *los ojos* by plural adjective. Elicit from students what they remember about forming plurals (add -*s* to a vowel and -*es* to a consonant). Put up the singular of the colour adjectives and elicit the plural forms.

2 Put the following sentences in the correct order. AT3.2; 7W4

Students produce an oral or written version of the sentences 1–6. In preparation, ask students to look at the first sentence and find the two colour adjectives (*azules, rubio*) – which is singular and which plural? Can they spot a singular and plural noun (*pelo, ojos*)? How do they know which adjective goes after which noun? Do the same with sentence 2 to ensure that all students have grasped the principle before allowing them to work on their own.

Answers

1 Tengo el pelo rubio y los ojos azules. **2** Tengo el pelo negro y los ojos negros. **3** Tengo el pelo rubio y los ojos verdes. **4** Tengo el pelo castaño y los ojos marrones. **5** Tengo el pelo castaño y los ojos negros. **6** Tengo el pelo gris y los ojos azules.

3 🔊 Escucha (1–5). ¿Cómo se llaman? AT1.2; 7L3

Students study the pictures and listen to each section of tape to determine who is speaking. They copy down the (first) letter of each name.

> **TRANSCRIPT** CD1, track 42
>
> **1** Hola. Tengo los ojos verdes y el pelo rubio.
> **2** ¿Qué tal? Yo tengo el pelo moreno y los ojos negros.
> **3** ¡Buenos días! Soy pelirroja y tengo los ojos azules.
> **4** ¡Hola! ¿Qué tal? Tengo el pelo rubio y los ojos marrones.
> **5** ¡Buenas tardes! Tengo el pelo negro y los ojos negros.

Answers

1 Ana **2** Cristóbal **3** María Luisa **4** José **5** Belén

Gramática: endings of adjectives 7W4

So far in this section, students have met masculine singular and plural adjectives (with *el pelo, los ojos*). This box also shows the endings of feminine adjectives. You will need to explain to students that *blanco* means 'white', *pecas* are 'freckles' and *la piel* is 'skin'. It also includes information on forming the plurals of adjectives. These are essentially the same as the plurals of nouns: add *-s* to a vowel and *-es* to a consonant. (The loss of the final accented vowel is highlighted later in Unit 3D, p.32.)

4 ✏️ Rellena los colores. AT4.1; 7W4

Students copy the sentences, writing in the correct form of the colour adjective. Only masculine adjectives are needed here.

Support

Provide a bilingual list of the colour adjectives in the singular on the board or OHT.

5a 📖 Une las descripciones y los dibujos. AT3.2; 7W8

Students match each description to its appropriate picture. There are a number of new words in here: *largo, liso, corto, blanco/a, ondulado, pequeños, rizado, morena, gafas, llevo*. If you wish to foster glossary or dictionary skills at this point, you might find the following useful:

- explain to students that nouns are usually found in the dictionary in their singular form (*el pelo*) and adjectives in their singular masculine form (*castaño*).
- provide a brief list of familiar nouns and adjectives from this and previous units on the board or OHT in the plural and ask students to work out the singular or singular masculine form, e.g. *grises, los ojos, verdes, negros, blancas, italianas, los españoles, azules*. Students may find it helpful to refer to the grammar box on page 29. Check their replies.

Answers

1 B **2** D **3** E **4** C **5** A

5b 💬 ¡extra! Elige una persona. Tu pareja adivina. Tú contestas solamente sí o no. AT2.2; 7L6

Students work in pairs, with A asking questions and B answering only *sí* or *no*. Fast-finishers can also practise using the third person singular *¿Tiene…?* (Does he/she have…?), choosing a person in the classroom to describe.

Extension

Encourage students to use the new adjectives denoting hair length and texture (*largo, corto, ondulado, liso, rizado* etc.), and to include whether the person they are describing wears glasses or not. You might like to give them the third person form of *'llevar' (No) lleva gafas* to help.

6 ✓ ✏️ Y tú, ¿cómo eres? Escribe tu descripción. 7T5, 7T6

Students write a short description of themselves, using the vocabulary grid and the examples from exercise 5a as a guide.

🔊 Pronunciación: j 7W6, 7L1, 7L6

Encourage students to listen to and practise the *j* sound as shown in the box. Other useful words for practice are: *abajo, ajo, caja, dejar, dibujo, jugar, mensaje, relajante, trabajo*.

Extension

The letter *g* when followed by the letter *e/i* makes the same sound, e.g. *inteligente, girafa, gente, gerbo, genial, argentino, agencia, giro*.

Plenary 7W4

✓ Focus on the agreement of adjectives. Ask students to work in pairs to formulate their own replies to the following questions, as if they were having to explain to an absent member of the class. Either put these on the board or OHT or give students a paper copy:

1 What is an adjective?
2 Can you give me three examples of adjectives in Spanish to help me understand?
3 I'm looking at exercise 1. Why do some adjectives end in *-s* and others don't?
4 Is *ojos* a noun or an adjective? How can you tell?
5 In English, the adjective comes before the noun: grey eyes, red hair. Is it the same in Spanish?
6 In exercise 5a, text 2, it says '*mi piel es blanca*' – why is it *blanca* and not *blanco*?

After checking students' explanations, ask them if there is anything about adjectives which still puzzles them or they're not sure of. You might like to have a 'comment' or '¡Socorro!' box on your desk into which students can post requests for help or clarification which can be dealt with anonymously in a subsequent lesson with the whole class or with the individual student.

Alternative plenary *(for lessons ending part-way through the section)* 7W1

✓ Brainstorm with students other topic areas in which it will be useful to know words to describe the colour of objects. Put up on the OHT or board the following nouns as headings, checking with students their English meanings and writing these underneath the Spanish for support: *el pelo, los ojos, el lápiz, los libros*. Give students a mixed list of singular and plural colour words (e.g. *gris, azules, negros, rojo, verdes, rubio, marrones, castaño, verde*). Ask students in pairs to allocate each adjective to as many of the nouns as appropriate – and elicit from them the rule that singular/plural adjectives match the noun they describe. Do an example or two with them, and set a time limit. When feeding back accept any correct answer, however humorous or unlikely (e.g. *el pelo azul*).

3C ¿Cómo son? pp. 30–31

Objectives:
- describe other physical aspects and personality
- use possessive adjectives
- link sentences

Key language: see p.55 for full list

Grammar:
- recognise subject pronouns
- possessive adjectives

Skills: Worksheet 26 (¡Así se hace! – reading aloud)

Resources: Visual 20 (Personality traits); CD1; *Just Click* CD-Rom.

Lesson starter 7L4, 7W1, 7W3

Put a copy of the following grid on the board or OHT as students arrive. Ask them to work out the odd one out (*Pilla al intruso*) in each horizontal and vertical line. Before they feed back their answers, remind them of the Spanish words they will need: ... *es (un) sustantivo, adjetivo, color, masculino, feminino, singular, plural, miembro de la familia* (7L4).

	1	2	3	4
A	padre	primo	hijo	madrastra
B	tía	gemelas	abuelo	padre
C	hermano	hermana	hermanastro	abuela
D	blanco	pelirrojo	azul	ojo

Answers

A *madrastra*, as it is only the feminine word; B *gemelas* is plural; C *abuela*, as the others words are all to do with brothers/sister; D *ojo* is the only noun; 1 *tía* is the only feminine word; 2 *pelirrojo* is the only adjective; 3 *azul* is a colour, the others are nouns; 4 *ojo* is not a family member.

Alternative lesson starter (for lessons starting part-way through the section) 7W1

As students come in, have a message on the board or OHP asking them to look through the vocabulary associated with family members, colours or hair/eyes in Units 3A and 3B. As you do the register, call students' names out in a random order – they have to answer with any Spanish word not previously mentioned by a student, and the class has to call out the English translation. This is easier for those at the start of the exercise than at the end – call names of more able students towards the end of the register.

Introduction

Focus students' attention on the pictures in exercise 1a – ask them to work out what aspect of size, shape, old/young or personality each of these represents. Opposites are presented in each case. Explain that this is the focus of the Unit.

1a 🔊 Escucha (1–5) y mira los dibujos. AT1.1, AT3.2; 7W1, 7W4, 7S1, 7T1, 7L4

Students listen and read. You might also like to use Visual 20 here for presenting or reinforcing the new language. To focus students' attention on the word order, compare the Spanish and English versions of the initial sentence (*Mi padre es alto*/My father is tall) and show how the adjective comes after the verb in both. As students listen and read, their task is to identify the adjective in each sentence and call them out to you at the end.

Support

Pause the tape after each sentence, and have students repeat each one with you to help them focus.

TRANSCRIPT   CD1, track 44

1   Mi padre es alto. Mi hermana es baja.
2   Mi tía es delgada. Mi tío es gordito.
3   Mi madre es habladora. Mi padre es callado.
4   Tengo dos primas. Ana María es simpática, pero Amelia es antipática.
5   Yo soy joven. Mi abuelo es viejo.

1b 📖 ¿Cómo son? Escribe en español e inglés. AT3.2; AT4.1, 7W7

Students write the family member and the Spanish and English adjectives which apply, using the glossary at the back of the book.

Support

Give students the Spanish and English adjectives in two columns on an A4 sheet in larger print, and allow them to match them up by tracing lines.

Extension

Encourage more able students and fast-finishers to work though the sentences in 1a and work out the Spanish words for the gender opposite to the one given. Start with the nouns, e.g. *mi padre – mi madre*. Given what they know about adjectives from Unit 3B (see grammar section page 29), can they work out the appropriate adjective as well for the altered gender, e.g. *alto – alta*?

Answers

hermana (sister) – *baja* (short); *tía* (aunt) – *delgada* (thin); *tío* (uncle) – *gordito* (fat); *madre* (mother) – *habladora* (talkative); *padre* (father) – *callado* (quiet); *primas* (female cousins) – *simpática* (nice), *antipática* (not nice); *yo* (I) – *joven* (young); *abuelo* (grandfather) – *viejo* (old).

Gramática: subject pronouns – I, you, he, she 7W2, 7W3, 7W5, 7S1

Read through the explanation with students, and add to their stock of words for use in language learning by introducing *el pronombre* (pronoun). For additional reinforcement, ask students to look back to exercise 1a, and replace each noun with the appropriate pronoun, modelling the first one as an example (e.g. *mi padre – él*).

Extension

If you wish to introduce the plural pronouns (*nosotros/as, vosotros/as, ellos/as, ustedes*) at this point as well, students could go back to the verb *llamarse* on page 26, and work out which pronoun is appropriate for each part of the verb paradigm.

2 📖 Encuentra los opuestos. AT3.1; 7W7

Students match the pairs of opposites. This could be done orally as a whole-class at first, then students could work in pairs for two minutes taking it in turns to say an adjective from the list, while their partner gives the opposite meaning.

Support

Write the matching pairs on the board or OHT.

Extension

More able students have to give the matching gender as well, e.g. A: ¡*baja*! B ¡*alta*!

Answers

alto/bajo, antipático/simpático, callado/hablador, delgado/gordito, joven/viejo.

3 🔊 Escucha (1–5). ¿Cómo se llaman? AT1.2; 7L3

Students listen and match the recorded descriptions to the pictures. Prepare for this exercise by asking students to brainstorm with you the words they think they might hear when the person in each picture is described. These can be written up on the board or OHT, and their English meanings checked. This will give students an opportunity to revisit colours of hair and eyes from Unit 3B, as well as the vocabulary for glasses and freckles.

Support

Work through each section of the recording one by one, repeating each several times before moving on. For further help, before the first playing, write up a few key identifying words or phrases from that section, and ask students to raise their hands when they hear these (e.g. 1 – *habladora, pelo rubio*).

Extension

After checking the answers, students could work orally in pairs or small groups: one begins to describe one of the pictures, and the other(s) give(s) the name as soon as they recognise who it is. As an alternative, the student could say who is being described as they start, and make one or more deliberate errors of content which their partner has to spot and chip in, e.g. A *José María es gordito y alto...* B *No, ¡bajo!* A *... y tiene el pelo marrón...* B *No, ¡rubio!*

TRANSCRIPT · CD1, track 45

1 ¡Hola! Voy a describir a mi hermana. Es muy alta y delgada, y muy habladora. Tiene el pelo largo y rubio.
2 Mi tío es bastante alto y callado. Tiene el pelo corto y negro.
3 Mi primo es gordito y bajo. Tiene el pelo rubio y pecas.
4 Mi madre no es muy alta, pero es bastante delgada. Es muy simpática y habladora. Es pelirroja y tiene el pelo largo y ondulado. ¡Lleva gafas!
5 Y yo, como ves, no soy muy alta y soy un poco gordita, pero no mucho. Mi pelo es largo y moreno, y mis ojos son verdes. ¡Y tengo pecas!

Answers

1 Alejandra **2** Pepe **3** José María **4** María Jesús **5** Inés

 Gramática: possessive adjectives 7W2, 7W4

The grammar explanation highlights possessive adjectives (*adjetivos posesivos*).

You might like to focus for the moment on 'my', 'your', 'his/her' and omit 'their' with some groups of students. You might find the following example helpful in getting across 'his'. Students could then suggest other names to you for a parallel paragraph beginning '*Mi amiga se llama...*' to reinforce the use of *su/s* for 'her':

Mi amigo se llama John. Tiene un padre, una madre y dos hermanas.

Su padre se llama Michael y su madre se llama Anne. Sus hermanas se llaman Kate y Sally.

4 ✏ Copy the sentences and write the correct possessive adjectives. 7W2, 7W4

Grammar practice in using possessive adjectives (*mi/mis/tu/tus/su/sus*). You will need to explain to students that there are several possible answers to numbers 3 and 6.

Answers

1 mi **2** tus **3** mis/sus **4** mis **5** tu **6** mi/su

5a ✏ Lee la carta y rellena los blancos. AT3.3, AT4.1; 7T1

Students either copy out the letter, substituting words for the picture icons, or write the Spanish for them in a list. In preparation, ask students to scan the letter and call out any words which reinforce the fact that he is talking about his family (e.g. *hermanos*).

Support

Give the answers on the board, OHT or paper in a jumbled order with one or two distractors. For those needing more help, give alternatives for each picture icon, in the correct order, and students have to underline the correct answer (e.g. for the first picture icon – *doce, trece, quince*).

Extension

Working orally in pairs, more able students or fast-finishers can produce another version with different possibilities for the pictures, e.g. *Me llamo Antonio y tengo catorce años.* 7T2, 7S3.

Answers

trece, gemelos, simpático, antipático, alta y delgada, padre, callado, viejos

5b ✓ ✏ ¡extra! Contesta al correo electrónico de Antonio. Describe a tu familia. AT4.4; 7S3, 7T6.

Students can now write a similar letter about their family, using Antonio's in 5a as a model.

Plenary

✓ Recap on the aims of the lesson (or unit objectives on page 30) and ask students how confident they feel about each one. They can raise both thumbs up to chest level for very confident, one thumb up for fairly confident, wobble a hand for so-so and use one or two thumbs down for not very confident at all. If students are facing you, you will be able to see their individual responses, but students will not feel exposed in front of the rest of the class. Congratulate students on the things they have understood, then choose the objective which appears to generate the least confidence and ask students to call out what they find difficult or don't. Pick the item which appears to be causing most difficulty and work on this immediately for five minutes so that students feel a sense of achievement in beginning to tackle it. Ask students who do feel more confident to contribute their understanding or share how they remember or learnt that item or concept. The other difficulties can inform your next lesson plan.

Alternative plenary *(for lessons ending part-way through the section)* 7W4

✓ Ask students to formulate a rule for forming the feminine of the new adjectives (exercise 2) met so far. As a follow-up, give them three minutes in pairs to invent another sentence containing an adjective. Have one of the pair read it aloud in Spanish and the rest of the class call out the translation.

Support

Put up the following examples to help: *Antonio es alto/Marta es alta. Julio es simpático/Alicia es simpática. Bernardo es joven/Clara es joven. Mi padre es hablador/Mi madre es habladora también.*

Extension

Ask students if they can work out the plural forms of the masculine and feminine adjectives, using the grammar table on page 29 or grammar section A3.1 at the back of the book to help.

3D ¿Tienes animales? page 32

Objectives:
• talk about pets
• learn more about how to make nouns plural
Key language: see p.55 for full list
Skills:
• apply language patterns to new words
• rules for stress (Worksheet 28 iextra!)
• compound sentences (Worksheet 25 Escribir)
Resources: Flashcards 10–20 (Pets); CD1; Worksheets 23 (Hablar), 25 (Escribir); *Just Click* CD-Rom.

Lesson starter 7W1

Refer students to the board or OHT after asking them to write down, in pairs, the Spanish for: four numbers between 1 and 15; four colours; four adjectives to describe height, size or character; the Spanish for 'I have' and 'have you (got)'. Ask students at random to call out their answers – other pairs who have this word have to strike it off their list. Award a point for any word in each category not written down by anyone else – who has the most?

Alternative lesson starter *(for lessons beginning part-way through the section)* 7W1, 7W4

With their books closed, flash up on the OHT or on card the following beginnings and endings of words for pets, and students have to call out the missing part to you: e.g. *ga-, cab-, ser-, -aya, -de colores, -ón, páj-, -ster, -per, -males, -uga*. This can also be done in pairs or small groups. To practise plurals, call out the singular pet (e.g. *una cobaya*) and students reply in a chorus with the plural. If you write the numbers 2–12 on the board, students can increase the quantity each time (T *una cobaya*, S *dos cobayas*; T *un pez*, S *tres peces*) etc.

Introduction

Explain that students will need to reuse the vocabulary from the lesson starter in the new work on pets.

1 🎧 Escucha y lee. AT1.1, AT3.2; 7W1, 7W4, 7S1, 7T1, 7L4

Students listen and follow the text. Flashcards 10–20 and games could also be used here to present the new language for pets.

Support

To help reinforce the vocabulary, call out the sentences below the pictures in random order, and students have to point to the relevant picture; then call out the start of any of the sentences (e.g. *Tengo un...*) and students call out another possible half from the page (e.g. *perro/caballo/ratón*).

Tengo un hámster.
Tengo un ratón.
Tengo un perro.
Tengo una cobaya.
Tengo un caballo.
Tengo tres pájaros.
Tengo una tortuga.
Tengo tres peces de colores.
Tengo dos gatos.
Tengo una serpiente.
No tengo animales.

2a 📖 Lee y une las frases. AT3.3; 7T1, 7L1

Students read the text and match up the sentence halves correctly.

Support

Familiarise students with the text by reading it aloud as students follow; stop every few words for the class to call out the next word. Then play a memory game. Students turn their books over and look at you; call out ten words, half of which are not in the text and the other half from the text. Students have to repeat aloud the ones which are, and remain silent for the ones which aren't – how many were listening carefully?

Answers

1 c **2** f **3** a **4** b **5** e **6** d

2b ☑ 🖉 ¿Y tú? ¿Tienes animales? ¿Cómo son? AT4.1–4.3; 7S3, 7T6

Students write about their own pets: this could range from a list or simple speech bubble, word-processed if liked, to a longer description using Paco's in exercise 2a as a model.

Support and extension

Either as additional exercise to stretch less able students or as a preparation for more able students before writing their own letter, write up the following English prompts for students, and ask them to adapt Paco's letter sentence by sentence, e.g. 'Paco has... two cats (Golfo is young, Peluche is old), five mice – they're very nice, a horse called Ramona and four goldfish. Has also got two horrible cats, called Siri and Miri.'

3 💬 Practica con tu pareja. ¿Qué tal tu memoria? AT2.1; 7L1, 7L2

In preparation for the speaking exercise, and to reinforce sound/spelling links, call out the Spanish for each pet while students try and write it down on paper or on a mini-whiteboard (books closed). Students then work orally in pairs to produce as long a list of pets as possible.

Gramática: plural nouns 7W4

Read through this section with students or allow them to do this at their own pace.

4 📖 Choose the appropriate word.

Answers

1 gato, cobayas **2** caballos **3** peces, hámster **4** perro **5** serpiente **6** ratones

Plenary 7W1

☑ Ask students to test each other in pairs on the vocabulary of this unit using the Resumen on page 33, awarding points for each correct answer. This could be extended to groups of three or four, where one student is in the 'hot seat' for a series of five questions from the others – who can get all five?

Support

Focus on the newly met vocabulary of pets to reduce the memory element.

Extension

Any questions from any unit up till now can be asked.

Alternative plenary *(for lessons ending part-way through the section)* 7W1

☑ Use some of the flashcard games. Place the cards out of sight, and students call out the Spanish for the animal they think is on the top of the pile – how many can they guess in a minute? Stick eight or more on the board as students chant the Spanish for each, then tap the cards rapidly in random order, calling out the Spanish for a pet. If it matches, students repeat it twice after you; if it doesn't, they call out 'no, no!'. Students can use the pictures in their textbooks from exercise 1 to do this in pairs – their aim is to ensure they and their partner can name them all correctly.

Resumen *(page 33)*

Give your students time to revise words by testing each other in pairs on the words in the Resumen. Give them ideas on how they can use the Resumen on their own, e.g. write down any five words which they always forget or find difficult. Focus on these five words, and see if they can remember them the next day.

¡Ahora, tú! *(pp. 122–123)*

Differentiated self-access reading and writing exercises: see page 37 for more information.

page 122

1 📖 **Who is it? Join the pictures to the descriptions.**

Answers

1 e   2 c   3 a   4 f   5 b   6 d.

2 💡 🖉 **Look at the family tree. Copy and fill in the gaps in the letter...**

Answers:

(in this order) me, quince, madre, treinta y nueve, Andrés, hermanos, tiene, diez, abuela, años, se llama, Carolina, Elena, gemelas.

3 💡 🖉 **Write a paragraph describing your family in as much detail as you can.**

Students complete the prompts with their own details.

page 123

1b 📖 **Say whether the sentences are true or false.**

Answers

1 V   2 M   3 M   4 V   5 M   6 V   7 M   8 V   9 M.

1c 🖉 **Correct the false sentences.**

Answers

2 La familia de Enrique es muy grande. **3** Enrique tiene un hermano. **5** Chábeli tiene los ojos marrones. **7** La madre de Enrique es alta. **9** Las tías de Enrique se llaman Victoria y Beatriz.

2 🖉 **Write what the young people are saying.**

Answers

1 Me llamo Inés. Tengo un perro marrón. **2** Me llamo Andrés. Tengo dos peces de colores rojos. **3** Me llamo Manolo. Tengo cuatro gatos grises. **4** Me llamo Esther. Tengo un pájaro verde. **5** Me llamo Paco. Tengo cuatro cobayas. Una cobaya es blanca y negra. Las otras tres cobayas son marrones. **6** Me llamo Inmaculada. Tengo una serpiente marrón y verde.

Worksheets Unit 3

19 **Descripciones** AT3.1; 7W1

Visuals: describing hair and eyes from Section B.

20 **¿Cómo eres?** AT3.1; 7W1

Visuals: describing personality traits from Section C.

21 **Resumen** AT3.1; 7W1

List of key language of the unit.

22 **Escuchar** AT1.1–2; 7L1, 7L2

1 Students learn to link a word with its written form by writing in the missing letter of each word so that it matches what they hear. Point out that just one letter can change the meaning of a word.

TRANSCRIPT
CD1, track 47

Ejemplo:
1 prima
2 padre
3 hermano
4 madrastra
5 hija
6 gemelos
7 sesenta

Answers

1 a   2 p   3 a   4 m   5 a   6 o   7 s

2a Students identify complete and incomplete utterances by putting a tick beside finished sentences and a cross beside unfinished ones. Model first using examples from earlier units like *En mi estuche tengo.../Tengo doce años/Mi cumpleaños es el doce de...*

TRANSCRIPT
CD1, track 48

Ejemplo:
1 ¡Hola! Me llamo...
2 Vivo con mi padre en Bilbao, en el norte de...
3 Mi madre vive en Madrid.
4 Tengo dos hermanas que se llaman...
5 Mi hermano se llama Carlos y tiene trece...
6 ¿Es verdad que tienes un hermano gemelo?
7 Tengo dos abuelos pero no tengo...
8 ¿Cómo es tu...?

Answers:

1 ✗   2 ✗   3 ✓   4 ✗   5 ✗   6 ✓   7 ✗   8 ✗

2b Students listen to the unfinished sentences and note the letter of the word(s) which best complete(s) each. Model first using examples suggested above in 1, giving a choice of possible endings, e.g. *En mi estuche tengo (un libro, una hermana, una regla).*

TRANSCRIPT

CD1, track 49

Ejemplo:
1 ¡Hola! Me llamo...
2 Vivo con mi padre en Bilbao, en el norte de...
3 Tengo dos hermanas que se llaman...
4 Mi hermano se llama Carlos y tiene trece...
5 Tengo dos abuelos pero no tengo...
6 ¿Cómo es tu...?

Answers

1 d **2** g **3** a **4** e **5** c **6** f

3 Students learn to recognise the context in which a passage is set. They write the number of the conversation appropriate to each setting. Check their understanding of the Spanish prompts, which have all been met in the Student's Book. Model with a few examples first, giving a restricted choice: *¿Cuántos años tienes tú? – edad, países, meses.*

TRANSCRIPT

CD1, track 50

1 Cuarenta y uno, cuarenta y dos, cuarenta y tres...
2 – ¡Hola! ¿Qué tal?
   – Bien. ¿Y tú?
3 ¿Inglés? No, no hablo inglés. Hablo español y un poco de francés.
4 ¡Escuchad! ¡Y mirad la pizarra, por favor!
5 Vivo en América Central. Soy mejicano.
6 Vivo en Granada con mi padre, mi madrastra y mi hermana.
7 A ver... Tengo un bolígrafo y una pluma, pero no tengo lápiz.

Answers

Instrucciones **4** Estuche **7** Números **1** Saludos **2** Cumpleaños (distractor) Nacionalidad **5** Familia **6** Idiomas **3**

23 Hablar AT2.2; 7W1, 7L6

Students work in pairs, using the A or B half of the sheet to talk about themselves and a brother or sister and pet(s). Explain to students that they can choose which figure to be, and the other is their brother or sister; and that they can choose the eye and hair colour and the personality characteristics.

Support

Write up the questions and the start of the answers, e.g.
¿Tienes padres? Sí, tengo.../No, no tengo...
¿Cómo se llama tu (madre)? Se llama...
¿Cuándo es tu cumpleaños? Es el... de...
¿Cómo se llama tu (gato/perro)? Se llama...
¿Cuántos años tiene? Tiene...
¿Cómo es (tu perro/gato)? Es...

Extension

You might like to brainstorm other questions which fast-finishers could ask and answer from previous units, with partners inventing replies (e.g. *¿Cuántos años tienes tú?, ¿Dónde vives?, ¿Eres francés/esa?*). Explain that this introduces an element of unpredictability, which will more accurately reflect a conversation with a Spanish person.

24 Leer 7W1, 7T1, 7W3, 7S2, 7T6

This worksheet focuses on cognates (*cognados*).

1 Students find the simple cognates, writing the English and Spanish down in pairs. You may prefer to instruct students to circle them on the sheet.

Extension

As a possible follow-up with more able groups, you might ask them to tell you which of these are adjectives (all except *carácter* and *en contacto*). Reminding them of the rule for the agreement of adjectives, ask them to work out in pairs what the masculine singular form is, explaining that this is the form they will need to look up in the dictionary.

Answers

1 divorced – *divorciados* **2** in contact – *en contacto* **3** identical – *idénticas* **4** character – *carácter* **5** optimistic – *optimista* **6** shy/timid – *tímida* **7** exotic – *exótico* **8** tropical – *tropicales.*

2 Ask students to use the different types of underlining to find the sentences which give information on each topic 1–5. Remind them that *padres* means 'parents' and *hermanos* is 'brothers and sisters', and the difference between *soy* (I am) and *es* (she is).

Answers

1 Mi madre se llama Paquita; mis padres están divorciados, y no estoy en contacto con mi padre Miguel. **2** Tengo una hermana gemela, Amaya. **3** Soy bastante alta y delgada, con el pelo largo, negro y ondulado, y tengo los ojos marrones. **4** Es un poco tímida y callada, pero es simpática. **5** También tengo un pájaro exótico y diez peces tropicales.

3 Students answer the simple questions in Spanish. Point out to them the hint below on how to reuse the language of the question in the answer. Check they remember that *quién* means 'who', and explain that *como* can also mean 'like'. Model a few examples, using the names of students in your group, e.g.

¿Cuántos años tiene Matthew? Matthew tiene doce años.
¿Dónde vive Rafik? Rafik vive en Leicester.
¿Cómo se llama la hermana de Claire? La hermana de Claire se llama Natalie.

Answers

1 Inés tiene trece años. **2** La familia vive en Santiago. **3** Su madre se llama Paquita. **4** No, Amaya es baja. **5** Inés no es tímida. **6** Amaya tiene los ojos verdes.

25 Escribir 7S6

This worksheet will help students improve their sentence construction.

1 Students select *y* or *pero* as appropriate.

Answers

1 La madre de Jason es extrovertida y es habladora. **2** Su padre es estricto pero (es) simpático. **3** Jason habla bien español y (habla) un poco de catalán. **4** Jodie es de Gales, pero no habla galés.

2 Students try and improve the paragraph by adding *que*. If they need reminding about *que*, you might find the following a useful preparation as a whole-class exercise. Put up the following sentences and ask students to join them with *que*:

1 *Juan tiene una hermana simpática. Se llama María.*
2 *Pili tiene un cobayo gordito, Mimi. Tiene dos años.*
3 *Javier tiene dos amigos. Se llaman Gonzalo y Sergio.*

Answers

There are many possibilities here: accept all versions which make sense.

3 You can also use *que* in the middle of a sentence to add extra information. Show students the example from exercise 3 with its two possible versions.

Now ask them to do the same with these examples:

1 *Su amigo Juan tiene doce años. Es alto y hablador.* (Su amigo Juan, que tiene doce años, es alto y hablador)
2 *Su padre es callado. Tiene el pelo rubio y lleva gafas.* (Su padre, que es callado, tiene el pelo rubio y lleva gafas).
3 *Su tío es bajo y gordito. Tiene un perro antipático.* (Su tío, que es bajo y gordito, tiene un perro antipático).

Answers

1 Su hermana Jodie, que tiene once años, es muy simpática.
2 Su madre, que es escocesa, es pelirroja y lleva gafas.
3 Su padre, que es profesor de inglés, habla también galés.

26 ¡Así se hace! 7T1, 7T2, 7L1

This reading sheet focuses on the micro skills needed to learn how to read aloud more accurately and confidently.

Firstly, ask students to underline all the words which have a letter *h* or *j*. Elicit their replies, write the relevant words on the board or OHT.

Answers

h: hola, hay, hija, Holanda, habladora
j: Juan, Japón, jefa, baja, ojos, pelirroja, japonesa, trabaja, Jaca, jueves, joven

Help students make sound/spelling links by eliciting from them the pronunciation rule for *h* and *j*. Model with words other than those used in the conversation (e.g. *junio, hermana, julio, hermanastro*).

Encourage students' ability to follow a written text. Read the conversation aloud, paying special attention to intonation, and encourage students to use their finger to follow the words, either horizontally under each word, or vertically to mark each new line. Stop several times and ask students to tell you what the next word is. Check their understanding of the meaning.

Ask students to work in pairs and practise reading aloud for points of pronunciation/shared reading of a scripted dialogue. You might like to encourage them to swop partners with other pairs for variety.

27 Gramática 7W3, 7W4, 7W7

This worksheet pulls together the adjectives from this unit, and gives students further practice in the pattern

of adjectival endings. You might like to reinforce the Spanish terminology: *adjetivo masculino, feminino, singular, plural,* and give students the phrases *¿Cómo termina (el adjetivo)? Termina en...*

The grammar explanation is broken down into two sections: the first dealing with adjectives ending in a vowel, the second with those ending in a consonant. Students underline, or copy out, the appropriate adjective, and in exercise 2, they work out the correct form.

Support

In exercise 2, read through the text with students, helping them work out whether they will need a masculine or feminine adjective, and whether it will be singular or plural – pronouns like *yo, ella* and verb markers like *soy, es, son* provide clues.

Extension

As an **¡extra!** exercise, explain that in the dictionary, adjectives *(adj.)* are given in their masculine singular form. Ask students to find the Spanish for the following: patient, honest, stupid, sensitive, hard-working, brave, lazy, kind, naughty, cheerful. They can write each out in their four possible forms, e.g. patient: *(ms) paciente, (fs) paciente, (mpl) pacientes, (fpl) pacientes.* For homework, they can choose any five new adjectives and incorporate them into a paragraph or five sentences.

Answers

1 rubio, alta, largo, delgada, guapa, verdes, simpática, inteligente
2 alta, delgada, marrones, corto, rubio, bajo, castaños, marrones, encantadoras, antipáticas, hablador, callado, buena.

28 ¡extra! 7W7

This worksheet presents and explains the Spanish rules for stress. Students often find it very empowering to learn that, once they know the rule, they can pronounce any Spanish word correctly even if they have not heard it before. Work through the exercises as suggested on the sheet. The vocabulary in exercise 4 is a useful addition to this unit.

Extension

You may wish to consolidate and explain further the rule for the loss of accent in some plurals (presented in the Student's Book on page 32). Give students the examples *ratón/ratones* and *jardín/jardines* – ask if they can work out, from the stress rule, why this is. Elicit their replies, and give them the following to put into the plural: *estación, avión, francés, autobús.* You

might like to also give them *joven*, which they've met in this unit, and ask how its plural might be pronounced, and therefore spelt (*jóvenes*).

Workbook A Unit 3

page 13 (Section A)

Answers

ex 1:
2 treinta y seis 3 veintinueve 4 sesenta y cuatro 5 cincuenta y cinco (sequence = +5, −3)

ex 2:
¡Hola! Soy Enrique. Tengo trece años y vivo en Toledo. Te presento a mi familia. Mi hermana Isabel tiene diecinueve años. Mi padre José tiene cincuenta y dos años. Mi madrastra Ana tiene cuarenta y cinco años. Roberto es el hijo de Ana. Tiene veinte años.

ex 3a:
1–b 2–c 3–a

ex 3b:
a Se llama Carlos. b Se llama Paco. c Se llama Molly.

page 14 (Section B)

Answers

ex 1:
1 ojo 2 rubio 3 pelo 4 gris 5 tengo 6 verde

ex 2a:
1 Me llamo Ignacio. Tengo el pelo corto y rubio, la piel muy clara y los ojos verdes.
2 Hola, soy Maite. Mi pelo es largo y castaño. Tengo los ojos grises y la piel morena.
3 Me llamo Eduardo. Llevo gafas y tengo los ojos verdes. Soy pelirrojo. Tengo el pelo rizado, y pecas grandes.
4 Soy Jaime. Llevo gafas muy pequeñas. Mis ojos son marrones. Tengo el pelo negro y la piel negra.
5 Me llamo Emilio. Tengo el pelo blanco y liso, la piel verde y los ojos rojos. No soy de aquí.

Note: exercise 3 is recorded on CD1, track 51.

page 15 (Section C)

Answers

ex 1:

s	i	m	p	á	t	i	c	o					
						a	n	t	i	p	á	t	i	c	o
				d	e	l	g	a	d	o			
	h	a	b	l	a	d	o	r					
			b	a	j	o							
	g	o	r	d	o								
	a	l	t	o									

¡extra!

otro adjetivo = callado (quiet)

ex 2a:

Hola, Caroline
Gracias por **tu** carta. ¿Cómo es tu familia?
Mi hermanastro Ignacio es **alto** y
antipático. Mi padre es bajo y **callado**.
Ignacio y mi padre son **gorditos. Mi**
madrastra es **habladora**, ella y mis
hermanas son delgadas y **simpáticas.**
Mis abuelos viven en mi casa. Son **viejos,**
habladores y muy simpáticos. Mi abuela
es **irlandesa.** ¿**Tus** abuelos son ingleses?
Nuria

ex 2b:

	Masculine	Feminine
Singular	simpático callado	irlandesa habladora
Plural	gordos viejos habladores	delgadas

page 16 (Section D)

Answers

ex 1a:

1 gato = cat **2** perro = dog
3 caballo = horse **4** cobaya = guinea
pig **5** hámster = hamster
6 serpiente = snake **7** pájaro = bird
8 pez de colores = goldfish

ex 1b: ¡extra!

M un gato, un perro, un caballo, un
hámster, un pájaro, un pez de colores;
F una cobaya, una serpiente

Note: exercise 2 is recorded on CD1,
track 53.

Workbook B Unit 3

page 13 (Section A)

Answers

ex 1:

1 cuarenta, cincuenta **2** treinta y seis,
cuarenta y cinco **3** veintinueve, treinta
y cinco **4** treinta y dos, sesenta y cuatro
5 cincuenta y cuatro, cincuenta y ocho

(sequence = +4, −3) **6** quince,
cuarenta y cinco (sequence = ×3, −3)

ex 2:

1b llamo Paco **2c** Me llamo Molly
3a Carlos

¡extra!

a Carlos. **b** Tiene una hermanastra que
tiene trece años. Vive en casa con su
madrastra y su padre. Se llama Paco.
c Tiene catorce años y es hija única. No
tiene hermanos. Se llama Molly.

page 14 (Section B)

Answers

ex 1: + ¡extra!

2 rubio = singular, rest = plurals
3 pelo = noun, rest = adjectives
4 gris = singular, rest = plurals
5 tengo = verb, rest = nouns
6 castaños = adjective ending in -o in
masculine singular, rest end in
consonant **7** pelo = singular, rest =
plurals **8** verde = can't have green
hair, rest = possible for hair

ex 2a:

Suggested solution

1 Tengo el pelo corto y rubio.
2 Mi pelo es largo y castaño.
3 Tengo los ojos grises y la piel
morena.
4 Llevo gafas y tengo los ojos negros.
5 Soy pelirrojo y tengo las pecas
grandes.
6 Llevo gafas muy pequeñas.
7 Tengo el pelo negro y la piel negra.

Note: ex 3 is recorded on CD1, track 52.

page 15 (Section C)

Answers

ex 1:

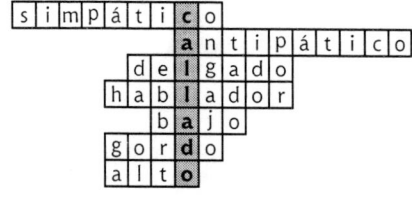

otro adjetivo = callado (quiet)

---

ex 2a:

Hola, Caroline
Gracias por **tu** primera carta. ¿Como es
tu familia? **Mi** hermanastro Ignacio es
alto y **antipático/callado.** Mi padre es
bajo y **callado/antipático.** Ignacio y **mi**
padre son **gordos. Mi** madrastra es
habladora, ella y **mis** hermanas son
delgadas y simpáticas. **Mis** abuelos
viven en **mi** casa. Son viejos, habladores
y muy **simpáticos. Mi** abuela es
irlandesa. ¿**Tus** abuelos son ingleses?
Nuria

¡extra!

(from) primera; alto, viejos; habladores;
irlandesa; ingleses; simpáticas

ex 2b:

	Masculine	Feminine
Singular	simpático antipático callado	irlandesa habladora primera
Plural	gordos simpáticos viejos habladores ingleses	delgadas simpáticas

page 16 (Section D)

Answers

ex 1a:

1 gato **5** hámster
2 perro **6** serpiente
3 caballo **7** pájaro
4 cobaya **8** pez de colores

ex 1b:

un gato = a cat; un perro = a dog; un
caballo = a horse; una cobaya = a
guinea pig; un hámster = a hamster;
una serpiente = a snake; un pájaro = a
bird; un pez de colores = a goldfish

ex 2: ¡extra!

afectuoso = affectionate;
hostil = hostile; amable = likeable;
desagradable = disagreeable; enorme =
enormous; minúsculo = minuscule (tiny);
feroz = fierce; domesticado = tame

Note: the adjectives in ex 2 **¡extra!**
are recorded on CD1, track 54.

Unidad 4 En el pueblo	Topic/Language/Culture	Grammar and skills	National Criteria
4A ¿Qué hay en tu pueblo? (pp. 34–35) **Objectives** • say where you live and what facilities there are • practise learning new vocabulary • learn how to pronounce v and b	*Vivo en una/la aldea, ciudad, capital, un/el pueblo, barrio de... en la costa, el norte de España* *¿Qué hay/no hay en...?* *Hay/No hay... un bar, una bolera, un cine, un colegio, una estación, un parque (de atracciones), una piscina, un polideportivo, una playa, un restaurante, un supermercado, una tienda, muchas cosas*	**Grammar** *hay/no hay* **Skills** Vocabulary learning skills **Pronunciation** *v* and *b*	**Attainment** AT1.2, AT2.2, AT3.2, AT4.1–3 **Framework objectives** 7W1, 7W8, 7T2, 7T4, 7T6, 7L1, 7L2 **Programmes of study** 1abc, 2abde, 3acd, 5ad **QCA Scheme of work** Language: Unit 5 Context: places in the town **Assessment for learning** Objectives, p.34 Ex 1c, p.35 Ex 2b + 3b, Plenary
4B ¿Cómo es? (pp. 36–37) **Objectives** • learn how to be a good language detective • describe what there is in your town or village • learn how to use modifiers	*¿Cómo es? Está en las montañas, es/está divertido, aburrido, grande, pequeño, ruidoso, tranquilo, bonito, feo, limpio, sucio, hay mucho tráfico, mucha industria, muchos cines, muchas tiendas*	**Grammar** *ser/estar* Modifiers *bastante, muy, demasiado* Use of *mucho/a, muchos/as* **Skills** Learn how to be a good language detective Learn how to link ideas using *porque* Develop memory skills in listening (Worksheet 31 *Escuchar*) Extend reading skills (Worksheet 37 *¡extra!*)	**Attainment** AT1.2, AT2.2, AT3.2, AT4.1–3 **Framework objectives** 7W1, 7W2, 7W3, 7W4, 7W5, 7T1, 7T3, 7T4, 7T5, 7T6, 7L2, 7L6 **Programmes of study** 1abc, 2abcde, 3acd, 5ade **QCA Scheme of work** Language: Unit 5 Context: places in the town **Assessment for learning** Objectives, p.37 Ex 3a + 3b, Plenary
4C ¿Se puede...? (pp. 38–39) **Objectives** • say what there is to do where you live • learn how to use a dictionary	*¿Qué se puede hacer en tu (pueblo)? Se puede... bailar, jugar, visitar, beber, comer, hacer, ver, ir, vivir*	**Grammar** *se puede* + infinitive **Skills** Dictionary – recognising verbs/nouns (Worksheet 35 *¡Así se hace!*)	**Attainment** AT1.2, AT2.1–3, AT3.2, AT4.1–4 **Framework objectives** 7W1, 7W2, 7W4, 7W5, 7W7, 7W8, 7T3, 7T4, 7L2, 7L4, 7L6, 7S3 **Programmes of study** 1abc, 2abcdefhj, 3bcd, 5ade **QCA Scheme of work** Language: Unit 5 Context: places in the town **Assessment for learning** Objectives, p.38 Ex3, p.39 Ex 6, Plenary
4D ¿Y tu opinión? (pp. 40–43) **Objectives** • say what you like and what you don't like, and why	*¿Te gusta...? me encanta, me gusta (mucho), no me gusta (nada), odio.* *¿Por qué?, porque....*	**Grammar** *gustar* *al (a + el)* **Skills** Asking questions (Worksheet 36 *Gramática*) Remembering language when listening (Worksheet 31 *Escuchar*) Recycling known language in new contexts (Worksheet 34 *Escribir*)	**Attainment** AT1.2–4, AT2.1–4, AT3.3, AT4.2–4 **Framework objectives** 7W1, 7W2, 7W4, 7W5, 7S1, 7S2, 7S3, 7S4, 7S8, 7T1, 7T6, 7L1, 7L2, 7L3, 7L5, 7L6 **Programmes of study** 1abc, 2abcdfh, 5abcdefghi **QCA Scheme of work** Language: Unit 6 Context: leisure activities **Assessment for learning** Objectives, p.40 Ex1.4 + 5, Plenary, All revision activities p.42

Other resources: *¡Ahora tú!* pp.124–125   WS 29–37   Flashcards 21–27   OHTs 8–9   WBA & B pp.18–22   Assessment units 3–4 (R & A file pp.120–123)   Just Click CD-Rom

4 En el pueblo

4A ¿Qué hay en tu pueblo?

pp. 34–35

Objectives:
- say where you live and what facilities there are
- practise learning new vocabulary
- learn how to pronounce *v* and *b*

Key language: see p.67 for full list

Grammar: Hay/No hay

Skills:
- practise learning new vocabulary
- (launch) learn how to pronounce *b* and *v*

Resources: OHT 8 (different types of places); OHT 9 (places in town); CD1; Workbooks A and B p.18; *Just Click* CD-Rom.

Lesson starter 7W8

As students come in, give each a piece of paper with between three and five of the following English cognates, and ask them to scan the texts and pictures in 1a to find the Spanish equivalents: bars, restaurants, a supermarket, the north, the capital, cinemas, a bowling alley, the coast, a park, a theme park. Fast-finishers can be asked to check the vocabulary section at the back of the book and note whether each of their words is masculine (*m.*) or feminine (*f.*). When you call out each English word in turn, all students with that word on their piece of paper call out the Spanish; remind them of the Spanish terms (*masculino, feminino*) for feeding back the genders.

Extension

Ask students to work out the singulars of the plural nouns, using the rules they already know.

Alternative lesson starter *(for lessons starting part-way through the section)*

Put up on the board or OHT a grid of sixteen squares, each containing either the beginning or end of eight Spanish words for places from those in the key language grid on page 35 (e.g. *par, nda, est* etc.). Without using their books, students have to match them up.

Support

Put a hyphen at the beginning or end of each part to help students (e.g. *-egio, bol-*).

Extension

Ask students to jot down whether each complete word will have *un* or *una* in front, using their memory or intelligent guesswork. You remind them that masculine words often end in *-o* and feminine ones in *-a*.

Introduction

Use the objectives at the top of the spread to help students focus on the content of the unit – what kind of places do they anticipate needing Spanish for to indicate what is in their town, or what kind of town they live in?

1a 🎧 Escucha (1–3) y lee. AT1.3; 7W1, 7T2, 7L2.

To present the new language of this exercise, both OHT 8 and 9 will be useful: OHT 8 relates to the first paragraph in each of the three sections and OHT 9 to the second. Students listen

and follow the texts. Use these for pronunciation practice by stopping the recording after each sentence and having students repeat. They could then be encouraged to read along with the tape in short sections.

¡Hola! Me llamo Susana. Vivo en el campo en una aldea. Está en Galicia en el norte de España. No hay mucho en la aldea. Hay dos restaurantes, unos bares, unas tiendas, un supermercado y un colegio.

¡Hola! ¿Qué tal? Soy Patricia. Vivo en la ciudad de Caracas, la capital de Venezuela. En mi barrio hay muchas cosas: cines, un parque, una bolera, una piscina y un polideportivo.

¡Hola! Me llamo María. Vivo en un pueblo en la costa. Se llama Salou. Hay un parque de atracciones cerca, playas bonitas, una estación y muchos restaurantes.

1b 💿 Escucha (1–10) y escribe el nombre de la persona. AT1.2; 7L1

In preparation, to help students familiarise themselves with the texts in 1a, give students a copy of OHT 9 and ask them to write the initial letter of each of the three names (Susana, Patricia, María) alongside each place found in the town or village of each of these three people. Students can then listen to the recording and identify who is speaking in each by writing S, P or M.

1 Vivo en una ciudad.
2 Hay un parque de atracciones.
3 En mi barrio hay un polideportivo.
4 Hay muchas cosas en mi barrio.
5 No hay mucho: solamente dos restaurantes, unos bares, unas tiendas, un supermercado y un colegio.
6 Hay muchos restaurantes.
7 No hay mucho en mi aldea.
8 Vivo en América del Sur.
9 Hay cines en mi barrio.
10 Vivo en el norte de España en una aldea.

Answers

1 P 2 M 3 P 4 P 5 S 6 M 7 S 8 P 9 P 10 S

1c ✓ 📖 Escribe si las frases son verdad (V) o mentira (M). AT3.2; 7T1, 7T3

Students decide if each statement is true or false. Fast-finishers can write a corrected version of the sentences they have labelled M.

Answers

1 V 2 M 3 M 4 M 5 V 6 V 7 M

2a ✍ ¿Qué hay/no hay en tu pueblo? Haz dos listas. AT4.1; 7W1, 7W2, 7T4

Students write a list of the places there are, or are not, in their area of the city or in their village or town. You may need to substitute *barrio* or *ciudad* for the *pueblo* of the instruction. First read through the Gramática section, halfway down the page, which highlights the absence of *un/a* after the negative *no hay*. Highlight the fact that *hay/no hay* are very useful cross-topic phrases.

Support

Give students a copy of OHT 9 and ask them to put a tick beside the pictures of places which do exist in their town/area, and a cross beside the ones which don't. They can then copy the appropriate word from the new language grid under each appropriate picture.

Extension

Students can use the dictionary to look for other places. Or you might like to give them the following English places and show them – by using one as an example – how you have to search through the relevant section to find the (compound) word or phrase you're looking for: railway station, petrol station, town hall, art gallery, shopping centre, playground, secondary school, market place.

2b ✓ ⚲ Compara con tu pareja. AT2.2; 7L6

A pairwork exercise in which students use the model given to explain what there is, or is not, in their own home town/village or area.

3a ✍ Copia la carta y rellena los espacios. AT4.1–2

Students replace each picture with the correct Spanish word.

Support

Give students the answers in a jumbled order.

Answers

aldea campo sur costa tienda restaurante colegio bar estación supermercado

Gramática: there is/there are – *hay* 7W2

Read through the grammar explanation with students, highlighting the use of *hay* and *no hay* in direct sentences and questions. You might like to give students some sample sentences in English, e.g. There is a sports centre/There aren't any parks/Is there a swimming pool?/Aren't there any supermarkets?

3b ✓ ✍ Escribe una carta sobre tu pueblo. Usa la carta en 3a como modelo. AT4.3; 7T6, 7T7

Using the paragraph in 3a as a model, students write a paragraph about their own area or home town/village.

Support

Students can simply copy the paragraph in 3a and substitute more appropriate single words.

Extension

Give more able students a short list of high-frequency words, e.g. *y, pero, soy, me llamo, vivo, cerca*, and ask them to incorporate them into their paragraph. If using *cerca* you might like to explain that *de* + *el* forms *del*.

4 ¡extra! ¡Así se hace! Learning vocabulary

Ask students to work in pairs and select between six and ten words from the unit they find difficult to remember, and work with their partner on pronouncing these, translating them and

practising the spelling. Remind them of useful techniques for learning vocabulary – look, cover, spell, check; being given the first half of the word and completing it; copying a list of the words with only the consonants in, then rewriting the list with the vowels in place from memory.

⚲ Pronunciacíon: *v* and *b*

Read the pronunciation tip before practising saying some words which contain the letters 'v' and 'b', e.g. *bien, bolígrafo, veinte, verde, polideportivo, Cuba, cobaya, vivir*.

Plenary *(for lessons ending part-way through the section)* 7W6, 7T2

✓ There are a number of words in the Key language grid to the right of exercise 2b which contain combinations of the *c* sound in Spanish: *ciudad, cine, atracciones, supermercado, colegio, piscina, estación*. Write these up on the board and ask students to formulate again the rule for pronouncing the letter *c*: soft 'th' when followed by *i/e*, and hard 'k' when followed by *a/o/u*, and a double *c* is hard, followed by soft. You might like to use the following words (a number from the rest of the unit) for further practice, either written up for students to work out the pronunciation or read aloud as students write down what they think the spelling is: *silencio, música, tráfico, sección, oficina, sucio, acción, comer, discoteca, hacer, pescado*.

4B ¿Cómo es? pp. 36–37

> **Objectives:**
> - learn how to be a good language detective
> - describe what there is in your town or village
> - learn how to use modifiers
>
> **Key language:** see p.67 for full list
> **Grammar:** the verbs *ser/estar* ('to be')
> **Skills:**
> - use modifiers 'quite', 'very', 'too'
> - learn how to be a good language detective
>
> **Resources:** Visual 29, Worksheets 31 (Escuchar – improving memory skills), 37 (¡extra! – reading skills); CD1; Workbooks A and B p.19; *Just Click* CD-Rom.

Lesson starter 7W3

Put the following three headings on the board or OHT: *adjetivo, sustantivo, verbo* and remind students of the meanings. Give students a time limit in which to allocate each of the words below to the correct group. This will help prepare them for the *¡Así se hace!* strategy and exercise 1, and revises known vocabulary. Suggested words: *hay, capital, costa, verde, vivo, bajo, tengo, barrio, soy, ciudad, alta, piscina*.

Answers

adjetivo – *verde, bajo, alta*; sustantivo – *capital, costa, barrio, ciudad, piscina*; verbo – *hay, vivo, tengo, soy*.

Alternative lesson starter *(for lessons starting part-way through the section)* 7W5

Write up the following English prompts: *to be, I am, you are, he/she is, they are* and the following parts of the two verbs 'to be' in random order: *está, ser, estás, soy, están, eres, es, estar, son, estoy*. Set students a time limit in which to find two Spanish verb parts for each English prompt. Students can then test each other in pairs, if liked.

Introduction

Highlight for students, from the objectives, the aim of being a good language detective, and learning how to use the modifiers *bastante* (quite), *muy* (very), *demasiado* (too). Ask them to give you some examples of English sentences containing these modifiers to check their understanding. If you have not used the starter, remind students of the concepts of noun (can put 'a' or 'the' in front), verb and adjective (describes a noun), and ask for examples in Spanish and English.

1 Escucha y lee. AT1.2, AT3.2; 7W1, 7W2, 7W4, 7T1, 7T3.

In preparation for this exercise, write up the words *paraíso, montaña, silencio, turista, tráfico* and give students two minutes in which to work out both how to pronounce these cognates, or near-cognates (*cognados*), and what their English meaning might be. To help them learn to anticipate and predict the content of a text, ask them the following questions. Where is this scene set? What do the pictures tell us? Who is speaking? Are there any contrasts or opposites being shown? What kinds of words in English do you think the speakers might be using? Are any words repeated? Students can then listen and follow the text.

Support

Play each section twice, and have students read aloud with the tape the second time to help them stay focused.

TRANSCRIPT　　　　　　　　　　**CD1, track 57**

– ¡Bienvenidos a Asturias!
– Paraíso natural: con campo, montaña y costa.
– Escucha el silencio... El campo es **muy** tranquilo. Hoy está **demasiado** ruidoso.
– Y las montañas son **muy** tranquilas. No son turísticas. Hoy están **demasiado** ruidosas.
– En la costa hay **muchos** turistas. La costa no es tranquila. Hoy está **demasiado** tranquila.
– Hoy los pueblos no están tranquilos, están **muy** ruidosos con mucho tráfico. ¡Hay **demasiado** tráfico!

 ¡Así se hace! 7W4

Read through the strategy, and ask students to find four different forms of the adjective *tranquilo* and three of the word *ruidoso*: can they work out why the endings of these adjectives change and which nouns they refer to? You might like to draw four columns headed *ms, fs, mpl, fpl* and write the different forms in the correct columns – can students work out what the other possible ending for *ruidoso* might be? Play the recording again and ask students to focus on the underlined modifiers – how do each of the phrases containing them translate into English?

Gramática: *ser* and *estar* – to be 7W5

Read through the grammar explanation with students, highlighting the use of *ser* to denote permanent characteristics and *estar* for temporary ones. You might like to give students some sample sentences in English, and ask them which verb they think they would need in Spanish, e.g. The city traffic is very noisy./This class is very noisy today!/The library is a quiet place to study./It is peaceful in the mountains./The town centre is very busy on Saturdays.

2a Lee y escribe un adjetivo para cada frase. AT3.2; 7S5, 7T4

Encourage students to use the vocabulary section if necessary to work out the meanings of the new words.

Extension

Highlight the use of *no... ni... ni* (neither/nor) in sentence 4 and ask students to formulate two or three other sentences using this construction.

Answers

1 ruidoso **2** feo **3** tranquilo **4** aburrido **5** grande
6 divertido

2b Escucha (1–6) y escribe los adjetivos correctos. AT1.2; 7L2

Students listen and write down the correct adjective(s). In preparation, play the tape and ask students to raise their hand every time they hear the word *es*: adjectives follow this word and it will help students focus. Stop the recording after each utterance so students have time to write down their answers.

Answers

1 aburrido **2** bonito y tranquilo **3** divertido **4** sucio y ruidoso
5 ruidoso **6** grande.

TRANSCRIPT　　　　　　　　　　**CD1, track 58**

1 Es muy aburrido. No hay ni bares ni discotecas.
2 Es bonito y tranquilo. No es ruidoso y hay un parque muy grande.
3 Hay muchas cosas. Es un pueblo muy divertido. Hay un polideportivo, una piscina y un parque de atracciones cerca del centro.
4 Es sucio y ruidoso. Hay mucha industria.
5 Es ruidoso y hay mucho tráfico.
6 Es muy, muy grande. Hay muchas estaciones, oficinas, muchos colegios, mucho tráfico...

3a Habla con tu pareja. Cambia las frases. AT2.2; 7S3, 7L6

Students work in pairs to talk about their home town, substituting other words for the italicised phrases.

3b Describe tu pueblo. ¿Cuántas frases puedes escribir en 5 minutos? AT4.2; 7T5, 7T6

Students use the grid to put together as many sentences about their home town or area as possible in the given time. Highlight the use of *porque* (because) or *pero* (but) to extend the sentences by giving a reason, and model first.

Plenary 7W4

☑ Ask students to formulate the rule for the formation of adjectival endings from exercise 1, and ask them to do the same with *mucho/a/os/as*. If liked, give them the following sentences and ask them to choose the correct part of *mucho*: **1** En el pueblo, no hay (*mucho*) tiendas **2** Hay (*mucho*) montañas cerca de la costa **3** En la ciudad, hay (*mucho*) restaurantes **4** No hay (*mucho*) silencio en el centro.

Alternative plenary (for lessons ending part-way through the section) 7W2, 7W5

☑ Focus on the uses of *ser/estar*, using language which students already know. Give them the following contexts from previous units, and ask them to work out which of the verbs 'to be' they would need in each of the following scenarios: saying what colour your pen is, asking where a student is, describing the character of your best friend, saying where your town is, talking about your hair and eye colour, saying how quiet or noisy your class is today.

4C ¿Se puede...? pp. 38–39

Objectives:
- say what there is to do where you live
- learn how to use a dictionary

Key language: see p.67 for full list
Grammar: infinitives
Skills: learn how to use a dictionary
Resources: CD1; Worksheet 35 (*¡Así se hace!* – using a dictionary); *Just Click* CD-Rom.

Lesson starter 7T3

Ask students to scan the sentences **a–f** in exercise 1 and, by the time you've taken the register, find the following: (**a**) six places they might find in a town or places of entertainment; (**b**) which sentences contain the Spanish for 'there isn't/aren't'; (**c**) how many times the Spanish for 'but' and 'and' is mentioned. (All this vocabulary is revision.) As an alternative, put up OHT 9 of places, each numbered, and ask students to write down the numbers of the places which are mentioned in each sentence **a–f** in exercise 1.

Answers

(**a**) supermercados, bares, discotecas, parque de atracciones, piscina, parque; (**b**) a, b, e, f; (**c**) *pero* ('but') occurs four times and there are is one occurrence of *y* ('and').

Alternative lesson starter *(for lessons starting part-way through the section)* **7W1, 7W4**

As you take the register, give students two minutes in silence to study the list of places in the language box on page 35, refreshing their memories as to which are masculine (*el, un*) and which are feminine (*la, una*). To prepare for the grammar work on page 39, call out a list of places, one by one. Allocate one wall of the classroom as the 'masculine' (*un/el*) side, and the opposite as the 'feminine' (*una/la*) side. Ask students to point to whichever side matches the gender of the place you mention. Useful places are: *colegio, tienda, supermercado, piscina, bolera, cine, restaurante, estación, polideportivo, iglesia, playa, bar.*

Support

The first time round, call out six words with *un/una* in front, then another six with *el/la*.

Introduction

Explain to students that the focus of the lesson is on saying what you can or can't do, where you live, and they will also learn the rule for saying 'to the' in Spanish.

1 🔊 **Escucha (a–f) y lee. Une las frases y los dibujos. AT1.2, AT3.2; 7W1, 7L2.**

Students listen to the recording, follow the text of sentences **a–f** and match them to the appropriate picture.

CD1, track 59

a No hay supermercados pero se puede comer bien.
b No hay bares pero se puede beber bien.
c Me encanta vivir en el campo. Se puede hacer muchas cosas.
d ¡Hola! En las montañas se puede hacer muchas cosas.
e No hay discotecas pero se puede bailar.
f No hay parque de atracciones pero mi amigo Pequeño Oso tiene una casa grande. Se puede ir a la piscina, ver una película y jugar en el parque.

Answers

a 2 **b** 3 **c** 6 **d** 1 **e** 4 **f** 5

🔅 **Gramática: *se puede* (you can) + infinitive 7W2**

Read through the grammar explanation with students and check their understanding.

2 ¡Así se hace! AT3.1; 7W8

Students use the dictionary to look up ten verbs. You might also like to use Worksheet 35 (¡Así se hace!) at this point.

Support

Some students might find it helpful to brainstorm a list of useful verbs in English with you first, like *to hire, to shop, to buy, to have breakfast, to go out, to arrive, to read, to write.*

3 ☑ 💿 **Escucha (1–5) y escribe las letras... AT1, AT2; 7L2**

Listening practice: students choose two speech bubbles for each section of tape.

Support

Play each section two or three times before moving on to the next.

CD1, track 60

1 – ¿Qué se puede hacer en tu pueblo?
– Bueno, se puede ir al polideportivo y a la piscina.
2 – ¿Qué se puede hacer en tu pueblo?
– Vamos a ver. Se puede jugar en el parque y comer en los restaurantes.
3 – ¿Qué se puede hacer en tu pueblo?
– Pues, se puede ir a la playa y visitar el parque de atracciones.
4 – ¿Qué se puede hacer en tu pueblo?
– Bueno, se puede ir a la piscina y a la bolera.
5 – ¿Qué se puede hacer en tu pueblo?
– Muchas cosas: se puede beber en los bares y bailar en las discotecas.

Answers

1 E,H **2** C,I **3** D,F **4** H,J **5** G,B

🔅 **Gramática: *a + el/la/los/las* – to the 7W2, 7W4**

Read through the explanation with students – students will find an example of *al* in the preceding exercise 3, speech bubble E.

4 Fill in the following gaps with the correct form of *al, a la, a los, a las.*

Students fill each gap with *al, a la, a los* or *a las.*

Support

Work through each sentence and help students note whether each noun is masculine, feminine, singular or plural.

Answers

1 al **2** a la **3** al **4** a la, a la **5** a los, a los **6** a las

5 ◯ Habla con tu pareja. Cambia las frases. AT2.3; 7S3, 7L6

Model the example with students, showing them how to alter the italicised phrases.

Support

Remind students that they can use the sentences in exercise 4 in their replies.

6 ☑ ✐ Mira el mapa y describe el pueblo. AT4.2–4; 7T4

Students use the information on the map to write about the town. Explain they can add in extra and imaginary detail as liked. Encourage them to think about which resources they can call on to find useful phrases and vocabulary (the exercises in the book, language boxes, Resumen, the glossary and a dictionary).

Support

Put the following sentences and pointers on the board or OHP to help students get started: *En el pueblo, hay muchos hoteles y...* (places in the town, p.35) *El pueblo es turístico y/pero...* (describing town, p.35 ex 3a) *Se puede ir al cine,...* (exercises and places, p.38 ex 1, p.39 ex 4)

Extension

Encourage more able students to include plenty of detail. Refer them to the descriptions on p.34, ex 1a, for ideas on how to begin. Either set them a minimum word or line limit, depending on the student or group, or encourage them to set a target for themselves of things to include, e.g. at least four adjectives, use *y/pero/que*, two verbs and two other places which they have looked up for themselves in the dictionary.

Plenary 7L4, 7W5

☑ Encourage students to think about how to improve the accuracy of their writing: checking for correct spellings, checking for the correct use of *un/una*, *el/la*, and the correct ending on adjectives. Give them the following piece of text, or part of it, omitting the underlining (here to highlight the errors) and ask them to work in pairs to spot and correct the mistakes. Which pair of students can find the most? (There are 18 in all.)

Hola! Me llamo Juana y viv̲e̲ en un̲a̲ pueblo en l̲a̲ w̲este de España. En mi ba̲rio hay un supe̲r ̲mercado, dos te̲indas y un colegio, pe̲rro en el t̲hentro hay much̲a̲s restaurantes, bares y hotel̲s por ̲que es muy turístico y divert̲eedo. Es un poco ri̲udoso también y hay much̲a̲ tráfico. Se puede visit̲ el cine, y bailar en e̲l discoteca.

Encourage students to put together a list of common mistakes on the board or OHT, and use this to correct a piece of their partner's written work. This list could be enlarged or developed into a poster for the wall to act as an aide-mémoire.

Alternative plenary *(for lessons ending part-way through the section)* 7W7

☑ Ask students to share useful ways of learning vocabulary, noting these on the board or OHT, and doing some examples. Encourage students to put these into practice with the infinitives at the bottom of the grammar section below exercise 1, p.38. Apart from look, cover, write, check, other exercises students might do could include writing out six verbs for their partner but omitting the vowels (e.g. *jgr*), and their partner has to write them

fully from memory, or writing the first part of the verb (e.g. *jug...*) and their partner has to complete it with the correct *-ar*, *-er* or *-ir*.

4D ¿Y tu opinión? page 40

Objectives:
• say what you like and what you don't like, and why
Key language: see p.67 for full list
Grammar: *gustar*
Resources: Flashcards 21–27; CD1; Worksheets 31 (Escuchar), 32 (Hablar), 34 (Escribir), 36 (Gramática); *Just Click* CD-Rom.

Lesson starter 7W4

Explain to students that, to achieve the objective in 4D, they will need to be familiar with singulars and plurals. Give students a brief time limit of 2–3 minutes to write a list of 6–8 types of town, area or places in the town, some of which are singular, some plural (e.g. *bares, cafetería, costa*). Instruct them to pass this to the student in front (or behind or near – not their usual partner) whose task is now to write the correct *el, la, los, las* in front and check the spelling inside another two minutes. Finally, working in pairs, students take it in turns to read out their list, an item at a time, while their partner listens carefully and calls out in Spanish ¡*singular!* or ¡*plural!*

Alternative lesson starter *(for lessons starting part-way through the section)* 7L5

Have the following sentences on the board or OHT as students arrive. Their task is to say which ones make sense, which ones don't, and alter the latter so that they do. This will also challenge their thinking skills. Fast-finishers can develop two or three of their own to contribute to the class.

1 *Me gusta mucho mi pueblo porque es bonito.*
2 *Odio mi barrio porque es divertido.*
3 *No me gusta vivir en la costa porque me encanta la playa.*
4 *No se puede nadar en la playa porque está sucia y fea.*
5 *Hay discotecas, cines, una piscina y polideportivo, y un parque de atracciones – no hay mucho para los jóvenes.*
6 *Me gusta mucho mi aldea porque es muy aburrido.*

When feeding back sentences corrected to make sense (nos. 2, 3, 5, 6), accept any version which does. Student contributions can be asked for at this point, and the rest of the class has to raise one hand for 'makes sense' and two for 'nonsense'. Give them the appropriate Spanish to call out: '*no, no tiene sentido*' and '*sí, tiene sentido*'.

Introduction

Ask students to look at the Key Language box on page 40 and work out, from the numbers of smiley/unsmiley faces with each Spanish phrase, what each phrase might convey.

1 ☑ ◉ Escucha (1–5). ¿Les gusta (☺) o no (☹)? AT3.2; 7L3

Students will need only to understand *(no) me gusta* for this exercise. Instruct students to draw a smiley face if the person likes where they live, and an unsmiley face if they don't. Fast-finishers can listen for a reason and note it in English or Spanish.

CD1, track 61

1 – Marisol, ¿te gusta tu ciudad?
   – Sí, me gusta porque es grande y bonita.
2 – Nacho, ¿te gusta tu pueblo?
   – No, no me gusta.
   – ¿Por qué?
   – Porque es pequeño y aburrido. ▶

3 – Anita, ¿te gusta tu pueblo?
– No, no me gusta. Es industrial, muy sucio y ruidoso.
4 – Julio, ¿te gusta tu ciudad?
– Sí, es bonita y tranquila.
5 – Lidia, ¿te gusta tu pueblo
– No, no me gusta porque es feo y sucio.

Answers

1 Marisol, ☺, grande, bonita
2 Nacho, ☹, pequeño, aburrido
3 Anita, ☹, industrial, sucio, ruidoso
4 Julio, ☺, bonita, tranquila
5 Lidia, ☹, feo, sucio

2 📖 Lee las 5 descripciones de un pueblo. Pon las descripciones en orden (positivo – negativo). AT3.3; 7T1

Students read the descriptions and order them from most positive to least. If you have not already presented the phrases for degrees of liking and disliking, then flashcards 21–27 will be useful here.

Support

Prepare students by asking them which key words will highlight a sentence about liking or not liking (*gusta, encanta, odio*). Ask them to scan down the texts and tell you where in each one they find these key words (*gusta* and *encanta* in the initial sentences; *odio* in the second).

Extension

For more able groups and fast-finishers, you might like to use the following exercise. The answers are in brackets.

Escribe el número o los números de la(s) frase(s) en que la persona dice...

a *No vivo cerca de la playa (4);* **b** *Vivo en una zona rural (3);* **c** *Mi pueblo no es divertido (2, 4);* **d** *No vivo cerca de la capital (2);* **e** *Se puede ver una película (1, 5).*

Answers

3, 5, 1, 4, 2.

3 💿 Escucha (1–5). ¿Les gusta o no? AT3.3; 7L3

Students listen out for the opinion of each person and draw the correct number of smiley/unsmiley faces as in the Key Language box on page 40 to illustrate the answer.

Extension

Write the statements from the Extension answers up on the board and ask students to note the number of the appropriate recording 1–5 (answers in brackets).

TRANSCRIPT

CD1, track 62

1 – ¿Te gusta el pueblo donde vives?
– Sí, hay mucho: parques, cines, bares. Se puede hacer muchas cosas. Me encanta.
2 – ¿Te gusta el pueblo donde vives?
– No, no me gusta.
– ¿Por qué?
– Es muy pequeño y aburrido. No me gusta.
3 – ¿Te gusta el pueblo donde vives?
– Sí, me gusta. Hay parques y la playa. Pues, sí. ▶

4 – ¿Te gusta el pueblo donde vives?
– No me gusta nada, nada, nada. Lo odio.
– Pero, ¿por qué?
– Es feo, sucio y ruidoso. Hay mucha industria, ¿sabes?
5 – ¿Te gusta el pueblo donde vives?
– Sí, me gusta mucho. Es bonito y tranquilo. Está en el campo y hay montañas cerca.

Answers

1 me encanta (☺☺☺) **2** no me gusta (☹) **3** me gusta (☺)
4 odio (☹☹☹) **5** me gusta mucho (☺☺)
(Extension) Es industrial (**4**) Hay mucho que hacer (**1**) Es ruidoso (**4**) Mi pueblo es pequeño (**2**) Vivo en un pueblo en la costa (**3**).

4 ✓ 💬 Habla con tu pareja AT2.2–4; 7L6

Students use the sample dialogue to ask others about their home town, and give their own replies. You will need to explain to students that, if using *odio*, they will need to repeat the type of town afterwards, e.g. *odio mi pueblo*. Remind them also that if they are speaking about *la ciudad/la aldea*, then the adjective will need to be feminine – *bonita, aburrida, ruidosa.*

Extension

With more able groups, you might like to introduce *lo/la odio* – I hate it. Students could write a short piece about what they think about their own home town giving reasons for it.

💡 Gramática: gustar 7W1, 7W2, 7W4, 7W5

Read through the grammar explanation and allow students to work out the rule for the ending -a/-an from the examples.

5 ✓ Write the correct form: gusta/gustan.

Students choose the correct form *gusta/gustan* in each sentence.

Answers

1 gusta **2** gustan **3** gustan **4** gustan **5** gusta

Plenary 7S1, 7S2

✓ Show students, by comparing a Spanish and English sentence, how the verb *gustar* functions literally (e.g. *Me gusta la ciudad*/To me, is pleasing the town), and how the word order is different to English. Do the same with a plural (e.g. *Me gustan las discotecas*/To me are pleasing...). Give students two minutes in which to generate a similar literal sentence either in English or a Spanish one based on the vocabulary of the unit (e.g. 'To me is pleasing the beach' or *No me gustan las tiendas*). Ask students at random to call out their sentence, and the rest of the class has to translate either into English or Spanish.

Alternative plenary *(for lessons ending part-way through the section)* 7W2, 7L5 7L6

✓ This would be a useful point at which to show students how to recycle known language in a different context. Ask students to look back at the unit and go to the list of infinitives in exercise 1, p.38. Using the question *¿Te gusta?* and the flashcards 21–27, show an example or two of how to use these with infinitives and previous nouns to generate questions and answers, e.g. *¿Te gusta visitar la costa/Me encanta ir a la costa.* Give students three or four minutes to invent as many questions as they can, beginning *¿Te gusta...?* Working in small groups, they take it in turns to ask someone else a question, who has to reply. Model first. Ask students in which other contexts they think these phrases will be useful.

Resumen *(page 41)*

Encourage your students to make active use of the Resumen when they do learning homeworks. Give your students practice in using the Resumen by occasionally making this a plenary task: if students use the Resumen in class, they are more likely to make use of it for homework too.

Repaso *(page 42)*

☑ This page revises work from Units 3 and 4.

1 🔊 **Escucha (1–4) e identifica un error o dos en las descripciones.** AT1.3; 7L3

TRANSCRIPT
CD2, track 01

1 – ¿Dónde está tu casa?
– Está en el campo en un sitio tranquilo y bonito.
– ¿Comó es? ¿Es grande?
– No, es pequeña.
2 – ¿Cómo es tu hermana?
– Es baja y guapa.
– ¿Tiene el pelo largo?
– Sí – largo y liso.
3 – ¿Como es tu pueblo?
– Es pequeño, sucio y hay mucho tráfico. No me gusta.
4 – ¿Tienes abuelos?
– Sí, tengo un abuelo.
– ¿Comó es?
– Es delgado. Habla mucho y es muy simpático.

Answers

1 The house is not in the country. It is big not small.
2 Girl is tall not short.
3 The town is large not small.
4 Grandfather is retiring not talkative.

2 📖 **Escribe los números.** AT3.1; 7W1

Students read the letter snake and decipher the numbers.

Answers

52, 63, 99, 34, 29, 100, 76, 50, 64, 1, 16.

3 ✏️ **Write the sentences in the singular.** AT4.2; 7W4

Answers

1 Mi primo es muy bonito 2 Mi abuelo tiene ochenta años 3 Tengo una serpiente 4 Me gusta el gato negro 5 Mi tío es viejo 6 El restaurante es limpio y muy tranquilo.

4 ✏️ **Copy the sentences and select the correct form of *gustar*.** 7W1, 7W4, 7W5

Students choose the correct form from the alternatives offered.

Answers

1 Me gustan mis hermanos 2 Me gusta Madrid 3 Me gustan los pueblos rurales 4 Me gusta mi hermanastra 5 Me gusta mi barrio.

5 ✏️ **Escribe 3 frases sobre tu familia y 3 frases sobre tu pueblo.**

Students write short sentences about their family and their home town.

Reading *(page 43)* AT3.3; 7C5

Board game practising physical characteristics, attractions in home town and personal information.

Ahora, tú! *(pp. 124–125)*

Differentiated self-access reading and writing exercises: see page 37 for more information.

1 📖 **Put the following words into the correct categories.**

Answers

Verbs: jugar, bailar, odiar, visitar, encantar, comer, ir, ver, gustar
Nouns: aldea, montañas, campo, playa, estación, ciudad, pueblo
Adjectives: feo, pequeño, sucio, limpio, divertido, bonito, inmenso
Modifiers: bastante, demasiado, muy

2 📖 **Write down the odd one out and say why.**

Answers

1 parque (man-made, the rest are natural) **2** odio (rest are modifiers) **3** hay (rest are verbs of liking/disliking) **4** sí (the only one which can be used as a reply) **5** fantástico (rest are negative) **6** polideportivo (others are plural) **7** barrio (rest are verbs in the infinitive form) **8** colegios (rest are singular).

3 📖 **Match up the two halves of the sentences.**

Answers

1 Es muy divertido ir al parque de atracciones. **2** Me encanta porque está en el campo **3** Es sucio y feo porque es muy industrial **4** Me gusta la aldea porque es pequeña **5** Es muy aburrido porque no hay ni cines, ni bares ni discotecas **6** Hay un colegio, una estación de trenes y dos tiendas.

4 ✏️ **Copy out the sentences and fill in the gaps.**

A variety of answers are possible here. Accept all those which fit grammatically and make sense.

page 125

1 📖 **Which town is each person writing about?**

Answers

a 2 **b** 3 **c** 1 (4 is a distractor)

2 ✏️ **Write a description of the remaining town.**

Sample answer might be: Yo vivo en la costa. Hay una playa, un camping, hoteles, restaurantes, bares, una bolera y un cine.

Worksheets Unit 4

29 En el pueblo AT3.1; 7W1

Visuals: Map of Mallorca and adjectives describing where you live.

30 Resumen AT3.1; 7W1

List of key language of the unit.

31 Escuchar 7L1, 7L2, 7L3

This worksheet aims to help students extend their ability to focus on and remember language. Work through the tips to the right of exercise 1 and elicit from students why they might be useful: concentrate better with eyes closed; not get distracted; not try to read and listen at the same time; really pay attention; useful to have a good memory for longer passages of listening.

1 Students listen and tick the sentence they hear.

TAPESCRIPT
CD2, track 02
1 Soy de un pueblo en la costa.
2 Mi familia vive cerca del centro.
3 Vivo en el noreste, en la montaña.

Answers

1 b **2** a **3** a

2 This exercise makes more demands on students' memory. They listen twice, then look and circle the places they heard.

TRANSCRIPT
CD2, track 03
1 – ¿Qué hay en el pueblo?
  – Pues, hay... restaurantes, tiendas...
2 – ¿Hay mucho en tu ciudad?
  – Sí, hay una playa, un parque, una bolera.... está bien.
3 – En tu ciudad, ¿qué hay?
  – Hay una piscina, dos o tres supermercados, tiendas, un polideportivo...

Answers

1 restaurantes, tiendas **2** una playa, un parque, una bolera **3** una piscina, supermercados, tiendas, un polideportivo

3 In this more challenging exercise, students need to listen carefully. Before listening, elicit from students which items of language they think they might hear in each description. Remind them to listen out for *no hay/no es*.

TRANSCRIPT
CD2, track 04
1 – Vives en una ciudad, ¿no?
  – Sí. Me gusta, porque hay muchas tiendas y es interesante.
  – ¿Hay un polideportivo?
  – No, no hay, pero hay una piscina.
  – ¿Es industrial?
  – No, está en la montaña y es bonita.
2 – ¿Te gusta vivir aquí?
  – Sí, porque está en la costa y me gusta la playa. Es un pueblo limpio, con varias tiendas y bares...
  – ¿Es un poco aburrido?
  – No, no es aburrido. Está bien.
3 – ¿Hay mucho que hacer aquí?
  – Sí. Por eso me gusta.
  – ¿Qué hay?
  – Hay tiendas, un cine, un polideportivo... y la playa, claro.
  – Me gusta vivir en la costa.
4 – ¿Dónde vives?
  – Vivo en la montaña.
  – ¿Te gusta?
  – Sí, es muy bonito.
  – ¿Qué hay?
  – Hay dos o tres bares... es todo. Es muy tranquilo, mi pueblo.
5 – ¿Cómo es la aldea donde vives?
  – No hay mucho. Un bar – es todo.
  – ¿Es aburrida?
  – No, porque toda mi familia vive aquí – mis primos, mis abuelos, mis tíos... Me gusta mucho vivir en el campo.

Answers

1 b **2** d **3** f **4** a **5** c

32 Hablar AT2.1–4; 7S3, 7L6

This worksheet gives students the opportunity to develop longer supported conversations, altering the underlined words, about the towns of Pollença, Port de Alcudia, Cala Sant Vicenc, Escorca y Muro. The artwork on it could also be used to generate a written conversation or a description of one or more of the towns.

Support

Develop students' familiarity with the symbols and artwork on the map before the pairwork, using the following whole-class exercises (which could also be done in pairs after modelling). Have students repeat the place names after you several times in preparation. Call out sentences indicating the type of town and position (e.g. *Vivo en una ciudad. Está en la costa, en el noreste*) and have students respond with the relevant place (e.g. *Port de Pollença*). Do the same with adjectives (e.g. T *Es ruidosa.* S *Port de Alcudia)*, with places (e.g. T *Hay un supermercado y una iglesia.* S *Muro*) and opinions (e.g. T

No me gusta el pueblo. S *Cala Sant Vicenc).*

Extension

Encourage more able students to add in other questions (e.g. age, birthday, family, nationality), to ask the questions in a different order and to give answers (e.g. *Vivo en un pueblo en la costa. Me gusta mucho*) which contain more information than the questioner is asking so he/she has to listen carefully and shape the next question accordingly.

33 Leer AT3.2–4; 7W1, 7T1, 7S3

This worksheet focuses on trying to work out the meaning of new words from the context. Students read Gabriel's description of his town and do the activities. The worksheet can be tackled at any time after students have worked on pages 34–35.

Answers

a **1** (el) centro comercial
  2 (la) mezquita
  3 (la) estación de trenes
  4 (la) estación de autobuses
  5 (los) almacenes grandes
  6 (el) río
  7 (el) hotel
  8 (la) comisaría
  9 (las) tiendas de regalos
  10 (el) mercado
  11 (la) plaza de toros
  12 (el) castillo
b ticks in boxes 1, 3, 6 and 8

34 Escribir AT4.2–4; 7W1, 7S3, 7T6

1 This first exercise combines expressions of liking/disliking with the infinitives met in the Student's Book originally with the expression *se puede*. Model for students how to form sentences using the grid. As a starter, work orally with the whole group, putting sentences into Spanish/English, e.g. T: You can visit the mountains. S: *Se puede visitar la montaña.*
T: *¡No me gusta mucho ir al colegio!* S: I don't like going to school much!

Check they understand the reason for the brackets and remind them of the rule *a + el = al*. Students could work orally in pairs for five minutes before tackling the writing exercise.

2a Students choose their own language to go in the gaps. The prompts in italics reminds them of the type of words and phrases they need. More able students could be encouraged, as suggested in 2b ¡extra!, to add adjectives to their nouns in order to give added interest and improve their writing.

35 ¡Así se hace! 7W1, 7W2, 7W7, 7W8

This worksheet alerts students to the dangers of using the dictionary carelessly, and reinforces the difference between verbs and nouns. The ¡extra! exercise requires students to also work out why they have made their choice: you might like to highlight how *se puede* is always followed by a verb in the infinitive, and that the presence of *un/una/unos/unas* or *el/la/los/las* indicates a noun will follow.

Answers

1 book – *sacar (una reserva)/reservar; libro (nm)*
breakfast – *desayunar; desayuno (nm)*
buy – *comprar; compra (nf)*
dance – *bailar; baile (nm)*
lunch – *almorzar, almuerzo (nm)/comida (nf)*
picnic – *ir de merienda/merendar; merienda (nf)*
shop – *ir de compras; tienda (nf)*
skate – *patinar; patín (nm)*
sleep – *dormir; sueño (nm)*
travel – *viajar; viaje (nm)*
watch – *mirar/observar; reloj (nm)*
walk – *andar/caminar; paseo (nm)/excursión (nf) a pie*
2 1 pescar **2** almacenes **3** patinar **4** ir en bicicleta **5** cruz

36 Gramática 7W5, 7S4, 7S8

These grammar exercises give further consolidation of the use of *al* (Student's Book p.39), and pull together the question words met so far. In the first exercise, students match the sentence halves correctly; in the second, they write the correct Spanish question word beside its English equivalent; in the third, they choose an appropriate question word for each of the sentences. This could lead on to oral work, asking and answering these questions, if liked, or students could write or word-process a dialogue incorporating them all, using an imaginary, fantasy or TV character.

Answers

1 1 e **2** d **3** a **4** f **5** b **6** c
2 what – *qué;* where – *dónde;* who – *quién;* how many – *cuántos;* when – *cuándo;* which – *cuál;* what... like/how *cómo*
3 1 Quién **2** Cuántos **3** Cuándo **4** Cuál **5** Cómo **6** Qué **7** Dónde **8** Qué **9** Cómo **10** Por qué

37 ¡extra! 7W3, 7W4, 7W8, 7T1, 7T3, 7T7

a Ask students to read through the text with a partner (aloud if liked: good pronunciation practice as there are a number of unknown words). Ask them to do the first exercise, setting a time limit. Elicit feedback – correct answer is **c**: reasons may include the more complex and flowery language, longer sentences (which do not mimic normal speech or informal writing patterns), quantity of information, the fact that it is a description.

b Check that students remember the rules for forming plurals of nouns (add *-s/-es*) and adjectives (these agree with the noun, so if they end in *-a* in the text their masculine singular form will end in *-o*). Model examples like *avenidas anchas, hoteles baratos, instalaciones deportivas.* Ask students whether they can tell the gender of the noun by looking at the adjectival ending (possible in this text with adjectives ending in *-o*). Instruct students to work at their own pace through the rest of the exercises in small groups or pairs.

Answers

c

Nouns (singular)	
el pueblo	village, small town
la provincia	province
la calle	street
la casa	house
el balcón	balcony
la flor	flower
el visitante	visitor
la iglesia	church
el convento	convent
el patio	patio
la procesión	procession
la semana	week

Adjectives (singular)	
blanco	white
típico	typical
célebre	famous
estrecho	narrow
tortuoso	winding
lleno	full
hermoso	pretty
extranjero	foreign
antiguo	old
precioso	pretty
pintoresco	picturesque
santo	holy
natural	natural

d An exercise which checks students' understanding of the text.

Answers

1 h **2** d **3** a **4** g **5** b **6** c **7** f

e An opportunity to reuse the new language. Encourage students to add the new vocabulary to their existing lists and to reuse them where possible in their next piece of writing. You might like to set them a target of 6–8 words.

Pruebas Unidades 3 y 4

R and A file pp.120–123

Prueba: Escuchar *(page 120)*
ex 1: AT1.2

Answers

Example: **1** train station **2** cinema
3 sports centre **4** bowling alley
5 beach **6** restaurant **7** shop
8 supermarket **9** school
10 fairground
Mark scheme: 1 mark for each correct answer.
Total: 9. 5+ shows evidence of performance at Level 2.

CD4, track 28
Ejemplo: **1** En mi pueblo hay una estación.
2 En mi aldea hay un cine.
3 En mi cuidad hay un polideportivo.
4 En mi barrio no hay bolera.
5 En mi pueblo no hay playa.
6 En mi cuidad hay muchos restaurantes.
7 En mi pueblo hay una pequeña tienda.
8 En mi aldea no hay supermercado.
9 En mi barrio hay un colegio.
10 En mi pueblo hay un parque de atracciones.

ex 2: AT1.2

Answers

2 short plump curly hair quiet
3 tall straight hair glasses quiet
Mark scheme: 1 mark for each correct answer.
Total: 8. 5+ shows evidence of performance at Level 2.
¡extra! (2) is called Catalina – is 12 years old – is from Barcelona – doesn't like noisy places (3) is called Miguel – has small eyes
Mark scheme: 1 mark for each correct piece of information.

CD4, track 29
Ejemplo: **1** ¡Hola! Me llamo Enrique. Tengo trece años y vivo en Madrid. Soy alto y bastante delgado. ¡También soy hablador! Llevo gafas.
►

2 Buenos días. Soy Catalina. Tengo doce años y soy de Barcelona. Soy una persona baja y bastante gordita, con el pelo rizado. Mi personalidad es callada. No me gustan los sitios ruidosos.

3 ¡Hola! Aquí Miguel. Soy muy alto y tengo el pelo liso. Tengo los ojos pequeños y llevo gafas. En general, soy bastante callado.

ex 3: AT1.2–3

Answers

Example **1**: cat **2** snake **3** dog **4** fish **5** tortoise **6** bird **7** mouse **8** hamster **9** horse
Mark scheme: 1 mark for each correct answer. 1 mark for each correct reason.
Total: 8. 5+ shows evidence of performance at Level 2.
8 marks shows evidence of performance at Level 3.

¡**extra!** +1 mark for additional details: Snakes are too big. Dogs are entertaining. Tortoises are quiet. Birds are quite noisy. Mice are nice. Hamsters are dirty. Horses are beautiful.

TRANSCRIPT
CD4, track 30

Ejemplo: **1** Me gustan mucho los gatos porque son muy limpios.
2 No me gustan las serpientes, son demasiado grandes.
3 Me encantan los perros, son divertidos.
4 No me gustan los peces de colores.
5 Me gustan mucho las tortugas porque son tranquilas.
6 Odio los pájaros – son bastante ruidosos.
7 Me gustan los ratones, son simpáticos.
8 No me gustan los hámsters porque son sucios.
9 Me encantan los caballos, son bonitos.

Prueba: Hablar (page 117)

ex 1: AT2.2

Answers

Example **1**: Tengo un hermano.
2 Tengo una hermana. **3** Es alta. **4** Es delgada. **5** Tiene el pelo moreno.
6 Lleva gafas. **7** Tiene dieciocho años.
8 Es habladora.
Mark scheme: 1 mark for each sentence which would be understood by a sympathetic native speaker.
Total: 7. 5+ shows evidence of performance at Level 2.

ex 2: AT2.2

Answers

Example **1**: Hay un cine, se puede ver una película. **2** Hay una discoteca, se puede bailar. **3** Hay un bar, se puede beber. **4** Hay un restaurante, se puede comer. **5** Hay un parque, se puede jugar.
Mark scheme: 2 marks for each sentence which would be understood by a sympathetic native speaker.
Total: 8. 5+ shows evidence of performance at Level 2.

¡**extra!** +1 mark for each extra correct point of information.

ex 3: AT2.3

Answers

Example **1**: Vivo en una aldea. **2** Vivo en una cuidad. **3** Está en la costa.
4 Hay mucho tráfico. **5** Me gusta porque es divertido.
Mark scheme: 2 marks for each sentence which would be understood by a sympathetic native speaker.
Total: 10. 7+ shows evidence of performance at Level 3.

¡**extra!** +1 mark for each extra correct point of information.

Prueba: Leer (page 122)

ex 1: AT3.2

Answers

Example: **1**c **2**a **3**e **4**f **5**d **6**g **7**b **8**h
Mark scheme: 1 mark for each correct answer.
Total: 7. 5+ shows evidence of performance at Level 2.

ex 2: AT3.2

Answers

1 Sucio ☺
2 Divertido ☺
3 Feo ☹
4 Demasiado grande ☹
5 Limpio ☺
6 Tranquilo ☺
7 Aburrido ☹
8 Bonito ☺
Mark scheme: 1 mark for each correct answer.
Total: 8. 6+ shows evidence of performance at Level 2.

ex 2: AT3.3

Answers

1 (3 details) Short, very slim, short red curly hair, blue eyes, no glasses, freckles.

2 (3 details) Mother, father, 2 twin sisters, brother, grandmother (who is old).
3 (2 details) Black cat + small green bird. Doesn't like the bird as it's too noisy.
4 (2 details) Lives in a small town/village in the mountains. He likes it. It's clean. He can play in the park.
Mark scheme: 1 mark for each correct answer.
Total: 10. 7+ shows evidence of performance at Level 3.

¡**extra!** Extra details score one mark each from the above lists. Students may also mention:

He is 14 years old. He is nice. He has lots of friends. He is very talkative.

Prueba: Escribir (page 123)

ex 1: AT4.1

Answers

Example **1**: en la discoteca **2** en los bares **3** en el cine **4** a la piscina **5** en restaurantes **6** en el parque
Mark scheme: 1 mark for each correct answer.
The words need not necessarily be absolutely correct but should be easily understood by a sympathetic native speaker.
Total: 5. 3+ shows evidence of performance at Level 1.

ex 2: AT4.2

Mark scheme: 2 marks for each correct answer. One may be given for a partially correct answer.
The words need not necessarily be absolutely correct but should be easily understood by a sympathetic native speaker.
Total: 10. 7+ shows evidence of performance at Level 2.

ex 3: AT4.3

Mark scheme: 1 mark for each correct answer.
The words need not necessarily be absolutely correct but should be easily understood by a sympathetic native speaker.
Total: 10. 7+ shows evidence of performance at Level 3.

¡**extra!** 1 extra mark for each extra correct detail added.

Workbook A Unit 4

page 18 (Section A)

Answers

ex 1:
2 Hay una estación en mi aldea.
3 Hay un polideportivo.

4 Hay un parque bonito y una piscina.
5 Hay playas y un parque de
atracciones.
6 Hay muchos supermercados.

ex 2:
un cine
una bolera
una estación
un parque
una piscina
una playa
un polideportivo

Note: the words listed in ex 3 are
recorded on CD2, track 05, for
pronunciation practice.

page 19 (Section B)

Answers

ex 1a:
1 d **2** c **3** b **4** a **5** e **6** h **7** g **8** f

ex 1b:
aburrido – divertido; tranquilo –
ruidoso; bonito – feo; grande –
pequeño

ex 2:
1 c **2** d **3** a **4** f **5** e **6** b

page 20 (Section C)

Answers

ex 1:
2 puede **3** ir **4** a **5** Se **6** bailar

ex 2:
2 al **3** a los **4** a la **5** al **6** a la

ex 3:
d Se puede visitar el campo. **e** Se puede
ir a las tiendas.

Note: ex 3 is recorded on CD2, track
07, for pronunciation practice.

page 21 (Section D)

Answers

ex 1a:
2 gustan **3** gusta **4** gustan **5** gusta
6 gustan

ex 1b:
2 encantan **3** encantan **4** encanta
5 encantan **6** encanta

ex 2a:
2 Me **3** encantan **4** Me gustan **5** Me
gusta... playa **6** Me encantan los cines

Note: the sentences in ex 2a are
recorded on CD2, track 08, for
pronunciation practice.

Workbook B Unit 4

page 18 (Section A)

Answers

ex 1:
2 No hay estación en mi aldea.
3 En mi barrio hay un polideportivo y
mi colegio.
4 Hay un parque bonito y una piscina
estupenda.
5 Hay playas bonitas y un parque de
atracciones.
6 En mi ciudad hay supermercados
enormes y muchas tiendas.

ex 2:
un cine
una bolera
el colegio
una estación
un parque
una piscina
una playa
un polideportivo
un parque de atracciones

Note: ex 3 is recorded on CD2, track
06, for pronunciation practice.

page 19 (Section B)

Answers

ex 1:
ruidoso – tranquilo; aburrido –
divertido; pequeño – grande; sucio –
limpio; feo – bonito

¡extra!
tranquilo (quiet) / ruidoso (noisy)
divertido (entertaining) / aburrido (boring)
grande (big) / pequeño (small)

bonito (pretty) / feo (ugly)
sucio (dirty) / limpio (clean)

ex 2a:
2 ruidosa **3** tranquilo **4** feo
5 divertido **6** bonitos **7** limpias
8 pequeños

ex 2b:
1 c **2** d **3** a **4** f **5** e **6** b **7** h **8** g

page 20 (Section C)

Answers

ex 1:
2 puede, bowling alley **3** ir, can **4** Se,
eat **5** los, to **6** bailar, discos **7** al,
amusement park **8** hacer, sports

ex 2:
2 al **3** a los **4** a la **5** a las **6** al **7** a la
8 al

page 21 (Section D)

Answers

ex 1a:
2 Me gustan **3** Me gusta **4** Me gustan
5 Me gusta **6** Me gustan

¡extra! **1** Me gusta mi colegio **2** Me
gusta la bolera **3** Me gustan los
restaurantes de mi barrio.

ex 1b:
2 Me encantan **3** Me encantan **4** Me
encanta **5** Me encantan **6** Me encanta

ex 2a:
2 Me gusta el parque **3** Me encantan
las montañas **4** Me gustan los parques
de atracciones **5** Me gusta la playa
6 Me encantan los cines

ex 2b:
4, 6, 1, 3, 5, 2

Note: the sentences in ex 2a are
recorded on CD2, track 09, for
pronunciation practice.

Unidad 5 En casa	Topic/Language/Culture	Grammar and skills	National Criteria
5A ¿Dónde vives? (pp. 44–45) **Objectives** • say what type of housing you live in • say how far a place is from something	types of housing: ¿Dónde vives? En una casa/un piso/una casa adosada/un chalet/en la (primera) planta adverbs: cerca de/lejos de/al lado de/delante de/detrás de/encima de/debajo de how far: a diez minutos/a cinco kilómetros locations: un pueblo/una avenida/una calle/en el campo/en la costa/en el centro de **Culture** living in flats v houses	**Grammar** a + distance and time de + article	**Attainment** AT1.3; AT2.2–4; AT3.1–3; AT4.1–4 **Framework objectives** 7W1, 7W2, 7W4, 7S1, 7S8, 7S9, 7T1, 7T2, 7T6, 7T7, 7L2, 7L3, 7L5, 7L6, 7C2 **Programmes of study** 1b, 2a, 2i, 2j **QCA scheme of work** Language: Unit 3 Contexts: Unit 3 **Assessment for learning** Objectives, p.45 Ex 4, OHTs 12A and 12B, Plenary
5B ¿Qué hay en tu casa? (pp. 46–47) **Objectives** • name rooms in the house • learn how to say 'my parents' room' • work out the meaning of new words	places in the house: el aseo, el comedor, el dormitorio, el garaje el jardín, el salón, la cocina, la terraza adverbs of position: abajo, arriba, a la derecha/izquierda receptive: más, menos	**Grammar** Possessive 'de' **Skills** How to work out the gist of a sentence by using context and finding similarities with English	**Attainment** AT1.2, 3.1–3, 4.2–4 **Framework objectives** 7W1, 7W2, 7W4, 7W7, 7W8, 7S1, 7S2, 7T1, 7T3, 7T4, 7T5, 7T6, 7L2, 8S1 **Programmes of study** 1b, 2e, 2g, 2h, 3b, 3c, 3d **QCA scheme of work** Language: Unit 3 Contexts: Unit 3 **Assessment for learning** Objectives, Plenary
5C Los muebles (pp. 48–49) **Objectives** • say what furniture there is in your home: say where things are • practise learning new vocabulary • learn how to pronounce z	**Key Language** (see p.51) Furniture: el sofá, la televisión. la lámpara, los sillones, la mesa, las sillas, la lavadora, la ducha, la cama, el armario, el equipo musical, el teléfono, le lavaplatos, la nevera, la cocina de gas, el ordenador prepositions of position: encima de, delante de, detrás de, al lado de, debajo de	**Grammar** Prepositions + de **Skills** How to learn vocabulary **Pronunciation** z	**Attainment** AT1.1–3, AT2.1–4, AT3.1–3, AT4.2–4 **Framework objectives** 7W1, 7W4, 7W6, 7W7, 7W8, 7S1, 7S3, 7S8, 7S9, 7L1, 7L3, 7L4 **Programmes of study** 1a, 2b, 3a **QCA scheme of work** Language: Unit 3 Context: Unit 3 **Assessment for learning** Objectives, p.48 Ex 1b + 2, p.49 Ex 5. Plenary
5D ¿Qué opinas tú? (pp. 50–51) **Objectives** • say what is good or bad about a place • revise ser and estar (to be)	conjunctions: porque, pero, y, and adverb también lo + adjective Relaunch: (no) me gusta, prefiero, me encanta	**Grammar** ser/estar lo + adj	**Attainment** AT1.3–4, AT2.3, AT3.1–4 AT4.2–4 **Framework objectives** 7W1, 7S2, 7S3, 7T1, 7T2, 7T5, 7L3, 7L5, 7L6 **Programmes of Study** 1b, 2j **QCA scheme of work** Language: Unit 3 Contexts: Unit 3 **Assessment for learning** Objectives, p.50 Ex 3. Plenary

Other resources: iAhora tú! pp.126–127   WS 38–47   OHTs 10–12   WBA & B pp.23–27   Just Click CD-Rom

5 En casa

5A ¿Dónde vives?

pp. 44–45

> **Objectives:**
> • say what type of housing you live in
> • say how far a place is from something
> **Key Language:** see p.79 for full list
> **Grammar:**
> • a + distance and time
> • de + article
> **Resources:** OHTs 10A and 10B (types of housing + overlay); OHT 11 (on foot, in car etc.); OHTs 12A and 12B (conversations); CD2; Worksheets 40 (Resumen), 46 (Gramática – de + article); Workbooks A and B p.23; *Just Click* CD-Rom.

On these pages students learn to say what types of housing they and other people live in, to discuss the location of the housing and to say how far away somewhere is.

To put this section in context, some of the following background may be useful. Traditionally in Spain most people rented flats and houses were less common. Many young people were unable to set up house on their own and were forced to live at home, with three generations living under the same roof. To some extent, this facilitated child care and other domestic arrangements (as well as care for the elderly and sick). However, a recent trend has been for city dwellers to move out to new towns (*urbanizaciones*) where housing is more affordable. The young family can no longer rely on the support of the extended family in the same way and often has the added pressures of commuting into the city (to earn the money to sustain such a lifestyle) and living in a place where others face similar challenges. It is interesting to compare the social problems that new towns such as Milton Keynes experienced. (7C2)

The tendency to move out of the city centres has been accompanied by a preference for houses rather than the high-rise flats that are still in evidence on the outskirts of major cities. Consequently, you see large numbers of terraced streets in these new towns and town planning that attempts to provide the necessary infrastructure in terms of transport and amenities.

Lesson starter

Revise places in the town by asking students to work in groups, brainstorming all the places they can remember. Which group can remember the most?

Alternative lesson starter *(for lessons starting part-way through the section)*

On the board write up various sentences giving good points and bad points for a house or location, e.g. *es pequeña, está en el centro, me gusta bastante, no me gusta.* Ask students to classify them under 'lo malo' and 'lo bueno' and to justify their answers.

Introduction

Use OHT 10A to present the names of the different types of dwelling and overlay 10B to present the written forms of the new words.

Use 10A on its own to point to each one in turn and say its name, getting the class and then individuals to repeat after you. Point to a picture and ask e.g. *Es una casa adosada o un piso?* Then point to a picture and ask an individual to tell you what it is.

Add overlay 10B and practise the sentences, then take away 10B, point to each picture in turn and say *Vivo en...* The class then supplies the words for each of the new locations.

Ask individuals to answer the question *¿Dónde vives?*

1a 🎧 Escucha (1–5) y lee. AT1.3; 7L3

The listening and reading presentation introduces the names of the different types of dwelling in the context of whereabouts in the town people live.

Students read the text and follow the recording. Although the context is new, some of the adjectives and other expressions will be familiar from the previous unit.

> **TRANSCRIPT** CD2, track 10
>
> 1 Me llamo Andrés y vivo en una casa en un pueblo pequeño.
> 2 ¡Hola! Soy Anita. Vivo en una casa adosada cerca de la capital.
> 3 Me llamo Nuria. Vivo en un un chalet en el campo.
> 4 Soy Nacho. Vivo en un bloque de pisos muy antiguo. Vivo en la primera planta.
> 5 Me presento. Soy Bea. Vivo en un piso moderno. El piso está en la planta baja.

Once students have listened to the recording and read the text, use OHT 10A to check comprehension. Point to a picture on the OHT and ask the class to supply the name of the person who lives in that type of house.

1b 🎧 Escucha (1–6). ¿Dónde viven? AT1.4; 7L3

This exercise offers an opportunity to listen out for the new language but is less structured. Students must first identify which type of home is mentioned in each exchange. Although the rubric asks where the people live, it will be best at this stage to concentrate on getting students to listen for one thing only at first. Ask students to try to add details such as which floor or where in the town at a subsequent 2nd or 3rd listening.

> **TRANSCRIPT** CD2, track 11
>
> 1 – ¿Dónde vives?
> – Pues, yo vivo en **un piso** en Barcelona. Vivo en la primera planta.
> – ¿Cómo es el piso?
> – Moderno, muy moderno.
> 2 – ¿Dónde vives?
> – Bueno, vivo en **una casa** en el norte de España, en Bilbao.
> 3 – ¿Dónde vives?
> – Yo vivo en **una casa adosada**. Es una casa pequeña en el centro.
> 4 – ¿Dónde vives?
> – Yo vivo en **un chalet**.
> – ¿Dónde está el chalet?
> – Está en la costa. Me gusta mucho.
> 5 – ¿Dónde vives?
> – Vivo en **un piso** en la planta baja.
> 6 – ¿Dónde vives?
> – Pues, vivo en **un bloque de pisos**.
> – Un bloque moderno.
> – No, muy antiguo. Vivo en la segunda planta.

Answers

1 en un piso (moderno), en Barcelona, en la primera planta **2** en una casa en el norte de España, en Bilbao **3** en una casa adosada, pequeña, en el centro **4** en un chalet, en la costa **5** en un piso en la planta baja **6** en un bloque de pisos (muy antiguo), en la segunda planta

2 ✑ Habla con tu pareja. Cambia las palabras. AT2.3

Pairwork based on language on types of houses presented in exercise 1 and the new vocabulary showing students how to say how far away something is in the Key Language box on page 44. Students take it in turns to ask and answer the two questions: 'Where do you live?' and 'How far is it from school?'

Gramática: de + el/la/los/las – from the 7W2, 7S8

An explanation of *de* + article. For further practice, see Worksheet 46 (Gramática).

3a 📖 Mira el plano. ¿Dónde está? Escribe la letra (a–d). AT3.3; 7T1

Students read a series of explanations about where Miguel and other members of his family live, and locate each person's dwelling on a town plan. The descriptions introduce some new prepositions and the expression *a* + time and distance. In most cases the dwelling mentioned does not belong to Miguel himself so a different expression of possession is used.

Before they start, discuss with students what things they are going to listen out for. They have already met both names for types of dwelling and for places in the town. These two details should on their own be enough for them to identify most locations. Thus in the first description *casa... centro... tiendas* should be sufficient. Ask students to read the descriptions and to find as many of the locations as they can. Having done so you can ask them to look at the *¿Dónde está?* grid which introduces two new adverbs and *a* + time and distance. At this stage they should be able to extrapolate what these new expressions mean.

Use OHT 11 (on foot, in car etc.) to present and practise expressions of distance. Choose locations near and far from the school to give examples of places that are five minutes away walking/in a car etc. Next ask students to think of other examples, for example how far away their house is from their friend's.

Now ask e.g. *La casa de Miguel está lejos del centro? ¿Está a cuántos minutos de las tiendas?* etc.

Ask individuals e.g. *¿Vives lejos del centro/cerca de la piscina?* etc.

Answers

1 c **2** a **3** b **4** d

3b 🎧 ¡extra! Escucha (1–5) y escribe la letra correcta (A–E), según el plano. AT1.4; 7L3

Five more listening descriptions relating to the map.

TRANSCRIPT CD2, track 12

1 La tienda de mi padre está muy cerca de la Plaza Mayor. Está al lado del Restaurante Sol. Está a diez minutos andando de la casa.
2 El supermercado está muy cerca de la casa de mis abuelos y cerca de los cines. Está a cinco minutos.
3 La estación de autobuses está muy cerca de la estación de trenes, a tres minutos andando.
4 El polideportivo está lejos del parque. Está a treinta minutos andando. Está cerca de la piscina.
5 La oficina de turismo no está muy cerca de la Plaza Mayor. Está cerca del parque y a diez minutos andando de la casa de mis tíos.

Answers

1 D **2** A **3** B **4** C **5** E

3c ✑ Habla con tu pareja sobre el plano. Cambia las palabras. AT2.4; 7T2, 7L5

Pairwork based on the town plan. The questions and answers require correct manipulation of *de* + article. Students first ask and answer the questions on the page and then adapt them to ask further questions. Thus once the exchange about Miguel's house has been completed, a further exchange can be constructed around his sister's flat.

4 ☑ ✎ ¿Dónde está tu casa? Escribe unas frases. AT4.3–5; 7T6, 7T7

Opportunity for writing practice. Students are invited to write a series of sentences about the location of their own homes.

Support

Less confident students may need a writing frame in order to produce a satisfactory piece of writing.

Extension

More able students could reuse phrases from e.g. Unit 4 – *Me gusta mucho, no es muy moderno* etc.

This exercise could be used for assessment.

Once they have finished a first draft but before they submit their work, encourage students to evaluate their work by looking over it for spelling, punctuation, verb endings, adjectival agreement, correct use of prepositions etc. This evaluation might be done in pairs.

✑ Extension AT 2.2–4; 7S9, 7L5, 7L6

Use OHTs 12A and 12B (Conversations) to practise all the language presented on the spread. Go through each conversation first with the class, discussing what you think might be said. When appropriate, place the overlays on the OHP to cue students into suitable questions and answers.

Ask students to work in pairs to prepare and practise one or more of the conversations. Remind them to work at their efforts before summoning you or the *asistente* to hear them.

This exercise could be used for assessment.

Plenary

☑ A chance to check comprehension of the tricky rule *de* + and or *a* + article. Ask pairs of students how they would explain it to an absent classmate and to produce one example.

Alternative plenary

☑ Recap on the objectives of the lesson and ask students how confident they feel about each one.

5B ¿Qué hay en tu casa?
pp. 46–47

Objectives:
• name rooms in the house
• learn how to say 'my parents' room'
• work out the meaning of new words
Key Language: see p.79 for full list
Grammar: possessive *de*
Skills: how to work out the gist of a sentence by using context and finding similarities with English
Resources: Visual 38 (plan of flat); CD2; Worksheets 38 (rooms), 40 (Resumen), 41 (Escuchar – selecting information), 46 (Gramática – the possessive de), 47 (¡**extra**! – working out meanings); Workbooks A and B p.24; *Just Click* CD-Rom.

On these pages students learn the names for the different rooms together with some useful adverbs of position. The possessive *de* is explained.

Lesson starter

Ask students to shut their books and work in groups to write down the names of as many family members as they can remember. Which group can remember the most?
This will be useful in reminding students of the different relationships mentioned in the first exercise.

Alternative starter *(for lessons starting part-way through the section)*

Put Visual 38 (plan of flat) on to OHP. Dotted around it put recognisable cut-outs of items of furniture taken from Worksheet Visual 39, e.g. bed, shower, armchair, sofa, wardrobe, cooker, chair, table, fridge, TV. Give students two minutes to look at the OHP and decide what the cut-outs are and which room each should go in, then point to each cut-out in turn, starting with the most recognisable and least transferable. Students shout out which room they think the item should go in. The names for the actual furniture items will be taught in the next section.

Introduction or reinforcement

You can either teach or reinforce the names of the places in the house using Visual 38 and Worksheet 38. On the OHT, point to each of three places in turn and say its name, asking the class and then individuals to repeat. Move on to pointing to a room and asking e.g. *¿La ducha o el comedor?* Finally point to a room and ask students to tell you its name. Now reinforce those three rooms by asking students to match up relevant pictures on the worksheet with the appropriate labels. Proceed in the same way for the other places on the sheet.

Teach *a la izquierda/derecha* by getting three class members to stand at the front and saying e.g. *Alison está a la izquierda de John.*

1 🎧 Escucha y lee. AT1.2, AT3.2; 7W7

Students listen to and read a simple presentation of the different locations in a flat. Play the CD and ask students to follow the presentation. After several playings, ask the class to repeat each utterance. Finally ask students to work in groups to act out the dialogue. Remind them to play special attention to intonation and flow. Ask groups of students to come out and act out the scene.

Support

Less able students may benefit from having met the new vocabulary via OHT and Worksheet (see above).

TRANSCRIPT   CD2, track 13

– ¡Hola! ¡Bienvenido! ¡Pasa, pasa!
– Aquí están el salón y el comedor.
– Y por aquí a la izquierda, la cocina.
– Y por aquí a la derecha está el cuarto de baño.
    … y el aseo.
– Aquí está tu dormitorio.
– ¡Muy bien!
– Hay una terraza y un jardín.
– Hay un garaje también.
– Está muy bien, gracias.

WS 41 (Escuchar) offers hints and practice on selective listening on this topic and revises types of dwelling as well.

2a 📖 Lee las cartas y mira los dibujos A–D en la página 47. ¿Quién habla? AT 3.3; 7T1

A reading comprehension matching exercise. The letters use a range of family and house language. *Arriba* and *abajo* are introduced. Note the inclusion of *más* and *menos* for receptive purposes at this stage.

If you are in a building with several floors, explain *arriba* and *abajo* by saying, while indicating up and down, e.g. *El gimnasio está arriba, la oficina de la señora Smith está abajo.*

Before they start, make sure that students realise that they have to match picture of family A–D + plan of dwelling a–d + description letter 1–3. One picture + plan will thus not have a matching letter.

Next discuss and make a list of the features that they need to look out for to do the matching: number of people in family, gender of writer, type of dwelling, number of bedrooms, size of bedroom etc.

Remind them not to jump to conclusions – the correct combinations can only be reached after they have considered ALL the possibilities.

Support

With less confident students read through the letters in class and make sure they have understood what is being said.

Answers

1 c A **2** b C **3** a B   (D and d are not matched)

Support/Extension

· For further practice of speaking, listening and reading, the 'trapdoor' exercise can be used. This is a whole-class exercise (although it could be easily modified for pairwork use) whereby the students see a passage with a number of pairs of options presented, e.g. *Hay tres/cinco dormitorios.* You decide in advance which is the correct one. Individual students volunteer to read out the passage, making decisions along the way. As soon as one of them makes a mistake, they fall through the trapdoor, and someone else tries. The object of the exercise is to read out the whole passage without making a mistake. Experience suggests that this results in high levels of concentration, engagement and challenge and, of course, plenty of repetition. This game can be used with any topic and the length and complexity of the passage can be adjusted to the different ability groups.

2b  Mira los planos a–d y las cartas en la página 46. ¿Quién habla?

Further reading practice. Students decide which of the house plans on page 47 correspond to Conchita, Sarah and Jorge.

Answers

a Jorge **b** Sarah **c** Conchita (**d** is not matched)

2c ¿Quién es? AT3.3; 7T1

Students decide to which of the letters in the previous exercise each statement corresponds. Again, they will need to read through the letters very carefully before making their choices.

Answers

1 Jorge **2** Sarah **3** Sarah **4** Conchita **5** Conchita
6 Conchita **7** Sarah

Extension

The exercise could be extended to pairwork. Students make a statement and their partner has to say who it is. More able students could do the exercise without the book from memory.

2d ¡extra! Escribe unas frases sobre la foto y el plan que sobran. AT4.4; 7T5

Students are invited to produce a 'letter' to correspond to photo **D** and plan **d** which were not matched in the previous exercise.

Support

With less able students this may be better done as an all-class exercise. Ask students to work in pairs first of all, and to decide what details need to be in the letter. Next ask them to try to produce some or all of these in Spanish, using the previous letters as a model to be adapted. Finally, pool the results and produce a letter on the board.

Gramática: de = of 7W2, 7S2, 8S1

This section alerts students to a clear difference between Spanish and English, the invariable use of *de* for possession.

To underline the pattern, write the Spanish example up on the board then write the English translation underneath. Draw lines to the phrases that correspond. This will underline the fact that the order is different too.

3a ¡Así se hace! Working out the meaning of new words 7W8, 7T1

An example of new language which students can largely work out from the context and the use of cognates. Encourage students to guess and to try to work out the meaning in pairs or groups.

There are more examples of adverts and hints about how to deal with them on Worksheet 47 (¡extra!).

3b ¡extra! ... Create an advert for your own house. AT3.3, AT4.3–4; 7T3, 7T4

Students trawl through the advert finding phrases to reuse before writing adverts for their own domiciles. This will involve noticing which language is different from a straight

description and trying to reproduce this. To underline the difference, get them to look back to the letter descriptions on the previous page and to compare the language and register of the two forms. The differences can be discussed in class.

4 Describe tu casa. AT4.3–4; 7T5, 7T6

Writing practice. See above. Students produce a 'straight' description of their dwelling. This can also allow for opinions, nearness to other locations etc.

Extension

For more imaginative practice, you could ask the students to design and describe *una casa ideal*.

Plenary

☑ In teams or pairs, students jot down as many words as they can remember in one minute.

Alternative plenary

☑ Students look back at the objectives of the unit and discuss in pairs what they have learnt for each one.

5C Los muebles
pp. 48–49

> **Objectives:**
> * say what furniture there is in your home; say where things are
> * practise learning new vocabulary
> * learn how to pronounce *z*
>
> **Key Language:** see p.79 for full list
> **Grammar:** prepositions + *de*
> **Skills:** how to learn vocabulary
> **Pronunciation:** *z*
> **Resources:** Visual 39, CD2; Worksheets 39 (furniture), 40 (Resumen), 42 (Hablar), 45 (¡Así se hace!), 46 (Gramática – prepositions); Workbooks A and B p.25; *Just Click* CD-Rom.

This section presents and practises furniture and other household items and some new prepositions. There are hints about vocabulary learning and practice of the sound *z*.

Lesson starter

A game to practise the possessive form. Everyone claps three times. You point to an individual at random. That person has to produce a phrase (the funnier the better) using *de*, e.g. *El bolígrafo de mi hermano, la casa de Jodie* etc. Everyone claps again and you choose the next person who must produce a new phrase.

Support

Variations on this could include: cuing students in by showing a flashcard/object and pointing to the 'owner' (*el caballo de Ben*); going round the class instead of picking people at random.

Extension

Make a whole sentence, e.g. *El bolígrafo de mi hermano es rojo, La casa de Jodie es pequeña.*

1a ¡Así se hace! **Learning new vocabulary** 7W1, 7W7

These hints for learning vocabulary are linked to the first exercise on the page – a grid depicting pictures and Spanish names for 16 household items.

Ask students to read the suggestions carefully. Tell them also to look for cognates, which are easier to recognise, then ask them to practise the sequence of LOOK, COVER etc. on the first line.

Remind them that to know a word they must be able to do four things: say it, translate it, spell it and use it in spoken and written Spanish.

There is a lot of new vocabulary here. Work in conjunction with the previous section. Concentrate on the strategies described on the page for learning vocabulary. Read the names of the items and ask students to repeat them chorally and individually.

Ask students to use the visual Worksheet 39 to practise identifying the items without their labels. A 16-picture noughts and crosses is much more successful than the 9-picture version in that it is high-scoring (every line of four is awarded a point) and unlikely to lead to a draw. Students say a number and the item.

A blank grid can be substituted for the one on the page once the students are familiar with the location of the items. Ask students to close their books, then point to a square and ask individuals to name the item that corresponds.

1b ☑ 💿 Escucha (1–4). Escribe el número de los muebles mencionados. AT1.3; 7L3

Listening identification of the new vocabulary in context. Students note down the numbers of the items of furniture they hear. Establish that each extract contains mention of several items. You will probably need to play the extracts several times each.

TRANSCRIPT CD2, track 14

1 – ¿Te gusta tu piso?
 – Sí, mucho.
 – ¿Qué hay en el salón?
 – Bueno, hay una televisión, un equipo de música, un sofá y dos sillones.
2 – ¿Hay un comedor?
 – Sí, con una mesa y tres sillas.
3 – Y, ¿en la cocina?
 – Hay una nevera, una cocina de gas, una lavadora y un lavaplatos.
4 – Y ¿en tu dormitorio?
 – Bueno, una cama y un armario. Y hay una lámpara y mi ordenador.

Answers

1 2, 11, 1, 4 **2** 5, 6 **3** 14, 15, 7, 13 **4** 9, 10, 3, 16
This exercise could be used for assessment.

2 ☑ 💬 Habla con tu pareja. AT2.3; 7S9

A pairwork exercise. Students ask and answer about what furniture and household items their partner has in different rooms. The example question uses *hay* and possessive *tu*.

Extension

The example answer just uses *hay* but could use the reply *mi...*

If appropriate, encourage students to work through the rooms in their own homes. If not, they can reply according to what would be in a typical room, e.g. *en la cocina hay...*

This exercise could be used for assessment.

3a 📖 Mira el dibujo y traduce las frases. AT3.3; 7W8

Students read and translate sentences that use new prepositions. This exercise is linked to the grammar explanation next to it. Students look at the pictures to get the meanings of the different prepositions before translating the same words in a set of sentences.

Answers

1 The cat is under the bed.
2 The lamp is on (top of) the table.
3 The computer is in front of the books.
4 The pencil case is behind the exercise book.
5 The CD is underneath the bed.
6 The sound system is next to the TV.

Gramática: prepositions + *de* 7W8

Once students have read through the presentation and produced some translations ask them what the difference is between the Spanish and English for e.g. 'under'. The answer is that while all the Spanish phrases use *de* (= of) most of their English equivalents do not.

Practise use of *de* + *el* etc. by getting students to say where the cat in the picture is: *encima de la mesa/delante de la mesa* etc. Next ask them to imagine that the cat is in/on/under the wardrobe: *en el armario/encima del armario/debajo del armario* etc.

WS 42 (Hablar) offers further practice of these adverbs in an information-gap exercise.

WS 46 (Gramática) has a further exercise on these adverbs.

3b 📖 Pon las frases en el orden correcto. AT3.3, AT4.3; 7S1

Students unscramble sentences on the same theme as the previous exercise. They will need to remember that each preposition needs a *de* after it.

Answers

1 El gato está debajo de la cama.
2 El teléfono está encima de la cama.
3 La regla está debajo del armario.
4 La mochila está en el armario.
5 El bolígrafo está al lado del teléfono.

4 💿 Escucha (1–6) y escribe el objeto y dónde está. AT2.3; 7L3

Students listen to a series of conversations and write out what the item mentioned is and where it is. The note-taking could be done in English if the students need more support. Tell them that you will play the track several times if necessary. Ask everyone to listen out for the object mentioned first and to note that down, then tell them to listen again for room and finally for the location within the room. You may like to get students to prepare a grid for their answers (see below) but note reservations.

TRANSCRIPT CD2, track 15

1 – ¡Mamá! ¿Dónde está mi libro de español?
 – ¡Ay! Está en la cocina.
 – ¿Dónde?
 – Encima de la mesa.
2 – ¡Mamá! ¿Dónde está mi mochila?
 – En la entrada delante de la puerta.
3 – ¡Mamá! ¿Dónde está mi bicicleta?
 – ¡Ay! Está detrás del garaje.
4 – ¡Mamá! ¿Dónde está mi bolígrafo?
 – ¡Ay! Está al lado de tu estuche en el salón.
5 – ¡Mamá! ¿Dónde están mis cuadernos?
 – ¡Ay! Están debajo de la mesa en el comedor.
6 – ¡Mamá! ¿Dónde está mi hermano?
 – ¿Tu hermano?
 – Sí, mi hermano, ¿dónde está?
 – No está en su dormitorio?
 – No, y no está en el piso.
 – ¡Ay! No lo sé.

Answers

This grid format might guide students' listening and help them to formulate their answers. However, the information doesn't all come in the same order and sometimes categories of information are missing.

	item	room	where?
1	libro de español	la cocina	encima de la mesa
2	mochila	la entrada	delante de la puerta
3	bicicleta	(el garaje)	detrás del garaje
4	bolígrafo	el salón	al lado del estuche
5	cuadernos	el comedor	debajo de la mesa
6	hermano	el dormitorio (no está)	el piso (no está)

5 ☑ 🖉 Describe dónde están unas cosas.
AT2.2–3, AT4.2–3; 7S3, 7S8

Students write sentences about a series of pictures, saying the name of the item, whereabouts it is, in which room it is in. This exercise requires the students to have understood the rule for using the new prepositions with *de + el*.

Support

Less confident students may require some additional support. Again, a grid like the one suggested below might be helpful, but note that this time the information is given in a different order.

Extension

More able students could produce further pictures and sentences of their own.

This exercise could be used for assessment

Pronunciación: *z* 7W6, 7L1, 7L6

Practice of the *z* sound. Encourage students to practise saying the examples aloud chorally and individually. Ask them if they can think of any further examples.

TRANSCRIPT CD2, track 16

plaza	diez
terraza	lápiz
izquierda	pizarra

En Zaragoza se ve la terraza a la izquierda desde la plaza.

WS 45 (¡Así se hace!) offers further listening, speaking and reading practice of this sound.

Plenary

☑ Reflect in groups on what they have learnt about dealing with unknown words. What strategies have they learnt? What strategies do they find most useful and what skills do they need to practise more?

Alternative plenary

☑ This unit has a number of different objectives so ask students to look back and consider in pairs or groups how well they think they have grasped each at different points. If you use coloured cards for grading difficulty you could go through the objectives one by one asking them to display a card according to whether they are very confident, quite confident or not confident.

5D ¿Qué opinas tú? page 50

Objectives:
* say what is good or bad about a place
* revise *ser* and *estar* (to be)
Key Language: see p.79 for full list
Grammar: *ser/estar*
Resources: CD2; Worksheets 40 (Resumen), 43 (Leer), 44 (Escribir); *Just Click* CD-Rom.

On the first of these pages students practise offering opinions and are alerted to the difference between *ser* and *estar*. There is some exposure to different conjunctions and the modifier *muy*. The page revises places in the town and adjectives to describe where you live by locating people's dwellings in a wider context.

	item		where?	room
1	el libro	está(n)	en la mesa	en el comedor
2	la mochila		detrás del sofá	en el salón
3	el ordenador		en la mesa	en el dormitorio
4	el equipo musical		al lado de la televisión	en el salón
5	el teléfono			en la entrada
6	la lámpara		encima de la televisión	en el salón
7	la lavadora			en el garaje

Lesson starter

Write up a series of adjectives on the board, e.g. *moderno, bonito, cómodo, tranquilo, nuevo, grande, pequeño, antiguo, turístico, interesante, aburrido*. As students come in tell them to choose which three best describe the area/town in which the school is situated. After (two) minutes ask students to call out the adjectives they think best apply. The volume of the reponse or a show of hands should show which are considered the most appropriate descriptions.

Alternative lesson starter *(for lessons starting part-way through the section)*

Using a model like the one below, on one side of the board write *lo bueno/malo es*; on the other side write a series of sentence endings. They can be as humorous as you like.

Students have two minutes to read through and decide which beginning best fits each ending.

Lo bueno es Lo malo es	que tengo tres hermanas que en mi casa no hay televisión que en el pueblo no hay cine que el colegio está cerca del centro que hay un ratón en la clase etc.

After two minutes point to an ending. The class must call out an appropriate beginning and then read out the rest of the sentence.

1 📖 Lee las opiniones. Escribe una cosa buena (*lo bueno*) o una cosa mala (*lo malo*) sobre las casas en inglés. AT3.3, AT4.2; 7T1

Reading practice. Recycling of *gustar* etc. A series of comments in which people talk about where they live and say what they like and don't like about it. The utterances use a selection of conjunctions.

Support

Less able students could be asked to cite only the specific items listed as *lo bueno/malo* (in bold below), rather than opinions as well. Most speakers cite good OR bad, not both.

Answers

1 **near friends' houses** (*lo bueno*) + it's big, likes a lot.
2 **small and modern** (*lo malo*) + prefers old houses, likes quite a lot.
3 **very quiet** (*lo malo*) + far from centre, very far from school, house is pretty and comfortable.
4 **close to cinemas and bars** (*lo bueno*) + it's close to the shops, central, loves.
5 **pretty and quiet** (*lo bueno*) + doesn't like a lot, prefers city.
6 **lots to do** (*lo bueno*), likes beach and sea.

Extension 7S3

Draw students' attention to the examples of *ser* and *estar*. You could recap and offer further explanation on the difference between these two verbs (see Student's Book p.37 for rule). Ask students to look at exercise 1 and to list the uses of the different verbs: *es grande y bonita/es una casa adosada/es muy tranquila/es que hay mucho que hacer; está cerca de las casas/está lejos del instituto/está en el centro* etc. Ask them to think about how these examples exemplify the rule given.

¡Así se hace! lo + adjective 7S3

The grammar presentation focuses on *lo* + adjective and asks students to say what the various examples given mean.

Answers

the interesting/difficult/boring thing (is...)

2a 💿 Escucha (1–5) y rellena el cuadro. AT1.3–4, AT3.4, AT4.3; 7L3

Listening presentation consisting of longer exchanges about where people live, leading to a written response. Students listen then fill in a previously copied or duplicated grid.

Support

Provide a duplicated grid for less confident students. All students will need to listen several times in order to complete the grid. Tell them to listen out for one type of information only on each listening.

TRANSCRIPT
CD2, track 17

1 – Pilar, ¿vives en una casa o en un piso?
  – Yo vivo en una casa adosada.
  – ¿Y cómo es la casa?
  – Pues, es bastante grande. Somos cuatro en casa, mis padres, mi hermana y yo.
  – ¿Quieres describir la casa un poco?
  – Sí. Hay tres dormitorios... una cocina-comedor, un salón, dos cuartos de baño arriba y hay una terraza.
  – Muy bien. ¿Te gusta la casa?
  – Sí, porque está cerca del centro. Lo bueno es que hay muchos autobuses. Sí, me gusta.
2 – José Luis, ¿vives en una casa o en un piso?
  – Vivo en un piso
  – ¿Cómo es?
  – Muy, muy pequeño. Demasiado pequeño. Hay un dormitorio solamente.
  – ¿Quieres describir el piso?
  – Bueno, hay una cocina-comedor, un pequeño salón, un cuarto de baño y un dormitorio.
  – ¿Hay una terraza?
  – No, ¡qué va!
3 – Marina, ¿vives en una casa?
  – No, vivo en un piso en el centro del pueblo.
  – ¿Te gusta?
  – No, no me gusta nada.
  – ¿Cómo es?
  – Es muy grande y bastante antiguo. Hay dos dormitorios, un salón-comedor, una cocina, un cuarto de baño y un aseo.
  – ¿Por qué no te gusta?
  – Porque es feo y ruidoso. Lo malo es el tráfico.
4 – Carlos, ¿vives en un piso?
  – No, vivo en una casa de dos plantas.
  – ¿Te gusta?
  – Sí, me gusta. Es muy bonita.
  – ¿Cuántos dormitorios hay?
  – Hay cuatro y un salón, un comedor, una cocina, dos cuartos de baño y un aseo.
  – ¿Hay una terraza?
  – Sí, eso es lo bueno.
5 – Charo, ¿dónde vives tú?
  – Pues, yo vivo en un piso de dos plantas.
  – ¿Quieres describirlo?
  – Sí, es grande y moderno y tiene cuatro dormitorios. Hay también dos cuartos de baño y un aseo.
  – ¿Hay comedor?
  – Sí, hay un salón y un comedor, una cocina y un dormitorio abajo y tres dormitorios arriba.
  – ¿Te gusta?
  – No. Es demasiado grande.

Answers

(The final column is to be filled in as part of the next exercise.)

	¿Vives en una casa o un piso?	¿Cómo es?	Tres detalles	¿Te gusta o no?	¡extra! ¿por qué?
1	casa (adosada)	bastante grande	3 dormitorios, cocina-comedor y salón	✓	cerca del centro, muchos autobuses
2	piso	muy/demasiado pequeño	1 dormitorio cocina-comedor, pequeño salón, cuarto de baño	–	–
3	piso (en el centro del pueblo)	muy grande, bastante antiguo	2 dormitorios, salón-comedor, cocina, cuarto de baño, aseo	✗	feo y ruidoso, el tráfico
4	casa (de dos plantas)	muy bonito	4 dormitorios, salón, comedor, cocina, 2 cuartos de baño, aseo	✓	muy bonito, terraza
5	piso (de dos plantas)	grande y moderno	4 dormitorios, 2 cuartos de baño, aseo, comedor, salón, cocina	✗	demasiado grande

2b ¡extra! Escucha otra vez y escribe por qué. AT3.4; 7L3

More able students listen again and fill in the final column of the grid – the reason for the person's likes or dislikes (see answers above).

3 Habla con tu pareja. Cambia las palabras. AT2.3–4; 7T2, 7L5, 7L6

A set of model questions and answers about where people live. It includes opinions and reasons.

This exercise could be used for assessment. Encourage students to practise and to evaluate their work, perhaps with some interim input from you or the *asistente*, before submitting it for a mark. This exercise could be used as preparation for the following one.

4 Describe tu casa/piso en 60 segundos (o más)... AT4.2–4; 7T5

A further writing exercise. Students write as much as they can about their own home in sixty seconds. They will need to draw heavily on their work on the previous question.

Resumen *(page 51)*

This section offers a resumé of all the vocabulary, grammar, skills and tips presented in the unit.

Plenary

Ask the class to look carefully at the Resumen. Go through it together. Does all the vocabulary now look familiar? Have they understood the grammar points? In speaking exercises, have they remembered about equal vowel values? Ask people to indicate whether they are happy, neutral or unhappy about each section by holding up appropriately coloured cards.

Ahora, tú! *(pp. 126–127)*

Differentiated self-access reading and writing exercises: see page 37 for more information.

page 126

1 Put the words in the box.

Answers

Furniture: armario, ordenador, baño, lavaplatos, nevera, sillón
Accommodation type: cocina, comedor, salón, entrada, dormitorio
Description: rural, moderno, cómodo, pequeño, bonito, grande, tranquilo

2 Find the odd one out and explain why.

Answers

1 cama – There is no bed in the living room
2 cocina de gas – There is no cooker in the bedroom
3 cocina de gas – It isn't a room
4 sillón – It isn't a location
5 cuarto de baño – It isn't a type of housing
6 entrada – It's inside a house/flat
7 televisión – It isn't a room

3 Copy the letter and fill in the splodges.

¡Hola. Me *llamo* Pepita. *Vivo* en una casa *pequeña* al lado del colegio. Me gusta la casa *porque* es muy *bonita*. Hay una entrada, *un* salón-comedor y *una* cocina. Hay tres dormitorios: el de *mis* padres, el dormitorio de mi hermana – *es* muy pequeño – y *mi* dormitorio. En mi dormitorio *hay* una cama y *un* armario. No hay televisión pero *hay* un ordenador.

4 Read the description and make a list of the number of rooms.

1 la entrada
2 un salón
3 un comedor
4 la cocina
5 el cuarto de baño
6 el aseo
7 una terraza
8 el dormitorio de sus abuelos
9 el dormitorio de sus padres
10 el cuarto de baño de sus abuelos
11 el dormitorio de Marco

page 127

1 📖 **Find the mistakes**

Vivo en **un chalet** en **la ciudad**. Hay **cuatro** dormitorios y dos cuartos de baño. En la planta baja hay la entrada, claro, y a la **izquierda** el salón. A la **derecha** hay el comedor y la cocina. En la **segunda** planta está el dormitorio de mis padres. Somos **siete** en la familia: mis padres, mis abuelos, **mis hermanas** y yo. El dormitorio de mis abuelos está en la **primera** planta. Mi dormitorio está en la segunda planta.

Hay un jardín y un garaje a la derecha. Pero **no hay terraza**.

2 ✏️ **Write two descriptions.**

House	Flat
Hay dos salones, una cocina, un comedor y cinco dormitorios. Hay muchos dormitorios. En la segunda planta hay tres dormitorios individuales. Hay dos cuartos de baño y un aseo. Me gusta porque es grande.	El piso está en la primera planta. Hay una cocina-comedor y un salón pequeño. Lo bueno es que es nuevo. Lo mal es que está en el centro de la ciudad. No me gusta porque es muy pequeño.

Worksheets Unit 5

38 La casa AT3.1; 7W1

Visuals and labels of rooms in house. Students cut out and stick labels to the correct rooms on the picture. This sheet can also be used for vocabulary-building and practice.

39 Los muebles AT3.1; 7W1

Mini-flashcards of household furniture to be cut up and matched to their labels. This sheet can also be used for vocabulary-building and practice.

40 Resumen AT3.1; 7W1

A useful worksheet version of the Unit Resumen. It can be used for homework and learning exercises.

41 Escuchar – Ways of listening AT 3.3; 7L2

This exercise offers practice in identifying type of dwelling, position, rooms etc.

a Students are guided to pick out just the information they need and to fill in the relevant boxes on the grid provided, with short notes and using abbreviations.

TRANSCRIPT

CD2, track 18

Ejemplo:

1 – ¿Dónde vives, Marcello?
  – Vivo en un piso.
  – ¿Y, dónde está?
  – Está cerca del centro.
  – ¿Cómo es?
  – … Está en el primer piso…
  – ¿Y qué hay?
  – Pues **no es muy grande**. Hay un salón, una cocina-comedor, dos dormitorios, un cuarto de baño y un aseo… ▶

2 – Y tú Marina, ¿dónde vives?
  – **Vivo con mis padres en un chalet.**
  – ¿Dónde está?
  – Está a cinco kilómetros del centro.
  – ¿Cómo es?
  – Pues… **es bastante grande**, con dos plantas. Tiene un salón, un comedor, una cocina, tres dormitorios, dos cuartos de baño y dos aseos. Y **el jardín es enorme**.

3 – ¿Vives en el centro, Carlos?
  – No, vivo en una casa en el campo.
  – **¿Es grande?**
  – **No.** Hay solamente un dormitorio y una cocina-comedor.
  – ¿Y un cuarto de baño?
  – No, hay un aseo pero no hay cuarto de baño.

4 – Lo bueno es que… ahora vivo en un bloque de pisos… a dos minutos de las tiendas. ▶

Mi piso es muy confortable… está en la segunda planta… Hay un dormitorio, un salón… una cocina-comedor y un cuarto de baño y un aseo **muy moderno. Me gusta mucho…**

5 – Vivo en una **pequeña** casa adosada a cinco minutos andando de la piscina.
  – ¿Y, cómo es tu casa?
  – Pues… **es muy bonita**… En la primera planta hay dos dormitorios, el cuarto de baño y el aseo. Y en la planta baja hay una cocina-comedor y un salón.
  – **Y tengo una pequeña terraza también.**

6 – Me gusta vivir en el centro. Tengo un piso en la tercera planta de **un bloque antiguo**.
  – ¿Cuántas habitaciones hay?
  – **Tengo solamente una habitación** – ¡es mi salón, mi dormitorio, mi cocina y mi comedor! ¡Es **muy cómodo**! Ah, y hay un cuarto de baño y un aseo también.

Answers

(The final column is to be filled in as part of the next exercise.)

	Type	Where situated	Which floor/ How many floors	Rooms
1	Flt	nr cent	1st	lvg, kit-dnr, 2 bds, bth, WC
2	Det hse	5 km cent	2	lvg, dng, kit, 3 bds, 2 bths, 2 WC
3	hse	country	–	1 bed, kit-dnr, WC
4	flt	2 mins shps	2nd	1 bed, lvg, kit-dnr, bth, WC
5	semi	5 mins pool	2	2 beds, bth, WC, lvg, kit-dnr
6	flt	cent	3rd	bed–lvg–kit–dnr, bth, WC

b An invitation to listen again for supplementary details (see items in bold in transcript).

42 Hablar AT2.3–4, AT4.3–4; 7L4

An information-gap exercise that practises the new prepositions and the furniture vocabulary. The worksheet also contains a final ¡extra! writing exercise.

Sometimes the difference lies in the item itself and sometimes in its position. Working in pairs students ask about and say where different items in the room are, ringing the items that are different.

Answers

La lámpara está encima de/en el armario.
Hay una televisión/un ordenador en la mesa.
El estuche está en/detrás de la mochila.
El cuaderno está en la silla/debajo de la silla.
El libro está en la cama/debajo de la cama.
Hay un lápiz/un bolígrafo encima del centro musical.

¡extra! Students work together to prepare six sentences, e.g. *En el dormitorio A la lámpara está encima del armario pero en el dormitorio B (la lámpara) está en el armario. En el dormitorio A hay un lápiz encima del centro musical, pero en el dormitorio B hay un bolígrafo encima del centro musical.*

43 Leer AT 2.3, AT 3.3, AT4.3; 7S2, 7T1, 7T2, 7L6

Reading comprehension on the theme of where you live. The worksheet also offers opportunities for follow-up linked speaking and writing exercises.

a Students read the information given by Ana about where she lives and deduce which questions Juan asked in order to elicit each piece of information. Generally the answers do not repeat the words of the questions so that students must think about the sense of each item.

Answers

1 e **2** f **3** b **4** d **5** h **6** c **7** g **8** a

b Once students have familiarised themselves with the gist of the conversation, they can think about preparing it for reading aloud in pairs.

c An invitation for students to produce their own spoken or written answers to Juan's questions.

44 Escribir AT4.2–3; 7S3

A writing frame giving information and opinions about where one lives.

a Students highlight or underline the options that apply to them.

b They use the information they have picked out to produce their own personalised accounts.

Support

Less confident students may need to use the sheet throughout the exercise, underlining their options as a class exercise, and then copying out their personalised account. The very unconfident would benefit from using ICT to copy and paste their choices on to a blank grid.

Extension

More confident students could use this sheet as an interim aid. Once they have thought about what they will write, take the sheet away and ask them to prepare their own accounts without it.

45 ¡Así se hace! AT1.1, AT2.1; 7W6, 7L1

This sheet offers further practice of the sound *z* and extends the scope to include the same sound as produced by the letter combinations *ce* and *ci*. (Framework 7W6 – Letters and sounds)

1a Students practise words with *z* then listen to check.

CD2, track 19

terraza	Ibiza	zapato
diez	Venezuela	zumo
plaza	haz	

1b Students look for five more words with the same sound/letter combination. Cues are given.

Possible answers

1 izquierda **2** lápiz **3** rizado **4** pez **5** marzo

2a Students practise words with *ce* and *ci* and listen to check.

CD2, track 20

piscina	centro	encima
habitación	cerca	cinco

2b Students follow cues to think of five more words with this sound/letter.

Possible answers

1 cine(ma) **2** cocina **3** once/doce

4 Francia **5** Valencia

3a Students underline all the examples of *z*, *ce* or *ci* in the text.

CD2, track 21

La madre de mi amiga Patricia es escocesa. Su padre es venezolano. Patricia tiene el pelo rizado y los ojos azules. Vive cerca del centro de Barcelona, a diez minutos de la piscina y a quince minutos de la plaza. En su piso hay cinco habitaciones. A la izquierda de la cocina hay una terraza donde hay dieciséis peces de colores.

3b Finally they practise reading the passage aloud then listen to check.

46 Gramática AT4.3; 7W4, 7S1

This sheet concentrates on the new prepositions and manipulating the phrases with *a* and *de* + *el/la* etc.

1 A reminder of the meanings of the new phrases. Students pair each one with the correct drawing.

Answers

1 e **2** c **3** b **4** d **5** a

2 A gap-filling exercise to practise *de* + *el/la* etc.

Answers

1 de la **2** del **3** de las **4** del **5** de la **6** del

3 A reminder about the possessive *de* and implications for word order.

Answers

1 el dormitorio de mi hermano **2** los bolígrafos de mi hermana **3** la casa de sus abuelos **4** el perro de sus primos **5** las serpientes de mi tío **6** la tía de tu amiga

47 ¡extra! AT3.3–4; 7W8, 7T3

A mixed-skill sheet that offers practice in reading and writing in a different register.

1 A set of property ads that use some unfamiliar words. Students first decide which property will suit each of the prospective buyers' requirements.

Answers

2 bf **3** ad **4** ce

2 Students are asked to write their own ads, using the ads given as models.

Suggested answers

1 Vendo casa, dos plantas, tres habitaciones, cocina y comedor, piscina y terraza.
2 Se vende piso, a diez minutos de la playa, dos dormitorios, dos cuartos de baño, cocina, salón y comedor. Garaje para un vehículo.
3 Casa adosada a cinco kilómetros de Benidorm. Tres habitaciones, cuarto de baño, cocina y salón-comedor, dos terrazas y patio. Jardín con piscina.

3 A suggestion that students write an ad for their own house.

Workbook A Unit 5

page 23 *(Section A)*

Answers

ex 1a:

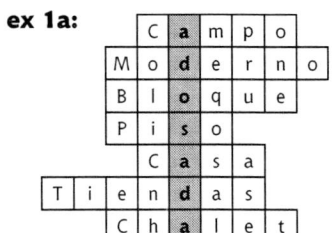

Revealed word = adosada

ex 1b:
1 campo 2 moderno 3 bloque 4 piso; tiendas 5 casa 6 chalet

ex 2:
1 d 2 a 3 f 4 b 5 c 6 e

ex 3:
1 c 2 a 3 b

page 24 *(Section B)*

Answers

ex 1a:
La planta baja:
el jardín (to the left of 'el garaje')
la cocina (to the right of 'el salón')
el comedor (to the right of 'la entrada')
La primera planta (clockwise):
el domitorio de Ignacio
el cuarto de baño
el dormitorio de Paca
el dormitorio de José
el aseo
el dormitorio de María
el dormitorio de la madre de Paca

ex 1b:
El dormitorio de Paca (Paca's bedroom)

page 25 *(Section C)*

Answers

ex 1:
televisión; cocina de gas; sillón; sofá; silla; lavaplatos; ducha; ordenador; lavadora

---

ex 2:
2 □ 3 ✓ 4 ↑ 5 → 6 ✗; ↓

ex 3:
c (= 'th' before *i* or *e*);
z (= 'th' before *a, o, u* or when at end of word)

Note: ex 3 is recorded on CD2, track 22, for pronunciation practice.

page 26 *(Section D)*

Answers

ex 1a:
1 delante 2 detrás 3 grande 4 al lado 5 al lado 6 moderna 7 debajo 8 tranquilo

ex 2:
1 es 2 Está 3 Es 4 Es 5 está 6 es

Workbook B Unit 5

page 23 *(Section A)*

Answers

ex 1a:
La planta baja:

		C	a	m	p	o	
	M	o	d	e	r	n	o
	B	l	o	q	u	e	
	P	i	s	o			
		C	a	s	a		
T	i	e	n	d	a	s	
	C	h	a	l	e	t	

ex 1b:
1 chalet, lives 2 campo, is 3 bloque, flats 4 casa, nearby 5 piso, house 6 adosada, house

ex 2:
1 d 2 a 3 e 4 b 5 c 6 f

¡extra!

a La casa está a diez minutos del bloque de pisos.
b La casa está cerca del aparcamiento.
c La casa está lejos del centro.

page 24 *(Section B)*

Answers

ex 1:
cuarto de baño = bathroom;
garaje = garage; cocina = kitchen;
comedor = dining room; salón = living room; terraza = terrace; jardín = garden

ex 2a:
El salón está abajo, <u>a la</u> izquierda de la cocina.
Aquí hay el cuarto de baño, a la <u>derecha</u> del dormitorio de Ignacio.

El aseo está a la derecha del <u>dormitorio</u> de María.
Hay un jardín a la <u>izquierda</u> del garaje.

ex 2b:
el jardín (to the left of 'el garaje')
la cocina (to the right of 'el salón')
el comedor (to the right of 'la entrada')
La primera planta (clockwise):
el domitorio de Ignacio
el cuarto de baño
el dormitorio de Paca
el dormitorio de José
el aseo
el dormitorio de María
el dormitorio de la madre de Paca

ex 2c:
El dormitorio de Paca (Paca's bedroom)

page 25 *(Section C)*

Answers

ex 1:
televisión; cocina de gas; sillón; sofá; silla; lavaplatos; ducha; ordenador; lavadora; cama; nevera; lámpara

ex 2:
2 de la 3 está, de 4 encima del 5 al lado de 6 no está

ex 3:
pez, en<u>c</u>ima, Rui<u>z</u>, terra<u>z</u>a, cru<u>c</u>e, pla<u>z</u>a, izquierda, <u>C</u>ecilia, <u>c</u>erca, ha<u>c</u>e, quin<u>c</u>e, die<u>z</u>, <u>c</u>inco, <u>c</u>ero

¡extra!

c (= 'th' before *i* or *e*);
z (= 'th' before *a, o, u* or when at end of word);
quick rule: c before *i* or *e* otherwise z

Note: ex 3 is recorded on CD2, track 23, for pronunciation practice.

page 26 *(Section D)*

Answers

ex 1a:
2 cerca, school 3 grande, is 4 lejos, town/city 5 al lado, flat 6 cómoda, moderna, too 7 delante, teatro, It is/It's 8 chalet, tranquilo, very

ex 2a:
1 es 2 Es 3 Está 4 Es 5 está 6 es 7 está 8 es, está

ex 2b:
1 goes with 2 5 goes with 3 6 goes with 4

¡extra!

7 The fantastic thing is that the house isn't far from the swimming pool.
8 The bad thing is that it's next to a disco.

Unidad 6 Tiempo libre	Topic/Language/Culture	Grammar and skills	National Criteria
6A ¿Qué te gusta hacer en tu tiempo libre? (pp. 52–53) **Objectives** • say what free time activities you like and do not like doing • read out aloud; practise intonation in questions	¿Te gusta...? jugar al fútbol/practicar la natación/salir con amigos/salir de compras/ir al cine/jugar al tenis/tocar el piano/escuchar música/navegar por Internet/ver la tele/ir al centro/hacer los deberes Relaunch: me gusta (mucho)/me encanta/odio/no me gusta **Culture** popular sports	**Grammar** gustar, encantar singular **Skills** Improving pronunciation Recognising questions	**Attainment** AT1.2–3, AT2.3–4, AT3.2–4, AT4.3–5 **Framework objectives** 7W5, 7W8, &S2, 7S3, 7S4, &T1, 7T2, 7T3, 7T4, 7T5, 7T6, 7L1, 7L3, 7L4, 7L5, 7C2, 8T6 **Programmes of study** 1b, 2a, 2b, 2c, 3c **QCA Scheme of work** Language: Unit 5; Context: Unit 4 **Assessment for learning** Objectives, p.53 Ex 3, Plenary
6B ¿Qué prefieres hacer en tu tiempo libre? (pp. 54–55) **Objectives** • give reasons for liking or not liking something • learn how to guess the meaning of new words from the context	giving opinions: prefiero/pienso que/creo que/en mi opinión es... aburrido/emocionante/barato/caro/ educativo/genial/un rollo en primavera/en verano/en otoño/en invierno Relaunch: me gusta (mucho)/me encanta/odio/no me gusta Relaunch: free time activities	**Grammar** preferir, pensar, creer, en mi opinión + infinitive **Skills** Listening for cognates Using context to guess meaning	**Attainment** AT1.3, AT2.2–4, AT3.3, AT4.2–4 **Framework objectives** 7W8, 7T1, 7T7, 7S2, 7S3, 7S9, 7L1, 7L3, 7L5, 7L6, 8S2 **Programmes of study** 3b, 3c **QCA Scheme of work** Language: Unit 5, Unit 6; Context: Unit 5, Unit 6 **Assessment for learning** Objectives, p.55 Ex 4b, Plenary
6C Mi semana (pp. 56–57) **Objectives** • say when and where you do activities • learn how to say 'on Monday'/'on Mondays' • use the present tense of stem-changing and irregular verbs	Days of the week ¿Qué día? lunes, martes, miércoles, jueves, viernes, sábado, domingo Times on the hour ¿A qué hora? A la una, a las dos etc. Relaunch: free time activities	**Grammar** Present tense of activity verbs Practico la natación el lunes/**los** lunes Stem-changing verbs	**Attainment** AT1.3, AT2.3–4, AT3.2, AT4.2–4 **Framework objectives** 7W1, 7W5, 7S2, 7S3, 7S9, 7T1, 7T4, 7T5, 7L3, 7L4, 8L3 **Programmes of study** 1b, 2f, 2i **QCA Scheme of work** Language: Unit 4 Context: Unit 4, Unit 5, Unit 6 **Assessment for learning** Objectives, p.56 Ex 1c, Plenary
6D ¿Dónde nos encontramos? (pp. 58–59) **Objectives** • learn how to arrange to meet • understand opening and closing times • learn how to pronounce t and d	¿Quieres/Te apetece?/Podemos... (ir al cine) Sí, No puedo/No tengo dinero/Estoy cansado ¿A qué hora abre/cierra? ¿Cuándo /Dónde nos encontramos? (En la puerta del cine) Relaunch: places in town, free time activities, days of the week, times	**Skills** Reading signs **Pronunciation** t and d	**Attainment** AT1.4, AT2.2–4, AT3.3, AT4.2–4 **Framework objectives** 7W6, 7W8, 7T1, 7T2, 7T3, 7T5, 7T6, 7L3, 7L5, 7L6 **Programmes of study** 1a, 1c, 2b, 2d **QCA Scheme of work** Language: Units 4, 5, 6, 9; Context: Unit 9 **Assessment for learning** Objectives, p.58 Ex 2a, p.59 Ex 3b, Plenary
6E Un fin de semana perfecto (pp. 60–63) **Objectives** • talk about plans for next weekend • use ir a + infinitive	¿Qué vas a hacer esta semana? (Voy a hacer los deberes) relaunch: free time activities, days of the week, times	**Grammar** Immediate future	**Attainment** AT 1.5, AT2.3–5, AT4.3–5 **Framework objectives** 7W5, 7T4, 7S9, 7L3, 7L5, 8W5 **Programmes of study** 1b, 2f, 3b **QCA Scheme of work** Language: Units 4, 5, 6, 9 Context: Unit 9 **Assessment for learning** Objectives, p.60 Ex 1b, Plenary. All revision activities p.62

Other resources: ¡Ahora tú! pp.128–129   WS 48–56   Flashcards 28–43   OHT 13   WBA & B pp.28–33   Assessment Units 5–6 (R & A file pp.124–127)   *Just Click* Just Click CD-Rom

6A ¿Qué te gusta hacer en tu tiempo libre?

pp. 52–53

> **Objectives:**
> - say what free time activities you like and do not like doing
> - read out loud; practise intonation in questions
>
> **Key Language:** see p.91 for full list
>
> **Grammar:**
> - *gustar, encantar*
> - forming questions
>
> **Skills:** how to improve pronunciation
>
> **Resources:** Flashcards 28–39 (free time activities ×12); Visual 48 (free time activities ×12); CD2; Worksheets 48 (Tiempo libre), 49 (Resumen), 55 (Gramática); Workbooks A and B p.28; *Just Click* CD-Rom.

On these pages words and phrases for different free time activities are presented and *gustar* and *encantar* are reintroduced. The grammar section looks at how to form a question.

Lesson starter

Drop on to the OHP a random selection of names and nouns that your students may have an opinion about and two further labels, one *Me gusta* and the other *No me gusta*. Draw a blank box on the OHT labelled *La sala 101*. Ask students to decide how they feel about each of the things you've written. After two minutes point to one entry and say e.g. David Beckham/Neighbours/*el español*. Students call out *me gusta* or *no me gusta* according to their preference. The entries that have more *no me gusta* shouts go into *La sala 101*.

Alternative lesson starter *(for lessons starting part-way through the section)*

Tell the class you're going to grade the pastimes according to popularity and they must decide which things they prefer to do. Hold up each flashcard in turn and get the class to call *me gusta* or *no me gusta*. Put the cards in order according to popularity.

Preliminary exercise

The first exercise uses *me gusta* and *no me gusta* and also *me encanta* and *me gusta mucho*. Students will have met all these terms in Unit 4 but they may need reminding. This could be done before you start as a follow-up and refinement of the starter exercise.

You may prefer to introduce the new vocabulary for the first exercise via Flashcards 28–39 or Visual 48, both of which depict all twelve activities. In either case present two or three new phrases at a time, moving from choral repetition to individual production.

1a ¡Así se hace! Reading out loud 7T2

Read the speech bubbles.

This skills explanation and exercise should be tackled in conjunction with the next one.

These two exercises can be used as an opportunity for self-assessment: students try to work out the meanings and check to see how many they get right.

1b ¿Qué les gusta hacer? Escucha (1–12) y une las frases con los dibujos. AT1.2, AT3.2; 7T1, 7L1

Listening and reading presentation of pastimes and revision of *me gusta, me gusta mucho* and *me encanta*. This exercise should be tackled in conjunction with the previous ¡Así se hace! explanation.

Students listen and try to match the balloons to the pictures. Most of the phrases should be identifiable because they contain cognates or words students have met before: *fútbol, música, tele, centro*. Encourage students to look for these before they start and to eliminate all the ones they are sure of.

> **TRANSCRIPT** CD2, track 24
>
> 1 Me gusta jugar al fútbol.
> 2 Me gusta mucho practicar la natación.
> 3 Me gusta salir con amigos.
> 4 Me encanta salir de compras.
> 5 Me gusta mucho ir al cine.
> 6 Me encanta jugar al tenis.
> 7 Me gusta tocar el piano.
> 8 Me encanta escuchar música.
> 9 Me gusta mucho navegar por Internet.
> 10 Me gusta ver la tele.
> 11 Me encanta ir al centro.
> 12 No me gusta hacer los deberes.

> **Answers**
>
> 1 a 2 c 3 e 4 g 5 h 6 b 7 i 8 d 9 j 10 f 11 l 12 k

Extension

Fast-finishers can be encouraged to rewrite the sentences, adapting them to their own opinions.

Gramática: *gustar/encantar* + infinitive 7W5

Encourage students first to work out the first person of the verbs *gustar* and *encantar* from the text in exercise 1.

The grammar box explains the use of the infinitive after the verbs *gustar* and *encantar*, and how the meaning differs when each word is followed by a noun or a verb in the infinitive. Point out to students that the infinitive is the name of the verb – the form you find in a dictionary.

When they are presented with the whole verb, they will need plenty of practice. The verb *gustar* tends to cause big difficulties, and it is important that students understand the grammatical formation.

2a Escucha (1–8). ¿Les gusta ☺, les gusta mucho ☺☺, o les encanta ☺☺☺? AT1.3; 7L3

Listening comprehension of *gustar/gustar mucho/encantar*. Students decide which of the three verbs is being used and put smileys accordingly. The last exchange uses two different verbs.

Extension

The exchanges actually use a full range of pronouns, not only all the singular ones given in the grammar section but all the plural forms as well. You may like to ask students to listen specifically for these.

TRANSCRIPT CD2, track 25

1 Me encanta navegar por Internet.
2 A mi hermano Juan le gusta mucho escuchar música.
3 A mi padre le encanta ir al cine.
4 Inés, ¿te gusta navegar por Internet?
5 Me gusta mucho tocar el piano.
6 A mi prima María le encanta salir con amigos.
7 A mi hermano le gusta mucho practicar la natación.
8 – Miguel Ángel, ¿te gusta jugar al tenis?
   – Sí, me gusta mucho.

Answers

1 ☺☺☺   5 ☺☺
2 ☺☺   6 ☺☺☺
3 ☺☺☺   7 ☺☺
4 ☺   8 you ☺, I ☺☺

2b ¡extra! Escucha otra vez. ¿Qué actividades les gustan mucho? AT1.3; 7L3

Students listen again and note just which pastimes are mentioned with *gustar mucho*. They may need to listen twice – once to note the relevant numbers and again to write the name of the pastime (abbreviated if necessary).

Answers

2 escuchar música 5 tocar el piano 7 practicar la natación
8 jugar al tenis

Extension

You could ask students to do the same for *gustar* and *encantar*.

3 ✓ Habla con tu pareja. AT2.3–4; 7T2, 7L4

Students work in pairs to follow and adapt the model conversation, asking and answering questions about their own likes and dislikes.

Once they have established and practised the sample format, encourage them to close their books and to speak spontaneously.

To encourage spontaneity ask students to swap partners and enact the conversation with a new person.

This exercise could be used for assessment.

The ¡Así se hace! hint is given in order to remind students to try to expand their conversations by using linking words like *y* and *pero*.

4a Lee el correo electrónico. Elige la respuesta correcta. AT3.4; 7W8, 7S2, 7T3, 7T4, 7C2

Reading comprehension of an email leading to a multiple-choice exercise.

This material provides an insight into attitudes to sports in Spain. Students should find it interesting to compare what they do with what Spanish youngsters do. Before embarking on the exercise start by asking students to work in groups and guess what sports they think Spanish people practise, and give a prize to those who guess the most popular sports.

This is one of the longest pieces of continuous writing that students will have encountered. Some of the vocabulary is new, e.g. *deporte, rápido, normalmente, nadie*. Some of these can be guessed as cognates or from the context. Some can be checked in the Resumen or dictionary. Instead of the infinitive the present tense of the verb *jugar* is used, as is *practico*. Encourage students to take their time reading the letter and to work in pairs or groups to try to extrapolate as much as possible. Once they have done this the multiple-choice options should provide further clarification.

Answers

1 a 2 b 3 a 4 c 5 a

4b ¡extra! Contesta al correo electrónico de Paco. Escribe qué deportes practicas, y tu opinión. AT4.3–5; 7T5, 8T6

Students respond to Paco's email. Remind them that they can recycle and adapt parts of the email. It may be useful to prepare an OHT version of the text. Let the class decide which bits can be reused as they stand, which can be adapted and which bits are not useful. Underline or highlight each category in a different colour.

5a ¡Así se hace! Intonation in questions AT1.2; 7S4, 7L1

Students decide whether what they hear is a question or a statement.

Listen (1–8) and write whether you hear a question (¿?) or not (¡!). Before listening to the recording, remind students that Spanish questions that don't use a question word have the same form as statements.

TRANSCRIPT CD2, track 26

1 ¿Te gusta jugar al fútbol?
2 ¡Me encanta salir con mis amigos!
3 ¡Odio quedarme en casa haciendo los deberes!
4 ¿Dónde juegas al tenis, en el polideportivo o en el parque?
5 ¿Sabes a qué hora vamos a ir de compras?
6 ¡Estoy muy cansado; no quiero ir a la piscina!
7 ¿Qué tal si vamos al centro?
8 ¿Prefieres jugar al hockey o al rugby?

Answers

1 ¿? 2 ¡! 3 ¡! 4 ¿? 5 ¿? 6 ¡! 7 ¿? 8 ¿?

5b Mira el ejercicio 1a. Habla con tu pareja. AT2.3; 7L5

A different slant on the exchange practised in exercise 3. This time students ask each other if they like doing specific activities. This gives a further chance to practise *me gusta/encanta* etc.

5c ¡extra! Write about your partner's likes and dislikes. AT2.4; 7S3, 7L5

This time students change the verb to the third person to discuss their partner's likes and dislikes. They also need to add *A...* at the front of their third person sentence.

Support

It may help to have an OHT or chart on the board showing first person forms and their equivalent third person forms. For less confident students stick to *me/le gusta* and *no me/le gusta*.

Plenary

☑ Ask students to close their books. Each group has two minutes to collect the largest and most accurately spelt list of free time activities.

Alternative plenary

☑ Divide the class into groups. Ask students to write down one fact they have learned then share it with the rest of the groups and finally with the class.

6B ¿Qué prefieres hacer en tu tiempo libre?

pp. 54–55

Objectives:
- give reasons for liking or not liking something
- learn how to guess the meaning of new words from the context

Key Language: see p.91 for full list

Grammar:
preferir, pensar, creer, en mi opinión + *infinitive*

Skills:
- listening for cognates
- using context to guess meaning

Resources: Visual 48, Flashcards 40–43 (four seasons); CD2; Worksheet 49 (Resumen); Workbooks A and B p.29; *Just Click* CD-Rom.

In this section free time activities and likes and dislikes are recycled but this time adding opinions and reasons for doing things, together with the names of the seasons. There are more hints about comprehension too.

Lesson starter

Use Flashcards 28–39 or Visual 48 to revise free time activities. Hold a flashcard facing you, students have to guess which one it is. The person who guesses correctly continues the game.

Or cover some or all of the items on Visual 48 and ask students to spend two minutes in groups trying to recall which activity fits in each of the covered spaces. The group that gets the most correct hits is the winner.

Alternative lesson starter *(for lessons starting part-way through the section)*

You hold up a flashcard and say e.g. *ir de compras – es aburrido*. Everyone claps three times then you point to an individual who must repeat the activity but change the adjective, e.g. *ir de compras – es educativo*. All clap three times and you point to someone else. When all the possible adjectives have been used for that activity, change the activity and start again.

1 💿 **Escucha (1–8) y lee.** AT1.3, AT3.3; 7T1, 7L1

A listening and reading exercise that represents pastimes, this time with some new expressions. *Es aburrido* should be familiar from Unit 4 but the others are new. Ask students to read the text and to try to guess the meaning of the new words from the pictures before checking in the box.

Once students have listened to the CD and are familiar with the new expressions, hold up a flashcard and ask e.g. *¿Te gusta salir con amigos?* The class and then individuals give you the answer in the book. Once you have practised the sentences in the book ask students to make further sentences along these lines that express their own opinions.

Support

To practise the new vocabulary, students could be asked to give a one-word opinion of activities mentioned by the teacher, e.g. *jugar al fútbol – divertido*.

Extension

Ask students to tell you how the opinions are linked to the pastime. Elicit the fact that in all cases but one the link is *porque* but one sentence uses *pero*.

TRANSCRIPT CD2, track 27

1 Me gusta jugar al tenis porque es divertido.
2 No me gusta practicar la natación porque es aburrido.
3 Me encanta ir al cine porque es emocionante.
4 Me gusta ir al centro porque es barato.
5 Me gusta mucho ir de compras pero es caro.
6 Me gusta navegar por Internet porque es educativo.
7 Me gusta salir con amigos porque es genial.
8 No me gusta tocar el piano porque es un rollo.

2a 💿 **Escucha (1–6). Escribe las actividades, y las opiniones.** AT1.3; 7L3

Listening practice. Students have to pick out the activity and the opinion mentioned each time. To facilitate note-taking you could agree a series of abbreviations or quick visuals for both categories. Play the CD several times, reminding students to listen first for the pastimes and, on a subsequent listening, for the opinions.

Extension

More able students could be asked to pick up other pieces of information (e.g. the expression used to give the opinion).

TRANSCRIPT CD2, track 28

1 ¡Hola! Soy María. No me gusta nada ir de compras porque es muy aburrido.
2 ¿Qué tal? Me llamo Miguel. Me encanta jugar al fútbol ¡es muy emocionante!
3 Soy Pedro. Me gusta mucho salir con mis amigos porque es genial.
4 ¡Buenos días! Me llamo Ismael, y mi pasatiempo favorito es escuchar música. Es muy divertido... ¡y barato!
5 ¡Hola! Soy Sara. No me gusta mucho tocar el piano porque es difícil y muy aburrido.
6 ¿Qué tal? Me llamo Elena. Mi pasatiempo favorito es ir al cine. Es muy emocionante pero un poco caro.

Answers

1 María, ir de compras, aburrido.
2 Miguel, jugar al fútbol, emocionante.
3 Pedro, salir con amigos, genial.
4 Ismael, escuchar música, divertido y barato.
5 Sara, tocar el piano, difícil y aburrido.
6 Elena, ir al cine, emocionante, caro.

2b 🔵 **¡extra! Escucha otra vez. ¿Cómo se dice en español...? AT1.3; 7L3**

Students listen again to the previous set of exchanges and pick out the Spanish for a series of English words.

Answers

because/porque; very/muy; my favourite pastime/mi pasatiempo favorito; a little/un poco

¡Así se hace! 7S2

Introduction of some new language for giving opinions and comparisons between the Spanish and English ways of constructing such sentences.

3 💬 **Habla con tu pareja. Da tus opiniones. AT2.2–4; 7S2, 7S3, 7L5, 8S2**

Students construct sentences on the opinion + pastime + connective + reason pattern to express their own opinions.

Support

Less confident students may need the above pattern to be built up on the board.

Extension

Encourage more confident students to use the new opinion phrases too, e.g. *Prefiero salir con amigos porque es barato.*

4a   **¡Así se hace! AT3.3; 7T1**

Reading presentation of seasons in the familiar context of opinions and pastimes.

To practise the new vocabulary ask students *¿Qué te gusta hacer en primavera?* Ask the class and then individuals to build up a list of things they like doing at different seasons.

Extension

More confident students can also prepare a list of what they don't like doing at different times of year, and say at which season they prefer doing certain activities.

Use flashcards 40–43 to present and practise the seasons. Use them in conjunction with the free time activity flashcards to build up sentences such as *Me gusta practicar la natación en verano (pero) no me gusta (practicar la natación) en invierno.*

4b ☑ ✏️ **¿Y tú? ¿Qué te gusta hacer en primavera, verano, otoño e invierno? AT2.2–4, AT4.2–4; 7S9, 7T7, 7L6**

Students prepare accounts of what they like doing when and why.

These accounts could be prepared as written exercises but students should then be encouraged to prepare and learn them for final oral delivery. Remind them to check their work and to practise saying the speech in pairs before saying it to you or the *asistente*.

Support

The teacher might want to provide a speaking/writing frame for less able students along the lines of:

me gusta no me gusta me encanta odio prefiero	ir al cine salir con amigos etc.	en verano etc.	porque pero	creo que es etc.	es aburrido etc.

(The greyed-out column could be omitted if too demanding). And:

me gusta me encanta	jugar al tenis etc.	en primavera etc.	pero	no me gusta odio prefiero	(jugar al tenis)	en verano etc.

Extension

More able students could be encouraged to prepare and learn by heart a mini-presentation on what they like doing, when and why.

This exercise could be used for assessment.

Plenary

☑ Students work in pairs and for each letter of the alphabet try to find a word featured in the section. There won't be a word for every letter but the pair who find words for the most letters are the winners.

Alternative plenary

☑ Discuss with students how they can memorise what they have learnt in Section B.

Collect ideas, e.g. 'What are you going to do to practise this before next lesson?'; 'How much practice do you think you'll need before you know this for ever?'

Add ideas of your own as necessary, e.g. 'Copy a longer sentence on to a piece of paper. Check you have spelt it correctly then fold it over so that the sentence can't be seen. The next day, try to write the same sentence below the fold. Check the spelling against the original sentence.'

6C Mi semana pp. 56–57

> **Objectives:**
> * say when and where you do activities
> * learn how to say 'on Monday'/'on Mondays'
> * use the present tense of stem-changing and irregular verbs
>
> **Key Language:** see p.91 for full list
> **Grammar:**
> * present tense of activity verbs
> * *practico* la natación **el lunes/los** lunes
> * stem-changing verbs
>
> **Resources:** CD2; Worksheets 49 (Resumen), 55 (Gramática), 56 (**¡extra!**); Workbooks A and B p.30; *Just Click* CD-Rom.

Within the context of free time activities, these pages present days of the week and times on the hour. Instead of using the activity verbs in the infinitive after *gustar* etc., students now learn to use them in the present tense. The new forms include some irregulars and stem-changers.

Lesson starter

Karaoke numbers. Get everyone singing the number song from Unit 1. Start with the CD then fade it down until the students are singing on their own. Divide the class into two groups and get the sides singing a verse each.

Alternative lesson starter *(for lessons starting part-way through the section)*

Working on their own, students have two minutes to write down all the words they can think of connected with the topic of the lesson (free time activities, times and days of the week).

When the time is up, students compare their list with that of their partner. They cross off any words they both thought of and score a point for any appropriate word their partner didn't think of. They must know the meanings of any words listed in English. The winner is the person with the most original words.

Introduction

Introduce the names of the days of the week orally, before the students see the spelling, to help them with the pronunciation. To do this, draw a 'diary page' on the board with just the first letter of each day on it. Once you have introduced all the names, practise them with choral repetition. Students could try to race each other in saying the seven days, or pairs of students could be timed saying the days in turns, to see which pair is fastest.

1a 💿 Mira la rutina semanal de María. El perro ha roto la agenda. Escucha (1–7) y pon en orden. AT1.3, AT3.2; 7T1, 7L3

Reading and listening presentation of the days of the week and times on the hour in the context of free time activities. Students listen and note the order of the activities. While the general gist should be clear, this presentation actually combines three new language points: exercises in the present tense, days of the week and times. Most students will need to deal with each of these separately.

If you have already introduced the days of the week as vocabulary items you will still need to elicit the fact that the way to say 'on (Mondays)' is *los (lunes)*. On a separate hearing, ask students to listen specifically for this formula. It is also explained in the Gramática section further down the page.

For the activities students will have met some of these verbs in the present, and all of them in the infinitive in the four previous pages. Remind them of the regular ending in *-o* for regular verbs in the present.

For work on the time see exercise 1c.

Extension

Once students are happy with all the new language, ask questions of the sort *¿qué actividad es el lunes a las cinco?* and 'have students read the answer?'

TRANSCRIPT   CD2, track 29

1 Los lunes voy de compras **con mi madre** a las cinco.
2 Los martes **normalmente** juego al tenis **con mi hermano y mi amiga Mélissa** a las cuatro.
3 Los miércoles navego por Internet a las nueve **de la noche**.
4 Los jueves voy al cine **con mi familia** a las cinco.
5 Los viernes salgo con mis amigos a las ocho.
6 Los sábados voy al centro **con mis amigos y mi novio** a las cuatro.
7 Los domingos **siempre** hago los deberes desde la una hasta las ocho.

Answers

lunes	Voy de compras – 5.00
martes	Juego al tenis – 4.00
miércoles	Navego por Internet – 9.00
jueves	Voy al cine – 5.00
viernes	Salgo con mis amigos – 8.00
sábado	Voy al centro – 4.00
domingo	Hago los deberes – 1.00–8.00

1b 💿 ¡extra! Escribe otra información. AT1.3; 7L3

Students listen again and note any extra information. You might want to prompt them in the right direction (who they do the activities with, what part of the day...).

Extension

The adverbs *normalmente* and *siempre* are new and could be used by more confident students in their accounts of their own routine.

Answers

See bold print in transcript.

Once students have listenened to the new phrases several times use Flashcards 28–39 to practise the new verb forms. Hold up a card and say e.g. *practico la natación*, encourage the class and then individuals to repeat. Build up three or four new phrases in this way, then hold up a card and ask e.g. *¿practico la natación o juego al tenis?* Elicit the correct phrase. Once a few of these new forms have been built up, say and write up e.g. *veo la tele, me gusta ver la tele* and ask students to tell you what the difference is. (If necessary ask students to look back to p.54 for a reminder of the gerund v infinitive difference.) Make sure that students realise that they are now talking about what they actually do rather than what they like doing.

¡Así se hace! Telling the time 7S2

Saying at what time, on the hour. This section should be dealt with in conjunction with the following exercise.

1c 💡 ☑ 💿 Listen again. How did María express the times? What did she say before the numbers? AT1.3; 7S2, 7L3

Students listen again to the recording, this time specifically for how to express time. Students have already heard the time in Spanish a few times. Ask students to tell you what the odd one out is (*a la una*) and why it's different.

Once students are clear about how times are expressed they listen again and note down the times that are mentioned. This can either be done in Spanish words, as in the example, or in figures.

The penultimate sentence does not give a time while in the last one a duration is given.

Extension

Ask students to listen and tell you what the time expression in the last sentence means, then ask them to make up other examples using the same construction.

This exercise could be used for assessment.

Answers

1 A las cinco (5.00) **2** A las cuatro (4.00) **3** A las nueve (9.00) **4** A las cinco (5.00) **5** A las nueve (9.00) **6** –
7 desde la una hasta las ocho (1.00–8.00) – uses the phrase desde... hasta (from... until)

2a 📝 Escribe tu diario. AT4.2–4; 7S9, 7T4, 7T5

Writing practice. Students now produce their own weekly diary.

Support

Some students may need a writing frame to help them.

Remind them that they can put more than one entry per day if required.

For less confident students omit the greyed-out columns.

lunes martes miércoles jueves viernes sábado domingo	practico la natación juego al tenis etc.	con mis amigos con mi hermana etc.	a la una a las dos etc.	en el polideportivo etc.

Extension

More able students could be encouraged to use a dictionary, to include activities they have not learned the Spanish for yet.

2b ◯ Habla con tu pareja. Di lo que hace cada día. AT2.2–4, AT4.2–4; 7S3, 7S9, 7L4, 7T5

Before doing the exercise students need to be familiar with the verb forms explained in the Grámatica section on page 57 and to be able to move between them.

Use the Flashcards 28–39 to practise asking and answering questions in the third person.

Ask a student *¿Qué haces el lunes?* Elicit the answer e.g. *Hago los deberes.*

Next ask the class *¿Qué hace (Kayleigh) el lunes?*

Elicit the answer *(Kayleigh) hace los deberes.*

Where appropriate, check students have remembered to change from *mis* to *sus amigos.*

Pairwork speaking and writing exercise.

Students ask their partners what they do on specific days of the week, make notes on the answers and write them up in the third person.

Make sure that students have understood this process before they start. To simplify their task they should make abbreviated notes on their partner's responses.

Gramática – on Monday, on Mondays 7S2

Explanation of the way to say 'on Monday', 'on Mondays'. Teachers will probably have asked students to look at this section while working on exercise 1.

Gramática – the present tense 7W5

This section first recaps on the regular -ar verbs. Encourage students to look back at the singular paradigm of these, as suggested.

The concept of stem-changing verbs is a difficult one and will need an in-depth explanation. Introduce it by encouraging students to look for the verb 'to play' on pages 52 and 53, and spot any differences in the spelling. Apart from the obvious ending change, they will notice the difference in the stem vowel. After that, the Grammar explanation and practice exercise 3 can follow.

3 📖 Rellena los espacios en blanco. AT3.2–3, AT4.2; 7W5

A series of gapped sentences into which students are required to insert the correct form of a stem-changing verb from the grammar section.

Answers

1	juega	4	juegan
2	haces	5	salgo
3	juegas	6	juega

WS 55 (Gramática) offers further practice of these types of verbs.

4a ✎ Rellena el diario. ¿Qué haces y a qué hora? Usa los dibujos. Añade información si puedes. AT4.3–4; 7T5

Students use a series of visual cues to write an account of what the speaker does through the week.

Support

Some students may be happier just dealing with the three categories: *Día*, *Actividad* and *¿A qué hora?*

Extension

The example suggests adding extra information not apparent from the picture. NB: Not all the basic answers lend themselves to the suggested extra categories of information.

Answers

Día	Actividad	¿Con quién?	¿Dónde?	¿A qué hora?
Los lunes	navego por Internet	con mis amigos	en mi dormitorio	a las siete
Los martes	juego al fútbol	con mi hermano	en el polideportivo	a las tres
Los miércoles	hago los deberes	con mi amiga	en mi dormitorio	a las cinco
Los jueves	veo la tele	con mi familia	en el salón	a las nueve
Los viernes	salgo con mis amigos	–	al centro	a las seis
Los sábados	voy al cine	con mi hermano	en el centro	a la una

¡Así se hace! Using language you already know 7W1

A reminder to recycle vocabulary from other topics. Before embarking on the next exercise, ask students to brainstorm what other vocabulary that they have learnt might be reused in the context of this topic (e.g. places in the town, rooms in the house, means of getting to places, family members, pets, opinions).

4b ◯ Habla con tu pareja. AT2.2–4; 7S9, 7T5, 7L4

This exercise can be used as a follow-up. It is actually an extension of exercise 2b. After students have written their own diary, including some of the extra information suggested in 4a, they interview their partners who should produce similar extra information about themselves.

4c ✎ ¡extra! ¿Y tu pareja? ¿Qué hace? AT4.2–4; 7S3, 7T5, 8L3

More able students could be encouraged to prepare a report on their partner's activities, in the third person, thus adapting what their partner said in the first person.

WS 56 ¡extra! offers a piece of more advanced reading on the topics of this and the preceding sections.

Plenary

☑ Ask students to look back at the objectives at the start of the section and to consider how well they think they have assimilated them. As you read out each objective, students hold up pieces of differently coloured card to show whether they are very confident, quite confident or not confident.

Alternative plenary

☑ Divide the class into groups. Ask students to write down three things that they have learnt, then to share it with the rest of the group and finally with the class.

6D ¿Dónde nos encontramos?

pp. 58–59

> **Objectives:**
> • learn how to arrange to meet
> • understand opening and closing times
> • learn how to pronounce t and d
> **Key Language:** see p.91 for full list
> **Skills:** reading signs
> **Pronunciation:** t and d
> **Resources:** OHT 13 (conversations about going out); CD2; Worksheets 49 (Resumen), 51 (Hablar), 52 (Leer), 53 (Escribir), 54 (¡Así se hace!); Workbooks A and B p.31; Just Click CD-Rom.

On these two pages students learn how to say at what time things open and close, to ask someone out and to arrange to meet.

Lesson starter

Ask students to work in groups to think of the names for all the places in town that people might want to go out to or where they might arrange to meet. After two minutes ask each group in turn to give you a name. The winning group is the one with the most names.

Alternative lesson starter (for lessons starting part-way through the section)

Give each pair of students a slip of paper as they come in. Ask pairs to make a set of 'odd one out' and to write it on the paper. Each pair then passes their effort on to the next pair who must solve it before passing it on again.

1 📖 Lee y une las frases. AT2.3, AT3.3; 7W8, 7T1, 7T3

This reading exercise uses a mixture of speech bubbles, notices and adverts. There is some new language, mostly single parts of verbs: *abrir, cerrar, apetecer, querer, poder, encontrarse,* and *cansado/a.* Generally, apart from the odd appearance in a rubric, the same single verb part is reused later in the section.

Support

You may prefer to treat the new verbs as lexical items at this stage. For instance, the reflexive is dealt with in detail in a later unit.

Extension

Students have already met another reflexive verb – *llamarse.* You may like to draw parallels with this and *encontrarse.*

Before they start, ask students to look through the presentation and to decide what sort of language they might expect to meet. Elicit the fact that the thought bubbles give information about opening times. From the pictures students should also grasp that the people are talking about going out and making arrangements.

Extension

Ask more able students to cover up the vocabulary on a first read-through.

Next ask students to read the frames through carefully to themselves several times. Establish what people think the gist of the story is, then brainstorm for extra details.

Finally ask some individuals to read the story aloud. This presentation could be learnt by heart and acted out, or adapted with some of the details being changed.

Students should now be ready to tackle the comprehension exercise, joining the two halves of sentences that paraphrase the events of the story, in the third person. To find the correct pairs students will have to look at the thought bubbles as well as the main photos. For number 7 they will need to be aware that *se* and *encuentran* go together.

Answers

1 e **2** c **3** a **4** b **5** g **6** d **7** f

2a ☑ 💿 Escucha (1–4). ¿Qué quieren hacer? ¿Dónde se encuentran y a qué hora? Copia y rellena el cuadro. AT1.4; 7L3

Students listen and fill in the grid. In the Actividad column they should write the activity the two people in each conversation end up doing. Offer the possibility for students to listen to the CD as many times as they need to, perhaps just filling in one column on each listening.

This exercise might be suitable for assessment.

> **TRANSCRIPT**   **CD2, track 30**
>
> **1** – Hola, Ismael. ¿Qué quieres hacer esta tarde?
> – No sé. ¿Quieres jugar al fútbol en el polideportivo?
> – Sí, muy bien. ¿Dónde nos encontramos?
> – ¿Qué tal en la entrada?
> – Muy bien. En la entrada a las tres. ¡Hasta luego!
> **2** – ¿Qué tal, Sara?
> – Muy bien. ¿Qué te apetece hacer esta tarde?
> – Podemos jugar al tenis en el parque.
> – No, el parque cierra a las cuatro.
> – Vale, entonces vamos al cine.
> – Muy bien. ¿Dónde nos encontramos?
> – En mi casa a las seis.
> – Perfecto, hasta luego.
> – Adiós
> **3** – Hola, Pedro
> – ¿Qué tal? Oye, ¿quieres salir esta tarde?
> – Sí, ¿quieres ir de compras?
> – No, no tengo dinero.
> – Bueno, entonces vamos al centro.
> – Muy bien. Nos encontramos en mi casa, ¿vale?
> – Muy bien. ¿A qué hora?
> – A las siete.   ▶

> **4** – ¡Hola, Pilar! ¿Tienes planes para esta tarde?
> – No, ¿qué quieres hacer?
> – Podemos jugar al fútbol en el polideportivo.
> – No, estoy muy cansada.
> – Entonces, ¿qué tal ver la tele en mi casa?
> – ¡Genial!. Nos encontramos en tu casa a las dos.
> – ¡Hasta luego!

Answers

	¿Actividad?	¿Dónde se encuentran?	¿Cuándo?	¡extra! ¿Problemas?
1	jugar al fútbol	polideportivo, en la entrada	a las tres	–
2	ir al cine	en mi casa	a las seis	parque cierra a las cuatro
3	ir al centro	en mi casa	a las siete	X no tiene dinero
4	ver la tele	en mi casa	a las dos	cansada

WS 51 (Hablar) offers an information-gap exercise on the same theme. It could be used from this point on.

To alert students to other possibilities, Worksheet 52 (Leer) uses a range of vocabulary from this and earlier topics in a series of rhyming exchanges.

2b ¡extra! Escucha otra vez. ¿Hay problemas? AT1.4; 7L3

The exercise can be further extended if students are asked to note down which plans are not accepted and the reasons for not accepting them. (See grid for answers.)

3a Lee el correo electrónico. Contesta a las preguntas en inglés. AT3.3; 7T1

This email reuses various formulae that have already been presented. In addition it introduces the expression ¿qué te parece? It ultimately provides a model for students to write similar messages of their own. As a first exercise, students answer questions on the email in English.

Answers

1 Going swimming or playing football at the sports centre.
2 In the entrance/foyer of the sports centre.
3 11 o'clock on Saturday.

3b ☑ ✑ ¡extra! Contesta al correo electrónico. Presenta un problema y sugiere un plan alternativo. AT4.3–4; 7T5, 7T6

This exercise would be suitable for assessment.

Students are invited to compose a reply to the email posing a problem and suggesting an alternative plan.

After they have written the mail, they could be encouraged to exchange them (randomly or not) and answer the one they receive, accepting the invitation or rejecting it, and giving reasons.

4 Q Habla con tu pareja. Mira las posibilidades. Inventa conversaciones. AT2.2–4; 7T2, 7L5

A multiple-choice flowchart that offers various possibilities based on the context of suggesting/accepting/refusing invitations.

Support

Practise different version of the conversations as a class exercise first of all before asking students to work in pairs. OHT 13 offers visual-only versions of the same sorts of conversation, which might be easier for less confident students.

Extension

Encourage more able students to work on their own in pairs preparing versions of these conversations which they can then act out without the text.

WS 53 (Escribir) also looks at the language needed for these sorts of situation.

Pronunciación: *t, d* 7W6, 7L6, 7L1

Students should practise these sounds with closed books, at least to begin with. Before putting them in words they could be asked to listen and repeat just individual syllables (*ta, te, ti, to, tu, pa, pe, pi, po, pu*), before doing the same with known words from the unit. Students listen to and repeat the following words, concentrating on *t* and *d*.

TRANSCRIPT CD2, track 31

polideportivo	tienes
martes	tres
tiendas	podemos

Extension

Students look for other words and test each other as to how accurately they are pronouncing the sounds.

WS 54 ¡Así se hace! also focuses on these two sounds.

Plenary

☑ Discuss with the class what they have learnt in this section and in what situations they think it would be useful if they went to Spain. (Inviting someone out you liked, refusing someone you didn't like etc.) What things do they now know how to say?

Alternative plenary

☑ Display groups of words from exercise 3 and ask students to choose and write down the one they consider the odd one out (in bold in the grid), e.g.

1	ir al cine; ver la tele; **muy bien**; ir de compras
2	en mi casa; delante de la entrada; en la puerta del cine; **a las tres**
3	a las siete; **a la una**; a las tres; a las ocho
4	no puedo; estoy cansado; **el lunes**; no tengo dinero
5	¿quieres ir al cine?; ¿te apetece ver la tele?; **el cine abre a las seis**; podemos jugar al fútbol

Invite students to call out the words they have written for *número uno*. If you hear different words being called out, challenge students to justify their choice. Repeat with *números 2, 3, 4* and *5*.

Support

Leave out *número 5* or more.

6E Un fin de semana perfecto
page 60

Objectives:
* talk about plans for next weekend
* use *ir a* + infinitive
Key Language: see p.91 for full list
Grammar: immediate future
Resources: CD2; Worksheets: 50 (Escuchar), 56
(¡extra!); Workbooks A and B p.32; *Just Click* CD-Rom.

On the first of these pages the immediate future is presented and practised in the now-familiar context of free time activities. The second page contains the usual resumé of the unit.

Lesson starter

On the board prepare a list of the verbs that feature in the free time activity vocabulary: *navegar, ir, ver, hacer, jugar, tocar, salir, practicar.* Ask students to work in pairs to copy them down and to think of at least one appropriate free time ending for each.

Alternative lesson starter *(for lessons starting part-way through the section)*

As above but instead of just the infinitive write *voy a navegar, voy a ir, voy a ver* etc. and ask students to finish the phrases as before.

Introduction

With the help of flashcards 28–39 and/or OHT 13, the teacher can present the plans for the future, in the first person to begin with.

Begin by establishing that you are talking about the future by pointing to or writing up a date several days in the future. Say *El sábado voy a ver la tele.* Get the class to repeat after you. Make sure that they are saying *voy a...* Now expand your utterance to two or three activities: *El sábado, voy a ver la tele, voy a salir con mis amigos* etc. Again get them to repeat. Now ask *¿y tú?* Encourage students to produce single utterances beginning with *voy a...* If necessary, prompt them with flashcards or the OHT.

1a ⊙ Escucha y lee. AT1.5, AT3.5; 7W5, 7L3, 8W5

If you haven't introduced the immediate future separately, this text could be used first of all as a purely listening text (students pick up as many plans as they can, ignoring for the time being the future continuous), or as a reading exercise (same sort of exercise).

Ask the class to look and listen as you play the CD. Play it several times if necessary. Ask them to tell you what the gist of the story is.

Ask them what they've noticed about the passage. (As well as the first person singular of *ir* it uses other persons of *ir* to form the immediate future.)

TRANSCRIPT CD2, track 32

– ¡Hola, Paco!
– ¡Hola, Sara!, ¿qué tal? ¿Qué vas a hacer el fin de semana?
– Bueno, el sábado por la mañana voy a dormir y después voy a ir al centro con Inés. Vamos a ir de compras.
– Y yo, por la mañana voy a jugar al fútbol en el polideportivo con mis amigos. Luego vamos a ir a la cafetería. ▶

– Mis padres van a ir al cine por la tarde, así que yo voy a ver la tele en mi casa. ¿Y tú? ¿Qué vas a hacer?
– Creo que voy a hacer mis deberes, y después mi hermano y yo vamos a jugar al tenis.
– ¿Y el domingo?
– Voy a ir al centro por la mañana. Por la tarde Luís y yo vamos a ir al cine y después voy a ir a mi cama temprano.
– Pues mi familia y yo vamos a ir a Madrid el domingo.
– ¡Qué bien! Los dos vamos a tener un fin de semana perfecto.
– Sí. ¡Estupendo!

1b 💡 ☑ 📖 Lee el texto. ¿Cómo se dicen las frases en español? AT3.5; 7S9

Students find in the text the corresponding Spanish sentences. Students will need to study the paradigm in the Gramática section before embarking on this exercise.

This exercise could be used for assessment.

Answers

1 Vamos a ir de compras.
2 Voy a dormir.
3 Voy a jugar al fútbol.
4 Vamos a ir a la cafetería.
5 Vamos a jugar al tenis.
6 Van a ir al cine.
7 Vamos a ir a Madrid.
8 ¿Qué vas a hacer?

Gramática: the immediate future 7W5, 8W5

Presentation of the paradigm of the immediate future with *jugar*. Students should study this section before doing exercise 1b.

Here are some extra phrases for students to translate:
1 I am going to go out with friends.
2 You (*sing.*) are going to go to town.
3 He is going to play tennis.
4 We are going to surf the net.
5 You (*pl.*) are going to do your homework.
6 They are going to go swimming.

WS 55 (Gramática) offers further work on this topic.

2 💬 Habla con tu pareja. Cambia las frases. AT2.3–5; 7S9, 7L5

A pairwork exercise that requires students to discuss their future plans.

Support

Help less confident students by offering them a frame of choices to get them started.

Extension

More confident students may be able to produce a more sustained and varied conversation, listing their plans for different days, using plural forms to talk about what they plan to do with other people and adding extra expressions (opinions, likes, dislikes etc.).

3 ✍ Escribe en el diario tu fin de semana perfecto. AT4.3–5; 7S9, 7L5

This is the written equivalent of the previous exercise.

Support

Again, help less confident students by offering them a frame of choices to get them started.

Extension

Students, particularly more able ones, should be encouraged to include as much extra information as possible. Dictionaries could be used at this stage.

Plenary

☑ Ask the class to look carefully at the Resumen. Go through it together. Does all the vocabulary now look familiar? Have they understood the grammar points? Ask students to indicate whether they are happy, neutral or unhappy about each section by holding up appropriately coloured cards.

Alternative plenary

☑ Ask students in pairs to explain the formation of the immediate future as if teaching it to someone who missed the lesson.

Resumen *(page 61)*

This section offers a resumé of all the vocabulary, grammar, skills and tips presented in the unit.

Repaso *(page 62)*

☑ This page revises work from Units 5 and 6.

1a 💿 Escucha (1–6). Une las personas con los dibujos. AT1.2–3; 7L3

Students listen and match each person's description of where they live with the appropriate picture.

TRANSCRIPT | **CD2, track 33**

1 ¡Hola! Soy María. Vivo en una casa muy bonita. Está en el campo, cerca de un pueblo.
2 ¿Qué tal? Soy Andrés. Vivo en una casa bastante pequeña, con mis padres y mi hermano Marco. Está en el centro de un pueblo muy pequeño que se llama Ronda. Es blanca.
3 ¡Buenas tardes! Soy Pepa. Vivo en una casa adosada. Está en una ciudad que se llama Granada.
4 ¡Qué tal! Soy Ana. Vivo con mis padres en un bloque de pisos. Yo vivo en la primera planta. Lo malo es que es muy antiguo. ¡A mí me gustan los pisos modernos!
5 ¡Hola! Soy Carlos. Vivo con mi hermana y mi perro en un piso muy moderno. Está en la segunda planta. ¡Me encanta mi piso!
6 ¡Buenos días! Me llamo Belén. Vivo en un chalet precioso. Está en la costa, cerca de la playa, y las vistas son magníficas. Vivo con mis padres y mi hermana Marta.

Answers

1 d 2 e 3 b 4 c 5 a 6 f

1b 💿 ¡extra! Escribe otros detalles. AT1.4–5; 7L3

Students listen again and note further details.

Answers

1 muy bonita, en el campo, cerca de un pueblo.
2 bastante pequeña, con padres y hermano, en el centro de un pueblo pequeño, se llama Ronda, blanca.
3 en la ciudad de Granada.
4 moderno, con hermano y perro, en la segunda planta.
5 precioso, en la costa, cerca de la playa, vistas magníficas, con padres y hermana.

2 ✏️ Contesta a las siguientes preguntas. AT4.3–5; 7S9, 7T5

Students answer a series of questions about themselves, including details of future plans.

The attainment target reached will depend on the fullness and accuracy of the answers.

3a 💬 Haz las preguntas en el ejercicio 2 a tu pareja. Anota sus respuestas. AT2.3–5; 7S9, 7L4

Students work in pairs to ask and answer the questions from the previous exercise. As they do this, each student should make notes on what the other one says. Again the exchange can provide opportunities for using a range of verb structures including the future.

3b 💬 ¡extra! Presenta a tu pareja al resto de la clase. AT2.3–5; 8L3

Students now relay to the rest of the class the information they have been given by their partner. This will entail re-reading and expanding any notes and changing the verb person to the third person. The attainment target reached will depend on the range and fullness of the account, fluency of delivery and grammatical accuracy.

4 📖 Pilla al intruso. AT3.1; 7W1

An odd man out exercise. The vocabulary is taken from Units 5 and 6.

Answers

1 natación (not a piece of furniture) 2 casa (not a sport)
3 cocina (not a type of building) 4 pueblo (not an adjective describing distance) 5 piso (not a room in the house).

Reading *(page 63)*
AT3.4; 7T1, 7T3, 7C3, 7C4

5 📖 Contesta a las preguntas en inglés.

A photo story about some teenage intrigues. Students read the story and answer a set of questions in English. In the text, the superlative form *cansadísima* is new but should be guessable. *Además* is new but not crucial. As well as *tener, tener que* is used with familiar pastime vocabulary. Students will need to understand this structure. They should be able to work it out from context or by checking in a dictionary.

Answers

1 Going swimming 2 She's very tired 3 The cinema 4 It's expensive and she has no money 5 Going to his house to watch TV 6 She's got a lot of homework 7 Go to play football together.

¡Ahora, tú! *(pp. 128–129)*

Differentiated self-access reading and writing exercises: see page 37 for more information.

page 128

1 📖 Match up the opinions.

Answers

1 b **2** a **3** c **4** e **5** h **6** f **7** d **8** g

3 ✏️ Put the words in the box into the following categories.

Adjectives	Places	Days	Seasons	Sports
aburrido barato divertido caro emocionante	polideportivo cine colegio	martes domingo miércoles jueves sábado lunes viernes	primavera verano otoño invierno	fútbol tenis natación

page 129

1 📖 Match up the questions.

Answers

1 e **2** d **3** g **4** f **5** c **6** a **7** b

3a 📖 Are the sentences true or false?

Answers

1 V **2** M **3** M **4** V **5** M **6** M **7** V **8** V

3b ✏️ Correct the false sentences.

2 Ignacio piensa que el fútbol es emocionante y divertido.
3 A Ignacio no le gusta ir de compras.
5 A Ignacio le encanta tocar el piano.
6 A Ignacio no le gusta escuchar la música de su grupo.

Worksheets Unit 6

48 Tiempo libre AT3.1; 7W1

At the start of work on pages 52–53 students can use the cards for practice in identifying the new phrases. Later on, during work on the same page, the visuals can be used for pairwork practice of *me gusta/encanta* + pastime phrases.

During work on pages 60–61 the cards can be used again for pairwork practice of *ir a* + pastime phrases.

49 Resumen AT3.1; 7W1

A useful worksheet version of the Unit Resumen. It can be used for homework and learning exercises.

50 Escuchar 7L3

This listening exercise requires students to listen twice to the same extracts, extracting different information each time. (Gist and detail.)

The extracts revise the pastime phrases from early in the unit and represent them in several forms: in the infinitive with *gustar, ir a, quiero* and as present tense verbs.

a Students listen to hear whether each person is going to do the activity mentioned or not.

b This time they make a note of what is said about the activity.

TRANSCRIPT

CD2, track 34

1 – Hola, Inés. ¿Vas a practicar la natación mañana?
 – No, no voy a practicar la natación esta semana – ¡es aburrido! Voy a salir de compras con Sara. Me encanta salir de compras – ¡es divertido! ▶

2 – Y tú, Paco, ¿qué vas a hacer, el viernes?
 – Voy a hacer los deberes. ¡Es un rollo!
 – ¿Y el sábado?
 – Voy a jugar al tenis.
 – ¡Jugar al tenis! ¿No es caro?
 – Sí, es caro, pero me gusta mucho.

3 – ¿José María? ¿Vas a ir al centro el sábado?
 – Sí, voy a ir al centro. Me encanta ir al centro los sábados – ¡es genial!
 – Podemos ir al cine después.
 – Ah, no quiero ir al cine – es demasiado caro. ▶

4 – ¡Dígame!
 – Sara, ¿que vas a hacer el domingo?
 – Voy a salir con amigos. Es divertido – ¡y es barato también!

5 – Elena, ¿quieres ver la tele?
 – No gracias, Papá – la tele es aburrida. Navego por Internet – es más educativo.

6 – ¡Miguel! ¡MIGUEL!
 – Sí, mamá.
 – ¿Qué haces?
 – Pues, escucho música… ¡Es emocionante!
 – ¡Miguel! ¡MIGUEL!
 – ¡Sí!
 – ¿Y tus ejercicios en el piano?
 – ¡Uf! Tocar el piano – ¡es un rollo!

Answers

	Inés	Paco	José María	Sara	Elena	Miguel
ir al centro			✓ genial			
ir al cine			✗ caro			
practicar la natación	✗ aburrido					
jugar al fútbol						
jugar al tenis		✓ caro				
tocar el piano						✗ rollo
salir con amigos				✓ divertido, barato		
salir de compras	✓ divertido					
ver la tele					✗ aburrido	
navegar por Internet					✓ educativo	
escuchar música						✓ emocionante
hacer los deberes		✗ rollo				

51 Hablar AT2.2–4; 7S9, 7L5

An information-gap exercise that practises places to go and pastime vocabulary, times and places to meet. It can be offered during work on pages 54–55. With the idea that the speakers are completing communal plans, the questions and answers call on the use of the first person plural of various familiar verbs. The example and the information box should cue students in to this form.

52 Leer AT3.3; 7T2

A poem to read and complete any time during or after work on pages 58–59.

1a The missing words are all rhymes so reading it aloud will help.

Answers

1 g 2 a 3 e 4 d 5 f 6 j 7 c 8 i 9 h
10 b

1b Once it is completed students can be encouraged to practise reading it aloud, perhaps working in pairs and dividing the lines up between them.

2 ¡extra!

Students are invited to make up further poems. Encourage them to look for rhymes in the glossary or in the Resumenes of previously completed units.

53 Escribir AT4.2–4; 7T6

A chance to do some creative writing. It can be attempted once students have worked on pages 58–59.

a Students are given a cartoon story with a set of blank balloons. The boxes at the bottom offer some possible choices. More adventurous students should be encouraged to go beyond these to produce versions of their own.

b,c Following the reminder at the top of the page, a suggestion that students compare what they have written, perhaps producing further differently worded versions.

54 ¡Así se hace! 7W7, 7L1

a The first exercise on this sheet tests students' aural comprehension of words containing the featured sounds 't' and 'd'. Students find and number the words as they hear them spoken. (7L1 – sound patterns)

TRANSCRIPT
CD2, track 35
1 discoteca
2 delante
3 apetece
4 dormitorio ▶

5 demasiado
6 tarde
7 treinta y tres
8 dentro
9 polideportivo
10 encanta
11 detrás
12 cómodo
13 tengo
14 tienda
15 antipático
16 andando
17 bonito
18 jardín
19 podemos
20 divertido
21 ordenador
22 cansado
23 adosada
24 gato
25 setenta

b As a preparation for the next exercise, students highlight the 't's and 'd's in the words on the page.

c A pairwork exercise that again requires students to practise the featured sounds in these words. The exercise also revises numbers. Students take it in turns to choose a number and say the corresponding word, paying particular attention to the 't' and 'd' sounds.

d ¡extra! Students are asked to identify and list the different parts of speech in the list.

Nouns: discoteca, dormitorio, gato, jardín, ordenador, polideportivo, tarde *(also adverb)*, tienda

Adjectives: adosada, antipático, bonito, cansado, cómodo, divertido

Verbs: andando, apetece, encanta, podemos, tengo

Prepositions: delante, dentro, detrás
Numbers: setenta, treinta y tres

55 Gramática 7W5

1 A reminder of how stem-changing verbs operate. Students complete the grid. The bold type reminds them which parts of the verb actually change their vowels.

	u>ue	e>ie	o>ue
	jugar *(to play)*	tener *(to have)*	poder *(to be able to)*
I	**juego**	tengo	**puedo**
you *(sing.)*	**juegas**	**tienes**	**puedes**
he/she/it	**juega**	**tiene**	**puede**
we	jugamos	tenemos	podemos
you *(pl.)*	jugáis	tenéis	podéis
they	**juegan**	**tienen**	**pueden**

2 More practice with the tricky intransitive verbs *gustar* and *encantar*. The exercise requires students to translate a series of sentences, reminding them that the English equivalent is not a literal translation. It also underlines other differences like there being only one word for 'you' in English and having to decide whether a third person singular verb in Spanish refers to 'he' or 'she'.

Answers

1 I like listening to music.
2 Do you like Spanish.
3 He/She likes going out with friends.
4 We like going to Barcelona.
5 He/She loves rock music.
6 Do you like dogs?

3 Practice in using the immediate future. Students fill in the right part of *ir* and the all-important *a*.

Answers

1 Voy a hacer mis deberes.
2 ¿Vas a escuchar la música?
3 Vamos a ir al cine.
4 Van a practicar la natación.
5 Vais a ver la tele.
6 ¿Va a jugar al fútbol?

56 ¡extra! AT3.4; 7T4

a An email that draws on the language of this and earlier units and introduces a limited amount of new time words (*entonces, después, luego, quedarse*). Students should be encouraged to guess the meanings of the new words and then to check them in a dictionary.

b Students decide whether a set of statements are true or false.

Answers

1 V 2 M 3 M 4 V 5 M 6 V

c Correction of the false sentences.

2 Miguel no sale martes porque hace sus deberes.
3 Juega al tenis y entonces va a casa.
5 Le encanta tocar el piano.

d A set of questions to answer on the email. The questions use the third person so students must use this in their answers too.

Suggested answers

1 Practica la natación a las cinco (entre las cinco y las siete).
2 Si no tiene dinero el jueves, escucha la música en (su) casa.
3 Después de jugar al tenis está muy cansado.
4 ¿Le gusta mucho tocar el piano. (Piensa que es genial.)
5 Sale de compras los sábados por la mañana con su madre.
6 Domingo va a ir al restaurante con su familia y entonces va a hacer sus deberes.

Pruebas Unidades 5 y 6

R and A file pp.124–127

Prueba: Escuchar *(page 124)*
ex 1: AT1.3

Answers

Example: watching TV **1**; swimming **5**; playing the piano **6**; surfing the net **2**; going to the cinema **3**; listening to music **10**; going to town **8**; playing tennis **7**; going out with friends **4**; shopping **9**; doing homework **11**
Mark scheme: 1 mark for each correct answer.
Total: 10. 8+ shows evidence of performance at Level 3.

TRANSCRIPT
CD4, track 31
Ejemplo: **1** Me gusta ver la tele.
   2 Me encanta navegar por Internet.
   3 Me gusta ir al cine.
   4 Los sábados, salgo con mis amigos.
   5 Los jueves, practico la natación.
   6 No me gusta tocar el piano.
   7 En verano, me gusta jugar al tenis.
   8 No me gusta mucho ir al centro.
   9 Me encanta salir de compras.
   10 Me encanta escuchar música.
   11 ¡Hago los deberes todos los días!

ex 2: AT1.4

Answers

Example: **a** 1 **b** 2 **c** 5 **d** 6 **e** 4 **f** 3
Mark scheme: 1 mark for each correct answer.
Total: 5. 3+ shows evidence of performance at Level 4.

TRANSCRIPT
CD4, track 32
Ejemplo: **1** En mi piso, hay dos dormitorios, una cocina, un salón y un cuarto de baño.
   2 En mi piso, hay tres dormitorios, una cocina, un comedor y un cuarto de baño. Hay un aseo aparte.
   3 En casa, tengo dos dormitorios, un cuarto de baño y una terraza con garaje.
   4 En mi piso hay tres dormitorios, una cocina y un cuarto de baño. También, tenemos un jardín con un pequeño garaje.
   5 Mi piso es muy pequeño. Solo hay un dormitorio, una cocina-comedor y una terraza al final.
   6 Yo vivo en un piso muy grande. Hay cuatro dormitorios, dos cocinas, dos cuartos de baño, un garaje doble y un jardín grande.

ex 3: AT1.4

Answers

1V **2**V **3**V **4**M **5**M **6**M **7**V **8**V **9**V **10**M **11**M
Mark scheme: 1 mark for each correct answer.
Total: 10. 7+ shows evidence of performance at Level 4.

¡**extra!** 1 mark for each extra correct piece of information: She lives in the centre of town. Bathroom is on the first floor. Dining room is on the ground floor. Living room is on the first floor. Sofa and armchairs are in the living room. Lamp is next to the computer. The whole family uses the computer. She loves the cinema. She's going to the cinema at 3.00 with her friends. She asks about your free time.

TRANSCRIPT
CD4, track 33
Hola me llamo Katia. Vivo en una gran casa adosada en el centro de la cuidad. En la primera planta hay cuatro dormitorios y un cuarto de baño. En la planta baja, hay un comedor, una cocina y un salón.

El salón es muy bonito porque hay un sofá, unos sillones, y una televisión, claro. Mis padres tienen un equipo de música. Al lado de la lámpara hay un ordenador para toda la familia. Me gusta mucho navegar por Internet y también me encanta el cine. El sábado a las tres, voy a ir al cine con mis amigos, y después vamos a jugar al tenis. Tú, ¿qué haces en tu tiempo libre?

Prueba: Hablar *(page 125)*
ex 1: AT2.3

Possible answers

2 La lámpara está encima de la mesa. OR La mesa está debajo de la lámpara.
3 El sillón está al lado del sofá. OR El sofá está al lado del sillón.
4 El lavaplatos está al lado de la nevera. OR La nevera está al lado del lavaplatos.
5 El teléfono está encima del equipo musical. OR El equipo musical está debajo del teléfono.
Mark scheme: 2 marks for each sentence which would be understood by a sympathetic native speaker – 1 for the two items and 1 for the está plus position.
Total: 8. 6+ shows evidence of performance at Level 3.

ex 2: AT2.4

Answers

Any answer which makes sense in context is acceptable.
Mark scheme: 1 mark for each sentence which would be understood by a sympathetic native speaker.
Total: 5. 3+ shows evidence of performance at Level 4.

ex 3: AT2.4

Answers

2 El jueves, voy a navegar por internet a las siete.
3 El miércoles, voy a jugar al tenis a las tres.
4 El domingo, voy a hacer mis deberes a las ocho.
5 El martes, voy a ver la tele a las seis.
Mark scheme: 3 marks for each sentence which would be understood by a sympathetic native speaker. 1 for the day expression, 1 for the future tense activity and 1 for the time expression.
Total: 12. 8+ shows evidence of performance at Level 4.

Prueba: Leer *(page 126)*
ex 1: AT3.2

Answers

2 Swimming pool: opens at 2.00, closes at 7.00, Monday or Thursday (the alternative day is a piece of additional information).
3 Sports centre: opens at 1.00, closes at 10.00, Tuesday or Wednesday (see above).

4 Park: opens at 9.00, closes at 6.00, Wednesday or Friday (see above).
Mark scheme: 1 mark for each correct part of the answer.
Total: 12. 8+ shows evidence of performance at Level 2.

¡extra! 1 mark for each additional piece of information.

ex 2: AT3.4

Possible answers

Town: on the coast, swimming pool near the centre, large park, shopping centre, beach, sports centre.
Activities at home: listening to music, surfing the net, playing/practising the guitar.
Questions: What do you do in your free time? Do you play sport? What do you like to do at home?
Mark scheme: 1 mark for each correct answer.
Total: 13. 10+ shows evidence of performance at Level 4.

¡extra! 1 mark for each additional piece of information. Covers all the above not already awarded a mark as a main answer.

Prueba: Escribir (page 127)
ex 1: AT4.4

Answers

Any activities from the unit which make sense in context are acceptable.
Mark scheme: 2 marks for each correct answer, 1 for the time expression and 1 for the future tense activity. The words must not necessarily be absolutely correct but should be easily understood by a sympathetic native speaker.
Total: 10. 7+ shows evidence of performance at Level 4 .

¡extra! 1 mark for each additional piece of information.

ex 2: AT4.4

Answers

Mark scheme: 1 mark for each correct answer. The words must not necessarily be absolutely correct but should be easily understood by a sympathetic native speaker.
Total: 5. 3+ shows evidence of performance at Level 4 .

ex 3: AT4.4

Answers

Mark scheme: 2 marks for each correct answer. The words must not

necessarily be absolutely correct but should be easily understood by a sympathetic native speaker.
Total: 10. 7+ shows evidence of performance at Level 4.

¡extra! 1 mark for each additional piece of information.

Workbook A Unit 6
page 28 (Section A)

Answers

ex 1a:
2 Me gusta mucho ver la tele.
3 Me gusta jugar al tenis.
4 No me gusta ir al cine.
5 Me encanta escuchar música.
6 Me gusta navegar por Internet.

ex 1b:
1 c **2** d **3** b **4** a **5** f **6** e

Note: 'music in questions' and ex 2a are recorded on CD2, tracks 36 and 37 respectively.

page 29 (Section B)

Answers

ex 1a:

e			g				e	
m	d	i	v	e	r	t	i	d	o
o				n	b			u
c				i	a			c
i			c	a	r	o		a
o				l	a			t
n					t			i
a					o			v
n	a	b	u	r	r	i	d	o
t								
e								

ex 1b:
Positive reasons: barato, educativo, genial, divertido, emocionante
Negative reasons: aburrido, caro

ex 2:
2 En primavera me gusta practicar la natación.
3 En otoño me gusta jugar al fútbol.
4 En invierno no me gusta ver la tele.
5 Prefiero ir al cine.
6 En verano no me gusta escuchar música.

page 30 (Section C)

Answers

ex 1:
1 voy de compras.
2 Juego al tenis.
3 Navego por Internet.
4 Voy al cine.

5 Salgo con mis amigos.
6 Voy al centro.
7 Hago los deberes.

ex 2a:
los lunes, los martes, los miércoles, los jueves, los viernes, los sábados, los domingos

ex 2b:
a 4 **b** 1 **c** 2 **d** 5 **e** 3

ex 2c:
1 Los <u>lunes</u>, juego al voleibol a las cinco. On Mondays I play volleyball at five o'clock.
2 Los martes, <u>voy</u> al cine a las siete. On <u>Tuesdays</u> I go to the cinema at seven o'clock.
3 Los miércoles, voy al centro <u>a las doce</u>. On Wednesdays <u>I go</u> to town at twelve o'clock.
4 <u>Los jueves</u>, hago mis deberes a las tres. On Thursdays I do <u>my homework</u> at three o'clock.
5 Los viernes, navego <u>por Internet</u>. On <u>Fridays</u> I surf the net.
6 Los sábados, salgo <u>con</u> mis amigos a las nueve. On Saturdays <u>I go out</u> with my friends at nine o'clock.

page 31 (Section D)

Answers

ex 1a:
2 f **3** a **4** e **5** b **6** d

ex 1b:
8,4　9,2　10,6　11,5　12,3

page 32 (Section E)

Answers

ex 1a:
1 d **2** c **3** a **4** e **5** b

ex 1b:
1 Voy a practicar la natación.
2 ¿Qué vas a hacer el sábado?
3 Va a tocar el piano.
4 Vamos a salir con amigos.
5 Va a ir al cine.
6 Voy a hacer mis deberes.

Workbook B Unit 6
page 28 (Section A)

Answers

ex 1a:
1 Alfredo, ¿te gusta escuchar música?
2 Me gusta mucho ver la tele y tocar la guitarra.
3 Me gusta jugar al voleibol.
4 ¿Qué te gusta hacer en tu tiempo libre?

5 Sí, me encanta la música pop.
6 Pedro, ¿qué deporte te gusta hacer?
7 No, no me gusta nada.
8 ¿Te gusta practicar la natación?

ex 1b:
1,5   4,2   6,3   8,7

Note: The 'intonation in questions' examples are recorded on CD2, track 38.

page 29 (Section B)

Answers

ex 1:

Positivo	Negativo
barato	aburrido
divertido	caro
educativo	estúpido
emocionante	fatal
enérgico	un rollo
genial	
interesante	

ex 2
2 En primavera me gusta practicar la natación.
3 En otoño me gusta jugar al fútbol.
4 En invierno no me gusta ver la tele, prefiero ir al cine.
5 En verano no me gusta escuchar música, prefiero salir con mis amigos.
6 En otoño me gusta tocar el piano.
7 En invierno no me gusta salir con mis amigos, prefiero ver la tele.

page 30 (Section C)

Answers

ex 1:
1 lunes, play, five **2** voy, a, Tuesdays
3 Los, a las doce, On, I go **4** Los jueves, my homework **5** por Internet, Fridays, I can

ex 2:
a **Stem-changing** verbs change the **u** in the infinitive to **ue** in some parts of the verb.
For example, j**u**gar (to play):
I play = j**ue**go
you play = j**ue**gas
he *or* she plays = j**ue**ga

b **Stem-changing** verbs change the **e** in the infinitive to **ie** in some parts of the verb.
For example, t**e**ner (to have):
I have = tengo (doesn't follow the rule!)
you have = t**ie**nes
he *or* she has = t**ie**ne

¡extra!
Stem-changing verbs change the **o** in the infinitive to **ue** in some parts of the verb.
For example, p**o**der (to be able):
I can = p**ue**do
you can = p**ue**des
he *or* she can = p**ue**de

Note: ex 3 is recorded on CD2, track 39, for pronunciation practice.

page 31 (Section D)

Answers

ex 1a:
1 c **2** f **3** a **4** e **5** b **6** d

ex 1b:
7,1   8,4   9,2   10,6   11,5   12,3

¡extra!
exhibition but here bookfair

ex 1c:
1 ¿Quieres escuchar música?
2 ¿Quieres salir?
3 ¿Quieres tocar el piano?
4 ¿Quieres ver la tele?
5 ¿Quieres navegar por Internet?

page 32 (Section E)

Answers

ex 1a:
2 f **3** a **4** h **5** g **6** b **7** e **8** c

ex 1b:
1 Va a tocar el piano a las nueve.
2 ¿Qué vas a hacer el sábado?
3 Van a jugar al tenis en el polideportivo por la tarde.
4 Vamos a salir con amigos.
5 Voy al cine con mi amigo Peter.

¡extra!
6 Va **a** ir al cine por la tarde.
7 Voy a **hacer** mis deberes a las siete.

Unidad 7 Tapas y bebidas	Topic/Language/Culture	Grammar and skills	National Criteria
7A ¿Adónde vamos? (pp. 64–65) **Objectives** ● say you are hungry or thirsty ● choose a place to have a drink ● learn how to sound Spanish using speech fillers	*tengo sed, hambre, frío, calor, sueño* *¿Qué quieres tomar?* *¿Algo frío o algo caliente?* *¿Adónde vamos?* *vamos a / podemos ir a...* *una cafetería, una heladería, un bar, un restaurante* *Sí, muy bien, está muy bien, está muy cerca, demasiado lejos, es muy / un poco caro / ruidoso* *Bueno, entonces, vamos a...*	**Grammar** *tener* + noun **Skills** Learn how to sound Spanish using fillers (**¡Así se hace!**) Listening for precise meaning (*WS60 Escuchar*)	**Attainment** AT1 Level 3; AT2 Level 4; AT3 Level 3 **Framework Objectives** 7W1, 7W2, 7W5, 7W7, 7S2, 7S4, 7T1, 7T2, 7T3, 7L2, 7L3, 7L6, 7C5 **Programmes of Study** 1abc, 2abdfh, 3bc, 4c, 5adi **QCA Scheme of Work** Language content: Unit 8 La comida Context: food and drink **Assessment for learning** Objectives, p.64 Ex 2b, p.65 Ex 4 & 5, Plenary
7B ¿Qué quieres beber? (pp. 66–67) **Objectives** ● say which drinks you want or prefer ● learn how to guess the meanings of new words ● learn how to say 'for me'	*¿Qué quieres/queréis tomar?* *¿Qué desean?* *quiero, para mí, ti, él, ella, usted* *No sé, ahora mismo* *una Coca-Cola, una Fanta de limón, un granizado de limón, un granizado de café, un té solo, un té con leche, un café solo, un batido de chocolate, un agua mineral con / sin gas, un chocolate caliente, un zumo de naranja*	**Grammar** *Querer* – full paradigm Disjunctive pronouns: *para mí, ti, él, ella, usted* **Skills** Guessing the meaning of new words from their context (**¡Así se hace!**)	**Attainment** AT1 level 3; AT2 Level 3; AT3 Levels 1–4 **Framework Objectives** 7W1, 7W2, 7W3, 7W4, 7W5, 7T1, 7T3, 7T4, 7T5, 7T6, 7L2, 7L6 **Programmes of Study** 1abc, 2abcde, 3acd, 5adei **QCA Scheme of Work** Language content: Unit 8 La comida Context: food and drink **Assessment for learning** Objectives, p.66 Ex1, p.67 Ex3a & 3b, Plenary
7C ¿Y de comer? (pp. 68–69) **Objectives** ● order a snack and pay the bill ● learn how to pronounce *ll* ● use the present tense of *-er* verbs	*una hamburguesa, un perrito caliente, un bocadillo de queso / atún / jamón, una ensalada, una tortilla española, una pizza, unos calamares, unas aceitunas, unas patatas bravas, unas patatas fritas* **Culture:** learning about Spanish tapas and snacks	**Grammar** Present tense regular *-er* verbs (*comer, beber*) **Skills** Using classroom language (Plenary) **Pronunciation** *ll*	**Attainment** AT1 Level 2; AT2 Levels 3–4; AT3 Level 2; AT4 Level 1 **Framework Objectives** 7W2, 7W3, 7W5, 7W6, 7W8, 7S2, 7S3, 7S4, 7S9, 7T1, 7T2, 7T3, 7T4, 7L1, 7L2, 7L4, 7L5, 7L6, 7C2, 7C4 **Programmes of Study** 1abc, 2abcdfh, 3abcd, 5abcdei **QCA Scheme of Work** Language content: Unit 8 La comida Context: food and drink **Assessment for learning** Objectives, p.69 Ex3, Plenary
7D Prefiero los calamares (pp. 70–71) **Objectives** ● compare drinks and snacks ● learn how to pronounce *rr*	*de beber / comer, prefiero la Coca-cola, el té, la carne, el pescado etc. porque....* *me gusta/n más .... soy vegetariano/a, me encanta/n...*	**Grammar** *querer / preferir* (*WS65 Gramática*) **Skills** Plurals of compound nouns (*WS63 Escribir*) **Pronunciation** *rr*	**Attainment** AT1 Level 3; AT2 Levels 3–4; AT3 Levels 3–4 **Framework Objectives** 7W2, 7W4, 7W5, 7S3, 7S6, 7T1, 7T2, 7T3, 7T5, 7T6, 7L3, 7L6 **Programmes of Study** 1abc, 2abcd; 3abcde, 5acdehi **QCA Scheme of Work** Language content: Unit 8 Context: likes, dislikes, preferences **Assessment for learning** Objectives, p.70 Ex3. Plenary

Other resources: *¡Ahora tú!* pp.130–131   WS 60–66   Flashcards 44–67   OHT 14   WBA & B pp.34–38   Assessment Units 7–8 (R & A file pp.128–131)   *Just Click* CD-Rom

7A ¿Adónde vamos?

pp. 64–65

Objectives:
- say that you are hungry or thirsty
- choose a place to have a drink
- learn how to sound Spanish using speech fillers

Key Language: see p.107 for full list

Grammar:
- use of *tener* 'to have' where English uses 'to be'

Skills: apply fillers in speech

Resources: Visual 57, Worksheet 60 (Escuchar – high-frequency words and precise meaning); CD 2; Workbooks A and B p.34; *Just Click* CD-Rom.

Lesson starter

Put up the following grid, items numbered 1–16. Explain that Unit 7A reuses words from Units 5 and 6. Students have to do two things with the grid – spot the four verbs (one in each horizontal line) and match up the other words into six pairs of opposites. (This will help them with exercise 2). They can write down the numbers.

1 ruidoso	2 quieres	3 lejos	4 caro
5 te apetece	6 un poco	7 divertido	8 un rollo
9 cerca	10 podemos	11 barato	12 muy
13 genial	14 aburrido	15 vamos	16 tranquilo

Answers

Verbs: 2, 5, 10, 15. Pairs of opposites: 1 + 16, 3 + 9, 4 + 11, 6 + 12, 7 + 14, 8 + 13.

Alternative lesson starter (for lessons starting part-way through the section)

Use the new language grid on p.65. Show students an example of *una invitación* (¿*Vamos a la cafetería? ¿Quieres ir al bar?*), *un problema* (*Es muy caro*) and *una solución* (*Bueno, entonces vamos a la cafetería cerca*). Call out a variety of invitations, problems and solutions based on the grid and on exercise 2a, and students call out one, either '*una invitación*' or '*un problema*' or '*una solución*' as appropriate.

Extension

Set a time limit for students to invent two of their own, which they take it in turns to call out to the whole class, who respond as before. Could also be done in smaller groups.

Introduction

Highlight the objectives at the top of the page in the Student's Book, explaining that the first one refers to exercise 1 and the second to exercise 2. Ask students to look at the pictures A–E in exercise 1 and work out in English what each person might be saying. Present the new Spanish phrases, having students repeat after you several times.

1 🎧 Escucha (1–5). ¿Cuál es el dibujo?
AT1.1; 7W1, 7W2, 7W7

Students listen and choose the appropriate picture for each section of the recording. Prepare students by calling out the key phrases for the pictures A–E whilst adding some extra language each time which students either know from a previous unit or can guess the meaning of, e.g. *Tengo sueño – voy a ir a mi dormitorio/Tengo hambre – quiero chocolate/Tengo sed – quiero un te o un café/Quiero ponerme un suéter porque tengo frío* etc. Students then call out the appropriate letter A–E.

Support

Play the recording through and ask students to raise a hand whenever they hear the word *tengo*. This will help them locate the key phrases faster on the next hearing.

Extension

On a subsequent hearing more able students can be asked to jot down in Spanish the item or place mentioned in each section, even if they're not sure of the meaning – given what they know about the rules for pronunciation, how are these words spelt? Pause the recording towards the end of each section just before the word students are listening for: *Coca-Cola, piscina, cama, abrigo.*

TRANSCRIPT CD2, track 40

1 – ¡Hola! ¿Qué tal?
– ¡Fatal! Tengo muchísima sed. ¿Tienes una Coca-Cola?
2 – ¡Buenos días! ¿Qué tal estás?
– Bien, pero... ¡qué hambre!
3 – ¡Hola, Marco!
– ¡Hola! ¡Uf, qué calor! Vamos a la piscina, ¿vale?
4 – ¡Tengo mucho sueño! Me voy a la cama.
5 – Uf, qué frío. ¿Dónde está mi abrigo?

Answers

1B **2**E **3**A **4**C **5**D

Gramática: *tener* + nouns 7W5, 7S2

Explain to students that where English uses the verb 'to be' ('I am cold, hot' etc.), Spanish uses the verb *tener* 'to have' (literally, 'I have heat, cold, hunger' etc.).

Extension

More able students can be reminded of the full paradigm of *tener* from Unit 3, and asked to do some quick-fire translation games: A Are you (*tú*) cold? B ¿*Tienes frío?*

2a 💿 Escucha y lee. AT1.3; 7T1, 7T2, 7T3, 7L2

Further presentation of the new language of the unit. You might like to use this text to focus students' attention on how easy/hard they perceive a text to be, and what factors make them think this. Ask them to feed back to you on a scale of 1 (easy) to 4 (hard) what they think of the text as they look at it. Next ask their reasons: is it the number of speech bubbles?; the quantity of language in each?; the perception that there are lots of new words?

To prepare students, read each speech bubble aloud as they follow the text, and ask them to repeat any words they hear/see which they don't feel they know the meaning of – they may be pleasantly surprised to realise that they do already know many of them from previous contexts. They can be asked to remember in which context these were originally met. As there are only two characters, this would be a useful text for practising reading aloud in pairs after hearing the recording several times.

TRANSCRIPT   CD2, track 41

– ¡Hola, Fede!
– ¿Qué tal, Isa?
– Mmm, muy bien. Oye, ¿te apetece tomar algo?
– Sí. ¿Qué quieres tomar, algo caliente o algo frío?
– Uf, tengo mucho calor. Prefiero tomar algo frío. ¿Te parece bien?
– Vale. Vamos a ver… ¿Quieres ir al bar de Manolo?
– No, es demasiado ruidoso.
– Bueno, entonces, si quieres, podemos ir a la cafetería Estrella.
– No, está bastante lejos. ¿Vamos a una heladería?
– Vale. ¿Qué heladerías te gustan?
– Mmm, me gusta la heladería Maki, y además está muy cerca.
– Pues, es un poco cara, pero está bien. ¡Vamos!
– ¡Muy bien!

2b ✔ 📖 Lee la conversación otra vez y contesta a las preguntas. AT3.3; 7S4

Highlight the question words here in sentences 1–6: *cómo, qué, cuál* and check students understand the meaning. You might like to preface this exercise by giving them a list of question words they've already met (*qué, cómo, cuándo, a qué hora, quién, porqué, dónde*) and ask them to match them up to a list of the English equivalents.

Remind students that they can use the same verb as in the question to start their answers. Model this first with an example like *¿Qué tal está Isa? Está muy bien.* You will need to give them *Van* (they are going) to answer question 5.

Answers

1 Se llaman Isa y Fede. **2** Isa prefiere tomar algo frío. **3** Es demasiado ruidoso. **4** Está bastante lejos. **5** Van a la heladería Maki. **6** Piensa que es un poco cara.

2c ¡Así se hace! 7C5

The fillers in the conversation are: *Mmm…; bueno* (well, fine); *oye* (listen); *vale* (OK); *vamos a ver* (let's see); *entonces* (in that case); *además* (and also/moreover/what's more); *está bien* (that's fine/OK). You might like to add *Pues…* (well, hm) to this list, which could be written up large for display to remind and encourage students to use them.

WS 60 (Escuchar) can be tackled from this point onwards.

3 🗣 Mira los dibujos. Habla con tu pareja. Usa el cuadro. AT2.4, 7L6

Students use the pictures to develop conversations with a partner.

Support

Work through the initial question in each picture with students, helping them formulate it and consolidate the pattern: **1** *¿Vamos a una cafetería?* **2** *¿Vamos a una heladería?* **3** *Vamos a un bar?* etc. before doing the same with the problems. Remind them that the *es* of *es demasiado caro* will change to *está* when saying something is too far away.

Extension

Students can invent their own, using the new language grid at the top of the page. Encourage them to incorporate some of the phrases from the previous page: *Tengo hambre/sed* and *¿Quieres?/Prefiero tomar algo frío/caliente.*

4 ✔ 💿 Escucha (1–4). ¿Qué sugerencias hay? ¿Cuál es la decisión final? AT1.3; 7L3

Students listen to the four conversations and note the suggestion and the decision. These could be noted under the headings: ?/✓.

Support

Give students a grid with some of the information already completed, e.g.

	?	✓
1	bar,.....................	restaurante
2	....	bar
3	bar	....
4	....	heladería

Extension

Ask students to listen for the reason given in each case. Fast-finishers could be given the following additional sentences to complete (answers are in brackets): **1** Miguel tiene… (hambre). **2** Pilar quiere tomar algo… (frío). **3** Ismael tiene mucha… (sed). **4** La joven va con su… (abuela).

TRANSCRIPT   CD2, track 42

1 – Hola, Miguel. ¿Te apetece tomar algo?
    – Sí, ¿vamos al bar?
    – Uy, no, está demasiado lejos. ¿Qué tal si vamos a la cafetería?
    – No, tengo hambre. Prefiero ir al restaurante.
    – Vale.
2 – ¡Buenas tardes, Elena!
    – ¡Hola, Pilar!
    – ¿Te apetece tomar algo?
    – Sí, me gustaría algo frío.
    – ¿Quieres ir a la heladería?
    – No, es demasiado caro.
    – Entonces, vamos al bar.
    – De acuerdo.
3 – ¡Ismael! ¿Cómo estás?
    – ¡Genial! Oye, ¿quieres tomar algo?
    – Sí, tengo mucha sed. ¿Qué tal si vamos al bar?
    – No, es muy ruidoso. Prefiero las cafeterías.
    – Bueno, podemos ir a la cafetería de mi padre que se llama Sevilla.
    – Muy bien, vamos.
4 – ¡Hola, abuela! ¿Te apetece tomar algo?
    – Bueno, ¿dónde quieres ir?
    – Podríamos ir a la cafetería El Sol.
    – No, está demasiado lejos. Tengo mucho calor, prefiero un helado.
    – Bueno, entonces vamos a la heladería.
    – Estupendo.

Answers

1 *Sug:* bar, cafetería. *Dec:* restaurante.
2 *Sug:* heladería. *Dec:* bar
3 *Sug:* bar. *Dec:* cafetería
4 *Sug:* cafetería. *Dec:* heladería.

5 ☑ 🖉 Lee el mensaje de texto. Contesta con otra sugerencia. AT4.3; 7T5, 7T6

Students read the message and write a reply, giving a reason as to why they don't want to go and offering an alternative suggestion. Remind students they can reuse *podemos* here, as in exercise 2a.

Support

Give students a selection of possible alternatives from which they can select (e.g. *es desmasiado ruidoso/está muy lejos/¿quieres ir…?*).

Plenary

☑ Ask students to look at the key language grid on page 65: which other expressions do they know/have they met in exercise 2 on page 64 which could go below the words *Vamos a…* to invite someone (*quieres/te apetece ir a…/quieres tomar algo frío/caliente en…*)? Write these up on the board or OHT. Ask students to work in groups of three: A invents a sentence using the grid (e.g. *¿Te apetece ir a una heladería?*), then B replies. C's role is to listen and check for errors (e.g. using *es* instead of *está*). Next B invites, and the other roles change accordingly. Encourage them to add fillers. Set a time limit – how many invitations can they generate in that time?

Alternative plenary *(for lessons ending part-way through the section)*

☑ List the fillers from exercise 2c, and ask students to turn back to the picture presentation from Unit 6D, exercise 1. Ask students to work in pairs to reread this conversation aloud several times, putting in appropriate fillers. Pairs of students may like to demonstrate their conversation to the class.

7B ¿Qué quieres beber?

pp. 66–67

> **Objectives:**
> * say what drinks you want or prefer
> * learn how to guess the meanings of new words
> * learn how to say 'for me'
>
> **Key Language:** see p.107 for full list
>
> **Grammar:**
> * *querer* (to want)
> * disjunctive pronouns
>
> **Skills:** understanding Spanish words from cognates, context etc.
>
> **Resources:** Visual 58 (*para mí* etc.); Flashcards 44–55; CD 2; Workbooks A and B p.35; *Just Click* CD-Rom.

Lesson starter

Use the *¡Así se hace!* strategy as the starter for the lesson. Read through this with students who, in pairs, work out the meaning of the Spanish for different types of drinks.

Alternative lesson starter *(for lessons starting part-way through the section)*

Remind students of the *algo frío/algo caliente* met in the previous unit. While you take the register, students work out which of these expressions is appropriate for each of the drinks on the list on page 66. After a few moments, call out the Spanish for the drinks in random order, and the class replies, e.g. T: *Un agua mineral con gas.* Ss: *¡Algo frío!* This can also be done in pairs or small groups.

Introduction

Explain the focus of the unit and highlight the skill of working out new language using what you already know and can apply in other contexts.

1 ☑ 💡 📖 Lee el menú. Escribe el español. AT3.1, 4.1; 7W1, 7W2, 7W8

Students write the matching Spanish phrase for each of the drinks 1–12. You might like to highlight *con* (with), *sin* (without): how might they ask for coffee with milk, a fizzy mineral water with lemon, tea with lemon?

Extension

Present *azúcar, tónica, (cubitos de) hielo* and encourage students to invent more combinations of drinks.

Answers

1 té con leche 2 café solo 3 té solo 4 batido de chocolate 5 Coca-Cola 6 chocolate caliente 7 granizado de limón 8 Fanta de limón 9 zumo de naranja 10 agua mineral con gas 11 agua mineral sin gas 12 batido de fresa

2a 💿 Escucha y lee la conversación. AT3.4; 7W1, 7T2, 7T4

Before playing the recording, ask students to work in groups of four (taking the roles of Tomás, Noelia, Victor and the Waiter/*Camarero*) to read through the conversation, using the pronunciation rules they know to work out how to say any new words. They can also use the vocabulary section at the back of the Student's Book and the Resumen to look up the meaning of any unfamiliar words. Ask them to produce a short summary in English of who asks for which drinks. Finally play the recording several times. The class can be split into four groups, each given a role and each group repeating their lines after the appropriate section on the recording (pause it after each utterance).

TRANSCRIPT   CD2, track 43

– Allí hay una mesa.
– Muy bien.
– Vamos.
– ¿Qué queréis tomar?
– No sé… ¿Qué hay?
– Hay Coca-Cola, Fanta, granizado, té, café, batidos, agua mineral, zumo de naranja…
– ¡Camarero!
– ¿Qué desean?
– Yo quiero un batido de chocolate. ¿Y para ti, Tomás?
– Para mí, un té con leche. ¿Y tú, Víctor?
– Quiero un granizado de limón.
– Entonces, un batido de chocolate, un té con leche y un granizado de limón. Ahora mismo.
– Muchas gracias.

2b **Encuentra el español. AT3.4; 7S2**

Students find the appropriate Spanish phrase for each of the English ones 1–9. Highlight, in checking the answers, how these may not be an exact translation.

Answers

1 ¿Qué desean? **2** ¿Qué queréis tomar? **3** ¡Camarero! **4** Para mí **5** Para ti **6** ¿Y tú? **7** No sé **8** ¿Qué hay? **9** Ahora mismo

Gramática: _querer_ – to want 7W2, 7W5

Show students how the stem changes in the verb _querer_: it may be helpful to write alongside each of its six parts the appropriate subject pronouns (_yo, tú_ etc.). You might like to ask students to turn back to the verb _jugar_ on page 57 to compare where the stem changes occur. The class can then work out, either together or in pairs first, what the six parts of the verb _preferir_ will be. Note that _preferir_, being an _-ir_ verb, will not follow the pattern of _querer_ in the _nosotros/as_ and _vosotros/as_ forms: these are _preferimos_ and _preferís_.

3a ✓ **Escucha (1–3). ¿Cuál es la lista apropiada? AT1.3; 7L3**

Students listen to the three conversations and work out how they relate to the lists in exercise 3. Tell students to mentally letter them A, B and C from left to right – they can write the number of the conversation and the letter of the list.

TRANSCRIPT   **CD2, track 44**

1 – Hola, ¿qué desean?
– Yo quiero té con limón.
– Yo, también.
– Para mí, un café con leche.
– María, ¿qué quieres?
– Una Fanta de naranja. ¡Tengo mucha sed!
– ¿Y para Pedro y Miguel Ángel?
– Para ellos, dos Coca-Colas.
2 – Hola, buenas tardes. ¿Qué desean?
– Para mí, un té con limón.
– Yo quiero una Coca-Cola, por favor.
– ¡Qué sed! Para mí, una Fanta.
– Pues yo tengo frío, así que quiero un café con leche.
– ¿Y para ti, Charo?
– Para mí, un té con limón.
3 – ¡Buenos días! ¿Qué desean?
– Vamos a ver. Para Andrés y Miguel, un café con leche y un té con limón, y para mí una Coca-Cola.
– Para mí una Fanta, por favor.
– Yo también quiero una Fanta, por favor. ¿Y vosotros?
– Para nosotros, un té con limón, y un café con leche.
– Muy bien, ahora mismo.

Answers

1A   2C   3B

3b ✓ 💬 **Escribe tu lista de bebidas y haz una conversación. AT2.3; 7T5, 7L6**

Students prepare a list of drinks and devise a conversation in groups in a café. Remind students that _quieres_ is used to one other teenager, and _queréis_ to two or more. A waiter would use _¿Qué desea?_ to one person and _¿Qué desean?_ to two or more.

Gramática: disjunctive pronouns 7W2

Students who are already familiar with subject pronouns may find it useful to compare these with the disjunctive ones: only _mí, ti_ and _ello_ are different. Visual 58 will be useful here.

Plenary 7W2

✓ Divide students into groups of four. Each student takes it in turn to name a drink, e.g. _un chocolate caliente_. Each then, in turn, has to invent a sentence which says who wants what in the group, using _para ti, para él/ella, para nosotros/as, para vosotros/as, para ellos/as_ (e.g. _Para vosotras, Alice y Clare, un chocolate caliente y un zumo de naranja/Para nosotros, John, un té solo y un agua mineral_ etc.). The drinks will be repeated, but the aim is for each student in the group to come up with a different disjunctive pronoun in each round. Once each student has invented a sentence, students begin again by naming a different drink. The grouping can be changed for variety by having one person change group after each round.

Alternative plenary (_for lessons ending part-way through the section_) **7W2, 7W7, 7L2**

✓ Encourage the development of memory skills using the following exercises (set this in the context of how much information a waiter has to hold in his head). Explain that you are going to name three drinks in Spanish: after a five-second pause you will ask the whole class to repeat them in the order in which you gave them. Brainstorm with students first what helps them to focus and remember, whether closing their eyes, repeating silently in their head, visualising the words or a picture of each item, etc. Point out that each of us will find some things work better than others. Repeat the series of three several times, using different items. Then challenge the class to extend this – either by increasing the number of items or the length of time they have to hold the list in memory before repeating. This can subsequently be done in small groups or pairs. Finally, help students to think about other places in the curriculum or their daily lives where this is a useful skill.

7C ¿Y de comer?
pp. 68–69

Objectives:
• order a snack and pay the bill
• learn how to pronounce '_ll_'
• use the present tense of _-er_ verbs
Key Language: see p.107 for full list
Grammar: use the present tense of _-er_ verbs
Resources: OHT 14 (sample conversation) and Visual 57 (mini-flashcards); Flashcards 56–67; Worksheet 61 (Hablar – ordering food and drink), 64 (_¡Así se hace!_ – _l, ll, r, rr_ sounds); CD 2; Workbooks A and B p.36; _Just Click_ CD-Rom.

Lesson starter 7W2, 7S2, 7T1, 7T3

Use the text of the song in exercise 1a as an opportunity to help students develop their scanning skills. Explain that it contains new items of language and a number of expressions they already know. Put up the following on the board or OHT and give them a time limit (3–4 mins) to locate the relevant information. There are 10 lines in the verse section. Tell students to allocate a number to each line (1–10). Exercise (answers in brackets):

Write the letter of the speech bubble(s) which mention(s)...
1 liking something? (1); **2** loving something? (2);
3 being hungry? (3, 9); **4** preferring something? (6, 10);
5 <u>not</u> being hungry? (7); **6** an English boy? (6).

Alternative lesson starter (*for lessons starting part-way through the section*)

Ask students to look at the language box for food items (top of page 68) and the one for drinks (top of page 66). Introduce *de comer/de beber*, writing them up where students can see them. You, and then members of the class, take it in turns to call out an item of food or drink and the class has to chorus correctly *de comer* or *de beber*.

Introduction 7C2

Check that students can identify in English the items in the pictures: some of them, like olives, squid rings and Spanish potato omelette may not be familiar to all students. When presenting the items of food, flashcards 56–67 may also be useful. Give students some cultural information on *tapas* and *tapas* bars. You might like to explain that *la tortilla española* is usually known in Spain as *la tortilla de patatas*, and is popular both as a *tapa* and inside a sandwich. *Patatas fritas* can mean both chips and potato crisps.

1a ⦿ Escucha y canta la canción AT1.3, 3.3; 7W2, 7T2, 7C4

Students listen to the song several times and then sing along. You might like to use this as pronunciation and reading-aloud practice first. Students could be given a gapped text of this song, with the food items missing, and asked to listen (books closed) and note these down in abbreviated form.

Support

If using a gapped text, give alternatives in the gaps and ask students to underline the one they hear.

TRANSCRIPT CD2, track 45

- ¿Te gustan los perritos calientes? Ahí hay un plato.
- Uy, sí, me encantan. Pero prefiero un bocadillo.

[estribillo]
Yo como ensalada
Tú comes mucho jamón
Comemos patatas fritas
Bebemos Fanta de limón
¡Ven a la fiesta a comer y beber!
¡Lo pasamos bomba – hay que ver!

- Tengo mucha hambre. ¿Hay hamburguesas?
- Hay con queso y sin queso. ¡Y hay patatas fritas!
[estribillo]

- Marisa, mira a aquel chico: ¡qué guapo es!
- Prefiero a su amigo. ¡Además es inglés!
[estribillo]

- No tengo mucha hambre... ¿hay aceitunas?
- No, pero hay tortillas.
[estribillo]

- ¿Hay patatas bravas? Tengo mucha hambre.
- Sí, pero prefiero un bocadillo grande.
[estribillo]

Gramática: regular -er verbs 7W2, 7W5

Read through with students the reminder of the formation of -er verbs. If they need practice, students can work in pairs or groups: one person says one of the subject pronouns, and the other(s) give(s) the matching part of the verb. Students can also find it helpful to write each part of the verb and each subject pronoun on small pieces of A4: one person points to a subject pronoun and says it, and the other locates the correct part of the verb and says it as they lay it alongside.

Support

Concentrate on those forms which students may need to use most actively: the *yo*, *tú* and *nosotros/as* forms.

Extension

Encourage students to play these oral grammar games with other -er verbs they met in the previous unit which are irregular in the *yo* form: *ver/hacer* (*veo/hago*).

1b 📖 ¿Qué hay de comer? Haz una lista. AT3.3, 4.1; 7T1

Students read the lyrics to the song on page 68 and make a list in Spanish of the food items mentioned. You might like to remind them to focus only on items to eat (not drink), and that they will need to take care with *no hay*!

Answers

perritos calientes, hamburguesas con y sin queso, patatas fritas, tortillas, patatas bravas, ensalada, jamón

1c ✎ Imagina que organizas una fiesta. Haz una lista de la comida y la bebida. AT4.1; 7W4, 7W8, 7T4

Encourage students to use a dictionary for this exercise to look up different types of filling for sandwiches and pizza toppings, as well as other items. Show them how these words will come after the *de*: *un bocadillo de salchichón, una pizza de queso y tomate*. You might like to use the first exercise on Worksheet 63 (Escribir) at this point to help with the formation of words with *de* and plurals of compound nouns.

2 📖 Une las cuentas con las conversaciones. AT3.2; 7T1

Ask students to work out what they think the phrases *la cuenta*, *¿me da la cuenta?, ¿cuánto es?* might be, given the replies below. Point out how Spanish uses *con* (which they have already met) to link the quantity of euros and the *céntimos*. Revise numbers 1–100 first, using counting games, e.g. count up in fives, back in tens, guess the number I'm thinking of (replying *más, menos* until students locate it correctly).

Answers

1E 2C 3B 4F 5A 6D

⦿ Pronunciación: ll 7W6, 7T2, 7L1

Students listen to the Castilian versions of the words listed. They can practise these as a whole class. You might like to use Worksheet *¡Así se hace!* (see below) at this point.

TRANSCRIPT CD2, track 46

tortilla, bocadillo, ella, bollo, botella, Sevilla, ellos, me llamo, ellas, caballo

---

3 ☑ 💬 ¡extra! Haz conversaciones en grupos de cuatro. AT2.3; 7W5, 7L6.

Students use the grid to invent and act out a conversation in a café. Remind students they can use fillers (see 7A) to stall for time, and highlight the use of *quisiera/me gustaría* as set phrases for expressing requests.

Support

You might find Worksheet 61 (Hablar) helpful at this point in providing students with a structured model which could be embroidered and expanded.

Extension

Encourage more able students to add in their own likes/dislikes as they talk with each other before ordering, using the previously met *me gusta/n, me encanta/n*.

Plenary 7L4, 7L5, 7L6

☑ Ask students to work in groups. Their task is to prepare 3–5 questions on the content of pages 68–69 which they will then put to other groups. Encourage them to think of different areas of learning, writing the headings on the board, e.g. grammar, pronunciation, spelling, meaning. Examples of each of these might be: (grammar) What is the *yo* form of *beber*?; (pronunciation) How you do pronounce this word: *t-o-r-t-i-l-l-a*?; (spelling) How do you spell *hamburguesa*?; (meaning) Give two ways of saying 'I want...' or 'I'd like...'. This would be a useful point at which to remind or teach students how to do this in Spanish using the following simple structures: *¿Cuál es la forma... del verbo...?; ¿Cómo se pronuncia la palabra...?; ¿Cómo se escribe...?; ¿Cómo se dice... en inglés/español?*

Alternative plenary *(for lessons ending part-way through the section)* 7W3, 7S4, 7S9

☑ Focus on helping students develop their ability to ask questions in Spanish. Remind them, using examples like *¿Tienes hermanos?, ¿Te gusta el té?*, that although we often use 'do you' in questions in English, this is not necessary in Spanish. Ask students to look at between three and six of the sentences sung in exercise 1a, and invent a question which could have generated that sentence. You might like to use the first as an example; though it already contains a question, other possible ones might be *¿Dónde hay un plato de perritos calientes?, ¿Dónde están los perritos calientes?*

Set a time limit – the class can share their findings when it expires.

7D Prefiero los calamares

p.70

> **Objectives:**
> * compare snacks and drinks
> * learn how to pronounce *rr*
> **Key Language:** see p.107 for full list
> **Grammar:**
> * comparative *más* + adjective
> * formation of plurals in compound nouns (Worksheet 63 Escribir – differences between plural and singular)
> **Skills:** reading using cues (Worksheet 62 Leer)
> **Resources:** Worksheets 62 (Leer – using cues), 63 (Escribir – plurals), 65 (Gramática – *querer/preferir*); CD 2; Workbooks A and B p.37; *Just Click CD-Rom.*

Lesson starter 7S1, 7S2

Use the speech bubbles in exercise 1a as a starter. Allocate a speech bubble to each pair of students and ask them to work out the meaning, using the vocabulary section if necessary, paying special attention to two things. Firstly, the word order – where is it different to English? Secondly, where does Spanish use *el/la/los/las* (the) where English doesn't? When eliciting replies, write up the examples where Spanish word order is different: in expressions of liking (*a mí me encanta/n, gusta/n...*) and where

adjectives follow the noun (*una tortilla española*). Spanish uses *el/la/los/las* with nouns after verbs of liking and preferring.

1a 🎧 Escucha y lee la conversación en el bar. Une las personas con las bandejas... AT3.3; 7W2, 7T1, 7T2

Tell the students to follow the text in the speech bubbles 1–4 as they listen. Discuss the pronunciation issues highlighted in the exercise. Play each sentence separately and repeat it yourself slowly so that students hear the pronunciation. Play the recording again and stop from time to time to ask a student for the next word. Students match the trays of food with the appropriate person. There are two distractors.

Answers

Antonio **D**   Alba **A**   Ignacio **C**   Jessica **F**

> TRANSCRIPT   CD2, track 47
>
> **Antonio:**
> 1 Yo tengo mucha sed. Prefiero la Coca-Cola, es más refrescante. Pues a mí me encanta la comida española. Para mí, una tortilla española.
> **Alba:**
> 2 Pues a mí me gustan las bebidas calientes, el té o el café. Voy a tomar un té con leche. De comer yo... prefiero la carne. Voy a tomar una hamburguesa con queso.
> **Ignacio:**
> 3 De beber me gusta mucho la Fanta. Quiero dos, por favor. Pues yo soy vegetariano, así que prefiero una ensalada.
> **Jessica:**
> 4 Pues a mí me encanta el chocolate. Uno, por favor. Y de comer... me gusta mucho el pescado, así que unos calamares.

1b 📖 Di si las frases son verdad (V) o mentira (M). AT3.3; 7T1, 7T3

Students decide if the sentences 1–10 are true or false.

Answers

1V   2M   3M   4V   5M   6V   7M   8V   9M   10V

Extension

Fast-finishers can correct the false phrases.

Answers

2 Antonio prefiere la Coca Cola.   3 Alba prefiere las bebidas calientes.   5 Jessica quiere un chocolate.   7 Ignacio es vegetariano.   9 Antonio prefiere la comida española.

2 ✏️ Escribe un párrafo... AT4.3–4; 7S6, 7T5, 7T6

Students use the grid to write a paragraph about their food and drink preferences, and reasons.

Support

Help students by giving them several sentences in English and asking them to find the parts of the sentence in different parts of the grid, e.g. To drink, I prefer tea because it's more refreshing.

Extension

Encourage students to work independently using the dictionary and previous met language (e.g. of nationality) to generate new phrases (e.g. *la comida italiana*).

Highlight the use of *así que* in the speech bubbles in 1a, and remind students of other conjunctions they know (*y, pero, además*) to produce more complex compound sentences.

3 ☑ ◯ Pregunta a tu pareja. AT2.3–4; 7L6

Students use the four questions to have a conversation with their partner on food and drink preferences. They can use the grid for support.

4 ◉ Pronunciación: *rr* 7W6, 7L1, 7L6

An opportunity to practise one of the most difficult sounds for English speakers – rolling the 'r'.

| CD2, track 48

perrito   arriba   párrafo

Plenary 7S3, 7L6

☑ Ask students to work out, in pairs, how to alter one of the speech bubbles in exercise 1a. Brainstorm first which elements can be changed, e.g. nouns (*sed → hambre, la Coca-Cola → el zumo de naranja*); adjectives (*la comida española → la comida italiana, las bebidas calientes → frías*); intensifiers (*me gustan más → me gustan mucho*); verbs (*gustan → encantan*). Each pair alters a speech bubble and reads it aloud to another pair who translate it.

Resumen *(page 71)*

The Resumen is a reference point for students at any time, and can be used by students, working in pairs, to revise vocabulary sections by section.

¡Ahora, tú! *(pp. 130–131)*

Differentiated self-access reading and writing exercises: see page 37 for more information.

page 130

1 💡 📖 Which is the odd one out?

Answers

1 tortilla 2 granizado 3 aceitunas 4 helado 5 cuatro
6 calamares

3 📖 Read the menu and answer the questions.

Answers

1 1,25€ 2 3,30€ 3 doce 4 quince 5–8 (student's own choice)

page 131

1 📖 Read the story and write whether the sentences are true or false.

Answers

1 verdad 2 mentira 3 verdad 4 mentira 5 mentira
6 verdad 7 mentira

3 📖 Match up the questions and the answers.

Answers

1e 2a 3h 4d 5b or g 6b or g 7c 8f

Worksheets Unit 7

57 Tapas y Bebidas AT3.1; 7W1

Visuals: buying food and drink in town from Section A

58 Disjunctive pronouns AT3.1; 7W1

Visuals: learning how to say 'for me/you/him/her/us' etc. from Section B.

59 Resumen AT3.1; 7W1

List of key language of the unit.

60 Escuchar AT3.2–4; 7L3

This worksheet helps students understand the importance of listening for high-frequency words for precise meaning. Explain to students that the 1a and 1b exercises are to help them listen more intently for detail. For 1a, ask students to tick the correct box when they hear each extract: *frío* or *caliente/calor*. Before playing the tape for 1b, use the board or OHP to highlight the difference between *tengo frío* (I am cold) and *(quiero) tomar algo frío* ((I want) to have something cold). Explain that it can

be very important to listen for the precise meaning: hearing *frío* or *calor/caliente* on its own is not enough – the verb before them is very important and changes the meaning. Students can now listen and do exercise 1b, distinguishing between *tengo* (T) and *tomar* (R).

| CD2, track 49

1a Ejemplo: **1**
 – ¡Hola, Merche!
 – ¡Iñigo! ¿Qué tal?
 – Bien. Pero tengo calor.
 – ¿Calor?
 – Sí, mucho.
2 – ¿Qué tal, Arancha?
 – Muy bien, gracias. Oye, ¿quieres tomar algo?
 – ¡Sí! Algo frío, por favor.
3 – Julio, ¿te apetece tomar algo?
 – Sí. Quiero algo caliente.
4 – Nuria, ¿vamos a la heladería?
 – ¡Buena idea! Tengo mucho calor.
5 – ¿Qué quieres tomar, Martín?
 – Mmm... no sé. Algo frío, me parece.
6 – ¿Qué tal, Javier?
 – Muy bien. Pero quiero tomar algo caliente. ¿Vamos a la cafetería?
 – Vale.

| CD2, track 50

1b Ejemplo: **1**
 – Felipe, ¿quieres tomar algo?
 – Sí, quiero tomar algo caliente, por favor.
2 – ¿Tienes frío, Beatriz?
 – Sí, tengo frío.
3 – ¿Qué tal, Úrsula?
 – Bien, pero tengo calor. ¿Vamos a la cafetería?
4 – ¿Qué quieres, Andrés?
 – No sé... Quiero tomar algo frío, pero no sé qué exactamente.
5 – Vamos a mi casa – ¿quieres venir?
 – Sí, quiero tomar algo caliente.
6 – ¿Qué te pasa, Carlos?
 – Nada. Es que tengo calor. ¿Vamos al bar?

Answers

1a 1 caliente/calor 2 frío
  3 caliente/calor 4 caliente/calor
  5 frío 6 caliente/calor
1b 1R 2T 3T 4R 5R 6T

2a Students listen and choose the correct two pieces of artwork for each conversation. The i*extra*! activity requires students to identify in which conversation each of the phrases a–f is said.

TRANSCRIPT
CD2, track 51

Ejemplo: **1**
- – ¿Vamos a la cafetería?
- – ¿Qué cafetería?
- – La cafetería Sol.
- – Buena idea. Está cerca.
- – ¡Menos mal – tengo calor! No quiero andar mucho...

2 – ¿Quieres tomar algo?
- – Sí, pero tengo hambre. ¿Vamos a un restaurante?
- – El restaurante Roma es barato.
- – ¡Perfecto – vámonos! ¿Qué quieres comer entonces?

3 – ¡Marcos!
- – ¡Hola! ¿Qué tal, Charo?
- – ¡Bien! Oye, ¿quieres tomar algo?
- – Vale. ¿Te apetece ir a la pizzería?
- – No sé... está un poco lejos. Quiero beber algo frío.
- – Bueno, una pizza para mí, ¡y una Coca-Cola para ti!
- – Vale. Vamos a la pizzería entonces.

4 – ¿Quieres tomar algo, Irene?
- – Sí – ¿vamos a la heladería?
- – ¿La heladería? Es muy cara.
- – Bueno, ¡yo te invito!
- – Gracias, pero quiero tomar algo caliente. ¿Por qué no vamos a mi casa...

5 – ¡Hola, Marisa!
- – ¡Hola, Miguel. ¿Qué tal?
- – Bien. ¡Pero tengo frío!
- – ¿Quieres tomar algo?
- – Vale. Pero ¿dónde?
- – ¿Vamos al bar?
- – Mmm... El problema es que es muy ruidoso.
- – Bueno, vamos a ver... Creo que hay una cafetería ...

Answers

2a: **1** D3 **2** B6 **3** E4 **4** A5 **5** C1

2b: ¡extra!
a5 **b**3 **c**1 **d**2 **e** distractor **f**4

61 Hablar AT3.4; 7L6

Students can use the framework given to practise two conversations. Fast-finishers can be asked to produce another, with different items of food and drink, following the same structure as given. More able students can be encouraged to do the ¡extra! exercise, which requires them to reuse language from earlier in the unit and cope with the unexpected.

62 Leer 7T1

As a starter, ask students to highlight in two different colours all the words which have something to do with foods/snacks and drinks. More able students could be asked to underline verbs which indicate these as well (tomar will cover both eating and

drinking). Fast-finishers could be asked to find the Spanish for places to eat.

Work through the hints with them: use the example Me gusta la cafetería porque es tranquilo/La cafetería no es muy tranquilo to remind them that to read for meaning does not mean spotting single words but reading the whole sentence. For the second hint, this example may be useful: Si quiero beber algo, voy al bar o a la taberna cerca de casa. Ask students what kind of word taberna is (snack, drink, place) and how do they know (because it is given as an alternative to bar so we can guess it's a place).

Answers

1 **1**B **2**B **3**C **4**A **5**C **6**D **7**D **8**B
2 **2** **1**g **2**c **3**f **4**b **5**e **6**a

63 Escribir 7W4, 7S3

This worksheet reinforces and extends students' understanding of plurals. Read through the bullet points with them, highlighting the formation of plural compound nouns and noun/adjective combinations. Explain that they will need these when ordering more than one of an item of food or drink, and often with gustar (e.g. me gustan las hamburguesas). Other examples you could work through on the board are: el zumo de naranja, una hamburguesa con queso, una bebida fría. Allow students to work at their own pace through the remaining exercise. They will find the Resumen on page 71 of the Student's Book helpful for other items of vocabulary.

Answers

1 Plural of compound noun, add -s/-es to the first word/part of the compound noun. For a noun + adjective, add -s/-es to the end of both noun and adjective.
1 los batidos de chocolate **2** los perritos calientes **3** las aguas minerales con gas **4** los zumos de naranja **5** las tortillas españolas **6** los bocadillos de jamón

64 ¡Así se hace! 7W6, 7L1

This worksheet reinforces the work done in the Student's Book on the sounds of the letter combinations r, rr, l, ll. Read through the introduction with students, giving some examples from recent previous units, e.g. (r, rr) – dormitorio, derecha, terraza, cierra; (l, ll) – televisión, lavadora, sillas, sillones. In exercise 1 students listen and identify the sounds, and in 2 they write in the missing letter or letters before practising their pronunciation in pairs or small groups. You might want to point out to students before starting exercise 2 that the r is often pronounced as a double rr when it is the first letter of a word.

TRANSCRIPT
CD2, track 52

1a Ejemplo: **1** para, para
Ejemplo: **2** parra, parra

3 buró, buró
4 burro, burro
5 quería, quería
6 querría, querría
7 carro, carro
8 caro, caro

Answers

1r **2**rr **3**r **4**rr **5**r **6**rr **7**rr **8**r

TRANSCRIPT
CD2, track 53

1b Ejemplo: **1** millón, millón

2 pilla, pilla   **5** calla, calla
3 pila, pila   **6** bolo, bolo
4 cala, cala   **7** bollo, bollo

Answers

1ll **2**ll **3**l **4**l **5**ll **6**l **7**ll

TRANSCRIPT
CD2, track 54

2a (Answers in bold with tapescript below)

1 ¡Mi **rutina** es muy aburrida!
2 Me **levanto** temprano.
3 Me **lavo rápidamente**.
4 Desayuno un **bollo** con mantequilla y un café.
5 Si **llueve**, voy al **colegio** en autobús.
6 A veces, **llego** tarde.
7 A las once, como **galletas** y **fruta**.
8 Cuando vuelvo a casa, **arreglo** mi habitación.
9 Luego, ceno **pollo** con verduras.
10 Hago mis deberes – ¡qué **pesadilla**!

65 Gramática 7W5

This worksheet gives further practice in the verbs querer and preferir. In the first exercise, students copy the parts of querer and preferir into the correct places in the table.

The second highlights the differences between the two verbs and, in the third, students underline the correct part of the verb in brackets. In the fourth, students choose the correct part of preferir.

Answers

1 querer: quiero, quiere, queréis;
preferir: prefieres, preferimos, prefieren

2 preferimos, preferís

3 (in this order) quiero, queréis, quieres, quieren, queremos, quiere

4 **1** prefiere **2** prefiero **3** prefieren **4** prefieres **5** preferimos **6** preferís.

66 ¡extra! 7W2, 7S4

Answers

1 Quisiera…, Voy a tomar…, Me gustaría…, Prefiero…, Quiero…, Para mí…

2 ¿Qué quieres tomar?, ¿Qué prefieres?, ¿Qué vas a tomar?, ¿Y para ti?

3 ¿Qué vais a tomar?, ¿Y para vosotros/as?, ¿Qué queréis tomar?, ¿Qué preferís?

4 ¿Qué desea (usted)?

5 ¿Qué desean (ustedes)?

Workbook A Unit 7

page 34 *(Section A)*

Answers

ex 1a:
1 ¿Tienes bastante calor?
2 Tengo mucho frío.
3 Tengo hambre.
4 Tengo trece años.
5 ¿Cuántos años tienes?

¡extra! & = e

ex 1b:
a2 **b**5 **c**4 **d**1 **e**3

ex 2a:
1 ¿Tienes doce o **trece** años? Are **you** twelve or thirteen?
2 **Tengo** frío. I'm cold.
3 Enrique tiene **mucha** hambre. Enrique is **very** hungry.
4 Tengo bastante **sed**. I am **quite** thirsty.
5 Tengo **poco** sueño. I'm not very **tired**.

page 35 *(Section B)*

Answers

ex 2a:
1 Para mí **2** ¿Qué quieres? **3** ¿Y para ti? **4** un batido **5** con leche **6** Quiero

ex 2b:
Sample answer
– ¿Qué quieres beber, Nuria?
– Quiero un agua mineral con gas.
– ¿Y para ti, Ana?
– Para mí, un batido de fresa.

– Y tú, Isa, ¿qué quieres?
– Para mí, un café con leche.

ex 3a:
– ¿Qué quieres beber, Jaime?
– Para *mí*, un batido de chocolate.
– ¿Y para *ti*, Ana?
– Quiero un agua mineral sin gas. ¿Y para ti?
– *Para mí*, un café solo.

Note: above conversation (3a) is recorded on CD2, track 55, for pronunciation practice.

page 36 *(Section C)*

Answers

ex 1:
3 Son doce euros con noventa.
4 Cuatro hamburguesas son ocho euros con veinte.
5 Tres pizzas y el agua mineral son diez euros con ochenta.
6 Calamares con ensalada y un batido son nueve euros con quince.

1d **2**f **3**a **4**e **5**c **6**b

ex 2:
1 bebo **2** comes **3** bebe **4** comemos **5** coméis **6** beben

page 37 *(Section D)*
ex 1b and ¡extra!:

Answers

1 true **2** false (he likes Italian, but prefers Mexican and Spanish) **3** true **4** false (it costs him 4,30€) **5** true **6** true **7** false (there's a choice of cheese, ham and tuna)

ex 1c:
1 prefiere **2** Prefiero **3** Preferimos **4** prefieren

Workbook B Unit 7

page 34 *(Section A)*

Answers

ex 1:
1 ¿Tienes doce o **trece** años? Are **you** twelve or thirteen? **2** **Tengo** frío. I'm cold. **3** Enrique tiene **mucha** hambre. Enrique is **very** hungry. **4** Tengo bastante **sed**. I am **quite** thirsty. **5** Tenemos mucho sueño. We're very **tired**. **6** Tienen **dos perros**. **They have** two dogs. **7** Tengo **bastante** calor. I'm quite **hot**.

ex 2:
1 Tengo mucho frío.
2 ¿Cuántos años tienes?
3 Tengo trece años.
4 ¿Tienes bastante calor?
5 Tengo hambre.
6 Tenemos demasiado calor.
7 Paco tiene mucho sueño.
8 Tengo mucha sed.

page 35 *(Section B)*

Answers

ex 1: ¡extra!:
mystery word = **chocolate**

ex 2a:
1c **2**h **3**f **4**e **5**a **6**g **7**b **8**d

ex 2c:
Note: the example given regarding vowel sounds is recorded on CD2, track 56, for reference. The conversation listed is recorded on CD2, track 57, for pronunciation practice.

page 36 *(Section C)*

Answers

ex 1:
1 Son doce euros con noventa.
2 Cuatro hamburguesas son ocho euros con veinte.
3 Tres pizzas y el agua mineral son diez euros con ochenta.
4 Calamares con ensalada y un batido son nueve euros con quince.
5 Dos tortillas y dos cocas son siete euros con cincuenta.
6 Tres bocadillos de queso son tres euros con cuarenta y cinco.

1a **2**e **3**c **4**b **5**f **6**d

ex 2:
como, come, coméis; beber, bebes, bebemos, beben

page 37 *(Section D)*

Answers

ex 1b:
1 prefiere **2** Prefiero **3** Preferimos **4** prefieren

ex 1c and 1d:
1 true **2** false (the good thing about eating together is that they can talk) **3** true **4** true **5** false (it costs him 4,30€) **6** true **7** true **8** false (there's a choice of cheese, ham and tuna and other things)

Unidad 8 La rutina diaria	Topic/Language/Culture	Grammar and skills	National Criteria
8A Tu rutina diaria (pp. 72–73) **Objectives** • say what you do in a typical day • learn how to use reflexive verbs • learn how to scan a text for information	¿Cuándo / A qué hora...? ...te despiertas / te levantas / te duchas / te vistes / desayunas / sales de casa / vuelves a casa / te relajas / cenas / haces los deberes / te acuestas? por la mañana, por la noche me levanto, me despierto, me ducho, me baño, me peino, desayuno, me lavo los dientes, me visto, salgo de casa, vuelvo a casa, me relajo, hago los deberes, ceno, me acuesto **Culture:** differences in routine	**Grammar** Reflexive verbs **Skills** Scanning a text for information (*¡Así se hace!*)	**Attainment** AT1 Level 2: AT2 Level 4: AT3 Levels 2–4; AT4 Levels 2–4 **Framework Objectives** 7W1, 7W2, 7W5, 7S4, 7S7, 7T1, 7T3, 7T4, 7L6, 7C2 **Programmes of Study** 1abc, 2abde, 3acd, 4cd, 5ad **QCA Scheme of Work** Language content: Unit 4 En casa Context: daily routine **Assessment for learning** Objectives, p.73 Ex 2a & b, p.74 Ex3a & 3b, WS72 Escribir Plenary
8B ¿Qué haces los fines de semana? (pp. 74–75) **Objectives** • say what you do at the weekend • recognise and use adverbs	¿Es diferente tu rutina los fines de semana? me quedo en la cama, (no) me pongo el uniforme entresemana, los fines de semana, los sábados, temprano, tarde rápidamente, lentamente, difícilmente, inmediatamente, fácilmente, evidentemente, tranquilamente, profundamente, completamente, útilmente	**Grammar** Recognise and use adverbs **Skills** Learn how to deal with unknown language. use adverbs in classroom language (WS75 *¡extra!*)	**Attainment** AT1 Level 3; AT2 Level 2; AT3 Level 3; AT4 Level 2 **Framework Objectives** 7W1, 7W2, 7W3, 7W7, 7S3, 7S7, 7T1, 7T2, 7T4, 7L1, 7L2, 7L4, 7L5, 7L6, 7C2 **Programmes of Study** 1abc, 2abcdef, 3bcd, 4cd, 5abde **QCA Scheme of Work** Language: Unit 6 Los pasatiempos Context: free time and hobbies **Assessment for learning** Objectives, p.75 Ex1b, Plenary
8C ¿Cuándo comes? (pp. 76–77) **Objectives** • talk about mealtimes and normal meals • compare mealtimes in England and Spain • learn how to pronounce qu + e or i	¿Qué / A qué hora... desayunas, almuerzas, comes, cenas? desayuno, almuerzo, ceno normalmente, a veces, también a las... entre las... y las... **Culture** Different patterns of mealtimes, items of food	**Grammar** más / menos... que more / less... than Time (Revision) **Skills** Read using clues (WS71 Leer) **Pronunciation** qu + e or i	**Attainment** AT1 Level 4; AT2 Levels 2–4; AT3 Level 4; AT4 Levels 1–4 **Framework Objectives** 7W1,7W2, 7W6, 7S1, 7S2, 7S3, 7S4, 7S9, 7T1, 7T3, 7T5, 7T6, 7L1, 7L2, 7L3, 7L4, 7L5, 7L6, 7C2 **Programmes of Study** 1abc, 2abcfi, 3bcde, 4bc, 5abcdei **QCA Scheme of Work** Language content: Unit 8 La comida Context: food and drink **Assessment for learning** Objectives, p.77 Ex3, 4a, 4b & c, Plenary
8D ¿Qué haces cuando llueve? (pp. 78–81) **Objectives** • describe the weather • say what you do depending on the weather • learn how to guess answers	(cuando) llueve, nieva, hay tormenta, hace sol, hace frío, hace buen tiempo, hace mal tiempo, hace calor, hiela... practico la natación, voy al cine / de compras / al centro, salgo con amigos, toco el piano, escucho música, navego por Internet, veo la tele, hago los deberes, me quedo en casa **Culture** Typical Spanish pupil's daily routine (p.63)	**Grammar** Clauses with cuando **Skills** Anticipate answers, forming questions (WS70 Hablar) Listening for detail (WS69 Escuchar) Expressions of time and frequency (WS73 *¡Así se hace!*)	**Attainment** AT1 Level 2, AT2 Levels 2–4, AT3 Level 2, AT4 Levels 2–4 **Framework Objectives** 7W1, 7W2, 7S3, 7S4, 7S7, 7L1, 7L2, 7L4, 7L5, 7T7, 7L3, 7L6 **Programmes of Study** 1abc, 2acdefg, 3e, 5a, bcdefhi **QCA Scheme of Work** Language content: Unit 5 En el pueblo Context: weather **Assessment for learning** Objectives, p.78 Ex2 & 3, Plenary, All revision activities p.80

Other resources: *¡Ahora tú!* pp.132–133   WS 67–75   Flashcards 68–91   WBA & B pp.39–42   Assessment Units 7–8 (R & A file pp.128–131)   Just Click CD-Rom

117

8A Tu rutina diaria

pp. 72–73

> **Objectives:**
> - say what you do in a typical day
> - learn how to use reflexive verbs
> - learn how to scan text for information
>
> **Key Language:** see p.117 for full list
>
> **Grammar:**
> - learn how to use reflexive verbs
>
> **Skills:** reading for gist
>
> **Resources:** Visual 67 (daily routine); Worksheets 72 (Escribir – daily routine), 74 (Gramática – reflexive verbs); CD3; Workbooks A and B p.39; *Just Click* CD-Rom.

Lesson starter 7T1, 7T3

(If students were not taught to tell the time with quarter to/past and half past in Unit 6, they will need to learn this first before tackling this unit).

Use the pictures A–L on page 72 for the starter. Explain to students that the starter will require them to ignore some information and scan rapidly for certain items – a useful life skill. Put the time phrases from the captions under the pictures A–L on the board in random order. Ask students to match these to the appropriate picture. Set a time limit: how fast can they do this and yet be accurate?

Answers

A a las siete y cuarto **B** a las ocho **C** de cinco a seis y media **D** a las siete **F** a las cuatro **G** a las nueve **H** a las diez **K** a las siete y media

Alternative lesson starter (for lessons starting part-way through the section) 7S4, 7W5

(Before exercise 3). Ask students to focus on captions A, D, E, G, H, I, J, L from exercise 1. Explain to them that the verbs in these are all -ar verbs, and ask students to work out the *tú* form of each of them, changing the *me* to *te* and altering the ending. Fast-finishers can work out the *tú* forms of verbs in speech bubbles B, F, C, K. Remind them that these verbs have irregularities and to check the grammar section at the back of the book. Set a time limit.

Introduction

Read the objectives at the top of the page, and ask students what kind of language they think each picture A–L conveys – what might María be saying in each?

1 🎧 Escucha y lee. Pon los dibujos en orden. AT1.2, 7W1, 7W2, 7W5

Students listen and read and put the pictures in the order that reflect María's daily routine. Subsequent oral exercises could include whole-class or pairwork in which one student reads a phrase 1–12 and the other(s) answer(s) with the letter of the matching picture, and vice versa. Visual 67 could be used for presentation of new language and for recognition/oral games.

Answers

D, A, I, K, L, E, B, F, C, J, G, H

CD3, track 01

> – ¿Cuál es tu rutina diaria, María?
> – Normalmente me despierto a las siete.
>   Después me levanto a las siete y cuarto.
>   Me ducho.
>   Me visto a las siete y media...
>   ... y desayuno.
>   Después, me peino y me lavo los dientes.
>   Salgo de casa a las ocho.
>   Normalmente vuelvo a casa a las cuatro...
>   ... y hago los deberes de cinco a seis y media.
>   Luego me relajo.
>   Siempre ceno con mi familia a las nueve.
>   Me acuesto a las diez.

💡 Gramática: reflexive verbs 7W1, 7W5

Read through the explanation with students, and check their understanding. Point out that the endings of these verbs are regular. You might like to use Worksheet 74 (Gramática) at this point.

Support

With some groups it may be enough to concentrate on the singulars only, or even just the active use of the *yo* form and passive understanding of the other singulars.

Extension

Some quick oral practice may help students in memorising these forms: initially with the book, and then without, one student can call out a verb form (e.g. *levantas*) and the other(s) call out the appropriate pronoun (e.g. *tú*). This could then be done in reverse (pronoun first, rest of verb given in reply) and extended to other regular verbs like *lavarse, ducharse, bañarse, peinarse, relajarse.*

2a ☑ 💬 Entrevista a tu pareja 7W5, 7S4, 7L6

Students use the question forms and sample answers to find out about the daily routine of their partner. Encourage them to note the appropriate times for use in exercise 2b.

Support

Allow students to use the book to do this, after modelling appropriate answers as students take it in turns to ask you the questions – they usually enjoy hearing about your own routine!

Extension

Encourage the student who is replying to the questions to do this without the book, listening carefully to the verb used in the question as a prompt for their reply.

2b ☑ ✏ ¡extra! Describe la rutina de tu pareja. 7W5, 7S4, 7L6

The list of verbs in the third person will allow students to describe to another person in the class the routine of the partner with whom they've worked. You might like to point out that these verbs could be used as questions too: *¿Cuándo se levanta? Se levanta a las...* Encourage students to add in the cross-topic words *por la mañana/tarde*, first checking where these might be used (e.g. *¿Te lavas los dientes por la noche?*; *¿Cuándo te duchas: por la mañana o por la tarde?*).

3a ☑ 💡 📖 Lee el correo electrónico y rellena el cuadro con las horas correctas.
AT3.4; 7T3, 7S7, 7T4, 7C2.

Students read the text about Antonio's routine and that of his sister. Students can be asked to use their dictionaries to collect together words from the text connected with the sequence of events (e.g. then, afterwards) or frequency (e.g. normally). (These are: *normalmente, más tarde, siempre, después/después de cenar, luego*).

Point out the ¡Así se hace! strategy to help students as they complete the grid with the correct times. You will need to tell them that if a time is not mentioned or cannot be deduced for one of the young people they can leave the box blank.

Answers

	Antonio	María
Se despierta	7.00	–
Se levanta	7.30	8.00
Desayuna	8.00	9.00
Sale de casa	8.30	9.00
Vuelve a casa	4.30	4.30
Cena	9.00	9.00
Se acuesta	11.00	10.00

To give them an additional focus, you might like to ask them to list the letters of the pictures A–L from exercise 1, and write the letter 'a' (for Antonio) and/or 'm' (for his sister María) alongside if the text mentions their doing that activity, e.g. A a+m, and an 'x' if that activity is not mentioned at all.

Answers

A a+m   B a+m   C a   D a   E x   F a+m   G a+m   H a+m
I a   J a   K x   L a+m

3b ☑ ✏ ¡extra! Contesta al correo electrónico de Antonio 7T5, 7T6, 7T7

More able students compose a reply to Antonio's letter. Prepare for this by dividing the class into groups of three students, each with a sheet of A4 on which to make a word web. One student notes down useful verbs for morning routine, up to arriving at school; the second notes down useful verbs for the afternoon and evening routine on the return from school; the third makes a list of useful connectives, sequencing and frequency words. These can then be checked as a whole group and any other words added which might be useful (e.g. first – *primero*; finally – *finalmente, por último*) before students begin their own drafts. Ask students to set themselves a personal challenge: do they need to be particularly careful about accuracy and verb endings?; do they need to try and use longer sentences?; is their previous work lacking in frequency and sequencing words?

Support

WS 72 Escribir could also be used at this point.

Plenary 7T7

☑ Ask students to look at a piece of writing which they have done recently with their partner with a view to evaluating its strengths and identifying one thing to improve on (this will ensure positive feedback). Brainstorm with them a list of what these things might be: accuracy of spelling, accuracy of verb endings, correct use of *el/la/los/las*, legibility of handwriting, correct use of exclamation and question marks at the beginning and end of sentences, sentence length (too short, reads in a staccato fashion) etc. Ask students to write these points down ('I did well at...'; 'In my next piece of writing I will...'). Make time after the next piece of writing to re-evaluate how well each student achieved his/her objective.

Alternative plenary *(for lessons ending part-way through the section)* 7W5

☑ Ask students to work in pairs or groups of three or four. They take it in turns, using their books if necessary, to call out a verb in the first, second or third person, and the others identify it by saying *yo, tú, él/ella.*

8B ¿Qué haces los fines de semana?
pp. 74–75

> **Objectives:**
> • say what you do at the weekend
> • recognise and use adverbs
> **Key Language:** see p.117 for full list
> **Grammar:** recognise and use adverbs
> **Skills:** how to deal with unknown language
> **Resources:** Worksheet 75 (¡extra! – classroom language); CD3; Workbooks A and B p.40; *Just Click* CD-Rom.

Lesson starter 7W7, 7T4, 7L1

Write the following adjectives on the board or OHT: *rápido, lento, inmediato, enérgico, tranquilo, fácil, completo, profundo, difícil, evidente* and ask students to work out how to pronounce these, paying particular attention to the accents, and rewrite them in alphabetical order. Explain to students that their second task is to look these up in the dictionary as fast as possible and jot down the meanings – are there any they can guess? Set a time limit.

Alternative lesson starter *(for lessons starting part-way through the section)* 7W1, 7W2

The following starter prepares students for listening exercise 2. Give students the following words on the OHT or board: *mucho, más, muy, temprano, tarde, no, bastante.* Check the English meanings with them, especially for *mucho/más/muy* which students often confuse, or have these written alongside the Spanish already. Setting a time limit, ask students to devise as many combinations of the words as they can which make sense, e.g. *muy tarde, no muy tarde* etc. Individual students feed back one combination at a time, the rest of the class checking their own lists and crossing off any expression mentioned by someone else – has anyone in the class thought of a combination which no one else has?

1a ⊙ Escucha (1–6) y lee la rutina de María. Une las frases con los dibujos. AT1.3, AT3.3; 7W1, 7T1, 7T2

After students listen to the tape once through, give them practice in reading aloud as a class. Every time you call out a student's name, they have to begin reading where the previous student ended. Allow them to read only a short sentence or half of a longer one to keep them on their toes. Mentally note words or sounds which cause problems, and practise these with the whole class afterwards. You might like to have students repeat each one five times, using the newly met words *rápidamente, lentamente,* to indicate how they are to repeat.

Use the ¡Así se hace! strategy to help students work out the meaning of each section. Students can then match each picture to the appropriate piece of text.

Answers

1F **2**C **3**E **4**B **5**A **6**D

TRANSCRIPT   CD3, track 02

– Hola, María. ¿Es diferente tu rutina los fines de semana?
– ¡Uy, sí, es muy diferente!

1 Los sábados me despierto a las nueve más o menos, pero no me levanto inmediatamente. Me quedo en la cama y me levanto a las diez y media.
Entresemana me despierto a las siete y me levanto a las siete y cuarto.

2 Después desayuno lentamente los sábados. Entresemana desayuno poco, y rápidamente, pero los sábados desayuno mucho.

3 Los sábados, después de desayunar, me relajo, veo la tele o escucho música tranquilamente.

4 Me visto lentamente a las once y media y salgo de casa a las doce.
De lunes a viernes me visto rápidamente a las siete y media y salgo de casa a las ocho.

5 Los sábados, vuelvo a casa por la tarde, a las seis, y a veces hago mis deberes a las siete. Entresemana vuelvo a las cuatro, y hago los deberes a las cinco.

6 Luego los sábados, veo la tele tranquilamente o navego por Internet. Entresemana me acuesto temprano, a las diez, pero los sábados me acuesto tarde, a las once y media o a las doce.

1b ☑ 📖 Copia el cuadro y rellena los detalles. AT3.3; 7T1

Students copy the grid and note the details.

Answers

	Se despierta	Se levanta	Desayuna	Vuelve a casa	Hace los deberes	Se acuesta
Entresemana	7.00	7.15	Poco, rápidamente	4.00	5.00	10.00
Los sábados	9.00	10.30	lentamente	6.00	7.00	11.30/ 12.00

Support

Provide a grid with some of the details completed, or ask partners to work together with one concentrating on *Entresemana* and the other on *Los sábados.*

Gramática: adverbs 7W2

Read through the grammar explanation with students, brainstorming a number of adverbs in English (quickly, hurriedly, happily, sadly etc.). Show the formation of adverbs from adjectives ending in -o and in a consonant. You might like to use the following for further examples: *franco, urgente, hábil.*

Extension

You might like to point out that there are two forms of the adverb from *rápido:* both *rápido* and *rápidamente* are current. As an alternative to *inmediatamente, en seguida* is frequently used.

1c Change the following adjectives into adverbs. 7W2

Using the rules from the Gramática, students work out the Spanish for the nine adverbs.

Extension

Ask students to invent five sentences using one of the adverbs from the list in each.

Answers

1 rápidamente **2** lentamente **3** difícilmente
4 inmediatamente **5** fácilmente **6** evidentemente
7 enérgicamente **8** profundamente **9** completamente

2 ⊙ Escucha (1–5) y rellena el cuadro con las horas correctas. AT3.3; 7L2

Students listen and note the times as required on the grid. Prepare students by asking them to listen to the recording first, without writing, and listen for the key expressions, raising one hand whenever they hear *me levanto* for Pedro, Inés and Daniel, and *me acuesto* for José and María Jesus.

Support

Pause the CD in between the morning and evening sections, repeating the words *el fin de semana* or *entresemana* as appropriate to help students locate where on the grid to write the information.

Answers

	Entresemana		Los fines de semana	
	Se levanta	Se acuesta	Se levanta	Se acuesta
Pedro	7.15	9.00	11.00	12.30
José	6.30	9.30	9.00	11.30
Inés	7.30	8.30	10.00	10.30
María Jesús	7.30	9.30	10.15	12.30
Daniel	7.15	10.00	10.30	11.45

TRANSCRIPT   CD3, track 03

1 – ¡Hola, Pedro! Háblame de tu rutina
– Bueno, entresemana, me levanto a las siete y cuarto, y me acuesto a las nueve.
– ¿Y los fines de semana?
– ¡Mucho más tarde! Normalmente me levanto a las once, y me acuesto a las doce y media. ▶

2 – ¿Qué tal, José?
 – Muy bien. ¿Y tú?
 – Fantástico. Dime ¿a qué hora te levantas los fines de semana?
 – Bueno, voy a la piscina, así que me levanto a las nueve, y como salgo con mis amigos, me acuesto a las once y media.
 – ¿Y entresemana?
 – Mucho más temprano. Me levanto a las seis y media, porque mi colegio está muy lejos, y me acuesto a las nueve y media.

3 – Buenas tardes, Inés.
 – Buenas tardes.
 – Dime, ¿a qué hora te levantas entresemana?
 – Normalmente me despierto a las siete, pero me levanto a las siete y media.
 – Y ¿a qué hora te acuestas?
 – Muy temprano, a las ocho y media.
 – ¿Y el fin de semana?
 – Bueno, normalmente me despierto a las diez, me levanto rápidamente, y me acuesto a las diez y media.

4 – ¡Hola, María Jesús!
 – Hola, ¿qué tal?
 – Vamos a ver. ¿A qué hora te levantas los fines de semana?
 – Normalmente, a las diez y cuarto, y me acuesto muy tarde, a las doce y media. ¡Me gusta mucho navegar por Internet!
 – ¿Y entresemana?
 – Bueno, me despierto a las siete y cuarto, y me levanto a las siete y media. Normalmente me acuesto bastante temprano, a las nueve y media.

5 – ¿Qué tal, Daniel?
 – Muy bien. ¿Y tú?
 – Estupendo. Háblame de tu rutina entresemana.
 – Siempre me levanto temprano, a las siete y cuarto, y me acuesto a las diez.
 – ¿Y los fines de semana?
 – ¡Mucho más tarde! Me levanto a las diez y media, y me acuesto bastante tarde, a las doce menos cuarto.

3a ◯ Sondeo de clase. Copia y rellena el cuadro. AT2.2; 7L6

Students make a copy of the grid, and ask each other about getting up and going to bed times in order to complete the grid.

Support

Limit this to asking five or six students only.

3b ✎ ¡extra! Escribe el resultado del sondeo. AT 4.2–3; 7S3

Students write up a summary of their survey. Remind students that the *ellos/ellas* form of the verb ends in *-an*. Encourage them to add the expressions *muy/bastante tarde* and *muy/bastante temprano*. You might also like to teach *antes/después de* with time.

Support

Provide a copy of the grid for 3a, with a framework for the summary results underneath, so that students only have to write in the appropriate number, e.g.
Por la mañana. Entresemana,...... personas se levantan antes de las 7.30. Y....... personas se levantan después de las 7.30.
Por la tarde. Entresemana,...... personas se acuestan antes de las 10.00. Y....... personas se acuestan después de las 10.00.

Plenary 7W2, 7S3

☑ Ask students to look back at Unit 6, and find or invent five sentences to which they can add an adverb, e.g. *Hago mis deberes rápidamente*. Students can then take it in turns to read out one of their sentences to the class and another student has to translate it into English. To keep the pace brisk, work against the clock – how many sentences does the class think they can say and translate in three minutes? How accurate is their estimate?

Alternative plenary *(for lessons ending part-way through the section)* 7W2, 7S7

☑ Ask students to reread the text in exercise 1 and in pairs find the Spanish for: 'on Saturdays', 'more or less', 'afterwards', 'during the week', 'after having breakfast', 'from Monday to Friday', 'sometimes'. As a follow-up, ask them to invent four sentences, each incorporating one of these.

Extension

Highlight the use of *después* and *después de* + infinitive. Ask students to brainstorm a list of other infinitives they know, e.g. *jugar, salir, ver, ir* and, as a whole class, build up a list of possible sentences using these which could enrich a description of their daily routine. With more able groups, show how the pronoun will change at the end of reflexive verbs, e.g. *después de levantar<u>me</u>, me visto...*

Answers

los sábados, más o menos, después, entresemana, después de desayunar, de lunes a viernes, a veces.

8C ¿Cuándo comes?

pp. 76–77

Objectives:
• talk about mealtimes and normal meals
• compare mealtimes in England and Spain
• learn how to pronounce *qu + e* or *i*
Key Language: see p.117 for full list
Grammar: *más/menos que*
Resources: Flashcards 68–82 (food items); Worksheet 71 (Leer – reading, using clues); CD3; Workbooks A and B p.41; *Just Click* CD-Rom.

Lesson starter 7W1, 7W6

Ask students to remind each other of the rule for stress in Spanish words, or elicit it as a whole-class exercise: in words ending in a vowel, the stress is on the penultimate (next to last) syllable; in words ending in a consonant, the stress is on the last syllable; where there is an accent, 'lean on' that syllable. Then ask students to work in pairs to decide how to pronounce the words next to the pictures on page 76, paying particular attention to the stress. They can then compare their decisions with another pair of students.

Alternative lesson starter *(for lessons starting part-way through the section)* 7W1

With their books closed, and working in silence in groups of four, ask each student to take a piece of paper and write on it one item of food or drink before passing it on to the next person in their group to add another. The word they add has to be a word which is not already on any of the lists. Set a time limit. Ask students in turn to read out their lists – other students strike out on their lists any item mentioned. Which group have items which no one else has thought of?

Introduction

Read the objectives with students and explain that food items, and information about mealtimes, are the focus. Explain the headings *desayuno, almuerzo, merienda, cena* above the pictures: what differences can they see already between meals in the two countries?

1 💡 📖 **Lee el texto 'En España y en Inglaterra'. Encuentra las expresiones en español. AT3.4; 7T1, 7T3, 7L2, 7C2**

Use the flashcards 68–82 and games to present the new language for items of food.

Students then read the text and find the Spanish equivalents for the English phrases 1–10. In preparation, you might like to highlight the construction *se* + third person (e.g. *se desayuna, se come*) to convey the impersonal 'one'/'they'/'we'. Ask students what the title and pictures tell them about the content then read the text aloud as they follow, raising their hands every time an item of food or drink is mentioned.

Answers

1 diferente **2** tostadas **3** pan con aceite **4** el almuerzo **5** entre las dos y las cuatro **6** casi todos los españoles van a casa **7** un primer plato **8** un plato principal **9** la cena es muy tarde **10** no comen mucho.

Gramática: comparatives 7W2

Introduce *más/menos... que*. You might like to give students the following sentences about the text in exercise 1. Their task is to insert *más* or *menos* in each gap as appropriate. (The answers are in brackets.)

1 En España se toma...... pan con aceite que en Inglaterra (*más*). **2** El almuerzo en Inglaterra es....... importante que en España (*menos*). **3** La cena española se toma...... tarde que en Inglaterra (*más*). **4** Se come..... en la cena española que en la cena inglesa. (*menos*). **5** Se toman....... platos en la cena en España que en el almuerzo (*más*).

2 📖 **Lee el texto 'Una entrevista'. ¿Verdad (V) o mentira (M)? AT3.4; 7S1, 7S2**

You might like to use the reading text first as the basis for consolidating students' understanding of word order, and using this to work out meaning. Remind students of the verbs *desayuno, almuerzo, tomo, como, ceno*, and that, as in English, these are often followed by an item of food/drink or a time (*a la/s...*). Ask students to read through the text and notice how many instances of each there are, what else follows these verbs and if it is the same word order as in English. Students then answer true or false to statements 1–7.

Answers

1V **2**M **3**M **4**V **5**M **6**M **7**V

3 ✓ 💿 **Escucha (1–4). ¿Qué toman, y a qué hora? Copia y rellena el cuadro. AT1.4; 7L3**

Students make a copy of the grid and note the times at which the four young people eat and what they eat. They will need to hear this a number of times in order to note all the information required.

Support

Play only one or two sections of the recording to reduce the amount students need to listen for. As an alternative, provide students with a list of the food items mentioned by Inés and Paco, and students write I or P beside each.

TRANSCRIPT CD3, track 04

1 – ¡Hola! Me llamo Inés. Normalmente desayuno poco, un café y unas galletas, a las siete de la mañana.
 – Siempre almuerzo en casa, a las dos. Normalmente como pollo o pasta.
 – No meriendo nunca, porque cenamos bastante temprano, a las ocho y media. Normalmente ceno ensalada y fruta.

2 – ¿Qué tal? Soy Paco. Te voy a hablar del horario de mis comidas. Desayuno bastante: un café con leche, cereales y dos tostadas. Normalmente desayuno con mi hermano a las ocho menos cuarto.
 – Tomamos el almuerzo bastante temprano en mi casa – a la una y media. Almuerzo pescado y verduras, o pizza.
 – Siempre meriendo a las seis y media, normalmente un té y dos galletas.
 – Y para cenar, me gusta comer una hamburguesa con patatas fritas. Normalmente cenamos a las diez.

3 – ¡Hola! ¿qué tal? Me llamo Pepa. Te voy a explicar lo que como cada día. Me gusta mucho el desayuno: tomo café con leche y pan con aceite, a las ocho de la mañana.
 – No almuerzo mucho, porque almuerzo en el instituto a la una y media. Tomo un trozo de pizza o una hamburguesa.
 – Siempre meriendo en casa a las seis: un té y algo de fruta.
 – Ceno en casa con mi familia a las nueve o nueve y media. Cenamos pollo y verduras, o pescado. De postre siempre tomamos fruta.

4 – Buenas tardes. Soy Pablo. No me gusta mucho desayunar, sólo tomo un vaso de leche antes de ir al instituto a las nueve.
 – ¡A la hora del almuerzo tengo mucha hambre! Como pasta con tomate, y después carne o pescado. En casa almorzamos a las dos. De postre tomo fruta, o en verano un helado.
 – Meriendo un té con tostadas a las cinco y media.
 – Y para cenar, normalmente como un perrito caliente o una hamburguesa con patatas. Ceno bastante tarde, a las nueve y media o a las diez.

Answers

		Inés	Paco	Pepa	Pablo
Desayuno	Hora	7	7.45	8.00	9.00
	Comida	Café, galletas	Café con leche, cereales, tostadas	Café con leche, pan con aceite	Vaso de leche
Almuerzo	Hora	2.00	1.30	1.30	2.00
	Comida	Pollo, pasta	Pescado, verduras, pizza	Pizza, hamburguesa	Pasta con tomate, carne, pescado, fruta, helado
Merienda	Hora	—	6.30	6.00	5.30
	Comida	—	Té, galletas	Té, fruta	Té, tostadas
Cena	Hora	8.30	10.00	9.00, 9.30	9.30, 10.00
	Comida	Ensalada, fruta	Hamburguesa, patatas fritas	Pollo, verduras, pescado, fruta	Perrito caliente, hamburguesa con patatas

4a ☑ ✍ Escribe un menú normal para ti y las horas correctas. AT4.2–4; 7T5, 7T6, 7L4

There are several graded possibilities for producing a piece of writing: the grid can be used to help students with the correct verb forms; they can produce a sentence or two for each mealtime, explaining when they eat and what they eat. Refer students back to the picture prompts on page 76 for useful vocabulary.

Support

At the simplest level, students could produce, with the help of ICT if liked, a list of what they eat under the heading for each meal, using as a model the vocabulary in *Gastronomía: En España y en Inglaterra* on page 76.

Extension

Set students the task of producing a piece of writing, independently, on their meals and mealtimes. Ask them to prepare this by working in small groups to produce a topic web of ideas, types of language and sources of support, e.g. 'things I eat and things I don't eat' (p.76, Resumen, dictionary, food and drink items from Unit 7); 'likes and dislikes' (Unit 7); 'differences between the week and weekend' (8A and 8B). They can also look back at the cross-topic words in each unit for useful high-frequency vocabulary.

4b ☑ 💬 Pregunta a tu pareja. AT2.3–4; 7L6

Students use the questions as the basis for a conversation with a partner.

Support

Work with students to elicit the possible start of each reply and write these prompts up on the board or OHT (e.g. *Desayuno... a las...*).

4c ☑ 💬 ¡extra! Presenta a tu pareja al resto de la clase. AT2.3–4; 7L6

Ask students to prepare a brief summary (lasting 60–90 seconds) which explains what their partner's eating routine and habits are. These can be presented within a group of five or six students rather than to the whole class if time is short. The sample answers will help students use the third person part of the verbs.

🎧 Pronunciación: *qu + e* or *i* 7W6, 7L1, 7L6

Students listen to the recording, practise the pronunciation of the *qu* sound, and memorise the tongue twister. Other useful words to read out while students try writing them down might be: *quiosco, quitar, quedar, química, quizá*. They might also enjoy *quiniela* (football pools), *quinqui* (delinquent) and *quisquilloso/a* (pernickety, touchy).

TRANSCRIPT CD3, track 05

| queso | quién | qué | quiero | quisiera |

¡Qué queso tan rico quiere Quique!

Plenary 7S4, 7S9, 7L4, 7L5, 7L6

☑ Remind students that when speaking to someone they don't know well or who is in a position of authority they need to use the *usted* form of the verb, and this is the same as the *el/ella* part. Ask students to work in groups of three or four to devise a list of questions they might ask you (or a visitor)

---

about your mealtimes and eating habits, e.g. *¿A qué hora desayuna usted?*; *¿Qué desayuna normalmente?* They may find it helpful to remember that the *el/ella/usted* form is almost always the same as the *tú* form, minus the final *-s*. Each group can feed back one question at a time as you write them on the board or OHT, until a complete list is obtained. You – or the Spanish assistant or another Spanish teacher – can then sit in the hot seat and reply to students' questions.

Finally, encourage students to think about occasions when they can use some of these in class in everyday conversation to you and to each other, e.g. *¿Qué almuerza(s) hoy?*; *¿A qué hora almuerza(s) hoy?*; *¿Toma(s)... hoy?*

Alternative plenary *(for lessons ending part-way through the section)* 7S3

☑ The text *En España y en Inglaterra* could act as a focus for teaching the skill of summarising in English or Spanish (Programme of study 2i). Put the following statements in English on paper or on an OHT, and ask students to divide them into two groups: those which contain the most important (key) points and those which contain additional detail.

1 The times of meals are very different in Spain to those in England. **2** The Spanish have white coffee and toast or bread for breakfast. **3** Lunch is the most important meal. **4** Lunch is eaten between two and four. **5** Most Spanish people go home for lunch. **6** The main dish is usually based around meat or fish. **7** Fruit is usually eaten as dessert. **8** The evening meal is eaten late, between nine and ten thirty. **9** People eat less at the evening meal. **10** The evening meal often consists of an omelette, vegetables and fruit. **11** Children also have a snack at about six or half six. **12** Popular snacks are a glass of milk and biscuits or a cake.

Elicit their replies and ask them to put the key points into a two-sentence summary.

Extension

Students can do this summary in Spanish, reusing and adapting the language from the text *En España y en Inglaterra*.

8D ¿Qué haces cuándo llueve?
page 78

> **Objectives:**
> - describe the weather
> - say what you do depending on the weather
> - learn how to guess answers
>
> **Key Language:** see p.117 for full list
>
> **Skills:**
> - anticipate answers
> - form questions
> - listen for detail
> - use time and frequency phrases
>
> **Resources:** Flashcards 83–91 (weather); Worksheets 70 (Hablar – questions), 69 (Escuchar – listening for detail), 73 (¡Así se hace! – time and frequency phrases); CD3; Workbooks A and B p.42; *Just Click* CD-Rom.

Lesson starter 7W1

Put up the following verbs, which students have met before in Unit 6, and ask them to complete each one in as many ways as they can within three minutes: *practico, juego, voy, algo, toco, escucho, navego, veo, hago, me quedo, leo.* Ask students in turn to read out one of their sentences. Everyone else repeats it and crosses it off their list.

1 📖 Une los dibujos y las frases AT3.2

Students match each sentence to its appropriate picture.

Answers

1F **2**H **3**E **4**G **5**D **6**C **7**I **8**A **9**B

2 ☑ 💡 💿 Escucha (1–9). ¿Qué actividades hacen según el tiempo? AT1.2; 7L3

Use the flashcards 83–91 to present the weather phrases, and use games to consolidate these and help students memorise them. Work through the ¡Así se hace! strategy with them, and allow students to note down which answers they anticipate hearing for four or five of the sentences 1–9. They then listen and complete these according to the information given in the recording: were they right in any of their guesses?

TRANSCRIPT   **CD3, track 06**

1 Cuando llueve, **veo la tele.**
2 Cuando nieva, **voy a esquiar.**
3 Cuando hay tormenta, **me quedo en la cama.**
4 Cuando hace sol, **voy al parque.**
5 Cuando hace frío, **navego por Internet.**
6 Cuando hace buen tiempo, **salgo con mis amigos.**
7 Cuando hace mal tiempo, **me quedo en casa.**
8 Cuando hace calor, **voy a la piscina.**
9 Cuando hiela, **voy a la pista de patinaje.**

Answers in bold in the recording.

3 ☑ ✏️ ¿Y tú? ¿Qué actividades haces? Escribe una lista. AT4.2–4; 7W2, 7T7

Using the phrases given in the box, students choose an activity for each type of weather and write a sentence to convey this.

✏️ Extension

Ask students to write two paragraphs, one describing what students do in good weather and one saying what they do when the weather is bad. They have to include at least six of the weather expressions A–I, as well as at least four verbs from the units on daily routine and food (8A–C), two adverbs (8B) and four of the following cross-topic phrases: *normalmente, entresemana, el fin de semana, a veces, en invierno, en verano.*

4a 💬 Pregunta a tu pareja y anota las respuestas. AT2.2; 7L6

Students use the formula *¿Qué haces cuando...?*, in conjunction with the weather phrases from exercise 2, to ask a partner about their activities in different types of weather.

4b ✏️ ¡extra! Escribe lo que hace tu pareja. AT4.2-4; 7T5

Students use the information gleaned in the speaking exercise to write up what their partner does in different types of weather with the help of the third person verbs in the box.

Plenary 7S3, 7S4, 7S7, 7L4, 7L5

☑ This exercise focuses on helping students reuse known language in other contexts and cope with the unexpected. Ask students to invent between four and six other questions each using a different verb and incorporating a weather phrase, e.g. *¿Sales mucho con tus amigos en invierno?*; *¿Qué te gusta hacer cuando hace calor?*; *¿Qué prefieres beber cuando hace frío?*; *¿A qué hora te levantas el fin de semana cuando hace sol?* Refer them back to Unit 6 for free time (pp. 52–63), Unit 7 for food and drink (pp. 64–71) and Unit 8 for daily routine (pp. 72–77). As a follow-up, have students work in groups of five or six to ask their questions and answer those of others. Brainstorm ways of coping with the unexpected and model some of these: asking for repetition (*Repite/Puedes repetir(lo) por favor*); repeating part of the question to let it sink in (*... ¿cuando hace sol?*); using fillers to give yourself time to think (*bueno, pues, es que...*).

Resumen *(page 79)*

Discuss with students how they can make use of this resource, e.g. as a reference point while working through a unit or as a list from which they can learn vocabulary:

• Students copy onto paper any three words or phrases from the list which they find difficult to remember and give you the pieces of paper.
• In the next lesson, you display a collated list of the problem words and students test each other on them in pairs.

Repaso *(page 80)*

☑ This revision page revises work from Units 7 and 8.

1 💿 Escucha (1–4) a los jóvenes. ¿Qué quieren comer y beber? Copia y completa el cuadro. AT1.4; 7L3.

Students copy the grid and note down the information required.

Answers

	Comida	Bebida	Precio
1	hamburguesa con queso, patatas fritas	Fanta de limón	5.60 euros
2	bocadillo de jamón, ensalada	agua mineral con gas	6.45 euros
3	un pincho de tortilla	Coca-Cola con limón	4.35 euros
4	aceitunas, patatas bravas, calamares	zumo de naranja, Coca-Cola 'light'	13.75 euros

---

TRANSCRIPT   **CD3, track 07**

1 – ¿Qué quiere de comer?
  – Bueno, creo que me gustaría una hamburguesa con queso y con patatas fritas. ¡Tengo mucha hambre!
  – ¿Y qué quiere de beber?
  – No sé, ¿tiene Coca-Cola?
  – No, pero hay Fanta de limón.
  – Bueno, pues una Fanta. ¿Cuánto es?
  – Son cinco euros con sesenta.
  – Gracias.
2 – ¡Hola! me gustaría pedir algo de comer.
  – Vale, ¿qué quiere?   ▶

– Me gustaría un bocadillo de jamón y una ensalada.
– Muy bien. ¿Qué quiere de beber?
– Un agua mineral con gas, por favor.
– Bien, son seis euros con cuarenta y cinco.
– Aquí tiene, gracias.
– Gracias a Vd.

3 – ¡Hola! ¿me pone una Coca-Cola con limón, por favor?
– Aquí tiene. ¿Algo más?
– Sí, me gustaría algo de comer. ¿Tiene tortilla de patatas?
– Sí, tenemos tortilla.
– Pues un pincho de tortilla, y la cuenta, por favor.
– Aquí tiene. Son cuatro euros con treinta y cinco.
– Gracias.

4 – ¡Hola! Me gustaría pedir, por favor.
– Sí, ¿que desea?
– Bueno, de comer me gustaría unas aceitunas y unas patatas bravas. Y para mí amigo unos calamares.
– ¿Y de beber?
– Yo quiero un zumo de naranja, y para mi amigo una Coca-Cola 'light'.
– Aquí tiene.
– ¿Cuánto es?
– A ver, son... sí, trece euros con setenta y cinco.
– Aquí tiene, gracias.

2 ✐ Mira la cuenta del restaurante *El Caracol*. Escribe la conversación y practica en grupos de cuatro. AT2.4; 7L6

Students use the items on the bill to invent a conversation in the café, playing the parts of customers and the waiter.

3a ✐ Imagina que eres María. Lee y contesta a las preguntas. A3.4; 7S3, 7T7

Students read the text and answer the questions as if they were María.

Answers

1 Mi bebida favorita es la Coca-cola light. **2** Me gusta desayunar té y cereales. **3** Entresemana me levanto a las siete y media. **4** Los sábados me levanto a las diez y media. **5** Entresemana salgo de casa a las ocho y media. **6** Normalmente ceno en casa. **7** Entresemana normalmente me acuesto a las nueve. **8** Los fines de semana me acuesto a las once y media o a las doce.

3b ✐ Contesta a las preguntas para ti y escribe un párrafo. Usa la letra de María como modelo. A4.4; 7S3, 7T7

Students use the example as a model for their own piece of writing about daily routine, which answers the questions 1–8.

Reading (page 81)
AT3.2–4; 7S2, 7T4

1 ✐ Contesta a las preguntas en inglés.

Students read the text, using a dictionary or the vocabulary section at the back of the Student's Book if necessary, and answer the questions in English.

Answers

1 María José. **2** 13 years old. **3** Granada in the south of Spain. **4** Goes swimming at seven. **5** Tea with milk and cereals. **6** Yes. **7** 8.45 a.m. **8** Very close to her home. **9** She is with friends. **10** Pizza and salad. **11** 4.00 p.m. **12** Piano classes, language lessons. **13** Chicken and vegetables, or pasta. **14** Relaxes, watches TV, surfs the Net, speaks to friends on the phone. On Saturdays she goes to the cinema or the shopping centre. **15** During the week, at 9.30 or 10.00 p.m. At the weekend, at 12 or 12.30 a.m.

2 ✐ Une las dos partes de las frases.

Students match up the sentence halves.

Answers

1h **2**c **3**b **4**f **5**d **6** **7**i **8**g

¡Ahora, tú! (pp 132–133)

Differentiated self-access reading and writing exercises: see page 37 for more information.

page 132

1 ✐ Put the sentences into the appropriate order.

Those answers that are in bold incorporate time phrases, which students are asked to translate in exercise 2.

Answers

6, **8**, 7, 2, 3, **10**, **11**, **4**, **1**, 9, **5**

2 ✐ Write the times from the sentences above in figures.

Answers

6 (Me despierto) 6.45; **8** (Me levanto) 7.00; **10** (Salgo de casa) 8.30; **11** (Vuelvo) 4.00; **4** (Deberes) 5.00–6.30; **1** (Ceno) 7.30; **5** (Me acuesto) 9.45.

4 ✐ Match up the questions and answers.

Answers

1d **2**c **3**b **4**a **5**e **6**f **7**g

page 133

1 ✐ Read the interview and answer the questions.

Answers

1 Se levanta a las diez o a las diez y media. **2** Se levanta a las siete o a las siete y media. **3** Desayuna pan tostado y un café. **4** Come a la una. **5** Le gusta comer un bocadillo de queso o una ensalada, y de postre una fruta. **6** Cena a las nueve, y le gusta la pasta. **7** Cena en un restaurante – pescado con verdura y un helado.

3 📖 **Put the words and sentences in the correct order.**

Answers (word order)

1 Me levanto a las siete y media. **2** Ceno pasta y una ensalada a las nueve. **3** Vuelvo a casa con mi hermano a las cuatro. **4** (Several possibilities) Hago los deberes y me relajo por la tarde delante de la tele/Hago los deberes delante de la tele y me relajo por la tarde/Por la tarde, hago mis deberes y me relajo delante de la tele. (etc.). **5** Me acuesto a las diez menos cuarto. **6** Desayuno un café con leche y tostadas.

Answers (sentence order)

1, 6, 3, 4, 2, 5

Worksheets Unit 8

WS 67 La rutina diaria AT3.1; 7W1

Visuals: daily routine from Section A.

WS 68 Resumen AT3.1; 7W1

List of key language of the unit.

WS 69 Escuchar 7L1, 7L2

This worksheet highlights the importance of accurate listening for detail.

1 Read through the initial points with students, using examples like *hermano/hermana, padre/madre, pescado/helado, casa/cara*. Set students a time limit for comparing the sounds in the italicised words before feeding back to you. Stress the importance of listening attentively. Play the recording twice while students underline the words they hear. Correct answers are underlined in the transcript below.

TRANSCRIPT
CD3, track 08

¿Mi rutina? Depende. Normalmente, me <u>levanto</u> bastante temprano. Desayuno pan con <u>aceite</u> y un café con leche. Almuerzo con la familia a las dos y media. Normalmente, comemos carne con <u>patatas</u> y verduras pero si hace mucho <u>calor</u> comemos un plato de <u>pescado</u>. Por la tarde, después de las clases, meriendo <u>un bocadillo</u>. Si salgo con mis <u>amigas</u>, tomamos <u>un chocolate</u> en el centro. También hay un bar que sirve tapas muy buenas de <u>atún</u>, y <u>perritos</u> calientes fenomenales.

2 Students listen carefully and note the letters of the appropriate pictures. Remind them not to make assumptions but to listen carefully to what is said – everyone's daily routine is different!

Answers

Paquita: a, c, g, b. Daniel: b, d, e, h.
Raquel: g, d, c, f.

TRANSCRIPT
CD3, track 09

1 – ¿Cómo es tu rutina, Paquita?
– Pues... me levanto, y luego me ducho.
– ¿No te bañas?
– No, me gusta más la ducha.
– ¿Y luego?
– Como algo – pan o un yogur con una bebida caliente.
– ¿Qué haces después?
– Me lavo los dientes, y después, depende si es un día de colegio o no...

2 – Daniel, ¿qué haces primero por la mañana?
– Me lavo los dientes.
– ¿Primero?
– Sí, siempre. Y luego me baño. No me gusta ducharme.
– ¿Y después de bañarte?
– Después, me visto. Me pongo vaqueros, un jersey...
– ¿Desayunas?
– No. Salgo de casa a las ocho. A veces, si tengo hambre, voy al bar de enfrente...

3 – Y tú, Raquel, ¿cómo es tu rutina?
– A las diez, tomo algo – un chocolate caliente, tal vez, o una tostada o como un poco de pan.
– ¿Te bañas o te duchas?
– Primero me relajo en el baño. Depués, me ducho.
– ¿Te bañas y te duchas? ¿Por qué?
– El agua del baño está caliente, y me gusta terminar con agua fría.
– ¿Y qué haces después?
– Me acuesto a las once, o a las once y media. A veces, leo un poco o veo la tele.

WS 70 Hablar 7S4

This worksheet includes all themes covered in the unit. The table at the bottom reminds students whether verbs are -ar, -er, or -ir, as the first person form does not show this. Stem-changing or irregular verbs are marked with an asterisk. Model some examples on the board or OHT first. Students can choose whichever question words are most appropriate – there may be several possibilities and more able students can be encouraged to explore these and write possible answers.

Possible Answers

1 ¿A qué hora/Cuándo te despiertas? **2** ¿A qué hora/Cuándo te levantas? **4** ¿Qué/Dónde/Con quién desayunas? **6** ¿A qué hora/Cuándo sales de casa? **7** ¿A qué hora/Cuándo vuelves a casa? **8** ¿Qué/Dónde/Cómo/Con quién meriendas? **9** ¿A qué hora/Cuándo haces los deberes? **12** ¿Qué/Dónde/A qué hora/Con quién cenas? **13** ¿A qué hora/Cuándo cómo/Dónde te relajas? **14** ¿A qué hora/Cuándo te acuestas?

WS 71 Leer 7T1

a As a starter, remind or elicit from students that many verbs to do with routine are reflexive in Spanish (*me despierto, me lavo* etc.) and brainstorm these. List verbs to do with eating and drinking (*comer/como* etc.) and highlight that these are not reflexive. Ask students to read through the text and underline all verbs once and reflexive ones twice. In preparation for the first exercise on the sheet, ask them to look at the extracts now – what does their underlining tell them about which extracts contain information about daily routine and which are about other things?

Answers

a2 **b**5 **c**3 **d**6 **e**1 **f**4

2 Students select the correct adverb for each gap.

Answers

1 inmediatamente **2** rápidamente **3** poco **4** fácilmente **5** tranquilamente **6** normalmente (Lentamente is over.)

WS 72 Escribir AT4.2–4.4; 7T5, 7T6

This worksheet gives students the opportunity to write according to their ability – from simple statements to longer and more detailed accounts from more able students. Shorter pieces of text could be word-processed then cut and stuck under the pictures; or students might like to scan the pictures and drop them into a longer text or 'mini-book'.

Extension

Encourage students to aim high, adding any details of food and drink they already know, and inventing other appropriate things if they like. You might like them to write in the third person for practice.

WS 73 ¡Así se hace! 7W2, 7S7

This worksheet gathers together time-related expressions which have been met in the unit and gives students an opportunity to incorporate them into some simple sentences. Remind them that there will be a number of possible options. More able students can be encouraged to develop the brief accounts into longer pieces of writing, using other daily routine verbs; you might like to set them the challenge of seeing who can use all of the time expressions appropriately!

Answers

1 **1** por la mañana **2** por la tarde **3** por la noche **4** el fin de semana **5** los fines de semana **6** durante la semana/entresemana **7** todos los días **8** luego **9** después **10** temprano/más temprano **11** tarde/más tarde **12** normalmente
2 There are a number of possibilities. Accept any which make sense.

WS 74 Gramática 7W5

This worksheet gives further practice in reflexive verbs. As a starter, you might like to write a vertical list on the board or OHP of the subject pronouns *yo, tú, él, ella, usted* etc. and list horizontally, in random order, the corresponding parts of the verb *lavar* (*lavo, lavas, lava* etc.). Ask students to work in pairs to match them up quickly. Highlight the endings, reminding students this is a regular *-ar* verb. Students can now tackle the exercises 1 and 2 on the worksheet. More able students tackling exercise 3 will be aided by the fact that it is clear how many letters are missing in each part of the verb.

Answers

1 me lavo, te lavas, se lava, nos lavamos, os laváis, se lavan.
2 te levantas, me peino, se baña, nos lavamos, me ducho, se relajan, se despierta, me quedo.

3

despertarse	acostarse	vestirse
me despiert**o**	me acuesto	me vist**o**
te despiertas	te acu**e**stas	te v**i**stes
se desp**ie**rta	se acuesta	**se** viste
nos despertamos	nos acostamos	nos vest**imos**
os despert**áis**	os acost**áis**	**os** vestís
se despiertan	se acu**e**stan	se vist**en**

WS 75 ¡extra! 7L2, 7W2, 7W3

This worksheet expands the use of adjectives and adverbs met in this unit of the Student's Book into the area of classroom language. It pulls together the vocabulary students need for giving their response to listening exercises.

1a Explain the purpose of the activities on the sheet, highlighting the fact that students have already met these words in other contexts and that there are no 'right' answers.

Play each extract twice before asking students to feed back in Spanish, using the simple headings on the sheet. If you have time to allow each student to give their opinion quickly, then write the headings on the board or OHT and build up columns of ticks underneath, so that students can see the range of views, e.g. T: *Número 1 – ¿qué opinas, James?* S: *Es bastante difícil.*

TRANSCRIPT

CD3, track 10

(slow and very clear)
1 – ¿A qué hora te levantas?
– Me levanto a las siete y me ducho.
– ¿Qué desayunas?
– No desayuno mucho: un café y una tostada.
– ¿A qué hora sales de casa?
– Salgo de casa a las ocho.

(At a medium pace, clear)
2 – ¿A qué hora vuelves a casa?
– Vuelvo de la oficina a las ocho de la tarde.
– Y luego, ¿qué haces?
– Me relajo un poco, veo la televisión y ceno con la familia.
– ¿Te acuestas temprano?
– Bastante sí. Me acuesto a las diez y media o a las once.

(Very fast, authentic)
3 – ¿A qué hora nos levantamos mañana, entonces?
– ¿A las siete o por ahí?
– ¡Qué va! Yo no soy madrugador como tú! Las nueve está bien, ¿no? ▶

– Para mí, sí. Como sabéis, soy trasnochadora y por la mañana estoy fatal.
– Oye, ¡no he venido aquí a este lugar tan precioso para pasar toda la mañana en la cama!
– Juan, tú puedes levantarte y ir por ahí...
– ¡... mientras nosotros, lirones, seguimos tranquilamente en la cama!
– ¡Qué vagas sois! ¡Y qué pérdido del tiempo pasar las vacaciones en la cama...!

(Medium-slow pace, clear)
4 – No me gusta acostarme temprano. Como paso todo el día trabajando con otras personas, explicando, charlando, animándoles, necesito una hora o dos de paz y tranquilidad antes de dormirme. No veo la tele ni siquiera escucho música. Prefiero leer o hacer algún tarea de la casa como planchar que no necesita mucha concentración. Así, me relajo.

1b Play the extracts again while students indicate in the grid the reasons for their opinion. Remind them they can have more than one reason – as long as these are not contradictory!

2a Check students understand the meanings of all the words in the grid. Do a sample example or two on the board or OHT, working from Spanish to English first, then the other way round, e.g. *Es un poco difícil porque no hablan claramente/*It's easy because there isn't any new vocabulary. Fast-finishers can practise orally with each other. With more able groups you might like to show them on the board or OHT how, when using two adverbs together, the first one loses the *-mente* ending, e.g. *Habla lenta y claramente.*

Answers

1 Es bastante fácil porque hablan lentamente. **2** Está bien porque no hay mucho vocabulario nuevo. **3** Es difícil porque hablan rápidamente. **4** Es muy fácil porque habla claramente. **5** Es un poco difícil porque hay vocabulario nuevo. **6** Está bien pero no habla muy claramente.

2b Finally, as extension, revisit classroom instructions – these could be brainstormed as a whole group. Ask students to work in groups and extend these by adding an appropriate adverb, e.g. *¡Sentaos rápidamente!* They might also find the adjectives *atento, cuidadoso* useful for forming additional adverbs.

Pruebas Unidades 7 y 8

R and A File pp.128–131

Prueba: Escuchar *(page 128)*

ex 1: AT1.3

Answers

Example **1**: ✗ cold   icy
2 ✗ hot   sunny
3 ✗ cold   ice   show
4 ✗ rain   stormy
5 ✗ hot   stormy
Mark scheme: 1 mark for each correct answer.
Total: 9. 6+ shows evidence of performance at Level 3.

TRANSCRIPT
CD4, track 34

– Muy buenos días señoras y señores oyentes. ¿Qué tiempo hace hoy en España?
Ejemplo: **1** Pues, en la costa, hace frío y hiela.
2 En la capital, en Madrid, hace mucho calor, con cuarenta grados y claro, también hace sol.
3 En las montanas, en el este, tenemos frío, ¡hiela y nieva!
4 Y en el norte, en Santander, llueve por la mañana y por la tarde tenemos mal tiempo con unas horas de tormenta.
5 Finalmente, en el sur, hace calor ¡como siempre! Pero por la noche tenemos tormenta.

ex 2: AT1.4

Answers

Example: tal
1 caliente
2 vamos
3 tomar
4 fresa
5 jamón
6 plato
7 té
8 hambre
Mark scheme: 1 mark for each correct answer.
Total: 8. 6+ shows evidence of performance at Level 4.

TRANSCRIPT
CD4, track 35

– Hola Elena. ¿Qué tal? ¿Te apetece tomar algo?
– Sí buena idea, hace frío hoy y tengo sed. Quiero tomar algo caliente.
– Entonces, vamos al bar El Forastero en la esquina.
– Y ¿qué vas a tomar? ▶

– Pues, no sé – me gustaría un batido de fresa. Y para comer, un bocadillo de jamón con patatas fritas. ¿Y tú?
– Para mí un plato de calamares y un té con limón.
– Vamos entonces – ¡ahora tengo hambre!

ex 3: AT1.4

Answers

Example: 7.00   wakes up
7.30   gets up
8.00   shower/puts on uniform/has breakfast
8.30   leaves house
9.00   arrives at school
5.00   goes home
6.00   does homework/listens to music/surfs the net
9.30   evening meal
11.00   goes to bed
Mark scheme: 1 mark for each correct answer.
Total: 8. 5+ shows evidence of performance at Level 4.

¡**extra!** 1 mark for each correct piece of information covering the above details not already awarded a mark (e.g. does homework for main mark, listens to music for the bonus).
Also: She is describing a school day. She has a hurried breakfast. She has toast and coffee with milk. Her parents have black coffee and cereals. She doesn't like either of these. She walks to school. She likes school. She has lots of friends. Her teachers are nice. She watches TV. She has a wash before bed.

TRANSCRIPT
CD4, track 36

Voy a describir un día típico: Normalmente, si es un día de colegio, me despierto a las siete y me levanto a las siete y media.

Me ducho a las ocho, me pongo el uniforme y después desayuno. Siempre desayuno rápidamente porque tengo prisa. Como tostadas y bebo un café con leche. Mis padres desayunan café sólo y cereales, pero a mí no me gustan.

Luego, salgo de casa a las ocho y media y voy al colegio a pie. Generalmente llego a las nueve. Me gusta mi colegio, tengo muchos amigos allí y los profesores son simpáticos. Vuelvo a casa a las cinco, hago los deberes en mi dormitorio a las seis y escucho música o navego por Internet. La familia cena a las nueve y media. Después, veo la tele, me lavo y me acuesto a las once.
¡Uf! ¡Qué día!

Prueba: Hablar *(page 129)*

ex 1: AT2.3

Answers

Example **1** Cuando hace sol, practico la natación.
2 Cuando hiela, veo la tele.
3 Cuando nieva, salgo con mis amigos.
4 Cuando llueve, me quedo en casa.
5 Cuando hace buen tiempo, juego al fútbol.
6 Cuando hace calor, juego al tenis.
Mark scheme: 2 marks for each sentence which would be understood by a sympathetic native speaker. 1 for the weather expression, 1 for the activity.
Total: 10. 7+ shows evidence of performance at Level 3.
2 marks each for each extra piece of information in a similar format.

ex 2: AT2.4

Answers

Any response which makes sense in context is acceptable.
Mark scheme: 1 mark for each sentence which would be understood by a sympathetic native speaker.
Total: 5. 3+ shows evidence of performance at Level 4.

ex 3: AT2.4

Answers

Any response which makes sense in context is acceptable.
Mark scheme: 2 marks for each sentence which would be understood by a sympathetic native speaker
Total: 10. 7+ shows evidence of performance at Level 4.
2 marks each for each extra piece of information in a similar format.

Prueba: Leer *(page 130)*

ex 1: AT3.3

Answers

1 Y **2** N **3** Y **4** Y **5** N
Mark scheme: 1 mark for each correct answer.
Total: 5. 3+ shows evidence of performance at Level 3.

ex 2: AT3.4

Answers

Example **1** E **2** I **3** E **4** I **5** E **6** E
Mark scheme: 2 marks for each correct answer.
Total: 10. 7+ shows evidence of performance at Level 4.

ex 3: AT3.4

Answers

Example **1**V **2**M **3**M **4**V **5**M **6**M **7**V **8**V **9**M **10**M **11**M
Mark scheme: 1 mark for each correct answer.
Total: 10. 7+ shows evidence of performance at Level 4.

¡extra! 1 mark for each phrase corrected in a manner which makes sense in context.

Prueba: Escribir *(page 131)*

ex 1: AT4.3

Answers

Example **1** Me gusta mucho la pizza.
2 Me gusta mucho la limonada.
3 Me encantan las patatas fritas.
4 No me gusta la carne.
5 Odio la fruta.
6 Me gusta mucho el yogur.
7 Me gusta mucho la leche.
Mark scheme: 2 marks for each correct answer, one for the opinion expression and one for the item of food or drink. The words need not necessarily be absolutely correct but should be easily understood by a sympathetic native speaker.
Total: 12. 8+ shows evidence of performance at Level 3 .

¡extra! 2 marks for each additional piece of information in a similar format.

ex 2: AT4.4

Answers

Any suitable responses which make sense in context are acceptable.
Mark scheme: 1 mark for each correct response. The words need not necessarily be absolutely correct but should be easily understood by a sympathetic native speaker.
Total: 7. 5+ shows evidence of performance at Level 4 .

¡extra! 1 mark for each additional piece of information.

ex 3: AT4.4

Answers

Any suitable responses which make sense in context are acceptable.
Mark scheme: 2 marks for each correct response. The words need not necessarily be absolutely correct but should be easily understood by a sympathetic native speaker.
Total: 6. 4+ shows evidence of performance at Level 4 .

¡extra! 1 mark for each additional piece of information.

Workbook A Unit 8

page 39 *(Section A)*

Answers

ex 1:
1c **2**d **3**f **4**e **5**b **6**a

ex 2a:
1 I have lunch at **one** o'clock.
2 I return home at three in the **afternoon**. **3** I go to **bed** at ten o'clock at night. **4** I have my evening meal at **half** past eight. **5** I leave home at **eight** in the **morning**. **6** I have breakfast at half past **seven**.

ex 2b:
6, 5, 1, 2, 4, 3

ex 3:
1 Me levanto **2** Me lavo los dientes **3** Salgo de casa **4** Vuelvo a casa **5** Me relajo **6** Me acuesto

page 40 *(Section B)*

Answers

ex 1:
me levant**o** I get up
te levant**as** you get up
se levant**a** he/she gets up
n**os** levant**amos** we get up
os levant**áis you** get up
se levant**an they** get up

ex 2:
¡Hola Mairéad!
Gracias por tu carta. Tu rutina diaria es interesante. Pero, ¿pasas el fin de semana <u>diferentemente</u>? Yo, sí. <u>Normalmente</u> me levanto a las seis, desayuno <u>rápidamente</u> y salgo de casa a las siete y media.

El fin de semana, comienzo el día <u>tranquilamente</u>. Desayuno <u>lentamente</u> y me visto <u>gradualmente</u>. Me gusta ir de compras; si tengo dos horas de tiempo libre, ¡gasto todo mi dinero <u>fácilmente</u>!

Paso los domingos <u>estupendamente</u>. Juego en un equipo femenino de fútbol. Y tú, ¿qué haces el fin de semana?

Un abrazo de tu amiga Josefina

ex 3:
1 e **2** M **3** o **4** s **5** c **6** e, a **7** t, u
New verb: Me acuesto

page 41 *(Section C)*

Answers

ex 1:

Desayuno	Almuerzo	Merienda	Cena
tostadas	pescado	pastel	pasta
café con leche	tortilla	galletas	pollo
pan con aceite	fruta	vaso de leche	verdura

ex 2:
1 en el comedor **2** a las dos y media **3** agua mineral con gas **4** comen pan **5** con verdura **6** con ensalada **7** una fruta

page 42 *(Section D)*

Answers

ex 1a:
1e **2**f **3**a **4**b **5**d **6**c

ex 1b:
1 Cuando hace calor voy **a** la playa.
2 Cuando llueve **hago** los deberes.
3 Cuando **hace** buen tiempo salgo con amigos.
4 Cuando hace frío **voy** al centro.
5 Cuando **hay** tormenta me quedo en casa.
6 Cuando hace sol **practico** la natación.

ex 2a:
1 Escucho música cuando hay tormenta.
2 Cuando llueve veo la tele.
3 Voy a la playa cuando hace calor.

ex 2b:
1 Navego por Internet cuando llueve.
2 Cuando hace buen tiempo salgo con mis amigos.
3 Voy al cine cuando hace mucho frío.

Workbook B Unit 8

page 39 *(Section A)*

Answers

ex 1a and 1b:

1	acos	tarse	**b** to go to bed
2	despe	rtarse	**f** to wake up
3	duchars	e	**c** to have a shower
4	leva	ntarse	**d** to get up
5	rel	ajarse	**a** to relax
6	vest	irse	**e** to get dressed

ex 2:
1 Almuerzo **a** la una. I have lunch at **one** o'clock. **2** Vuelvo a casa a las **tres** de la tarde. I return home at three in the **afternoon**. **3** Me acuesto a las diez **de** la noche. I go to **bed** at ten o'clock at night. **4** Ceno **a** las ocho y media. I have my evening meal at **half** past eight. **5** Salgo de **casa** a las ocho de la mañana. I leave home at **eight** in the **morning**. **6** Desayuno a las siete y **media**. I have **breakfast** at half past seven.

ex 3:
1 Me levanto **2** Desayuno **3** Me lavo los dientes **4** Salgo de casa **5** Almuerzo **6** Vuelvo a casa **7** Hago mis deberes **8** Ceno **9** Me relajo **10** Me acuesto

page 40 (Section B)

Answers

ex 1:

me levant**o**	I get up
te levant**as**	you get up
se levant**a**	he/she gets up
nos levant**amos**	we get up
os levant**áis**	you get up
se levant**an**	they get up

ex 2:

Querida Mairéad

Gracias por tu carta. Tu rutina diaria es interesante. Pero, ¿pasas el fin de semana <u>diferentemente</u>? Yo, sí. <u>Normalmente</u> toda la familia se levanta a las seis. Desayunamos <u>rápidamente</u> y salimos de casa a las siete y media. El fin de semana, comienzo el día <u>tranquilamente</u>. Desayuno <u>lentamente</u> y me visto <u>gradualmente</u>. Me gusta <u>mucho</u> ir de compras; si tengo dos horas de tiempo libre, ¡gasto todo mi dinero <u>fácilmente</u>!

Paso los domingos <u>estupendamente</u>. Juego en un equipo femenino de fútbol. Y tú, ¿qué haces el fin de semana? Un abrazo de tu amiga Josefina

¡extra! Mucho

ex 3:
1d **2**c **3**a **4**b **5**f **6**a

page 41 (Section C)

Answers

ex 1:

Desayuno	Almuerzo	Merienda	Cena
tostadas	pescado	pastel	pasta
café con leche	tortilla	batido	pollo
pan con aceite	fruta	vaso de leche	carne
	yogur	galletas	verdura

ex 2:
1 Fede y Juliana comen en el comedor.
2 Almuerzan a las dos y media.
3 Beben un vaso de agua mineral con gas.
4 Comen pan.
5 Fede toma pollo con verdura.
6 Juliana come pescado con ensalada.
7 Después Fede va a tomar una fruta, y Juliana va a tomar un yogur.

page 42 (Section D)

Answers

ex 1a:
1e **2**f **3**a **4**b **5**d **6**c

ex 1b:
1 Cuando **hace** calor Eduardo y su hermana **van** a la piscina.
2 Cuando **llueve** no se puede jugar **al** tenis.
3 Cuando hace buen **tiempo** me **gusta** mucho hacer ciclismo.
4 Cuando **hace frío** vamos al centro comercial.
5 Cuando hay **tormenta** Enrique prefiere **quedarse** en casa.
6 Cuando hace viento **se puede** practicar windsurf.

¡extra! It is windy.

ex 2:
1 Navegan por Internet cuando llueve.
2 Cuando hace buen tiempo ¿sales con tus amigos?
3 Voy al cine cuando hace mucho frío.

Unidad 9 El cole	Topic/Language/Culture	Grammar and skills	National Criteria
9A ¿Cómo es el colegio? (pp.82–83) **Objectives:** • learn about schools in Spain • talk about your school • use numbers 1–1000	*el instituto femenino / masculino / mixto / privado / un colegio secundario* *el alumno / la alumna* *el profesor / la profesora* *Aquí está(n)... el aula, la biblioteca, el campo de deportes / de fútbol, el comedor, el despacho del director, el gimnasio, el vestuario, los laboratorios, el patio, la piscina, la sala de profesores* Higher numbers 100–1000 **Culture** Spanish school system	**Grammar** Forming higher numbers **Skills** Linking phrases working with higher numbers	**Attainment** AT1.1–4, AT2.1–4, AT4.3–4 **Framework objectives** 7W2, 7S2, 7S3, 7S6, 7T1, 7T5, 7L2, 7L3, 8W2, 8S2 **Programmes of Study** 1b, 2a **QCA Scheme of Work** Language: Unit 7 Context: Unit 5 **Assessment for learning** Objectives, p.83 Ex3a & b, Ex 4, Plenary
9B El horario (pp.84–85) **Objectives:** • talk about your timetable • learn more about how to say the time • make longer sentences using 'firstly', 'then'	School subjects: *¿Qué tienes/tenemos?* *Tengo... dibujo, inglés, deporte, geografía, matemáticas, español, alemán, informática, tecnología, historia, gimnasia, biología, ciencias, cocina, física, química, biología, religión, música de la(s)... hasta la(s)...* Time connectives: *entonces, finalmente, luego, primero, también, después*	**Grammar** Time between the hours **Skills:** Connecting short sentences and phrases with time connectives	**Attainment** AT1 Level 3: AT2 Levels 2–4; AT3 Level 3: AT4 Levels 2–4 **Framework objectives** 7W1, 7W6, 7W7, 7S3, 7S7, 7T1, 7T5, 7T6, 7L2, 7L3, 7L4, 7L5, 7L6 **Programmes of Study** 2f, 2j **QCA Scheme of work** Language: Unit 3, Unit 6 Context: Unit 5 **Assessment for learning** Objectives, p.85 Ex2a & 3b, Plenary
9C: Un día típico (pp.86–87) **Objectives** • talk about your daily routine • say how often you do something • learn how to read Spanish handwriting	Daily routine: *empezar, terminar, durar, llegar, volver* *ir al club de ajedrez / atletismo / arte / baloncesto / fútbol / informática / teatro / baloncesto / fotografía* *ir al coro/ a la orquesta* Expressions of frequency: *una vez/dos veces a la semana/al día/al mes, todos los días, los fines de semana, los martes* **Culture** Spanish school organisation	**Skills** How to read Spanish handwriting **Pronunciation** All sounds	**Attainment** AT1 Level 4; AT2 Levels 2–4, AT3 Level 4, AT4 Levels 3–4 **Framework objectives** 7W6, 7T1, 7T2, 7T6, 7S3, 7L1, 7L3, 7C2 **Programmes of Study** 1a, 1c, 2b, 2f, 3b **QCA Scheme of work** Language: Unit 6 Context: Unit 5 **Assessment for learning** Objectives, p. 87 Ex2c, Plenary
9D ¿Qué opinas tú? (pp.88–89) **Objectives** • Say what subjects you like and dislike, and why • Use e (and) before i/hi and u (or) before o/ho	*es (super)fácil, difícil, útil, interesante, aburrido, divertido, (no) se me da(n) bien* *Mi(s) asignatura(s) favorita(s) es (son)...* *Mi profesor(a) es simpático/a, divertido/a* Revision of *(no) me gusta(n) mucho, me encanta(n), odio etc. porque...*	**Grammar** *y > e* before *i/hi* *o > u* before *o/ho* **Skills** Learning vocabulary in context	**Attainment** AT1 Level 3: AT2 Level 4: AT3 Levels 3–4: AT4 Levels 3–4 **Framework objectives** 7W1, 7W6, 7T1, 7T5, 7L1, 7L2, 7L3 **Programmes of study** 2d, 3b, 5c **QCA Scheme of work** Language: Unit 5 Context: Unit 5 **Assessment for learning** Objectives, p.88 Ex1a & 1c, Plenary

Other resources: *¡Ahora tú!* pp.134–135   WS 76–84   OHTs 15A & B   WBA & B pp.44–48   Assessment Units 9–10 (R & A file pp.132–135)   *Just Click* Just Click CD-Rom

9A ¿Cómo es el colegio?

pp. 82–83

> **Objectives:**
> - learn about schools in Spain
> - talk abou~~~
> - use num~~~
>
> **Key Langua~~~**
> **Grammar:**
> - forming h~~~
>
> **Skills:**
> - linking ph~~~
> - working w~~~
>
> **Resources:** O~~~ ~~~rlay);
> Visual 76, CD3~~~ ~~~44;
> (Escuchar), 83 ~~~
> *Just Click* CD-R~~~

[handwritten note:] I place on trip to fil

Lesson starter

An exercise to remi~~~ ~~~ow
already (1–100). W~~~
between 1 and 100 ~~~

As they come in, ask ~~~dents to think about putting them in
numerical order in their heads. After two minutes ask them to
say the numbers together in the correct order.

Alternative lesson starter *(for lessons starting part-way through the section)*

As above or any other starter lessons with numbers (see Unit 1
TB34), but choose numbers between 100 and 1000.

Introduction

You may wish to teach the names for the places in the school
separately before embarking on the first exercise. These can
be presented and practised using OHTs 15 A & B. First show
just the pictures. Teach the names of two or three at a time,
saying them and getting the class and then individuals to
repeat and then produce them. Once you are confident of
students' pronunciation, add the overlay with text.

1a 🔘 Escucha y mira las fotos. AT1.4, AT3.4; 7T1, 7L2

A photo story about a girl's first day at school. The students
follow the photo story and listen to the same exchanges on CD.

Play the CD several times and ask students to follow in their
books. Next play it in sections, asking the class and then
individuals to repeat the extracts. Finally some students may
be able to act out some or all of the exchanges without
looking at their books.

> **TRANSCRIPT** CD3, track 11
>
> – ¡Hola! ¿Es tu primer día?
> – Sí. Soy Nuria Alvarez.
> – Bueno, bienvenida al Colegio Santa María. Te
>   enseñamos el colegio.
> – Aquí está el patio y detrás el campo de deportes.
> – Y aquí la biblioteca y los ordenadores. ▶

> – A la derecha está la sala de profesores… y a la izquierda
>   el despacho del Director.
> – Aquí están los laboratorios.
> – Aquí están el gimnasio y los vestuarios.
> – Y el comedor.
> – Finalmente, el aula y el profesor.

¡Así se hace! Linking words 7W2, 7S6, 8W2

A reminder about linking clauses to form longer sentences.
Ask students to look in the photo story for examples of *y* and
of the other connectives mentioned.

1b 💬 Describe los colegios siguientes. AT2.3–4; 7S3, 8W2, 8S2

A pairwork or full-class exercise. Students are given a grid
showing details of four other schools. From this they must
supply descriptions. The photo story provides the vocabulary
and the example provides a pattern.

Before they start make it clear that they should only list the
ticked and crossed items and that they should disregard the
blanks. It will be easier if they list the facilities in the order in
which they appear on the grid.

Support

Less confident students should concentrate on producing the list
of facilities the school has and has not got. For these students
this exercise may work better as a whole-class exercise.

Extension

More confident students can extend their answers to include
examples of *pero* and *también*.

> **Possible answers**
>
> A: Hay un patio, una piscina, un comedor, aulas y laboratorios
>   (también). (Pero) No hay gimnasio.
> B: Hay un patio pero no hay piscina. Hay laboratorios y un
>   gimnasio. Hay/Y una biblioteca (también).
> C: No hay patio. (Pero) hay un comedor, aulas, un gimnasio,
>   un campo de deportes y una biblioteca.
> D: Hay un patio, una piscina y un comedor pero no hay
>   laboratorios. Hay un gimnasio y una biblioteca
>   (también).

1c 🔘 Escucha (1–4). Escribe la letra del colegio. AT1.3; 7L3

The students listen to a series of descriptions and write down
the number of the school described each time.

> **Answers**
>
> **1**C **2**D **3**B **4**A

> **TRANSCRIPT** CD3, track 12
>
> **1** – Bueno, hay una biblioteca, un comedor y muchas
>   aulas. No hay patio pero hay un gimnasio. También
>   hay un campo de deportes. ▶

2 – ¿Qué hay en tu colegio?
– Pues, hay una biblioteca, una piscina y un gimnasio.
– ¿Algo más?
– Sí, un patio.
– ¿Hay laboratorios?
– No, no hay.

3 – ¿Qué hay en tu colegio?
– Hay un gimnasio, un patio, una biblioteca y laboratorios.
– ¿Hay piscina?
– No.

4 – Hay patio, piscina, comedor, aulas y laboratorios. No hay gimnasio.

2a ¡Así se hace! High numbers AT2.2; 7S2, 7W2

A reminder of the importance of saying and understanding numbers. It cannot be stressed enough how important numbers are. They frequently come up in examination questions and can make the difference of one grade at GCSE. Many students are unreasonably worried particularly by higher numbers. So familiarisation with the rules for these and regular practice of higher numbers in different skills can only be a good thing. Students take turns with their partner to say a series of numbers over 100 for them to practise in pairs. This exercise can be returned to several times.

Support

For less confident students start by asking them to produce the numbers separately (100, 11, 200, 22 etc.) before asking them to put them together.

Answers

ciento once, dos cientos veintidós, trescientos treinta y tres, cuatrocientos cuarenta y cuatro, quinientos cincuenta y cinco, seiscientos sesenta y seis, setecientos setenta y siete, ochocientos ochenta y ocho, novecientos noventa y nueve.

ciento veintitrés, doscientos treinta y cuatro, trescientos cuarenta y cinco, cuatrocientos cincuenta y seis, quinientos sesenta y siete, seiscientos setenta y ocho, setecientos ochenta y nueve.

2b Escucha (1–5). Identifica los números. AT1.1; 7L3

Students listen to a series of dialogues containing numbers and identify the number they hear from a selection on the page. To check their work, they will need to have written down each number as they hear it.

Answers

1 1700 **2** 250 **3** 650 **4** 1900 **5** 1430

TRANSCRIPT CD3, track 13

1 – ¿Cuántos alumnos hay en tu colegio?
– Hay aproximadamente mil setecientos.
2 – ¿Cuántos alumnos hay en tu escuela?
– Es pequeña. Hay solamente doscientos cincuenta alumnos.
3 – ¿Cuántos alumnos hay en tu colegio?
– Hay seiscientos cincuenta.
4 – ¿Cuántos alumnos hay en tu colegio?
– Hay mil novecientos.
5 – ¿Cuántos alumnos hay en tu colegio?
– Hay exactamente mil cuatrocientos treinta.

3a Une las preguntas y las respuestas. AT3.3; 7T1

A matching exercise. All the questions deal with the topic of school and are the sorts of things that might have been asked of the writer of the email in 4. This exercise could be used for assessment

Answers

1e **2**b **3**d **4**a **5**c

3b Habla con tu pareja y usa las preguntas en 3a. Adapta tus respuestas. AT2.3–4; 7S3

Students work in pairs to ask and answer the questions from the previous exercise.

Extension

Students can write up their own personalised answers to the questions in 3a in order to produce an account like the sample one below.

A suggestion for more confident students that they extend the question and answer format to make an interview. If necessary, before they start, discuss with them the things they will need to add or could add (name, age, domicile etc.). The results could be taped and used for assessment.

Gramática: Los números AT3.1; 7S2

Introduction of the rules for forming higher numbers. Students are asked to write the high numbers cited as words in exercise 4 first as figures then as words in English. This exercise should alert them to similarities and differences in the way of forming numbers in the two languages.

Answers

1200 (one thousand two hundred); 800 (eight hundred)

The first exercise on Worksheet 78 (Escuchar) deals with higher numbers.

4 Lee y usa las frases que son útiles para describir tu colegio. AT3.4; AT4.4; 7S3, 7T5

Students read an email and then adapt it to write a similar message about their own school. The email is also used to introduce higher numbers. It should be considered in conjunction with the Gramática section that follows and work on the two sections can be interspersed. Ask students to read it through for gist first. Check that they have understood the general content. Before they can produce their own version of the email they will need to understand how higher numbers work so they should work on the Gramática section too.

To prepare for adapting this email make an OHT of it or give students a copy of the text on the page.

Support

Work through the text with the class underlining or highlighting the words or phrases that can be recycled.

Extension

Ask them to underline or highlight words and phrases that might be useful to them. This can contribute to their 'fichero personal' that they can be encouraged to build up over the years.

Plenary

☑ Everyone writes down five numbers between 150 and 200. The teacher reads out random numbers in the series (keep a check of the ones you've said). Students check off any that they hear from their list. The first person to have checked off all their numbers and to read them back correctly is the winner.

Alternative plenary

☑ In pairs or groups, students make a set of word cards with school facilities in Spanish, e.g. *el comedor* on one card and their English translations on the other. They can then play pelmanism.

Extension

Students put the words into sentences, e.g. *Aquí está el comedor* or *A la derecha/izquierda está el comedor*, and identify patterns.

9B El horario

pp. 84–85

Objectives:
- talk about your timetable
- learn more about how to say the time
- make longer sentences using 'firstly', 'then...'

Key Language: see p.131 for full list

Grammar:
- time between the hours

Skills:
- connecting short sentences and phrases with time connectives

Resources: Visual 76 (school subjects); CD3; Worksheets 77 (Resumen), 78 (Escuchar), 79 (Hablar), 80 (Leer), 83 (Gramática); Workbooks A and B p.45; A 'prop' clock; *Just Click* CD-Rom.

Lesson starter

Write up all the times on the hour between 1.00 and 12.00 in words but in jumbled order. Students have one minute to work in pairs to reorder them. After one minute students call out the times in the correct order.

Alternative starter *(for lessons starting part-way through the section)*

Write up all the times between 1.00 and 2.00 at five-minute intervals in words in jumbled order. Students have two minutes to work in pairs to reorder them. After two minutes students call out the times in the correct order.

Introduction 7W7

Use Visual 76 and then Worksheet 76 to introduce the school subject vocabulary.

Use the OHT to move from presenting a few subjects and getting the class to repeat them to individual student production of the different subjects. Students can then work in pairs using the mini-flashcards to say and match the pictures and spellings.

1a 💿 Escucha (1–5) y apunta el número de las asignaturas. AT1.3; 7L3

A series of short exchanges about different subjects. From their books, students choose and note down the numbers corresponding to the subjects that they hear.

The exchanges use the various time connectives that are featured on the page.

Support

Before you start, practise the number–subject matches. You say a subject and students must say the number, or you say a number and they say the subject.

This preparation can also be done in pairs.

Answers

1 8, 3, 14, 5, 15
2 9, 4, 1, 16, 11, 17
3 13, 2
4 13, 9
5 9, 7, 1, 12, 17

TRANSCRIPT
CD3, track 14

1 – ¿Qué tienes hoy?
– Hoy tengo gimnasia, biología, música, química y religión.
2 – ¿Qué tenemos hoy?
– Vamos a ver... primero inglés, luego física. Después del recreo, tenemos geografía, cocina y, por la tarde, francés y matemáticas. Me gusta francés.
3 – Oye, Paco. ¿Qué tenemos esta tarde?
– Bueno, tenemos tecnología e historia.
– Bien.
4 – ¿Es hoy cuando tenemos tecnología e inglés?
– Sí, tonta.
– Entonces es mi día favorito.
5 – Hoy tenemos primero tecnología, ¿no?
– No, primero inglés, luego deporte, geografía, dibujo y matemáticas.

1b 💿 Escucha otra vez y mira el horario. ¿Qué día es? AT1.3; 7L3

The students look at a school timetable and listen again to the set of exchanges. They identify which day of the week it is according to the timetable. The conversations use the expressions *por la mañana/por la tarde* and the adverb *después*, and this language is essential in order to do the exercise. To focus students' attention on it, ask them to look at the timetable and go through the subjects for Monday saying: *Por la mañana hay inglés, después hay deporte, después geografía* etc. Write the featured expressions on the board and ask them to tell you what they think they mean. Next ask them to give you a similar list for Tuesday.

Support

It would be helpful to revise the days of the week with less able students before embarking on this exercise.

Extension

This presentation doesn't use the connectives that were presented in the previous exercise (*primero, luego* etc.); however, they will be needed in the next exercise so you could incorporate them into your catalogue of what lessons are on a particular day.

Answers

1 miércoles **2** jueves **3** martes **4** viernes **5** lunes

It would be helpful for students to write out theur own school timetables in Spanish at this point. Worksheet 79 (Hablar) has a template for students to do this.

1c ⌕ Habla con tu pareja. Usa el horario y adivina el día. AT2.3–4; 7L4, 7L5

Pairwork. Based on their own timetables, the students ask each other questions to find out what day it is. An alternative is for students to say what they have (in any order) and their partner has to guess which day it is. They get three points if they only get one clue, two points if they need two clues and one point if they need three.

For example:

> *Tengo inglés.*
> *Es jueves.*
> *No. Tengo inglés y matemáticas.*
> *Es jueves.*
> *No. Tengo inglés, matemáticas y deporte.*
> *Es lunes.*
> *Sí, un punto.*

For further practice, students can work in pairs to use the information-gap exercise on Worksheet 79 (Hablar).

2a ☑ 📖 Une las frases con los relojes. AT3.3; 7T1

A matching exercise. Students read a series of sentences and look for the subject and time that correspond with each. The times on the minute are new but the subject should help with identification. Note that three different forms of *tener* are used. This exercise should be tackled in conjunction with the grammar explanation that follows. This exercise could be used for assessment.

Answers

1E 2C 3I 4H 5B 6D 7A 8J 9G 10F

Gramática: *la hora* 7W1

Exercise 2a leads into the grammar explanation on telling the time in five-minute intervals.

Use a 'prop' clock to practise these and other times on the minute, chorally and with individuals. Common mistakes will be to confuse *diez* and *doce*, *seis* and *siete*, and *once* with *una*.

WS 78 (Escuchar) and 83 (Gramática) have a further explanation and exercises on times. Worksheet 79 (Hablar) is an information-gap exercise revolving around timetables, with reference to days, lessons and times.

A further exercise might consist of the students making up their own domino game with written times and clocks, e.g.

 las dos y cuarto

 la una y veinte

2b Draw a clock and put in the *y cinco, y diez* etc... AT 4.2; 7T6

A suggestion that students produce their own written record of these new times.

Support

For students who may find difficulty conceptualising this suggestion a blank sheet with a series of clocks showing all the times between 1.00 and 2.00 at five-minute intervals could be offered for them to fill in.

2c ⌕ ¡extra! Gimnasia mental. Practica con tu pareja. AT2.2; 7L6

A pairwork exercise that encourages students to practise the times in two ways. In addition to the two simple ideas in the Students' Book, students could count up (or backwards) increasing the interval by five minutes each time, e.g. *a las siete, a las siete y cinco, a las siete y cuarto, a las siete y media...*

By taking turns and working against the clock or to set a record students can be engaged in some very quick and focused pairwork.

3a ⌕ Describe tu horario a tu pareja. ¿Cuántos segundos puedes hablar sin pausa?... AT2.3–4; 7S3, 7L6

Students are invited to talk about their own timetable on the model of the one on the page. They should be encouraged to plan what they are going to say and to use as many connectives and adverbs as possible.

Support

Less confident students may benefit from a writing/speaking frame version of this exercise. Once they have established their own version they could then memorise it for oral production.

3b ☑ ✎ Escribe tu horario. AT4.2-4; 7T5

Students can now consolidate their practice by writing a description of one day of their timetable. Encourage them to redraft their account using ICT. They can also build on it in subsequent spreads. This exercise could be used for assessment.

3c ✎ ¡extra! Da más detalles. Escribe qué haces antes y después del cole. AT4.4; 7T5

Students are encouraged to add additional information about what they do before and after school.

¡Así se hace! Structuring sentences 7W1, 7S7

A reminder of the new time connectives that were introduced in exercise 1a. The example offers a model for the kind of writing students could aspire to. As in exercise 2a, different forms of *tener* are used.

Plenary

☑ Give students a few seconds to think of how many lesson names they can remember. Next ask who can name at least one lesson (all hands should go up), then ask who can remember two, and three. At various points stop and challenge students to list the lessons they remember.

Alternative plenary

☑ In pairs, students explain the rules for telling the time in Spanish, e.g. *menos* for 'to' as in 'in ten to ten' and *y* for 'past' as in 'ten past ten'. Give extra points for the students who remember that you have to use *a la* for one o'clock.

9C Un día típico

pp. 86–87

> **Objectives:**
> • talk about your daily routine
> • say how often you do something
> **Key Language:** see p.131 for full list
> **Pronunciation:**
> • all sounds
> **Skills:**
> • how to read Spanish handwriting
> **Resources:** CD3; Worksheets 77 (Resumen), 78
> (Escuchar), 81 (Escribir); Workbooks A and B p.46;
> *Just Click* CD-Rom.

This spread introduces verbs to do with daily routine and relaunches some freetime activity vocabulary. Some expressions of frequency are introduced. The section revisits the Spanish alphabet and introduces Spanish handwriting.

Lesson starter

Depending on the number of students in the class, to the first (twelve) students to arrive give out the twelve freetime flashcards 28–39 from Unit 6. To the next (twelve) students, give out twelve labels to go with the twelve activities. Each student has to find his/her visual or written match. If you know that there are going to be say thirty students in the lesson, make three extra pictures and three extra labels to depict three associated activities (e.g. *tocar la guitarra, hacer los deberes de inglés, jugar al baloncesto*).

Some of these exercises or variations on them feature on these pages as school-based exercises.

Alternative starter *(for lessons starting part-way through the section)*

Ask students to work in pairs or groups to brainstorm as many Spanish words for different types of clubs as they can. They have learnt nine different ones on the page; they may be able to add to this list with words from earlier units (e.g. *cocina, animales, natación*).

1a 🔘 Escucha y lee. Pon las fotos en orden. AT1.4, AT3.4; 7T1, 7L3

Students first listen to and read an account of a girl's day then order the photos according to what she says. The visuals all contain time and other clues. While some of the language is new (verbs: *empezar, llegar, durar, terminar, cantar*; types of clubs: *ajedrez* etc.), other language items will be familiar from other contexts (food, freetime activities).

It is worth pointing out that in Spain and elsewhere it is common to open schools on a two- or even three-shift system. This both optimises the use of space and facilities and allows those students who have to work to support themselves an opportunity to work and study.

TRANSCRIPT   CD3, track 15

> Soy Ana. Llego al cole a las ocho. Voy en autobús. Hablo con mis amigos en el patio. Las clases empiezan a las ocho y media. Las clases duran una hora.
>
> A las diez y media hay recreo. Voy al comedor y tomo un bocadillo. Hay clases desde las once hasta la una. ▶

> Vivo cerca y voy a casa a comer con mi madre. Hay actividades pero prefiero volver a casa.
>
> Vuelvo a las tres y media. Termino las clases a las cinco y media. Hay actividades después. Por ejemplo, hay un club de fotografía. Hay equipos de fútbol y de baloncesto. Canto en el coro y toco la flauta en la orquesta.
>
> Vuelvo a casa a las siete y hago mis deberes. Ceno a las diez.

Answers

5, 3, 2, 4, 6, 1

1b 📖 Contesta a las preguntas en inglés. AT3.4; 7T1

Further comprehension practice of the previous exercise. Students answer in English a series of questions on the account. Only a few of the questions can be answered by looking at the pictures. To glean all the information they will have to read the account carefully.

Answers

1 8.00 **2** talks to her friends in the playground **3** 8.30 **4** 10.30 **5** 1.00 **6** no (at home with her mother) **7** 3.30 **8** 5.30 **9** sings in the choir and plays the flute in the orchestra **10** 7.00 **11** does her homework

1c 🖊 ¡extra! Contesta a las preguntas para ti en español. AT4.3–4; 7S3

Having based their previous answers on Ana's description, students now answer the questions in exercise 1b for themselves in Spanish. Remind them to look in Ana's letter for model answers to be adapted.

Support

If the students need support, part of the answers could be provided.

Extension

More confident students could amalgamate their answers to form a continuous account, like Ana's.

WS 81 (Escribir) offers tips and examples on producing a piece of writing of this type.

2a 🔘 Escucha (1–8). ¿Qué actividades? AT1.4; 7L3

Students listen and write down the letters of the activities mentioned.

The exchanges use various known verbs to go with the activities: *ir a, gustar, jugar, practicar, hacer*, and a couple of new ones: *interesar* (on the analogy of *gustar*) and *cantar*. Ask students where they have heard the familiar verbs before (in the freetime activity language in Unit 6).

Various phrases of frequency are also introduced: *¿Cuántas veces?..., ... veces a la semana/al mes, el fin de semana*.

TRANSCRIPT
CD3, track 16

1 – ¿Qué actividades haces en el colegio?
 – Bueno, hay un club de teatro.
 – ¿Te gusta?
 – Sí, mucho.
 – ¿Cuándo vas?
 – Una vez a la semana los martes.
2 – ¿Qué actividades haces en el colegio?
 – Yo juego en el equipo de fútbol.
 – ¿Cuándo practicas?
 – Dos veces a la semana.
 – ¿Qué días?
 – Jueves y viernes. Juego con mis amigos los fines de semana también.
3 – ¿Qué actividades haces en el colegio?
 – Voy al club de fotografía.
 – ¿Cuándo es?
 – Los lunes.
4 – ¿Qué actividades haces en el colegio?
 – Me interesan los ordenadores. Voy al club de informática todos los días.
5 – ¿Qué actividades haces en el colegio?
 – Canto en el coro y toco en la orquesta.
 – ¿Cuántas veces a la semana vas?
 – Dos veces: lunes y miércoles.
6 – ¿Qué actividades haces en el colegio?
 – Voy al club de arte.
 – ¿Cuándo vas?
 – Los viernes.
7 – ¿Qué actividades haces en el colegio?
 – Yo juego mucho al baloncesto.
 – ¿Juegas en el equipo?
 – Sí. Juego dos veces a la semana: los martes y jueves.
8 – ¿Qué actividades haces en el colegio?
 – En verano practico el atletismo.
 – ¿Cuántas veces al mes?
 – Cuatro veces al mes con el club: tres horas los fines de semana.

Answers

1c **2**a **3**i **4**b **5**e **6**g **7**h **8**f

2b ⏺ Escucha otra vez. ¿Cuándo? AT1.4; 7L3

As further listening practice, students note down which day(s) they do a particular activity. Remind them of the rule about *el/los* + day.

Answers

1B **2**A **3**H **4**C **5**G **6**D **7**F **8**E

Extension

Ask students to listen again to see how each person expresses the number of times a week (*una vez/dos veces a la semana* etc.).

Practise the new language by asking students: *¿Qué actividades haces en el colegio?*

Elicit answers like *Practico el atletismo, Juego al fútbol, Canto en el coro…*

Support

With less able students establish the pattern: *Voy al club de informática/arte/fútbol* etc.

2c ☑ 🗨 Habla con tu pareja. Cambia las frases. AT2.2–4; 7S3, 7T2

Pairwork speaking practice. The example gives a structure and the grid presents patterns for students to construct the different activity phrases.

Support

Less confident students may need to stick to the choices given.

Extension

Encourage students to make up as many sentences as they can and to add as much detail as possible. This exercise would be suitable for assessment.

Gramática: on Mondays 7W2

A reminder about how to say e.g. on Monday(s). Encourage students to use the plural form in their exchanges.

3 📖 Lee la carta y compara el horario de los dos estudiantes. Haz una lista de las diferencias. AT3.4; 7T1, 7C2

Reading accounts of a typical day for two Spanish students. Students are asked to read the two accounts and note the differences. One student has a part-time job and attends school in the afternoon and evening, the other one has no job and attends during the day. The two accounts differ in content and the order in which items are mentioned.

The accounts offer interesting cultural insights into the shift systems operated by some schools.

A range of new language items are used (including time connectives) together with some from earlier units.

Ask students to read through the two accounts for gist and to tell you what they've noticed.

Support

For less confident students a set of questions in English may be useful, e.g. What time do they each get up?, How do they travel?, Where does Isabel/Pedro go in the morning?

Differences could initially be expressed in English. Otherwise, as in the example on the page, students could be asked to pick out and list similar phrases that give different details.

Possible answers

Isabel	Pedro
gets up 6.30	gets up 6.00
hasn't got a job	works as a barman
walks to school	gets bus to work
starts classes at 8.30	starts work at 8.00, finishes at 2.00
break lasts half an hour	goes to school in the afternoon
classes till 5.30	break lasts 15 minutes
goes to basketball club	classes till 10.30
gets home at 7.00 and	likes music and sports but no time
does homework	to do them
	no time for homework – studies at weekends

WS 78 (Escuchar) has a multiple-choice exercise on the same topic.

Plenary

☑ Students work in pairs, and for each letter of the alphabet try to think of *one* word they have just learnt in the lesson.

Alternative plenary

☑ Display the learning objectives of the section to work out how well they think they have learned/understood each objective: well (green), a bit unsure (orange), not well (red). This enables you to see which areas need extra work.

9D ¿Qué opinas tú?

page 88

> **Objectives:**
> - say what subjects you like and dislike, and why
> - use e ('and') before i/hi and u ('or') before o/ho
>
> **Key Language:** see p.131 for full list
>
> **Grammar:**
> - y > e before i/hi
> - o > u before o/ho
>
> **Skills:**
> - learning vocabulary in context
>
> **Resources:** CD3; Worksheets 77 (Resumen), 82 (¡Así se hace!), 84 (¡extra!); Workbooks A & B p.47; *Just Click* CD-Rom.

Lesson starter

On the board, put up a series of odd one out word groups. Students work in pairs or groups to find the exceptions. It would be helpful if some of these featured school subjects since these reappear in this section.

Here is a possible set of words to use.

1 inglés, francés, física, **piscina**
2 profesor, alumno, **coro**, director
3 campo de deportes, gimnasia, **geografía**, laboratorio
4 sábado, **religión**, martes, jueves
5 atletismo, **aula**, ajedrez, arte
6 **polideportivo**, tranquilo, aburrido, ruidoso

Alternative lesson starter *(for lessons starting part-way through the section)*

Students have two minutes to think of all the words and expressions they can to do with liking and disliking.

1a ☑ 🎧 Escucha las opiniones. Hay cinco errores. Escribe el número de las frases falsas. AT 1.3, AT3 3; 7L2, 7L3

Students read ten sentences giving opinions about teachers and lessons. They then listen to a taped version of the sentences in which some details are different, and note the sentences that have been changed. Two of the sentences contain examples of y > e.

First give the class some time to read the sentences on the page.

Students now have to listen actively to the sentences to pick out the changes that have been made. They will need to listen carefully as the change is often quite small, so play the CD several times. Emphasise the fact that at first they only have to listen for a change, they don't have to say what it is.

This exercise could be used for assessment.

TRANSCRIPT CD3, track 17

1 Me gusta mucho la **física**. El profesor es muy divertido.
2 No me gusta el alemán porque es muy aburrido.
3 Me gusta mucho la tecnología. Es útil e **interesante**.
4 Se me dan bien las matemáticas pero son **difíciles**.
5 Mi día favorito es el sábado. No hay colegio.
6 Me gustan los jueves. Tengo francés e inglés.
7 Mis asignaturas favoritas son informática e historia.
8 No se me da bien la física. Es superdifícil.
9 Mi profesor de religión **no** es muy simpático.
10 **Me gusta** el deporte.

Answers

The changed sentences are: 1, 3, 4, 9, 10.

Once students have identified the changes, encourage them to listen again to say what they are.

Gramática: y > e 7W6

Changing y > e, o > u

Ask students to read this section and then to look back and find the examples of y > e. Encourage them to try saying e.g. *francés e inglés* and then *francés y inglés*, to demonstrate why the change has been made. Do the same thing for o > u.

1b 📖 Pon las frases en orden para hacer un diálogo. AT 3.4; 7T1

Re-ordering some questions and answers to make a meaningful dialogue.

The dialogue falls into three clusters, with the sentences only being jumbled within their own cluster. Each cluster contains an initial question and a general answer, a second question *¿por qué?*, and a second answer always containing the word *porque* and giving reasons.

If students realise this, the exercise will seem less daunting.

Answer

¿Cuál es tu día favorito en el colegio?
Es el martes.
¿Por qué?
Porque hay inglés e historia. Me gustan los profesores de inglés e historia.

¿Cuál es tu asignatura favorita?
Inglés.
¿Por qué?
Me encanta el inglés porque es divertido y muy interesante.

¿Qué asignaturas no te gustan?
Física y química.
¿Por qué?
Odio la física y la química porque son difíciles y aburridas.

1c ☑ 💬 Habla con tu pareja. Usa las preguntas en 1b. Da más detalles. AT 2.4; 7S3, 7L6, 8L4

Once students have reordered the conversation they could memorise it for oral presentation.

Support

Make an OHT or board copy of the finished conversation, go through it with the class underlining the bits that can stay the same (the questions) and the bits in the answers that could be changed.

Extension

Encourage students to change details to reflect their own situations, and to add extra language like adverbs of frequency.

This exercise could be used for assessment.

2 *Contrarreloj.* **¿Cuántas frases puedes hacer en un minuto?** AT4.3–4; 7T5

A timed writing exercise. Working from a grid, students produce as many sentences as possible in one minute.

Support

Start less confident students off with a couple of examples.

3 **¡extra! Learning a word means being able to say it...** AT4.3; 7W1

A reminder about learning vocabulary in context. Students are given a set of words connected with the topic and invited to use them in sentences.

Plenary

☑ Ask the class to look carefully at the Resumen. Go through it together. Does all the vocabulary now look familiar? Have they understood the grammar points? Ask people to indicate whether they are happy, neutral or unhappy about each section by holding up appropriately coloured cards.

Resumen *(page 89)*

This section offers a resumé of all the vocabulary, grammar, skills and tips presented in the unit.

¡Ahora, tú! *(pp. 134–135)*

Differentiated self-access reading and writing exercises: see page 37 for more information.

page 134

1 **Read the letter about Juanjo's school and make a list of its facilities.**

aulas, salas de ordenadores, salas de música, salas de arte, una biblioteca, un comedor, unas oficinas administrativas, una zona deportiva, una piscina, un campo de fútbol, una cancha de baloncesto y voleibol, laboratorios de física, química y biología.

2 **Look at Mariluz's timetable. Correct the six mistakes in the letter.**

Tengo **siete** clases al día. Las clases duran **cincuenta** minutos. Por la tarde tengo física, **dibujo** y deporte. ...luego a las nueve y veinte tengo química. Después del recreo tengo **historia**. Termino a las cuatro **menos** diez.

3 **Fill the gaps with words from the box.**

1 alumnos 2 divertido 3 aulas 4 francés 5 se me da bien 6 instituto 7 es 8 religión 9 asignaturas 10 son 11 llego

page 135

1 **Separate the sentences to make two letters – one positive, the other negative.**

positive	negative
• Me encanta el colegio. • Se me da bien el dibujo. Es fácil y divertido. • Mi profesora de francés es muy simpática y me gusta mucho. • Me gustan los lunes. Voy al club de informática. Es muy interesante. • Estudio mucho en casa y hago tres horas de deberes por la noche.	• Odio mi colegio. No voy a un club y no hago actividades extracurriculares. Son aburridas y estúpidas. Prefiero jugar con mis amigos. • Es aburrido y las asignaturas no son útiles. • Las matemáticas son difíciles y no se me dan bien. Odio la química y la biología es muy complicada. • No me gusta levantarme por la mañana, prefiero quedarme en la cama. • Mis profesores no son simpáticos. Son muy severos.

2 **Are you a good student?**

A multiple-choice questionnaire based around school, revising language from the unit. Once students have chosen their answers, they add up their scores and consult the points system to find out what kind of student they are.

Worksheets Unit 9

76 Las asignaturas 7W1

These mini-flashcards of school subjects can be constructed and used for vocabulary checking and question and answer during and after work on pages 84–85

77 Resumen AT3.1; 7W1

List of key language of the unit

78 Escuchar 7L2, 7L3

This sheet contains three separate exercises:

1 A multiple-choice involving high numbers. Students listen to each exchange and underline or highlight the number that they hear. The exchanges vary in context. This exercise can be done at any time during work on pages 82–83

CD3, track 18

1 – ¿Cuántos alumnos hay en el colegio?
– En el colegio... a ver... Tenemos setecientos setenta alumnos.
2 – Y ¿cuántos profesores tiene, señor?
– Pues... de profesores hay... ciento trece.
3 – ¿En qué año nació, señora?
– Nací en el año mil novecientos nueve.
4 – ¡Psst! ¿Cuál es la solución?
– Creo que es cuatro mil, trescientos setenta y dos.
5 – ...¡Uff!
– Quinientos metros. ¡Bravo!
6 – Cristobal Colón llegó a América en el año mil cuatrocientos noventa y dos.

Answers

1 b **2** a **3** a **4** c **5** b **6** c

2 A more demanding exercise. This time students hear six times mentioned and must fill them in on the blank clocks provided. These exchanges are slightly longer than in the previous exercise. This exercise can be done at any time during work on pages 84–85.

CD3, track 19

1 – José, ¿a qué hora tenemos física?
– Mmm. Es lunes... el lunes tenemos física... a las tres y media.

2 – ¿Tenemos mátematicas hoy?
– Sí, claro.
– ¿La clase empieza a qué hora?
– … a las diez y veinte.
3 – ¿La piscina está abierta el miércoles?
– Creo que sí. A ver… Sí, sí. El miércoles abre a las siete y cuarto.
4 – ¿Quieres venir al cine con nosotros?
– Sí. ¿A qué hora?
– Nos encontramos en la puerta del cine a las ocho menos cuarto.
5 – ¿Cuándo vuelves a casa normalmente, Maite?
– Oh… depende… Si voy andando vuelvo a las siete menos veinticinco.
6 – ¿La telenovela ha empezado?
– Todavía no, solamente son las ocho menos cinco.

Answers

1 3.30 **2** 10.20 **3** 7.15 **4** 7.45
5 6.35 **6** 7.55

3   This piece of listening contains information similar to that in exercise 1a on page 86, but sometimes the material is worded differently and offers more information. The answers are in bold with the tapescript below.

TRANSCRIPT

CD3, track 20

¡Hola! Soy Rafa y tengo catorce años. Voy al colegio Carlos Quinto en Valencia. Normalmente llego al cole a las ocho **y diez**. Si hace buen tiempo voy **andando**. Cuando llego al patio juego al **baloncesto** con mis amigos. Las clases empiezan a las ocho y **veinte** y duran una hora. A las diez y veinte hay recreo. Voy al comedor con mi amigo Juan y comemos **un sandwich**. Por la mañana hay clases hasta la una menos **diez**, y con la mayoría de mis amigos comemos en el colegio. Soy miembro del equipo de **fútbol** y practico los **lunes** por la tarde. Termino las clases a las cuatro **menos cuarto**. Después, voy al club de **arte**. Vuelvo a casa a las seis y veinte, bebo algo y voy a mí dormitorio para **hacer los deberes**. Cenamos a las diez y **media** y después me acuesto.

79 Hablar 7L5

An information-gap exercise based on a timetable. It can be tackled during work on pages 84–85. Some of the subjects are filled in on both timetables and, for ease of spelling, the missing ones are the more frequent subjects that appear elsewhere on the sheet.

More able students could vary their questions by asking e.g. *¿Qué tenemos después de la comida?*

Completed grid

	lunes	martes	miércoles	jueves	viernes
9.00–10.00	matemáticas	alemán	inglés	inglés	matemáticas
10.00–11.00	deporte	inglés	biología	geografía	gimnasia
11.00–11.30			RECREO		
11.30–12.30	historia	lengua	informática	física	español
12.30–1.30	religión	matemáticas	tecnología	cocina	francés
1.30–3.30			Comida		
3.30–4.30	inglés	tecnología	química	francés	dibujo
4.30–5.30	español	geografía	matemáticas	dibujo	música

80 Leer 7W6

This sheet concentrates on reading identification of words, using familiar letter strings and syllables. It features the subject words from pages 84–85, a number of which share common suffixes: *-és, -ica, -ía* which can help identification.

1   A warm-up exercise. The hidden vertical word is *COLEGIO*.

2   An invitation to make a similar puzzle, using a different hidden word. Students work in pairs or groups, sharing their results with other groups. Some may like to go on to 'hide' other words in a similar fashion.

3   A word square that contains 18 school subject words. The box reminds students to look for familiar letter strings.

Answers

		Q		H	I	S	T	O	R	I	A	
D	I	B	U	J	O					E	N		L
	F		Í	S	I	C	A			S	G		E
	M		N					P	L		N
	I		F	C	O	C	I	N	A	È		G
	C		O					Ñ	S		U
F	A		R		B	I	O	L	O	G	Í	A
R	R		M					L	E	
M	A	T	E	M	Á	T	I	C	A	S		O
N	L		T	E	C	N	O	L	O	G	Í	A
C	I			D	E	P	O	R	T	E
É	G		C						A
S	I		A	L	E	M	Á	N		F
	Ó	H	I	S	T	O	R	I	A	Í
	N		C	I	E	N	C	I	A	S

81 Escribir 7T6, 7T7

1a and **1b**. Three accounts given by different people about their schools. Students highlight each corresponding set of information in a different colour, noticing variations in wording, order of presentation and omissions. They can then use the three accounts as models for their accounts about their own school. Can be tackled during work on pages 86–87.

2   A blank proforma for students to fill in with their own personalised timetable.

Use this worksheet during work on pages 84–85.

82 ¡Así se hace! 7L1

This sheet focuses on the need to differentiate between certain pairs of sounds/letters, using pairs of Spanish words containing the sounds *r/rr, l/ll, n/ñ, b/v, t/d* (Framework 7L1 – Listening for inferences). In a series of exercises, students progress from identifying the sound they hear to repeating, pronouncing and saying the words.

The nature of exercises a–c makes them very suitable for individual home listening and pronunciation practice.

a   Students highlight which word of each pair they actually hear.

TRANSCRIPT

CD3, track 21

1 perro
2 talla
3 piña
4 tarda
5 barra
6 vano
7 ceno
8 cierra
9 hielo
10 jarra
11 sello
12 largo
13 llama
14 mala
15 pera
16 polo

b This time students hear both words in each pair and try to pronounce each one as they hear it.

TRANSCRIPT

CD3, track 22

1	pero	perro
2	talla	tala
3	pina	piña
4	tarta	tarda
5	barra	vara
6	baño	vano
7	ceño	ceno
8	cera	cierra
9	hielo	ello
10	jarra	jara
11	celo	sello
12	largo	lago
13	llama	lana
14	mala	malla
15	pera	perra
16	pollo	polo

c A repeat of the CD extract for b. This time students try to say each word before they hear it, listening to check.

d Students work in pairs, taking it in turns to pronounce each word of each pair.

83 Grámatica

The grammar sheet concentrates on numbers and times. All the exercises bring up when and where to use *y*.

1 In large numbers, the word for 'and' is needed between tens and units in Spanish.

2 Various reminders about forming numbers between 100 and 999 (pages 82–83).

Answers

1 trescientos setenta y tres **2** quinientos sesenta y uno **3** novecientos tres **4** ciento **5** setecientos veintiuno **6** ciento cincuenta y seis

3 Students now manipulate numbers with nouns, taking into account the adjectival agreement needed (pages 82–83).

Answers

1 quinientas veinte alumnas
2 seiscientos treinta y uno profesores
3 tres cientas setenta y tres aulas
4 seiscientos dieciseis colegios
5 mil doscientos tres campos de fútbol.
6 dos mil setecientas diecinueve bibliotecas.

4 An exercise on the time (pages 84–85).

Answers

1 (A) las dos y veinte **2** (A) las cuatro menos veinte **3** (A) las ocho menos cuarto **4** (A) las once y cinco **5** (A) las nueve menos veinticinco **6** (A) la una y cuarto

84 ¡extra!

A giant crossword that brings in vocabulary from earlier units too.

Solution

Workbook A Unit 9

page 44 (Section A)

Answers

ex 1a:
novecientos setenta y seis; ochocientos cincuenta y dos; quinientos cuarenta y tres; seiscientos treinta y cuatro

ex 1b:
976 (novecientos setenta y seis)
852 (ochocientos cincuenta y dos)
543 (quinientos cuarenta y tres)
634 (seiscientos treinta y cuatro)

¡extra! ochocientos setenta y tres

page 45 (Section B)

Answers

ex 1a:

	lunes	martes	miércoles	jueves	viernes
8.45	geografía	matemáticas	química	historia	física
9.45	inglés	matemáticas	física	francés	biología
10.45	recreo				
11.15	música	biología	matemáticas	español	francés
12.15	química	historia	religión	inglés	religión
1.15	comida				
3.30	biología	español	español	dibujo	deporte
4.30 – 5.30	dibujo	tecnología	música	deporte	inglés

6 ¡extra! Tenemos religión el miércoles y el *viernes* a las doce y *cuarto*.

ex 2:
a 7 **b** 2 **c** 4 **d** 1 **e** 6 **f** 3 **g** 5 **h** 8

page 46 (Section C)

Answers

ex 1:
1 b **2** b **3** a **4** a **5** b

ex 2:
Note: the picture story is recorded on CD3, track 23, for pronunciation practice.

page 47 (Section D)

Answers

ex 1a:

ex 1b:
otro adjetivo = difícil

ex 2:
1 e **2** d **3** a **4** c **5** b

ex 3:
1 – e **2** – y **3** – e **4** – y **5** – e

Workbook B Unit 9

page 44 *(Section A)*

Answers

ex 1a and 1b:
mil novecientos setenta y seis (1976);
mil ochocientos sesenta y cinco (1865);
mil setecientos cincuenta y cuatro
(1754);
mil seiscientos cuarenta y tres (1643);
mil quinientos treinta y dos (1532)

ex 1b ¡extra! :
1421 – mil cuatrocientos veintiuno
(1532 less 111)

page 45 *(Section B)*

Answers

ex 1:
1c 2a 3d 4e 5b

ex 2:

	lunes	martes	miércoles	jueves	viernes
8.45	geografía	matemáticas	química	historia	física
9.45	inglés	matemáticas	física	francés	biología
10.45	recreo				
11.15	música	biología	matemáticas	español	francés
12.15	química	historia	religión	inglés	religión
1.15	comida				
3.30	biología	español	español	dibujo	deporte
4.30 – 5.30	dibujo	tecnología	música	deporte	inglés

¡extra! Tenemos religión *el* miércoles y también el *viernes* a las *doce* y *cuarto*.

page 46 *(Section C)*

Answers

ex 1:
1b 2b 3a 4a 5b

ex 2:
Note: the picture story is recorded on CD3, track 24, for pronunciation practice.

page 47 *(Section D)*

Answers

ex 1a:

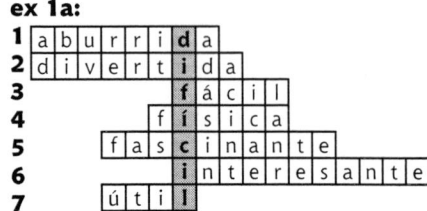

ex 1b:
otro adjetivo = difícil

ex 2:
1e 2d 3a 4c 5b

ex 3:
Suggested solutions
2 Me gustan las matemáticas y el inglés.
3 El viernes tengo física e historia.
4 La historia es interesante y útil.
5 La física es divertida e interesante.

Unidad 10 En la oficina de turismo	Topic/Language/Culture	Grammar and skills	National Criteria
10A ¿Tiene un folleto, por favor? (pp.90–91) **Objectives** • ask for information at the tourist office • learn how to use the polite 'you'	¿Tiene(n) usted(es)...? / Me da.... / Quisiera... por favor? un plano / un mapa / un horario / un folleto de la ciudad / región / del pueblo una lista de trenes / autobuses / excursiones / hoteles / hostales / campings / restaurantes Voy a pasar quince días / un mes / un fin de semana Vamos a alojarnos en un hotel / hostal / camping ¿Qué hay de interés para visitar? ¿Hay... Muy señor mío (Le) escribo para pedir información sobre... Necesito información sobre... Agradeciéndole de antemano, le saluda atentamente **Culture** using polite forms formal letters	**Grammar** *usted, ustedes* Immediate future **Skills** Memorising and adapting dialogues	**Attainment** AT1 Level 3; AT2 Levels 3–4; AT3 Levels 3–5; AT4 Levels 3–5 **Framework objectives** 7W5, 7S2, 7S3, 7T1, 7T2, 7T5, 7T6, 7L2, 7L6, 7C2, 7C5 **Programmes of study** 2e, 2f, 3a, 4a, 5h **QCA Scheme of work** Language and contexts: Unit 8 **Assessment for learning** Objectives, p.91 Ex1b, Plenary
10B ¿Por dónde se va? (pp.92–93) **Objectives:** • ask the way and give directions • say where places are • learn how to use polite commands	¿Por dónde se va a la a la / al ... el aparcamiento, el ayuntamiento, el castillo, el monumento, el museo, el palacio, el puerto, el hotel, la catedral, la comisaría, la iglesia, la plaza, la playa, Correos siga todo recto, baje la calle / avenida, cruce la plaza / el puente, está a la izquierda / derecha, tuerza a la izquierda / derecha, tome la primera / segunda / tercera calle a la izquierda / derecha **Culture** polite commands	**Grammar** polite commands	**Attainment** AT1 Levels 2–4; AT2 Levels 3–4; AT3 Level 4: AT4 Levels 3–4 **Framework objectives** 7W5, 7S2, 7S3, 7T5, 7L3, 7L6, 7C5 **Programmes of study** 2a, 2e, 5i **QCA Scheme of work** Language and contexts: Unit 8 **Assessment for learning** Objectives, p93 Ex3a, Plenary
10C ¿Qué hay de interés? (pp.94–95) **Objectives** • ask about places of interest • ask about opening and closing times • revise ways of understanding new words	¿Qué hay de interés? la naturaleza, la historia, las fiestas, los edificios religiosos el arte, la costa, la arquitectura la catedral , los jardines, los museos, las ruinas, el castillo, el paisaje, las montañas, la mezquita, las iglesias, el palacio, el casco antiguo, el alcázar, el acueducto ¿A qué hora se abre / se cierra? Está abierto / cerrado **Culture** Learn about some tourist centres in Spain	**Skills:** Assessing texts Using a dictionary Understanding new words (preterite) in context **Pronunciation:** Revision of vowel sounds	**8Attainment** AT1 Level 4: AT2 Levels 3–5; AT3 Level 4 **Framework objectives** 7W6, 7W8, 7S2, 7S3, 7T1, 7T4, 7L2, 7L3 7C1, 8C1 **Programmes of study** 1a, 2a, 2b, 2h, 3b, 3d, 4a **QCA Scheme of work** Language and contexts: Unit 8 **Assessment for learning** Objectives, p.95 Ex3, Plenary
10D ¿Qué hiciste? (pp.96–100) **Objectives** • say what you did on holiday • recognise the preterite tense • use the preterite of ir (to go)	¿Qué hiciste? visité el parque de atracciones, fui a la piscina / a la playa / al cine / al estadio / de compras comí en el restaurante, vi un partido de fútbol / una película, tomé el sol, leí un libro, jugué con videojuegos, hablé por teléfono, escribí unas tarjetas, escuché música, saqué fotos, cené, visité, me gustó Preterite of ir ayer	**Grammar** Preterite tense	**Attainment** AT1 Level 5: AT3 Levels 4–5 **Framework objectives** 7W2, 7S7, 7T1, 7L3, 8W5, 8S7 **Programmes of study** 1b, 3b **QCA Scheme of work** Language Units 8 and 10 Context: Unit 8 **Assessment for learning** Objectives, p.96 Ex1b, Plenary. All revision activities p.98

Other resources: *¡Ahora tú!* pp.136–137   WS 85–94   Flashcards 92–105   OHT 16–17   WBA & B pp.49–53   Assessment Units 9–10 (R & A file pp.132–135)   Just Click CD-Rom

10A ¿Tiene un folleto, por favor?

pp. 90–91

> **Objectives:**
> - ask for information at the tourist office
> - learn how to use the polite 'you'
>
> **Key Language:** see p.143 for full list
>
> **Grammar:**
> - usted, ustedes
>
> **Skills:**
> - memorising and adapting dialogues
> - working with higher numbers
>
> **Resources:** OHT 16A and B (tourist office conversation and overlay); CD3; Worksheets 87 (Resumen), 89 (Hablar), 91 (Escribir); Workbooks A and B p.49; Just Click CD-Rom.

Lesson starter

On the board/OHT have ready a list of print items found at tourist offices, e.g. *un horario de trenes, un mapa de la región, una lista de restaurantes, un folleto de excursiones, un plano de la ciudad.* You can use each of the category words several times, depending on what items of realia you have available or what you have downloaded from the Internet. So, for example, you might list *un folleto de hoteles, un folleto de excursiones* and *un folleto de festivales.* Try to aim for about ten to twelve items. Depending on what you have available, have ready an envelope for each group containing one or a selection of realia of the items you have listed. Ask students to open their envelopes and to see what they have got from the list on the board. After two minutes ask e.g. *¿Qué grupo tiene (un plano de la ciudad)?* The first group to respond with the correct items gets a point. An incorrect submission loses a point.

Alternative lesson starter *(for lessons starting part-way through the section)*

Ask students to work in pairs and to make as many phrases in two minutes as possible from the Key Language grid in exercise 1b. They can use their imagination and be inventive but the results must make sense. Go round and ask pairs to submit a suggestion which you write up. Anyone else with that one ticks it. The pair with the largest number of feasible suggestions is the winner.

Introduction

Use items of realia as described above to practise the names of at least some of the items mentioned in the next exercise. Hold up e.g. a timetable and ask *¿Es un horario de trenes o un horario de autobuses?* or show a map of a town and ask *¿Es un plano de la ciudad o un mapa de la región?* Work towards students producing the new vocabulary items.

1a ✎ Escucha (1–6) y lee. Empareja los diálogos y los dibujos. AT1.3, AT3.3; 7T1, 7T2, 7L2

A listening, reading and matching exercise. The students first follow the dialogues in their books while listening to them on CD. Once they have done this they try to find an appropriate picture for each exchange.

Explain that there are two different exercises here and that you would like them simply to listen and follow the dialogues first.

Support

Use realia items as described above to reinforce comprehension.

Extension

More confident students could listen again with their books closed and tell you what is requested in each case.

TRANSCRIPT · CD3, track 25

1 – Hola, buenos días.
  – Buenos días.
  – ¿Tiene usted un plano de la ciudad?
  – Aquí tiene. ¿Algo más?
  – Sí. Una lista de hoteles, por favor.
  – Vale.
  – Gracias.
  – Adiós.
2 – Buenas tardes.
  – Buenas tardes.
  – ¿Tiene un folleto de excursiones, por favor?
  – Sí. Aquí tiene.
  – ¿Y tiene una lista de restaurantes?
  – Sí, señorita.
  – Gracias. Adiós.
  – Adiós.
3 – ¡Hola!
  – ¡Hola! ¿Tiene usted un mapa de la región?
  – Sí. Y estamos aquí.
  – Gracias.
  – Adiós.
4 – Buenos días. ¿Tiene un horario de trenes?
  – ¿Para ir a Madrid?
  – Sí.
  – ¿Algo más.
  – No, nada más. Gracias, adiós.
5 – Por favor, ¿tiene una lista de restaurantes?
  – No, pero aquí hay un plano de la ciudad y hay unos restaurantes.
  – Vale, ¿y un folleto de excursiones?
  – Lo siento, no hay.
  – Vale, adiós.
6 – ¿Tiene un horario de trenes?
  – No hay estación. ¿Quiere usted un horario de autobuses?
  – Sí, gracias.
  – Adiós.

Once students have listened to the exchanges ask them to read them again and to decide which picture goes with each. Remind students not to jump to conclusions; some of the exchanges demand identification of the right combination of items, and in two cases the enquirer doesn't receive what he/she asks for.

Answers

1 B **2** C **3** A **4** F **5** E **6** D

Once the exercises have been completed you could ask different pairs to prepare and act out a dialogue.

Gramática: *usted* – 'you' 7W5, 7C5

An explanation of the polite 'you' form.

You may like to explain the origins of *usted* in order to give students a reason for the use of the third person. *Usted* is a contraction of *vuestra merced* ('your worship'). Ask them to imagine a butler saying 'Does your worship want some tea?' They should then see that the form of the verb 'does' corresponds to the third person.

In fact, since the subject pronoun in Spanish is used only for emphasis, the dialogues in 1a do not actually use the word *usted* or *ustedes*. However, they do all use the third person singular form.

To consolidate the *tú/usted* difference, offer a set of 'familiar' sentences and ask students to tell you which verb person each uses, or if they are polite or informal.

Here are some possible choices:
1 ¿Cuántos años tienes?
2 ¿Quiere algo más?
3 ¿Va usted a Madrid?
4 ¿Tiene un plano de metro?
5 ¿Hablas inglés?
6 ¿Vas al cine?

Students will have met these or similar questions in earlier units and can be asked to say to whom each might be addressed.

1b ☑ ◯ Habla con tu pareja y cambia las palabras. AT2.3–4; 7S3, 7T2, 7T5

Students build up tourist office dialogues, using a grid of key language.

This exercise should be performed in conjunction with the following ¡Así se hace! advice.

OHTs 16A and B present a series of visual and written cues for building up these conversations. They can be used with or without the overlay to help students produce and practise different versions of the exchanges.

Support

☑ Worksheet 89 (Hablar) offers a set of visual cues to enable students to build up a dialogue from memory.

Extension

Encourage more able students to ring the changes with the ways of asking for things identified in the ¡Así se hace! section. There are examples of all these in exercise 1a.

All these dialogues could be practised and reworked for assessment purposes.

¡Así se hace! Practising dialogues 7S3, 7T2, 7T5

This section offers advice on how to practise dialogues by memorising and adapting language, and highlights the four different ways of asking for things that have been presented.

The following six dialogues are alternative versions of those presented in exercise 1a. You may find them useful to illustrate the fact that you can ask for the same information in a number of different ways, perhaps by reading one version aloud while asking students to follow the text of the other.

1 – Buenos días. Un plano de la ciudad, por favor.
 – Aquí tiene. ¿Algo más?
 – Sí, una lista de hoteles.
 – Lo siento, no tenemos.
 – Gracias, adiós.
2 – Buenas tardes.
 – Buenas tardes. ¿Qué desea?

 – Un folleto de monumentos históricos.
 – Vale, aquí tiene.
 – Gracias. Adiós.
3 – Un horario de trenes, por favor.
 – Muy bien. Vamos a ver. ¿Algo más?
 – Sí, una lista de restaurantes.
 – Muy bien.
 – Adiós.
4 – ¿Hay un camping por aquí?
 – Sí, señora. Hay varios. ¿Quiere una lista de campings?
 – Sí, por favor y un plano del pueblo.
5 – Buenos días.
 – ¿Qué desea?
 – Me da un mapa de la región y una lista de hoteles, por favor.
 – Un mapa y una lista. Vale.
 – Adiós y gracias.
6 – ¡Hola! Quisiera un horario de trenes, por favor.
 – Vale. ¿Algo más?
 – No, nada más, gracias.

1c ◯ ¡extra!

After reading through the ¡Así se hace! section and discussing the six dialogues above, students practise the four different ways of asking for things with a partner, using vocabulary learnt in previous units.

2a 📖 Lee y rellena el cuadro. AT3.5, 7S2; 7T1, 7C2, 7C5

A pair of formal letters asking for tourist information. Students should read them for gist before copying and filling in the grid offering specific details. (Tell them to make the **Necesita** box bigger than the others which only require single word answers.)

Draw their attention to the formal beginnings and endings of the letters and discuss with them what they might mean and what their equivalents would be in English. (An alternative beginning would be *Muy señor mío/señora mía*.)

Besides the beginnings and ends both letters use other formulae (*le ruego me envíe…, información sobre…, vamos a quedarnos…*) which can be reused later.

Both letters use the immediate future.

Extension

More able students could write down other details as well. Students could do some research of their own on one or more of the places mentioned in the letters.

Answers

Nombre	Destino	Mes	Tiempo	Necesita
Ursula	Bogotá	julio	una semana	lista de hoteles, plano de ciudad, folleto de actividades y excursiones
Marisol	Cantabria	agosto	15 días	mapa de la provincia, lista de campings, folleto sobre Santander y Santillana

Preliminary exercise

It may be useful to revise *ir a* separately before embarking on this exercise. Use the flashcards 28–39 to practise ¿Qué vas a hacer? Voy a jugar al tenis/ir de compras, etc.

Next ask two students *¿Qué vais a hacer?* Elicit the answer *Vamos a...*

Ask studénts to refer if necessary to Grammar section B5.

2b ✎ ¡extra! Escribe una carta electrónica a una oficina de turismo. AT4.5; 7T5

This exercise combines the grammar practice of the previous exercise and the ability to produce the set phrases presented in the letters in 2a. The phrases they can reuse are highlighted in the letters.

Discuss with the class which tourist offices they will write to. You could then send selected completed letters off and display any information and material received.

Support

WS 91 (Escribir) offers a useful writing frame for just such a formal letter.

Plenary

☑ On the board or OHT display the following trap-door exercise letter. In all cases the alternatives should be written one above the other. You decide in advance which alternatives are correct. Ask the class to read the letter aloud, pausing at each choice while you ask an individual to choose an answer. A wrong answer means that that student goes through the trap door and the class starts at the beginning again, remembering what has gone before. This is a good finishing exercise and encourages concentration on the part of the class as well as plenty of repetition. Students could also do the exercise in pairs, noting their choices and counting up the number of lives lost when you supply the correct choices at the end.

Estimado señor,

Le escribo para pedir información sobre Málaga/Madrid. Voy/ Vamos a pasar un mes/una semana en la ciudad/la región en abril /octubre. Voy/Vamos a quedarme/quedarnos en un hotel/un hostal.

Le ruego me envíe un plano/un mapa, una lista de hoteles/hostales, una lista de restaurantes y un folleto de excursiones/atracciones.

Atentamente suyo, Marta Mateo.

Extension

Ask students what other expressions in Spanish would be useful to know when asking for information.

Plenary *(for lessons part-way through the section)*

In pairs, students explain the use and formation of *usted*.

10B ¿Por dónde se va?

pp. 92–93

> **Objectives:**
> * ask the way and give directions
> * say where places are
> * learn how to use polite commands
> **Key Language:** see p.143 for full list
> **Grammar:**
> * polite commands
> **Skills:**
> * memorising and adapting dialogues
> * working with higher numbers
> **Resources:** Visual 84 and OHT 17 (directions); CD3; Worksheets 85 (direction visuals), 87 (Resumen), 93 (Gramática); Workbooks A and B p.50; *Just Click* CD-Rom.

On these pages more places in the town and directions are presented and students learn how to form polite commands and when to use them.

Lesson starter

Drop on to the OHP OHT 9. Ask students to work in groups. They have just two minutes to recall as many of the places in the town as possible. They must try to provide the correct spelling and gender for each. After two minutes ask students to put their hands up with suggestions. Any student providing a place name with the correct spelling and gender gets a point.

Alternative lesson starter *(for lessons starting part-way through the section)*

On the board write up a series of directions from the door to individuals' places, e.g *siga todo recto; tome el segundo pasillo a la izquerda; es la tercera silla a la derecha.*

Students must work out to whom each one refers.

1 💿 Escucha (1–8). Mira el plano y escribe la letra. AT1.2; 7L3

Students look at the map and identify the places that they hear.

> **TRANSCRIPT**
> CD3, track 26
>
> 1 Perdone, ¿por dónde se va al museo, por favor?
> 2 La comisaría, ¿dónde está?
> 3 Buenos días, ¿por dónde se va a Correos?
> 4 ¿La iglesia Santa Ana está por aquí?
> 5 Perdone, ¿dónde está la catedral, por favor?
> 6 Por favor, ¿el aparcamiento?
> 7 Quisiera saber dónde está el ayuntamiento.
> 8 Perdone, ¿por dónde se va al puerto?

> **Answers**
> **1** G (museum) **2** F (police station) **3** H (post office) **4** K (church)
> **5** J (cathedral) **6** M (car park) **7** L (town hall) **8** D (port)

Preliminary exercise

Use Visual 85 or OHT 17 and your own actions to introduce and practise directions. Once a few basic ones have been introduced, ask a student to be a robot, with first you and then other class members giving directions.

If appropriate, move on to asking the class to build up a set of directions for how to get from e.g. the school to the centre of town or from one public building to another.

Ordinal numbers have already been encountered in the context of e.g. floors of a block of flats and lessons. They only appear here in the feminine form but students may recall e.g. *el primer/segundo piso.* Ordinal numbers are dealt with in section D1.2 of the grammar section of the Student's Book. The Gramática worksheet 93 has information and an exercise on this point.

The mini-flashcards on Worksheet 85 can be used for pairwork practice and for vocabulary building.

2 💿 Escucha (1–8) y escribe la(s) letra(s). AT1.3; 7L3

A more advanced set of listening items that revise the place names and introduce directions. Some of the directions use more than one instruction so students should be alerted to the need to put down more than one answer. To do this exercise students will need to be able to differentiate between

Está/Tuerza/Tome la primera/segunda/tercera calle a la derecha, so it is not enough just to identify a single word, e.g. *izquierda.*

Support

Less confident students will benefit from a lot of prior practice with teacher and student actions and with Visual 85 and/or OHT 17. They may also need to listen several times.

Extension

Fast-finishers could note down the destinations as well.

TRANSCRIPT
CD3, track 27

1 – ¿Por dónde se va a la iglesia Santa Ana?
  – Tome la primera calle a la izquierda.
  – Gracias.
2 – ¿Por dónde se va al puerto?
  – Tome la tercera calle a la izquierda.
3 – ¿Por dónde se va al Monumento Murillo?
  – Cruce la plaza y siga todo recto.
4 – ¿Por dónde se va a la catedral?
  – Tome la primera calle a la izquierda y cruce el puente.
5 – ¿Por dónde se va al palacio?
  – Tuerza a la derecha, después tome la segunda calle a la derecha.
6 – ¿Por dónde se va al aparcamiento?
  – Está a la derecha.
7 – ¿Por dónde se va a Correos?
  – Tome la segunda calle a la derecha. Está a la derecha.
8 – ¿Por dónde se va al castillo?
  – Baje la calle, tome la segunda calle a la derecha y está a la izquierda.

Answers

1 I **2** M **3** C, A **4** I, D **5** G, K **6** F **7** K, F **8** B, K, E

Gramática: commands 7W5, 7C5

An explanation of the use and formation of polite commands. To practise this form, give students a list of familiar regular verbs, including some direction ones and ask them to produce the singular polite command for each.

Here are some suggestions: *abrir, bajar, comer, mirar, tomar.*

3a ☑ 💿 Escucha (1–7). Mira el plano y sigue las direcciones. ¿Adónde van?
AT1.4; 7L3

Students listen to another set of instructions, following on the map and noting the destinations.

Support

Less confident students will need time to follow each instruction and provision to hear each extract several times.

Extension

More able students could work in pairs, taking it in turns to produce further sets of instructions for their partners to guess. This exercise could be used for assessment.

TRANSCRIPT
CD3, track 28

1 Baje la calle, tome la segunda calle a la derecha y tuerza a la izquierda.
2 Tome la segunda calle a la izquierda y está a la derecha.
3 Baje la calle. Cruce la plaza y siga todo recto. ▶

4 Siga todo recto. Tome la primera calle a la izquierda. Está a la derecha.
5 Tome la primera calle a la derecha y está a la izquierda.
6 Tome la primera calle a la izquierda y está al final.
7 Tome la tercera calle a la izquierda y suba la calle y siga todo recto.

Answers

1 al castillo **2** a la comisaría **3** al monumento **4** a la iglesia
5 al ayuntamiento **6** a la catedral **7** al puerto

3b 💬 Habla con tu pareja. Usa el plano.
AT2.3–4; 7S3, 7L6

Students use the town plan to ask and answer questions about how to get to places.

Encourage students to practise the sample dialogue so that they can say it and then adapt it without looking, thereafter using the visual cues on the map.

Extension

Encourage more able students to build up to longer exchanges by recycling and adding questions and answers like *¿Está lejos? No, está a cinco minutos andando, ¿Puede repetir por favor?*

4 ✏️ Escribe direcciones para un amigo español. AT4. 4; 7T5

From a series of instructions in English, students construct Spanish versions.

As the example indicates, rather than a literal translation, students need to concentrate on putting over the gist of the information.

Suggested answers

2 Cruce el puente, baje la calle, tuerza a la derecha y tome la segunda calle a la izquierda.
3 Siga todo recto, y está a la izquierda al lado del cine.
4 Tome la tercera calle a la derecha y tuerza a la izquierda. Está todo recto.
5 Baje la calle, tuerza a la derecha y (luego) a la izquierda. Está a la derecha.

5a 📖 Une las frases y los dibujos. AT3.4; 7S2

Students match the sentences with the correct pictures.

Answers

1 C **2** D **3** A **4** G **5** B **6** E **7** F

5b ✏️ ¡extra! Escribe direcciones de tu colegio a tu casa para un amigo español.
AT4.3–4, 7T5

Writing practice. Students produce directions for getting from school to their home and how far it is. If students have very long and complicated journeys you may prefer to substitute another pair of locations.

Support

By choosing pairs of locations like school–town centre, MacDonalds–Woolworths, you can work on this initially as a class exercise before asking students to work in pairs or groups to produce their own written version.

Plenary

☑ First ask the class to recap on the use of the formal command, building up an explanation for an absent classmate. Then ask them to work in groups. Each group has two minutes to prepare a list of three famous people whom they would address formally and three whom they would address informally.

At the end of the two minutes compare notes. Give points to the groups with the most ingenious/hilarious suggestions.

Alternative plenary

☑ Display some or all learning objectives for the section on the board and students say whether they are confident (green card), quite confident (orange card) or not confident (red card) that they have mastered them.

10C ¿Qué hay de interés?

pp. 94–95

> **Objectives:**
> • ask about places of interest
> • ask about opening and closing times
> • revise ways of understanding new words
> **Key Language:** see p.143 for full list
> **Skills:**
> • assessing texts
> • using a dictionary
> **Pronunciation:**
> • revision of vowel sounds
> **Resources:** CD3; Worksheets 87 (Resumen), 90 (Leer); Workbooks A and B p.51; *Just Click* CD-Rom.

On these two pages students learn vocabulary for places of interest, opening and closing times are dealt with, there are tips on how to deal with longer texts and pronunciation of vowel sounds is revisited.

Lesson starter

On the board write a list of possible reasons tourists might come to your town or region. Ask students to work in groups or pairs to rate them in order.

Depending on the time you want to spend and the confidence of the students, reasons (taken from the pages) might include some of the following:

la naturaleza
la historia
las fiestas
los edificios religiosos
el arte
la costa
la arquitectura
la catedral
los jardines
los museos
las ruinas
el castillo
el paisaje
las montañas
la mezquita
las iglesias
el Palacio

At the end of two minutes ask each group in turn to give you their numbered list. Write the numbers next to each attraction and at the end compare the results.

Alternative lesson starter *(for lessons starting partway through the section)*

Ask students to work in groups and to make a list of three to five reasons (along the lines of those mentioned on the page) for visiting the town or region.

1 💡 📖 **Mira la información sobre cuatro ciudades. Une las ciudades con las personas A–D.** AT3.4; 7T1, 7T4, 7C1, 8C1

A set of four brochure-type descriptions of different places in Spain, to be matched to four different people's touristic requirements. Each account is supported by a photo.

This exercise should be tackled in conjunction with the *¡Así se hace!* section.

Students could work in groups for this exercise. Ask them to start by reading the *¡Así se hace!* section. They should then read through each account carefully and look at the accompanying photo. As the advice suggests, they should discuss any new vocabulary, first looking for similarities with English and only then looking up any problem words.

Once they have read the four accounts, ask different groups to give you the gist of one of them.

Now ask them to look at the tourists' requirements. There is a vocabulary box for some of the new vocabulary (all preterite forms – these will be featured in the next section.) Once again, when they have finished, ask groups to give you the gist of each person's requirements.

Finally ask students to match each person with the most appropriate destination.

Answers

A Sevilla **B** Andorra **C** Sitges **D** Segovia

Extension

These accounts could provide a launching pad for students to find out more about each place, perhaps by writing to tourist boards or searching on the Internet.

¡Así se hace! 7S2, 7T1, 7T4

Communication strategies for reading comprehension. As the last instruction suggests, if students read through this section (again) before embarking on exercise 2 they can assess their success on exercise 1 and plan strategies for dealing with 2.

Preliminary exercise

Revise the time and the days of the week by asking e.g. *¿Qué día hay una clase de geografía?*, *¿A qué hora hay francés?*

Revise the 24-hour clock by first asking students to give you the Spanish for 9.00, 11.30 etc., and then by asking them to give you the 24-hour equivalent for these.

2 🎧 **Escucha (1–4). ¿Qué hay de interés?** AT1.4; 7L3

A series of exchanges in which people in a tourist office ask and say what there is to visit and see. Students list the places that they hear each time. They can write in English or Spanish.

Support

Play the extracts as many times as necessary for students to take notes.

Extension

More able students could provide a piece of extra information about each exchange.

TRANSCRIPT **CD3, track 29**

1 – Buenos días.
– Buenos días. ¿Qué desea?
– Vamos a pasar una semana aquí. ¿Me puede decir qué hay de interés?
– Pues, hay un palacio, un castillo y una catedral.
– ¿Y para los niños?
– Hay un parque de atracciones muy cerca.
– Gracias.

2 – Perdón, señor.
– ¿Sí?
– Vamos a pasar unos días aquí. ¿Qué hay de interés?
– Bueno, hay muchos museos, hay parques, hay el puerto que es muy bonito.
– Gracias. ¿Tiene un folleto?
– Sí, tome.
– Gracias.

3 – Buenas tardes.
– Buenas tardes.
– ¿Me puede decir qué hay de interés aquí?
– Sí, señor. Hay una catedral, unas iglesias, hay un castillo y un museo muy importante.
– Gracias.
– De nada, adiós.

4 – ¿Qué hay de interés, por favor?
– Hay un palacio muy grande, hay un ayuntamiento muy antiguo y también hay jardines y parques.
– Gracias.
– Adiós.

Answers

1 palacio, castillo, catedral, parque de atracciones **2** museos, parques, puerto **3** catedral, iglesias, castillo, museo **4** palacio, ayuntamiento, jardines, parques

3 ☑ 📖 ¿Verdad (V) o mentira (M)? AT3.4; 7W8, 7T1, 7T4

Students look at a collection of data about opening and closing times and then decide whether a series of statements about them are true or false.

To offer a contrast in register, while the ads are in typical ad shorthand and use adjectives like *cerrado* and *gratuito*, the questions use verbs like *abrirse*, *cerrarse*, and *visitar*. *Abrir* and *cerrar* should be familiar from Unit 6.

Ask students to work in pairs or groups and to read through the ads for gist, then ask them to make notes on each ad. To focus their efforts ask them to look back to the ¡Así se hace! section on the previous spread. Much of the language should be known from other contexts. They should notice that the same type of language is repeated in all four. While some of the information should be clear, they will need to guess e.g. *festivo*, *gratuito*, from the context. *Cerrado* can be extrapolated from *cerrar*. Anything they can't work out they can look up in the dictionary. Check for the meaning of *escultura* (sculpture, not culture).

Now ask the class to look at the questions. What are the basic verbs? (*se abre/cierra/puede visitar*). Check the implication of the *se* form, which varies according to the verb (it opens/closes, you can visit (literally it can be visited)).

Next ask the groups to use their notes to answer the questions.

Extension

More able students could change the incorrect statements.

Answers

1V **2**V **3**M (el museo está cerrado los lunes) **4**M (el museo está cerrado los domingos por la tarde) **5**M (el museo se abre a las cuatro de la tarde).

This exercise could be used for assessment.

WS 90 (Leer) offers a comprehension exercise based on opening and closing time information.

4 ◯ Habla con tu pareja. Usa la información en 3. Cambia las palabras. AT.2.3–5; 7S3

Students make conversations by adapting the model given and by referring back to the previous exercise.

Extension

More able students could add questions like *¿Cuánto es?* and *¿Se puede visitar (el lunes)?*

Pronunciation: vowel sounds 7W6, 7L1, 7L6

Revision of the vowel sounds in Spanish with a reminder that, unlike English vowel sounds, Spanish vowels each have a fixed value. Once students have read the notes they can practise the sample sentences in pairs.

TRANSCRIPT **CD3, track 30**

Ana y Alicia van andando a Alicante.
Enrique y Ernesto son elefantes enormes.
Visitan iglesias interesantes en Ibiza.
¡Hola Olivia! ¡Hola Alonso!
La unidad más útil es la unidad uno.

Plenary

☑ Give students in pairs a copy of the sentences from the pronunciation box. First, they go through and underline all vowels. They then circle any letters or parts of words that they are not sure how to pronounce. Finally, go through the words together as a class, sorting out any pronunciation problems.

Plenary (for the more able)

☑ The 24- versus 12-hour clock can be a source of confusion. This may have been demonstrated during the lesson. Ask students to think of /give a rule that works for them and to put their hand up to tell you. Explain that everyone may have a different strategy. On the board write down as many of the rules offered as you think are helpful, e.g.

1.00 → 13.00
2.00 → 14.00
3.00 → 15.00
4.00 → 16.00

1.00 ADD TWO = 13.00

Remember the 6.00 news is at 18.00 and work backwards and forwards.

Draw a clock face and write the two lots of numbers round the edge.

Alternative plenary

☑ Display the Section D objectives on an OHT. In groups, students note down what they have learnt for each point then report back.

10D ¿Qué hiciste?

page 96

Objectives:
- say what you did on holiday
- recognise the preterite tense
- use the preterite of *ir* (to go)

Key Language: see p.143 for full list

Grammar:
- the preterite tense

Resources: Visual 86 (freetime activities for practising preterite); CD3; Worksheets 87 Resumen, 88 (Escuchar), 92 (*¡Así se hace!*), 93 (Gramática), 94 (*¡extra!*); Workbooks A and B p.52; *Just Click* CD-Rom.

In the context of holiday activities, these pages present a selection of high-frequency first person preterite forms together with the full preterite paradigm of *ir*. There is incidental listening exposure to other persons of high-frequency verbs.

Lesson starter

As students come in give out slips of paper showing either a key word or phrase or a picture clue. Students must find the person with the matching picture or word(s).

The words and phrases are all taken from page 96 and could include: *el parque de atracciones, la piscina, música, compras, el restaurante, una película, un partido de fútbol, un libro, teléfono, una tarjeta, el sol, videojuegos, Internet*. Pictures can be easily drawn symbols.

When everyone has found their partner ask people to come to the front, and show and say their word and picture before sitting down.

Alternative lesson starter *(for lessons starting part-way through the section)*

Use the words and phrases listed above but instead of pictures, students match them up to the correct verb: *fui a, fui de, leí, jugué con, escuché, navegué por, escribí, visité, tomé, comí en, hablé por, vi, vi* (only use the last two if you have a large class).

When everyone has found their partner, ask people to come to the front and say their complete sentence before sitting down.

Introduction

First ask students to tell you what tenses they have learnt in Spanish. Recap the fact that they have learnt how to talk about what they are doing or habitually do, and how to say what they are going to do. From flashcards 28–39 use the music, shopping, cinema and net ones to revise these two tenses.

Ask students what other tense would be useful. Elicit the fact that it's useful to be able to talk about what you've done. Now use Visual 86 to present and practise the new freetime

activities with the preterite. Start with the four that correspond to the activities mentioned in the previous paragraph (*escuché música, navegué por Internet, fui al cine, fui de compras*). Build up until students are able to react to most of the cards.

1a 📖 Lee y escribe los números de las actividades que se mencionan. AT3.5; 7S7, 7T1

Students read a set of postcards written in the preterite and match the activities mentioned in each to a series of visuals.

Provided that the new language has been presented and practised via the OHT, this exercise should be fairly straightforward.

This exercise should be presented in conjunction with the first part of the Gramática section.

Answers

A 12, 9, 8, 2   **B** 7, 2, 3, 6   **C** 4, 11, 5, 10, 13

1b ☑ 💿 Escucha (1–4). Escribe los números de las actividades que se mencionan. Apunta información extra si puedes. AT1.5; 7L3, 8W5, 8S7

Students listen to a series of exchanges about what people did on holiday trips. Referring back to the pictures in exercise 1a they note the activities they hear mentioned.

This exercise could be used for assessment.

Answers

1 1, 7, 2   **2** 4, 11, 10   **3** 1   **4** 6, 2

TRANSCRIPT   CD3, track 31

1 – ¡Hola, Maite!
– ¡Hola! ¿Qué tal?
– Bien, bien.
– ¿Qué hiciste en Córdoba?
– Bueno, visité la catedral y unos museos durante el día.
– ¿Y por la noche?
– Fui al cine un día.
– ¿Qué viste?
– Una película de terror.
– ¿Comiste en casa de tus abuelos?
– No, fuimos a comer a restaurantes. Es más fácil para mis abuelos.

2 – ¡Hola!
– ¡Hola, Juan!
– ¿Qué hiciste ayer?
– Pues, pasé todo el día en casa. Leí un libro de inglés, navegué por Internet y jugué con mi hermano.
– ¿Es todo?
– Sí, ah, no. Escribí una tarjeta a mi amiga.
– Aha.

3 – ¿Qué hiciste en la ciudad?
– Visité mucho: monumentos, palacios, iglesias y la catedral.
– ¿Visitaste un museo?
– Sí visité el museo de arte moderno.
– Muy bien.

4 – Oye, ayer, ¿fuiste a la playa?
– Sí, claro. Fui por la mañana y pasé todo el día allí. Tomé el sol y luego comí en un restaurante que está en la playa.
– ¡Estupendo!

WS 88 (Escuchar) offers more listening practice of the preterite together with revision of times and opinions.

Gramática: the preterite tense 8W5, 8S7

Once students have identified the new verbs in exercise 1a and matched each up to its picture, ask them to look back at the exercise and to give you the preterite forms of the verbs asked for.

Taking *visitar*, *comer* and *escribir* as regular examples of three verb families, see what rules the students come up with for forming the first person of the preterite verbs. Ask students to tell you why they think *navegué* and *jugué* have a *u* before the final *e*. Explain that the preterite forms of *ver* (*vi*) and *ir* (*fui*) must be learnt as irregulars.

At this stage students are only given the paradigm of one (irregular) preterite: *ir*.

WS 93 (Gramática) offers further explanation and practice of the preterite.

2a 📖 Rellena los espacios con *fui, fuiste, fue o fuimos.* AT3.4; 8S7

Students read a gapped postcard and fill in the missing verbs.

Answers

fui, fuimos, fuimos, fui, fue, fuimos, fuimos, fuiste

WS 94 (¡extra!) focuses on tense and time markers and provides further reading exposure to the preterite as well as revision of other tenses.

Plenary

☑ **WS 92** (¡Así se hace!) focuses on high-frequency words and would make a good plenary lesson exercise for students working together in groups, perhaps with different groups being allocated different sections of the sheet to work on.

Alternative plenary

☑ Alternatively ask the class to look carefully at the Resumen. Go through it together. Does all the vocabulary now look familiar? Have they understood the grammar points? Ask people to indicate whether they are happy, neutral or unhappy about each section by holding up appropriately coloured cards.

Resumen *(page 97)*

This section offers a resumé of all the vocabulary, grammar, skills and tips presented in the unit.

Repaso *(page 98)*

☑ This page revises work from Units 9 and 10.

1 💿 Escucha (1–4). Mira los horarios de Conchita, Alejandro e Isabel. ¿De quién es el horario? AT1.3; 7L3

Students listen to a series of short exchanges and decide to which each one refers.

Answers

1 Alejandro **2** Isabel **3** Alejandro **4** Conchita

TRANSCRIPT

TRANSCRIPT CD3, track 32

1 Los martes no me gustan mucho. Tengo tecnología por la mañana. Por la tarde tengo geografía e historia. La historia no se me da bien.

2 Los martes por la tarde tengo clases de historia y tecnología. Odio la tecnología.

3 Los lunes por la mañana tengo clase de dibujo y luego informática. Me encanta la informática.

4 Me gustan los lunes. Tengo tres clases de ciencias: dos por la mañana y una por la tarde. Hay deporte también por la mañana. No tengo clase de matemáticas. Para mí las matemáticas son superdifíciles. Hay informática antes de comer. Es fácil y muy interesante.

2 💬 Haz diálogos con tu pareja basados en los horarios arriba. AT2.3–5; 7 7S9, 7L3

A pairwork exercise based on the timetables in exercise 1.

3 📖 Mira la información turística en la página 99. ¿Adónde fueron los turistas? AT3.5; 7T1, 7T3

Students read a set of holiday accounts and assess them for gist before matching them to an assemblage of details about different attractions.

Answers

a Pueblo de Montjuich **b** Fuente Mágica **c** Sagrada Familia **d** Port Aventura

4 ✏️ Rellena los espacios. AT4.4; 7T6

Students fill in the gaps in a text with a mixture of nouns, numbers, and times to complete their own account of their school and school routine.

Reading *(page 99)*
AT3.4; 7S2

1 📖 Mira la información sobre Barcelona. Di si las frases son verdad (V) o mentira (M). Corrige las frases falsas.

A set of true/false questions on the ads for attractions in Barcelona. Once students have done them, they are asked to correct the false statements.

Answers

1V **2**V **3**V **4**V **5**M (La Sagrada Familia está abierta los domingos) **6**V

2 📖 Escribe los precios para los turistas siguientes. AT3.4; 7S2

A series of visual cues to get students to work out prices for the attractions. The students will have to read through the admission details very carefully.

Answers

1 40€ **2** – **3** 24€ **4** 21€ **5** 50€ **6** 31,70€ (28€ for 4 adults + 3,70€ for a child)

¡Ahora, tú! *(pp. 136–137)*

Differentiated self-access reading and writing exercises: see page 37 for more information.

page 136

1 📖 **Replace the images with the correct vocabulary.**

quince días/agosto/plan de la ciudad/mapa de la región/lista de campings/un folleto/y una lista de restaurantes

2 📖 **Look at the town plan and follow the directions...**

Answers

1 C, G **2** K, J **3** C, D

page 137

1 ✏️ **Using the town plan on page 136, write directions for your partner.**

Students take turns to write out directions that lead their partners to a location of their choice on the map.

2 💡 📖 **Join up the two parts of the sentences.**

Answers

Vi una película muy buena.
Tomé el sol en la playa.
Leí un libro de ciencia ficción.

Visité el museo de la ciudad.
Escribí postales a mis amigos.
Comí con mi familia en restaurantes muy buenos.
Fui a un partido de fútbol.

3 💡 📖 **Be a detective. Read what the friends say. Who is the culprit?**

A challenging reading activity which focuses on recognition of the *yo* and *nosotros* forms of the preterite tense. Ask students to read through the statements from all the house guests and make notes in English of their activities, paying particular attention to any times mentioned. Conchita, Rafa, Pepe, Jorge, Helena and Juan all have stories which can be corroborated by someone else. Therefore, Isabel, by a process of elimination, is the most likely culprit of the murder. (She says she went to the kitchen at 2.20 for a glass of milk and went back to her bedroom *without speaking to anyone*. Both Conchita and Jorge were in the kitchen at the time and make no mention in their statements of having seen her).

Answer

Isabel

4 ✏️ **Answer the detective's questions.**

1 Fui a la cama a la una y media.
2 Fui a la cama a la una con Rafa.
3 No fui a la cocina.
4 Vi a Jorge en la cocina pero no vi a Isabel.
5 Vi a Juan en el salón.
6 Vi una película en la televisión.
7 Fui a la cama a las tres.

Worksheets Unit 10

85 **¿Por dónde se va? AT3.1; 7W1**

Twelve visual symbols and matching captions to help practise and learn directions (pages 92–93).

86 **¿Qué hiciste? AT3.1; 7W1**

Twelve visuals and matching captions to help teach holiday activities (preterite tense) from Section D.

87 **Resumen AT3.1; 7W1**

Students may paste this into their exercise books, so that they have a reference for e.g. when doing homework.

88 **Escuchar AT1.5; 7S7, 8S7**

a, b and **c** This exercise combines work on places of interest (pages 94–95) and the preterite (pages 96–97). As the instructions suggest, it is advisable for students to listen to the conversation at least twice, if not three times. The instructions use ordinal numbers and the third person of the preterite, while the dialogue uses first and second persons. As well as offering listening recognition of preterites the exercise revises opinions and times of day.

TRANSCRIPT

CD3, track 33

– ¡Hola, Ana! ¿Qué tal las vacaciones? ¿Qué hiciste?
– Pues llegué el lunes por la mañana y fui en seguida a la playa y tomé el sol... ¡Estupendo!

El martes... a ver... hizo mal tiempo así que por la tarde fui al cine y vi una película de terror. No me gustó mucho. Fue un poco aburrida.

El miércoles hizo de nuevo buen tiempo. Por la tarde visité el palacio viejo con Julio. Fue muy interesante. ▶

El jueves por la mañana Julio y yo fuimos al parque de atracciones.

Saqué muchas fotos. Era muy ruidoso, pero ¡qué divertido!

El viernes por la noche cené en un restaurante pero la comida no fue muy buena y no comí mucho.

El sábado por la noche no salí. Escribí unas postales y leí un libro. ¡Qué rollo!

El domingo por la tarde volví a casa. Llamé a mis amigas y navegué por Internet. Es tranquilo pero ¡me gusta estar en casa!

Answers

	What she did	Time of day	Her opinion
lunes	arrived, went to beach, sunbathed	morning	great
martes	went to cinema, saw horror film	afternoon	boring, didn't like it
miércoles	visited old palace	afternoon	very interesting
jueves	went to theme park, took photos	morning	fun!
viernes	went to restaurant, didn't eat much	evening	not very good
sábado	didn't go out, wrote cards and read book	evening	boring
domingo	came home, phoned friends and went on the Internet	afternoon	quiet, but good to be home

89 Hablar AT2.3–4, 7L6

A set of visual cues to support the set of sample Tourist Office dialogues on pages 90–91. This sheet would be particularly useful for those students who are unable to make the leap from reading to ad-libbing. More able students can be encouraged to add extra details like the reason why there isn't a brochure or map of something.

The dialogue can be practised and worked on as part of an assessment exercise.

90 Leer AT3.4; 7T1

An exercise based on pages 94–95 and using some authentic-style notices about opening and closing times.

a Students first check the meanings of some recurring key words.

Answers

abierto – open; cerrado – shut; (días) festivos – holidays; días laborables – working days; excepto – except; renovación – restoration/repairs; todos los días – every day

b A reading comprehension exercise using cues, where students can be helped by context and layout. Students decide whether various places will be open on the days and at the times mentioned.

Answers

See Table below.

91 Escribir AT4.3–5; 7T6

This writing frame supports work on pages 90–91, allowing students to write their own personalised formal letters.

1 Students produce a letter by choosing available options from the writing frame.

Answer

Muy señor mío,

Le escribo para pedir información sobre Madrid. Voy a pasar una semana en la ciudad con mi familia en abril. Vamos a alojarnos en un hotel. Le ruego me envíe un plano, una lista de restaurantes y un folleto de excursiones.

Atentamente...

2 Students are invited to decide upon and write their own letter. Less confident students should be encouraged to choose from the options in the frame; more confident ones may prefer to choose more freely, using the frame as a model.

92 ¡Así se hace! 7W2

This sheet concentrates on the importance of high-frequency words, and underlines the fact that these useful words may be rendered in different ways depending upon where they occur.

a Students find the missing word for each boxed set of phrases.

Answers

1 hace **2** tiene **3** qué **4** hay **5** a **6** es **7** está **8** en **9** de **10** por

b Students provide translations for the different phrases featured, thus underlining the fact that these words may be rendered differently according to context.

93 Grámatica

The first section of this sheet deals with the ordinal numbers featured on pages 92–93. Students are reminded about the formation of ordinals 1–10 and of the fact that they must agree.

1 In this exercise students are given the number and the abbreviation of the ordinal needed. This cues them for the agreement.

Answers

1 tercero; cuarta **2** quinta; primera **3** segundo; sexta

2 The context now goes beyond directions into other uses of these forms. In this exercise, students are asked to supply the correct ordinal number, ensuring that it agrees with the nouns listed.

Answers

1 tercer **2** séptimo **3** quinta **4** segundo **5** sexta **6** cuarto

The third section of this sheet deals with the preterite and in particular the first person forms that have been introduced on page 96.

3a Students match some preterite forms with their infinitives.

3b They identify those preterite forms that are regular (irregularities shown in bold). The pattern among those verbs whose infinitive ends in -gar is that in the preterite these verbs take -gué in order to retain the hard g sound.

Answers

See Table on page 154

94 ¡extra! AT3.5; 7S7, 8S7

Focus on time markers and tense recognition as an aid to comprehension

a A suggestion that students first of all check any time markers they are not sure of: anteayer, pasado mañana have already been given as examples but others such as mañana as 'tomorrow' and próximo may need checking.

b Students order Conchi's thoughts in time sequence. There is only one possible order, as even sentences 10 and 11 have an y to establish internal order.

Answers

1 El año pasado, fui a Chile de vacaciones.
2 En abril, visité Santiago de Compostela con mis padres.
3 El mes pasado, llovió mucho aquí en Galicia.
4 La semana pasada, recibí una carta de mi amiga venezolana.
5 El lunes, vi una entrevista muy interesante en Antena 3.
6 Anteayer, tuve una clase de física muy interesante.
7 Ayer por la mañana, bebí una Coca-Cola en un bar con mis amigos.
8 Ayer por la noche, hice un montón de deberes.
9 Hoy, a las once de la mañana, llamé a mi abuela en Madrid.
10 Ahora navego por Internet y
11 En este momento escribo mi diario.
12 Hoy, a las once de la noche, voy a escuchar música en mi dormitorio.
13 Mañana por la mañana, voy a levantarme a las seis y media.
14 Mañana por la tarde, voy a salir de compras con mi madre.

	swimming pool	zoo	museum	water world	restaurant	castle	theme park
An ordinary Monday in August at 3.00 pm	✗	✗	✗	✓	✓	✗	✓
A Saturday in October at 10.00 am	✓	✓	✗	✗	✗	✗	✓
Tues 1st January (a public holiday) at 4.00 pm	✓	✗	✗	✗	✓	✓	✓
A Sunday in April at midday	✓	✓	✗	✓	✗	✓	✓

Table to Grámatica 93, 3b

infinitive	ir	sacar	hacer	llegar	tomar	llamar	jugar	navegar	ver
preterite	**fui**	**saqué**	**hice**	**llegué**	tomé	llamé	**jugué**	**navegué**	vi

15 Mañana a las once de la noche, voy a ver mi telenovela preferida en la tele.

16 Pasado mañana, voy a cenar en un restaurante con mis tíos.

17 El miércoles, voy a jugar al voleibol en el polideportivo.

18 La próxima semana, voy a comprar unos peces de colores.

19 En enero, voy a las Islas Canarias con mi familia.

20 El próximo año voy a hablar muy bien inglés.

Pruebas Unidades 9 y 10

R and A File pp.132–135

Prueba: Escuchar *(page 132)*

ex 1: AT1.4

Answers

1 Monumento **2** Comisaría **3** Puerto **4** Catedral **5** Museo **6** Castillo **7** Iglesia **8** Ayuntamiento

Mark scheme: 1 mark for each correct answer.

Total: 7. 5+ shows evidence of performance at Level 4.

CD4, track 37

Ejemplo: **1** Siga todo recto, cruce la plaza y está al final.

2 Siga todo recto, tome la segunda calle a la izquierda y está a la derecha.

3 Baje por esta calle hasta la Plaza Mayor y tuerza a la izquierda. Siga todo recto.

4 Tome la primera calle a la izquierda. Pase la iglesia. Siga todo recto.

5 Baje la calle, tome la segunda calle a la derecha y está a la izquierda.

6 Baje la calle, tome la segunda calle a la derecha y tuerza a la izquierda.

7 Siga todo recto. Tome la primera calle a la izquierda. Está a la derecha.

8 Tome la primera calle a la derecha, siga todo recto y está a la izquierda.

ex 2: AT1.4

Answers

1 9.00 **2** deporte **3** matemáticas **4** 12.15 **5** 3.30 **6** química

Mark scheme: 1 mark for each correct answer.

Total: 6. 4+ shows evidence of performance at Level 4.

¡extra! 1 mark for each correct piece of information which can include: Likes school. School is quite big. Nice teachers. Interesting lessons. Plays basketball. Goes swimming. Likes maths. Good at calculations/sums. Finds English difficult. Favourite subject is chemistry. One or two hours homework. Does homework listening to music.

CD4, track 38

En general, me gusta mi colegio, es bastante grande pero los profesores son simpáticos y las clases me interesan. Por ejemplo, el lunes pasado, desde las nueve hasta el recreo, tuve deporte – normalmente juego al baloncesto o practico la natación. Después del recreo, tuve una hora de matemáticas. Me gustan bastante porque soy fuerte en cálculo. Fui a una clase de historia a las doce y cuarto. Por la tarde a las tres y media, estudié inglés -¡lo encuentro muy difícil! Y finalmente una hora de química que es mi asignatura preferida. Siempre tengo una o dos horas de deberes también, que hago en casa mientras escucho música.

ex 3: AT1.5

Answers

ISABEL: Last year, went to Paris by plane and loved it.

MARTÍN: On Thursday, went to a party at his uncle's house by car and had fun.

LUCI: In July, went to the coast by bus and it was boring.

Mark scheme: 1 mark for each correct answer.

Total: 12. 8+ shows evidence of performance at Level 5.

¡extra! 1 mark for each additional piece of information from: Isabel Went with her family. She stayed in a hotel near the centre. It's a beautiful city. Lots to do. Martín Mother will pick him up after school. It's his cousin's birthday. His cousin is the same age as him. They get on well together. Luci Went with her friends. The bus goes from the library. Bus was late. It rained (nearly) all day.

CD4, track 39

Ejemplo:
Fui a Barcelona el fin de semana pasado. Fuimos en metro a la estación en el centro y pasamos todo el día en el famoso parque de atracciones. Me gustó mucho.

Isabel
El año pasado fui con mi familia a París. Fuimos en avión y nos alojamos en un hotel cerca del centro. Me encantó porque es una ciudad muy bonita y hay mucho que hacer.

Martín
El jueves, después del colegio, mi madre va a recogerme en coche porque voy a asistir a una fiesta en casa de mi tío. Vamos a celebrar el cumpleaños de mi primo. Va a ser muy divertido. Mis primos tienen la misma edad que yo y nos llevamos bien.

Luci
En julio, mis amigas y yo fuimos a la costa. Cogimos el autobús que sale de la biblioteca pero hubo un problema y llegó tarde. Entonces, cuando llegamos por fin, llovió casi todo el día y tuvimos que volver a casa sin hacer nada. ¡Qué día más aburrido!

Prueba: Hablar *(page 133)*

ex 1: AT2.4

Mark scheme: 1 mark for each sentence which would be understood by a sympathetic native speaker.

Total: 9. 6+ shows evidence of performance at Level 4.

ex 2: AT2.4

Mark scheme: 1 mark for each sentence which would be understood by a sympathetic native speaker.

Total: 10. 7+ shows evidence of performance at Level 4.

ex 3: AT2.5

Mark scheme: 2 marks for each sentence which would be understood by a sympathetic native speaker

Total: 6. 4+ shows evidence of performance at Level 5.

¡extra! 2 marks each for each extra piece of information in a similar format.

Prueba: Leer (page 134)

ex 1: AT3.3

Answers

Example **1**c **2**a **3**b **4**e **5**d
Mark scheme: 2 marks for each correct answer.
Total: 8. 5+ shows evidence of performance at Level 3.

ex 2: AT3.4

Answers

Ticks next to: Cathedral Shopping centre Museum Castle Bull ring Restaurant Industry
Mark scheme: 1 mark for each correct answer.
Total: 7. 5+ shows evidence of performance at Level 4.

¡extra! 1 mark for each additional piece of information which can include: Capital of Aragón. Popular with Spanish and foreign tourists. Cathedral recently restored. Fiestas in October

ex 3: AT3.5

Answers

Example Marisa Díaz
2 Barcelona/Cataluña **3** 15 días/2 semanas **4** la familia **5** en mayo
6 información sobre hoteles – lista de precios – plano de la ciudad – folleto de excursiones – horario de trenes – horario de autobuses
Mark scheme: 1 mark for each correct answer.
Total: 10. 7+ shows evidence of performance at Level 5.

¡extra! 1 mark for each additional correct piece of information. Can include any of the above choices not already awarded a mark as well as: Hotel en el centro de la ciudad. Le gusta la historia y comer en restaurantes típicos.

Prueba: Escribir (page 135)

ex 1: AT4.4

The words need not necessarily be absolutely correct but should be easily understood by a sympathetic native speaker.
Total: 6. 4+ shows evidence of performance at Level 4.

¡extra! 1 mark for each additional piece of information in a similar format.

ex 2: AT4.4

Mark scheme: 1 mark for each correct piece of information. The words need not necessarily be absolutely correct but should be easily understood by a sympathetic native speaker.
Total: 7. 5+ shows evidence of performance at Level 4.

ex 3: AT4.5

Mark scheme: 2 marks for each point covered in the letter. The words need not necessarily be absolutely correct but should be easily understood by a sympathetic native speaker.
Total: 12. 8+ shows evidence of performance at Level 5.

¡extra! 2 marks for each additional piece of information in a similar format.

Workbook A Unit 10

page 49 (Section A)

Answers

ex 1a:
tardes
Adiós
horario
gracias
plano
más
Tiene
folleto

ex 1b:
– Buenos días.
– Buenos días. Una lista de hoteles y campings, por favor.
– Aquí tiene.
– Gracias, adiós.
– Adiós.

ex 2d:
Note: the conversation 2a is recorded on CD3, track 34, for pronunciation practice.

page 50 (Section B)

Answers

ex 1:
1 el aparcamiento **2** el ayuntamiento
3 el castillo **4** la comisaría **5** Correos
6 el puerto **7** la catedral **8** el palacio
9 la iglesia **10** el monumento

ex 2a:
1d **2**c **3**a **4**e **5**b

ex 2b:
1 todo **2** izquierda **3** segunda, cruce
4 a, está **5** Tome, derecha

page 51 (Section C)

Answers

ex 1:
1 Museo de Cera **2** waxworks (of world's most famous people) **3** Plaza de Recoletos **4** Colón **5** from 10.00 to 2.30 **6** 4.30 – 8.30 pm Mon to Fri **7** telephone number

ex 2:
MUSEO ÁNGEL NIETO
Motos y **trofeos** del campeón de motociclismo
Calle Pedro Bosch
Metro: Méndez Alvaro
Visita de 11:00 a **18:00** horas
Domingos de 11:00 a 15:00 **horas**
miércoles **cerrado**
Teléfono 91 468 02 24

page 52 (Section D)

Answers

ex 1a:

leí	I read
escribí	I wrote
comí	I ate
escuché	I listened
visité	I visited
fui	I went
vi	I saw
hablé	I spoke

ex 1b:
1 Fui **2** Comí **3** Visité **4** Escribí
5 Vi **6** Navegué

ex 2:
Past tense

visité	I visited
escuché	I listened
comí	I ate
escribí	I wrote
fui	I went
leí	I read
navegué	I surfed
vi	I saw

Workbook B Unit 10

page 49 (Section A)

Answers

ex 1:
b Buenas tardes.
e Buenas tardes. ¿Tiene una lista de cines, por favor?
a Sí, aquí tiene.
c Gracias, adiós.
d Adiós.

c Buenos días.
e Buenos días. Quisiera un horario de autobuses.
b Aquí tiene. ¿Algo más?

a No, gracias. Adiós.
d Adiós.

b Buenos días. Un plano del centro, por favor.
e Aquí tiene. ¿Algo más?
a Sí. ¿Tiene un folleto de conciertos?
d Por supuesto. Aquí tiene.
c Gracias, adiós.
f De nada. Adiós.

d Buenos días. ¿Qué quiere?
g Una lista de hoteles y campings, por favor.
f Aquí tiene. ¿Algo más?
a Quisiera también un folleto de excursiones.
c Aquí tiene.
e Gracias, adiós.
b Adiós.

ex 2d:
Note: the conversation 2a is recorded on CD3, track 35, for pronunciation practice.

page 50 *(Section B)*

Answers

ex 1:
1 el aparcamiento – car park   **2** el ayuntamiento – town hall   **3** el castillo – castle   **4** la comisaría – police station   **5** Correos – post office   **6** el puerto – port   **7** la catedral – cathedral   **8** el palacio – palace   **9** la iglesia – church   **10** el monumento – monument

ex 2a:
1d   **2**c   **3**a   **4**e   **5**b

ex 2b:
1 Baje la calle y siga todo recto.
2 Baje la calle y tuerza a la izquierda.
3 Tome la segunda a la izquierda y cruce el puente.
4 Tuerza a la izquierda y está a mano derecha.
5 Tome la tercera a la derecha y cruce la plaza.

page 51 *(Section C)*

Answers

ex 1:
1 Museo de Cera
2 personajes de cera
3 en la Plaza de Recoletos
4 a quinientos metros
5 10:00–14:30h
6 sí, 4:30–8:30 lunes–viernes

ex 2:
MUSEO **ÁNGEL NIETO**
Motos y trofeos del campeón de **motociclismo**
Calle **Pedro Bosch**
Metro: **Méndez Alvaro**
Visita de 11:00 a **18:00** horas
Domingos de **11:00** a 15:00 **horas**
Cerrado **miércoles**
Telf. **91 468 02 24**

page 52 *(Section D)*

Answers

ex 1a:

comí	I ate
escuché	I listened
leí	I read
visité	I visited
vi	I saw
fui	I went
hablé	I spoke
escribí	I wrote

ex 1b:
1 Fui   **2** Comí   **3** Visité   **4** Escribí   **5** Vi   **6** Navegué

ex 2:
1 comí   **2** fui   **3** comí   **4** leí   **5** fui

Unidad 11 La ropa	Topic/Language/Culture	Grammar and skills	National Criteria
11A ¿Qué ropa te gusta? (pp. 100–101) **Objectives** • say what you like and don't like wearing • revise rules on the use of adjectives; say more / less than	me gusta llevar... unos pantalones (un pantalón), unos vaqueros, una camisa, una camiseta, una chaqueta, una falda, un vestido, un abrigo, unos calcetines, unas medias, unos zapatos, unas botas, unas zapatillas de deporte, un jersey (no) me gusta(n) mucho, me encanta(n), detesto, odio, prefiero + llevar ... porque pienso/creo que ... es / son un poco / bastante / muy / demasiado elegante(s), bonito/a/os/as, precioso/a/os/as, cómodo/a/os/as, horrible(s), incómodo/a/os/as, formal/es	**Grammar** me gusta(n) + noun (Revision) Agreement of adjectives (Revision) More/less than (Revision) Adverbs (Revision) **Skills** Developing memory skills when listening (WS 97 Escuchar)	**Attainment** AT1 Level 4; AT2 Levels 2–4; AT3 Levels 1–4; AT4 Levels 2–4 **Framework Objectives** 7W1, 7W2, 7W3, 7W4, 7S3, 7S6, 7T4, 7T5, 7T6, 7L2, 7L3, 7C1 **Programmes of Study** 1abc, 2abcdfh, 3bcde, 5acdef **QCA Scheme of Work** Language content: Unit 2 agreement of adjectives Context: other information abut themselves **Assessment for learning** Objectives, p.100 Ex 2 & 3, p.101 Ex 4a & b, Ex 5a & b, Plenary
11B ¿Qué llevaste ayer? (pp.102–103) **Objectives** • say what you like wearing for different occasions; say what you wore yesterday • use the preterite tense of llevar	¿Qué llevas / prefieres llevar en tus vacaciones? me gusta / me encanta / prefiero llevar... de rayas, de flores, de lunares, de manga corta, de manga larga, de cuadros, azul oscuro, azul claro los zapatos de tacón alto, los zapatos planos, las sandalias, un bañador, unas gafas de sol, una gorra, un sombrero, una bufanda, unos guantes para mis vacaciones, cuando hace frío, los fines de semana, cuando salgo con mis amigos, en verano, en invierno, al colegio ayer llevé...	**Grammar** The preterite tense of llevar, de + noun, e.g. un vestido de rayas (¡extra! only) **Skills** Writing longer sentences (Ex 4 p. 103) Expressions of time and occasion (WS99 Leer) Adjectival word order (WS100 Escribir) Listen for detail (WS101 ¡Así se hace!)	**Attainment** AT1 Level 4; AT2 Levels 4–5; AT3 Levels 3–4; AT4 Levels 4–5 **Framework Objectives** 7W1, 7W2, 7W4, 7W5, 7S1, 7S2, 7S3, 7S4, 7S5, 7S6, 7S7, 7T2, 7T3, 7T4, 7T5, 7T6, 7L1, 7L2, 7L3, 7L6 **Programmes of Study** 1abc, 2abcfhi, 3bcd, 5acde **QCA Scheme of Work** Language content: Unit 6: likes, preferences Context: clothes **Assessment for learning** Objectives, p.103 Ex 3a & 4, Plenary
11C ¿Me lo puedo probar? (pp.104–105) **Objectives** • learn what to say when you shop for clothes • learn how to use object pronouns • learn how to listen for detail	¿Qué desea(n)? Me gustaría / Busco... ¿De qué talla? ¿Qué talla usa? ¿De qué color? Aquí tiene talla pequeña, mediana, grande, talla (38) ¿Me lo / la / los / las puedo probar? ¿Puedo probármelo? ¿Cómo le quedan? ¿Le quedan bien? (Muy) bien, gracias Me lo / la / los / las llevo Lo dejo, gracias Está demasiado pequeño / grande / holgado / grande / corto / largo / ajustado ¿Tiene la talla...? ¿Lo / la / los / las tiene en (negro)...? ¿Lo / la / los / las tiene en (rojo)? Tenemos la talla (42) ¿Cuánto es? son...	**Grammar** Direct object pronouns lo, la, los, las **Skills** Listen for detail	**Attainment** AT1 Level 4; AT2 Level 4; AT3 Level 4 **Framework Objectives** 7W1, 7W2, 7W4, 7W5, 7W8, 7S2, 7S3, 7S9, 7T1, 7T3, 7L3, 7L4, 7L5, 7L6 **Programmes of Study** 1abc, 2abcdefh, 3bcd, 5abdef **QCA Scheme of Work** Language content: Unit 10 De compras Context: shopping for clothes **Assessment for learning** Objectives, p.105 Ex 2a & 3, Plenary
11D Me encantan los monopatines (pp.106–107) **Objectives** • talk about skateboards and mountain bikes • use known vocabulary in different contexts, e.g. adverts	el monopatín, la bicicleta de montaña ¡Qué guay!	**Skills** Use known vocabulary in different contexts **Pronunciation** j, z, (r)r, v, b	**Attainment** AT3 Level 4; AT4 Levels 2–4 **Framework Objectives** 7W1, 7W4, 7W6, 7W7, 7W8, 7S3, 7S8, 7T4, 7T6, 7L1, 7C1 **Programmes of Study** 1abc, 2befj, 3bcde, 5df **QCA Scheme of Work** Context: hobbies and free time **Assessment for learning** Objectives, p.106 Ex 2, Plenary

Other resources: ¡Ahora tú! pp.138–139   WS 95–103   OHTs 18–19   WBA & B pp.54–58   Assessment Units 11–12 (R & A file pp.136–139)   WBA & B pp.54–58   🔵 Just Click CD-Rom

11 La ropa

11A ¿Qué ropa te gusta?

pp. 100–101

> **Objectives:**
> - say what you like and don't like wearing
> - revise rules on the use of adjectives; say more/less than
>
> **Key Language:** see p.157 for full list
>
> **Grammar:**
> - revise rules on the use of adjectives
> - say more/less than
>
> **Skills:**
> - adding emphasis to adjectives, listening for detail (Worksheet 97)
>
> **Resources:** Visual 95 (clothing items); Flashcards 92–105 (clothing items); Worksheets 97 (Escuchar – improving memory skills when listening), 102 (Gramática – adjectives of colour); CD4; Workbooks A and B p.54; *Just Click* CD-Rom.

Lesson starter 7W1, 7W2

To revise colours, put up the following colour combinations on the board or OHT and ask students to write down the Spanish word for the colour which these combinations make. 1 *azul + amarillo*, 2 *rojo + amarillo*, 3 *negro + blanco*, 4 *rojo + blanco*, 5 *lila + naranja*. (**Answers** 1 *verde*, 2 *naranja*, 3 *gris*, 4 *rosa*, 5 *marrón*.) For some groups you might like to do this the other way round, giving them the final colour and asking them to jot down the Spanish for two colours which will result in these. You might like to add the following questions (answers in brackets) or read them out afterwards, giving students – perhaps in groups – one minute in which to jot down their reply to each. Write down/Name three Spanish adjectives of colour which...

1 change from an *-o* ending in the masculine to *-a* in the feminine (any three of *rojo, amarillo, negro, blanco*); 2 change in the plural but have the same form in the masculine and feminine singular (*azul, verde, marrón*); 3 never change at all (*rosa, lila, naranja*).

Alternative lesson starter *(for lessons starting part-way through the section)* 7W1, 7W2

Use exercise 4a as the basis for the starter. Ask students to skim through the texts, spotting those verbs which, in different forms, indicate degrees of liking, disliking or expressing an opinion. (Text 1: *me gusta mucho, me encanta.* Text 2: *me encantan, me gusta, detesto, creo que.* Text 3: *me gusta mucho, creo que, prefiero.*) As a follow-up, you might like to ask students how to adapt some of these to indicate 'I quite like...', 'I don't like... very much', 'I like... a little'.

Introduction

Introduce the objectives at the top of the page and ask students how many garments in the list 1–14 they can work out the English for, using their knowledge of the colours to locate each item.

1 📖 Une los dibujos con las palabras.
AT3.1; AT 7T1

Present the new language for clothes either using OHT 32,

flashcards 92–105 or the exercise suggested in the Introduction. If using the latter, ask students to work out how to pronounce them before they hear the new language from you: remind them of the work they did in Unit 7C on the double letters *ll* and *rr*. Students write down the matching numbers and letters.

Answers

1B **2**C **3**L **4**J **5**I **6**F **7**K **8**G **9**H **10**N **11**E **12**A **13**D **14**M

2 ☑ 💿 Escucha (1–5). ¿Qué ropa les gusta ☺ o no les gusta ☹? AT1.4; 7W2, 7W4, 7L3

Prepare students for this exercise by revising the expressions of liking and disliking in the grid. Remind them of the use of *gusta/encanta* for singular (*el/la*) items, and *gustan/encantan* for plural (*los/las*) ones. Ask them for the Spanish for a lot (*mucho*), a little (*un poco*), quite (*bastante*). If they do not already know *no... nada*, introduce this here as an alternative to *odio/detesto* as it is used in the recording. Ask students to combine these phrases of liking and disliking with the items 1–14 in exercise 1 to indicate their opinion, e.g. *Me gustan mucho los pantalones negros; No me gusta nada el jersey amarillo.* Students could work through the list with a partner, expressing an opinion on alternate items. When they have familiarised themselves with these expressions, students listen to the recording and note the likes and dislikes of each person.

Support

Students may find it easier to use a partially completed grid along the following lines, which limits the number of things they have to listen for each time.

	Ropa	*Color*	☺	☹
INÉS	vaqueros		✓	
		negros		✓

Answers

1 Inés – ☺ vaqueros azules, ☹ vestidos negros
2 Juan – ☺ jerseys rojos y vaqueros, ☹ camisas blancas
3 Francisca – ☺ falda roja, ☹ abrigo gris
4 Fede – ☺ chaquetas azules, ☹ botas
5 Paco – ☺ camisas, ☹ camisetas de colores

TRANSCRIPT   CD4, track 01

1 ¡Hola! me llamo Inés. Me encantan los vaqueros, especialmente los vaqueros azules, pero no me gusta nada llevar vestidos. ¡Y odio los vestidos negros!
2 ¿Qué tal? Soy Juan. Me encantan los jerseys, especialmente de color rojo. También me gustan mucho los vaqueros. No me gustan nada las camisas blancas; son demasiado formales.
3 ¿Qué tal? Soy Francisca. Vamos a ver, de ropa, me gusta mucho llevar faldas. Tengo una falda roja que me encanta. Pero no me gustan nada los abrigos. ¡Odio mi abrigo gris! ►

> **4** ¡Hola! Soy Fede. Bueno, me gustan mucho las chaquetas azules. ¡Creo que son muy elegantes! Pero odio las botas. Son muy incómodas.
> **5** ¡Buenos días! Soy Paco. ¿Sabes lo que prefiero llevar? Me encantan las camisas, son preciosas. Pero no me gustan nada las camisetas de colores, son horribles.

3 ☑ 🖉 ¿Y tú? ¿Qué prefieres? Escribe un párrafo. AT 3.2–4; 7S3, 7S6, 7T5

Students write a paragraph about their clothes preferences, using the grid at the bottom of the page. Check they know the meaning of the adjectives. If liked, students could hear the recording from exercise 2 again, listening out for these and raising a hand when they hear them. Are there any in the grid which are not on the tape (*cómodo, bonito*). Highlight the use of *pienso/creo que* for giving opinions. Check that students remember how to form the feminine and plurals of adjectives – the Gramática on page 101 may be useful here. You may find the suggestion for an alternative plenary (see below) provides a useful preparatory exercise at this point.

4a ☑ 📖 Empareja las descripciones y los dibujos. AT3.4; 7W3, 7T4

Students match each description to its appropriate picture. Remind students of the comparative (*comparativo*) *más/menos... que* which they have already met in Unit 8C p.77.

Answers

1C **2**D **3**A

4b ☑ 🖉 Describe el otro dibujo. AT4.2–4; 7S6, 7T6

Students write a short paragraph which includes the clothes items in the remaining picture B. They can choose whether to express likes or dislikes. Highlight how the sentences in 4a are made longer by using connectives (*conjunción/palabra conjunctiva*) like *y, pero, porque, también*, and encourage students to do the same.

Support

Students can simply list the items of clothing, with the colour adjective if they can, and write beside each a phrase of liking or disliking, e.g. *Vaqueros negros – me gustan*.

5a ☑ 💬 Habla con tu pareja. AT2.2–4; 7S6, 7T6, 7L6

Students work in pairs to say what they like or don't like wearing, along the lines suggested.

5b ☑ 💬 ¡extra! Presenta a otra pareja. AT2–4; 7S6, 7T6, 7L6

Invite students to explain what their partner likes/dislikes, using the third person. Remind them that if using a name with *gustar*, they will need to use the personal *a* in front of it, e.g. *A Sarah le gusta llevar...*

Plenary 7W3

☑ You might like to use the texts in exercise 4a to reinforce Spanish language learning words. Students will have met *verbo, infinitivo, pronombre, sustantivo, adjetivo, singular, plural, masculino, feminino*. You might like to add *conjunción*

or *palabra conjunctiva* (for words like *y, pero, con*) and *comparativo* (for *más/menos que*). Using the texts in 4a, call these out in turn: students have to find a matching word and respond – there may be a variety of answers, e.g. T: *¡Sustantivo!* Ss: *¡Camiseta!; ¡Dibujo!; ¡Grupo!* Set students a challenge: can they find words to match combinations like *sustantivo plural masculino* (e.g. *vaqueros*), *pronombre y verbo singular* (e.g. *me gusta*), *verbo en el infinitivo* (*llevar*), *adjetivo singular feminino* (e.g. *favorita*). Students can then do this in pairs for each other.

Alternative plenary *(for lessons ending part-way through the section)* 7S3, 7S6

☑ Use the key language grid below exercise 3 on page 100. Model for the class a sentence like the following and ask students to give you the English as you say it section by section: T: *Me gusta mucho llevar...* (S. I really like wearing) *mis vaqueros azules...* (S. my blue jeans) *porque...* (S. because) *son...* (S. they are) *muy cómodos* (S. very comfortable). Students can now do this in pairs or groups for each other.

Extension

Students can subsequently work from English to Spanish.

11B ¿Qué llevaste ayer?

pp. 102–103

> **Objectives:**
> * say what you like wearing for different occasions; say what you wore yesterday
> * use the preterite tense of *llevar*
>
> **Key Language:** see p.157 for full list
> **Grammar:**
> * preterite tense of *llevar*
>
> **Skills:**
> * developing better memory skills when listening
>
> **Resources:** OHT 18 (patterns in clothes); Worksheets 99 (Leer – expressions of time and occasion), 101 (*¡Así se hace!* – listening for detail), 100 (Escribir – word order); CD4; Workbooks A and B p.55; *Just Click* CD-Rom.

Lesson starter 7W1

In advance, prepare slips of paper which contain previously met phrases in Spanish indicating occasions and their translations in English. Put the Spanish ones on coloured paper so you can see who is holding one later on. The following might be suitable phrases (there are 15 here to cover the average class size): *cuando salgo con mis amigos, cuando voy al colegio, si voy a la playa, cuando voy a la piscina, si juego al fútbol, en invierno, en verano, el fin de semana, cuando me acuesto, cuando hace calor, cuando hace frío, cuando hago deporte en el colegio, cuando voy de compras, si llueve, si voy a la discoteca*. Give one to each student as they enter the classroom, and allow them a few moments to work out a translation either into English or Spanish. As you take the register, each student reads out whatever is on their piece of paper and whoever has the translation has to read it aloud. At the end, collect all the pieces of paper and call out the Spanish and English phrases rapidly for the whole class to reply with the translation.

Alternative lesson starter *(for lessons starting part-way through the section)* **7S7**

Ask students to scan Inés's letter in exercise 2 for phrases which inidicate *when* (time of day, year, weather or occasion) she wears different types of clothes: how many can they find? There are three places in the text when there are two of these next to each other: which ones are they? *(los fines de semana/cuando juego al tenis; cuando salgo con mis amigos/por la noche; en invierno cuando hace frío).* Can they invent another two like this?

Introduction

Read through the objectives with students. Remind them that they have already met the *yo* form of the preterite in Unit 10D and check their understanding of its meaning.

1a ⏺ Escucha y lee el diálogo. AT1.4, 3.4; 7T2, 7L1, 7L2

Students listen and read the conversations about holiday clothes. You might like to use this text for practice in reading aloud. On the second time of hearing, focus on the intonation for questions, stopping the tape so that students can repeat the question asked as accurately as possible. On a subsequent hearing, students can read aloud the whole passage (one half in María's role, the other in Pablo's). Five or six times, lower the volume for five or ten seconds and then bring it back up again – have students kept pace with the recorded voices?

> TRANSCRIPT CD4, track 02
>
> – ¡Hola, María!
> – ¿Qué tal, Pablo?
> – Muy bien, María. ¿Te vas pronto de vacaciones?
> – Sí, el martes, ¡qué bien! Ya tengo toda mi ropa lista.
> – ¿Qué llevas en tus vacaciones?
> – Pues me gusta llevar pantalones cortos verdes, una camiseta blanca de tirantes y sandalias.
>   Y cuando voy a la playa, en verano, me gusta mucho llevar unas gafas de sol, un bañador de muchos colores y una gorra roja.
>   ¿Y tú? ¿Qué prefieres llevar en tus vacaciones?
> – Bueno, me gusta también llevar gafas de sol, pero... llevo normalmente un abrigo gris, guantes azules, un sombrero de lana de colores, una bufanda naranja y unas botas negras.
>   Pero el año pasado llevé unos pantalones azules y un abrigo azul: toda la ropa azul. ¡Aburrido!
> – Pero... ¿adónde vas de vacaciones normalmente, Pablo?
> – Normalmente voy a esquiar a la montaña... ¡en invierno!
> – ¡Ah, claro!

1b 💡 📖 Busca las palabras en el texto, AT 3.4; 7T3, 7T4

Students look for the Spanish equivalent of the phrases 1–9 in the text above.

Encourage students to use the glossary or the dictionary to look up meanings. Ask them to summarise the text briefly in English, explaining why María has been confused.

Answers

1 de vacaciones **2** tengo toda mi ropa lista **3** una camisa blanca de tirantes **4** sandalias **5** cuando voy a la playa **6** de muchos colores **7** llevo normalmente **8** el año pasado llevé... **9** ¿Adónde vas de vacaciones normalmente?

1c 📖 Lee el texto otra vez. Di si las frases son verdad (V) or mentira (F). AT3.3; 7W2, 7S2, 7S7, 7T3

Students reread the text, then the statements 1–10 and decide whether each is true or false. This is a useful point at which to remind students of the negative *no... nunca* (never) as it appears in sentence 6. Ask students to scan the questions to get an idea of their content. How many are about María? How many about Pablo? What is the focus of each? Students can write 'C' if clothes are mentioned, 'P' if a place is mentioned and 'T' if it includes a time phrase. Explain this will help them focus on the detail of each question and they are more likely to be able to say whether it is true or false.

Answers

1M **2**V **3**M **4**M **5**V **6**V **7**V **8**M **9**M **10**M

1d ✏ ¡extra! Corrige las frases falsas. AT4.2; 7S3

Students write a corrected version of the false statements. Use the first sentence to show students how to reuse the language of the question in the answer.

Answers

1 María va de vacaciones el martes. **3** María prefiere llevar una camisa blanca de tirantes. **4** A María le gustan las sandalias. **8** Pablo lleva una bufanda naranja. **9** Pablo llevó pantalones azules el año pasado. **10** Pablo va de vacaciones a la montaña normalmente.

2 📖 ¡extra! Lee la carta. Une las palabras subrayadas con los dibujos. AT3.4; 7W4, 7W8

Students read the longer text and match the underlined words to the pictures 1–10. Use this an opportunity for developing dictionary skills. Ask students to look at the underlined phrases: which contain only nouns and which have noun + adjective? How can they tell? (Two nouns are not usually found together, the adjective follows the noun). Elicit from students the rule for forming the plurals of nouns and adjectives and ask them to apply it in reverse: what will they actually look up in the dictionary for nouns like *rayas, flores, lunares,* and adjectives like *corta, larga, planos?*

Answers

de rayas **9**, de tacón alto **5**, de flores **4**, de lunares **8**, de manga corta **7**, de manga larga **6**, zapatos planos **3**, azul oscuro **2**, rosa claro **10**, de cuadros **1**.

3a ☑ ⏺ Escucha (1–3). ¿Qué ropa llevaron ayer? Empareja con los dibujos A–D. ¡extra! Describe el otro dibujo. AT3.4; 7L3

Students listen to the recording and choose the picture which best matches each of the three descriptions. There will be one left over. As an extension exercise, ask students to describe the remaining picture (A).

Answers

1C **2**D **3**B

TRANSCRIPT CD4, track 03

1 – Ayer al colegio llevé una camisa blanca y una chaqueta gris. También llevé una falda de cuadros grises y rojos. ¡No me gusta nada!

2 – ¡Hola! Ayer llevé pantalones cortos y una camiseta de manga corta. ¡Hizo mucho calor! También llevé una gorra de mi equipo de fútbol, el Real Madrid, y llevé zapatillas de deporte blancas y rojas. Normalmente llevo sandalias, pero cuando practico deporte con mis amigos llevo zapatillas de deporte.

3 – ¿Qué tal? Me encanta la ropa de invierno. Ayer llevé un jersey, mi jersey favorito es de color lila. También llevé un abrigo negro, y unos vaqueros azules. Llevé zapatos de tacón alto.

Gramática: the preterite of -ar verbs 7W5

Read through this section with students, which presents the regular preterite tense of -ar verbs in the singular. Which of these did they meet in exercises 1a and 1c?

Extension

Remind students they have already met the verbs *visitar* (Unit 10), *escuchar, navegar, jugar, practicar*: can they put these into the preterite tense orally? With more able groups, you could ask them to write down the *yo* form, explaining they will have to make changes to the spelling of some of the verbs in order to keep the sound. Model with *jugar* – what letter needs inserting to keep the *g* sound hard?

3b ◯ Habla con tu pareja. AT2.4–5; 7W1, 7W5, 7S3, 7S4, 7S6, 7L6

Using the model provided by the speech bubbles, students exchange information about what they wore yesterday. To extend the possibilities, brainstorm other useful phrases, e.g *el (sábado) por la noche, el fin de semana, para hacer deporte, para ir de compras*.

Support

List these time markers on the board or OHT for visual support.

Extension

Remind students that they met the preterite tense of the verb *ir* in Unit 10D. How could they make the following sentences indicate past time: *cuando voy al colegio, cuando voy de compras, cuando voy a la playa*. What other ones can they invent? Encourage them to generate longer questions with two past tenses, e.g. *¿Qué llevaste el fin de semana cuando fuiste de compras?*

4 ☑ ✐ Escribe qué ropa prefieres llevar. Usa la carta de Inés como modelo si quieres. AT4.2–5; 7T5, 7T6

Using Inés's letter for ideas and structures, students write a description of the clothes they prefer to wear, which includes a variety of additional detail (pattern, heel height, sleeve length etc.). Encourage them to develop longer pieces of writing by asking for a short paragraph on each of four of the occasions given in the new language grid (*para mis vacaciones* etc.).

Extension

Encourage students to add a reference to past time: *llevé... (cuando fui...)*, which will increases their NC level in writing.

Plenary 7W5, 7L2, 7L3

☑ Remind students that they also know the present tense of -ar verbs and set them the challenge in pairs of working these out for the whole paradigm *yo, tú* etc. of the verb *llevar*. (See the grammar section B1 on page 144.) Set a tight time limit. Elicit their answers and write these up on the board or OHT alongside the preterite tense of *llevar*. Point out that the *nosotoros/as* form is the same in each – how would students know which time frame was meant? (Presence of expressions of time, e.g. *normalmente, hoy, ayer, el año pasado*, and the context.)

To consolidate these, the following exercises might be useful; they can also be done in pairs after being modelled with the whole class. For recognition practice, call out one part of the verb (e.g. *yo llevé*) and students reply in chorus with *presente* or *pasado* (or *normalmente/ayer*). Give an oral sequence of these, present and preterite mixed, and students have to repeat only the past, e.g. *llevo, llevé, llevastéis* etc. Make it more challenging by omitting the subject pronoun, covering up one of the paradigms, in pairwork having one of the students sitting with his/her back to the board or OHT to encourage memory skills.

Alternative plenary *(for lessons ending part-way through the section)* 7S1, 7S4

☑ Use the sentences in exercise 1c to develop students' ability to form questions. Write up the followng four question words and ask students to give you the English meanings: *adónde, cuando, qué, quién*. Using the first sentence as an example, work with students to develop two or three questions which might have generated sentence 1 in reply, e.g. *¿Adónde va María el fin de semana?*; *¿Cuándo va María de vacaciones?*; *¿Quién va de vacaciones el fin de semana?* Highlight the change in word order: after the question word comes the verb. Set students the task of selecting two or three sentences (or allocate these to different rows or groups in the classroom) from the list 3–10 in exercise 1c and generating as many questions for each as they can. They can then be shared together as a whole class.

11C ¿Me lo puedo probar?

pp. 104–105

Objectives:
- learn what to say when you shop for clothes
- learn how to use object pronouns
- learn how to listen for detail

Key Language: see p.157 for full list

Grammar:
- learn how to use direct object pronouns 'it' and 'them'

Skills:
- learn how to listen for detail

Resources: OHT 19A and B (shopping conversation + overlay); Worksheets 98 (Hablar – buying clothes), 103 (¡extra! – position of object pronouns); CD4; Workbooks A and B p.56; *Just Click* CD-Rom.

Lesson starter 7W5, 7W8

A 'language detective' exercise: put the up following verbs (from exercise 1a) on the board or OHT: *busco, creo, quedan, están, tiene, llevo, son, usa*. Some of these students know, some they haven't met. Their challenge within five minutes is to find/work out the infinitive form of each verb and its meaning. Use as examples *compra, vende* and *deseo*: can they tell whether these verbs end in *-ar*, *-er* or *-ir*? (With *compra* they know it must be an *-ar* verb, *vende* could be an *-er/-ir* verb, and *deseo* could be any of these: they'll just have to search for its listing in the dictionary).

Fast-finishers can work out the meaning of the verbs in English in the form they are written on the board or OHT.

Alternative lesson starter (for lessons starting part-way through the section) 7W1, 7S2, 7S3

Use exercise **2a** as a basis for the starter. Ask students to look back at the picture story on page 104 and find sentences from it which match each of the headings in the grid, e.g. *Ropa/color: Busco unos pantalones. ¿Los tiene en negro?* As a follow-up, students take any three of them and alter at least one detail to make a new sentence, e.g. *Busco una falda. ¿La tiene en azul?* Students read their sentences back to the class, with a different volunteer or designated student, giving a translation each time.

1a 🔵 Escucha y lee la conversación en una tienda de ropa. AT3.4, 7T1, 7T3

Prepare for this exercise by asking students to brainstorm what phrases they think they might hear the Spanish for – what do the pictures suggest? You might like to use the shopping conversation on OHT 19 in preparation or for consolidation afterwards.

TRANSCRIPT   CD4, track 04

- Buenos días, ¿qué desea?
- Hola. Busco unos pantalones, por favor.
- Muy bien, ¿qué talla usa?
- No estoy segura: la treinta y ocho, creo.
- ¿De qué color le gustaría?
- ¿Los tiene en negro?
- -Sí, aquí tiene
- ¿Me los puedo probar?
- Por supuesto, el probador está a la derecha.
- ¿Te quedan bien?
- No, están un poco ajustados. ¿Los tiene en la talla 40?
- Sí, pero en azul.
- A ver... sí, me gustan. Me los llevo. ¿Cuánto son?
- Son 30€.
- Aquí tiene. Gracias, adiós.
- Adiós

1b 📖 Lee la conversación otra vez. Contesta a las preguntas en inglés. AT3.4; 7S2

Students reread the conversation and answer the questions in English. Highlight the use of *los* to mean 'them' (referring to the *pantalones*). Explain to students that they are normally used to seeing *los* before a noun and meaning 'the': here, before a verb, it means 'them'. Can they find the four occasions in the conversation where this happens? (*los tiene en negro, los puedo probar, los tiene en la talla 40, me los llevo*).

Answers

1 trousers **2** black **3** 38 **4** on the right **5** a bit tight **6** a blue pair in size 40 **7** 30 euros

🔔 Gramática: direct object pronouns 'it' and 'them'

Work through the information and suggested exercises with students. You might like to use Worksheet 103 (**¡extra!**) at this point. Although the later exercises are designed as extension, the first two are suitable for most groups.

2a ☑ 🔵 Escucha (1–4) y copia y rellena el cuadro. AT1.4; 7L3

Students make a copy of the grid and complete it as they listen to the recording. Check that they know the vocabulary for *pequeño, grande, ajustado, hogado, corto, largo*.

Support

Give students a copy of the grid on which to write. Reduce the amount of information they have to listen for: either let them choose one or two columns to listen for each time, or allocate these to different rows/groups of students so that as a whole class all the information is obtained.

Answers

Ropa/color	Talla	¿Problema?	Precio	¿Lo compra?
1 vaqueros azul claro	42	un poco grandes	36€	sí
2 abrigo gris claro	44	caro	140€	no
3 vestido blanco o amarillo	42	demasiado ajustado y un poco corto	–	no
4 jersey, rojo o azul	46	no, es perfecto	40€	sí

TRANSCRIPT   CD4, track 05

1 – ¡Hola! Busco unos vaqueros, por favor.
- ¿De qué color?
- Azul claro, de la talla 42
- Bien, aquí tiene. ¿Cómo le quedan?
- Me están un poco grandes. ¿Los tiene en la talla 40?
- Sí, aquí están.
- ¿Cuánto son?
- Son 36€
- Perfecto, me los llevo. Gracias, adiós.
2 – Buenas tardes. Me gustaría un abrigo, por favor, de la talla 44
- Bien, tenemos en azul oscuro y en gris claro
- Prefiero el gris claro. ¿Me lo puedo probar?
- Sí claro. ¿Cómo le queda?
- Es perfecto. ¿Cuánto vale?
- Son 140€.
- ¡Uf! ¡Qué caro! Lo dejo, gracias.
3 – ¡Hola! Buenos días. Quisiera un vestido, por favor.
- ¿De qué color le gustaría?
- No sé, quizás blanco o amarillo.
- Bueno, tenemos éste en blanco. ¿Qué talla usa?
- La 42. ¿Me lo puedo probar?
- Sí, claro. El probador está a la derecha... ¿Cómo le queda?
- Es demasiado ajustado, y un poco corto. ¿Hay otro más largo?
- No, lo siento.
- Bueno, entonces lo dejo. Gracias.
4 – -Buenas tardes. Busco un jersey, en la talla 46.
- ¿Sabe qué color le gustaría?
- Sí, lo quiero en rojo o en azul.
- Bueno, tenemos este de lana roja, que es precioso. ¿Se lo quiere probar?
- Sí gracias.
- ¿Qué tal le queda?
- Es perfecto. ¿Cuánto cuesta?
- Son 45€, pero tiene un descuento de 5€, así que 40€.
- Perfecto. Me lo llevo.

2b 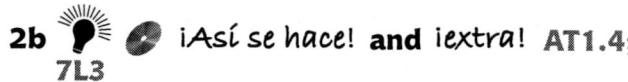 ¡Así se hace! and ¡extra! AT1.4; 7L3

Students listen for the language used for asking for items, how much an item costs and whether it fits or not. When feeding back replies, explain to students that when asking about cost, they may need the plural form 'they cost/are': *son, cuestan, valen.*

Answers

Asking for items (3 ways): *Busco, Me gustaría, Quisiera*
Cost (3 ways): *¿Cuanto es?, ¿Cuánto vale?, ¿Cuánto cuesta?*
Fit (2 ways): *¿Cómo le queda?, ¿Cómo le quedan?*
Discount: *un descuento*

3 ☑ ⬭ Habla con tu pareja AT2.4; 7L6

Students use the flowchart grid to invent a conversation in a clothes shop. Work through it with them, helping them to work out when they will need to alter the object pronouns and the adjectival endings.

Plenary 7W5, 7W8, 7S9, 7L4, 7L5, 7L6

☑ Refer back to the use of *puedo probar* in the Gramática, highlighting the fact that the second verb is always in its infinitive form. Using their dictionaries, ask students to look up infinitives of appropriate verbs to formulate as many classroom requests as they can within the time limit you set, e.g. *¿Puedo abrir la ventana?* Collect these together on the board or OHT afterwards and make a large copy (or ask students to) for classroom display. Encourage and reward students who use Spanish in the classroom spontaneously for real communication.

Alternative plenary *(for lessons ending part-way through the section)* 7W2. 7W4

☑ Give further practice in using *el/la/los/las* with classroom items, first as a whole class then in pairs, e.g. T: *James, ¿tienes el diccionario?* J: *Sí, lo tengo aquí.*

Support

Revise genders of classroom items first and write them up in columns under *el/la/los/las* so that, where it would be natural to use *tu* (*libro de texto*), students have a quick reference point for remembering the gender. Point out that the words for 'it' and 'them' are the same as the words for 'the', except for *el* which becomes *lo.*

11D ¡Me encantan los monopatines!

page 106

Objectives:
- talk about skateboards and mountain bikes
- use known vocabulary in different contexts, e.g. adverts

Key Language: see p.157 for full list

Skills:
- reading adverts for gist

Resources: CD4; Workbooks A and B p.57; *Just Click* CD-Rom.

Lesson starter 7W1

Set the scene for students: they are shortly going to look at two adverts for a mountain bike and a skateboard. What words do they know already which they think they might find in the adverts? Give the following categories to each group

and allow them three minutes to brainstorm Spanish words on flipchart paper: *palabras relacionadas con a) el color, b) el precio, c) otros adjetivos* (e.g. size, pattern). Have them feed back their results and then skim-read the advert: how many did they anticipate correctly?

1 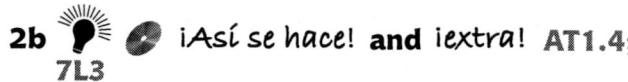 📖 Lee y encuentra las palabras de abajo. AT3.4; 7W8, 7T4

Students read the text and find the Spanish equivalent of the English phrases 1–11. Ask them to use the dictionary to look up the meanings of *tabla, rueda, fuerte, salto, cambio, marcha, rayo.* Their task is to choose the meaning which best fits the context here and write down any two other meanings of each of these words. Feed back the results: what is the lesson here about using a dictionary?

Answers

1 el último modelo **2** monopatín **3** diablo **4** tabla **5** pintura brillante **6** las ruedas **7** envidia **8** bicicleta de montaña **9** cinco marchas **10** ligero **11** ¡tú escoges!

2 ☑ ✏️ Escribe tu propio anuncio... Puedes usar el diccionario... AT4.2–4; 7T6

Students write an advert of their own for a skateboard or mountain bicycle. You might like to extend this to any item students choose. If you have Spanish magazines, students will enjoy looking at these for ideas and extra vocabulary.

Support

You might find the ideas in the Plenary helpful here.

Pronunciación: j z (r)r v b. 7W6, 7L1, 7L6
🎧 Escucha (1–5) y repite.

This recording focuses on the *j, z, (r)r, v, b* sounds. You might like to have some fun with these – say each sentence in turn with a very British accent, mispronouncing the unfamiliar *z, rr, j, ll* sounds, and ask students to tell you what is wrong. Encourage them also to focus on the vowel sounds and hear the difference between their local sound for *a, e, i, o,u* and the Spanish ones. Play the recording several times and have students listen carefully and repeat after each hearing.

TRANSCRIPT   CD4, track 06

1 Quiero unos **z**apatos **r**ojos.
2 **B**usco un **j**ersey **v**erde.
3 Me gustaría un a**b**rigo naran**j**a.
4 ¿Tienes una go**rr**a **r**osa o a**z**ul?
5 **V**oy a comprar unas **z**apatillas de deporte ma**rr**ones o **v**erdes.

Plenary 7W1, 7S3, 7S8

☑ Ask students to produce attention-grabbing headlines for an item – the kind of language which often goes in a flash-bubble and is designed to attract your attention. Remind them of the use of *extra* in the adverts in exercise 1 and introduce them to *super*. What might the Spanish be for: extra-light, supersoft, extra strong, super shiny, super-resistant? They might also like the expressions: *¡oferta especial!, ¡ganga!, ¡no te lo pierdas!* Work through an example with them, e.g. *¿Ganga? ¡Sí! Monopatín superbrillante, extrafuerte, increíblemente barata – precio absurdo. ¡Última semana!* Remind them too of the need to put question marks and exclamation marks upside down at the start of the sentence. Set a time limit and have students read out their heading to the rest of the class with plenty of expression! This exercise is also a good opportunity for creating ICT work and display material.

Resumen *(page 107)*

Give students time to test each other on the vocabulary on the Resumen page. Give students practice with matching Spanish words to the English equivalents by asking students for words which are part of a phrase, e.g. *¿Cómo se dice en inglés, zapatos?, ¿Cómo se dice en inglés, gafas de sol?, ¿Cómo se dice en español, pink?, ¿Cómo se dice en español, size?*

¡Ahora, tú! *(pp. 138–139)*

Differentiated self-access reading and writing exercises: see page 37 for more information.

page 138

1 📖 **Put the sentences in the appropriate order.**

Answers

5, 10, 1, 6, 8, 4, 3, 12, 11, 9, 13, 7, 2

2 ✏️ **Describe the other items of clothing.**

An open-ended writing exercise where students are asked to write descriptions of the clothing shown in the shop window.

3 💿 **Read the e-mail from Paula.**

Answers

1c 2b 3a 4a 5a

page 139

1 💿 **Join the descriptions to the items of clothing.**

Answers

1c 2h 3g 4i 5a 6d

2 💡💿 **Read the descriptions and write the Spanish words.**

Answers

1 falda **2** gorra **3** camiseta **4** vaqueros **5** abrigo **6** zapatos **7** camisa **8** calcetines **9** vestido **10** medias **11** chaqueta **12** guantes

Worksheets Unit 11

95 **La ropa** AT3.1; 7W1

Visuals: items of clothing from Section A.

96 **Resumen** AT3.1; 7W1

List of key language from the unit.

97 **Escuchar** 7L2

1 This worksheet gives students practice in listening and remembering what they've heard – encouraging them to focus and hold information in their heads. Before playing the recording for exercise 1, explain that students are not to write their answers until you tell them. Depending on your group, you can allow students to listen once or twice before writing, and count aloud (increasing from 5 up to 10) when the recording has stopped and before you instruct them to write.

Answers

Felipe **b** Amalia **d, e** Unai **f, a**
Paquita **c, f, d** Javier **a, e, g**

CD4, track 07

Felipe
– ¿Mi ropa preferida? Mi jersey rojo. Es un regalo de mi novia.

Amalia
– Sobre todo, me gustan mis botas. Son de cuero y son muy cómodas.
También me gusta mi camiseta negra. ▶

Unai
– ¿Qué prefiero llevar? Prefiero mi chaqueta, que es negra... También me gustan mis vaqueros.

Paquita
– Si salgo con mis amigos, me gusta llevar una camisa blanca, con una chaqueta... y mis botas.

Javier
– Los fines de semana, me gusta llevar vaqueros, con una camiseta, y mis zapatillas de deporte.

2 This second exercise encourages students to hold items in their memory for longer despite hearing other language which may interfere or distract. The items increase in length and complexity. Explain the purpose to students and share useful strategies. Encourage students to experiment with either looking at the list of words and mentally ticking them off as they listen or, as an alternative, closing their eyes to listen hard for any adjectives and then looking at the list when the tape has stopped – which works best for them? Did anyone try anything else which was successful?

Answers

a preciosa **b** formales **c** cómodo
d bonito **e** incómodo

CD4, track 08

a – ¿Es nueva, la chaqueta?
– Sí.
– Es muy bonita.
– ¡Qué elegante! ¿Te gusta a ti?
– Sí, mucho. Es muy cómoda.

b – ¿Qué pasa? ¿No te gustan mis botas?
– No, ¡son horribles!
– Pues, yo creo que son bonitas.
– ¿De verdad?
– ¡Sí! Son un poco incómodas, porque son nuevas, pero me gustan.

c – ¡Oye, Marta! Me gusta tu vestido. Es precioso.
– Sí, es muy elegante.
– ¡Gracias!
– ¿Adónde vas?
– ¿Vas a la discoteca?
– No, voy a casa de los abuelos para cenar. Les gusta si llevo algo más formal.

d – ¿Qué llevas para la fiesta esta tarde?
– No sé. Quiero ponerme un pantalón pero todos mis pantalones son horribles.
– ¡Qué va! Ese pantalón marrón es precioso.
– No sé...
– ¿Por qué no te gusta?
– No me gusta mucho el color. Y además, es muy incómodo. Es un poco pequeño, creo.

e – No sé que ponerme para ir al restaurante el sábado.
– Tu vestido azul está bien.

– Sí, es elegante, pero no sé si es demasiado formal.
– ¿Qué restaurante es?
– El Gallo, en la calle San Martín. Y después vamos al club de enfrente para bailar.
– Mejor llevar algo cómodo, entonces, si vas a bailar, ¿no?
– Sí, pero ese vestido es un poco viejo... No sé. Tal vez me voy a comprar algo nuevo.

3 Students now combine the previous two exercises, identifying correctly the item and noting down two adjectives for each. Explain to students they will not hear them mentioned in the order they are on the page and there will be one left over. Encourage them to reuse successful strategies from the previous exercises. To increase the difficulty, you might like to encourage students not to write until they've heard each section in its entirety, and you might like to have a time delay of 5–10 seconds before allowing them to write. More able students can be encouraged to try and write the adjective with its correct ending as heard on the recording.

Answers

(Heard in this order. The distractor is **d**.) **c** bonitos, cómodos   **a** precioso, elegante   **b** horrible, incómodo, ajustado   **e** bonitas, cómodas

TRANSCRIPT

CD4, track 09

1 – ¡Mamá! ¿Sabes dónde están mis calcetines?
– ¿Cuáles?
– Los azules. Son muy bonitos y cómodos.
– Ni idea, Ana.

2 – ¿Este es tu abrigo, Papá?
– Sí.
– Es precioso. Póntelo, para que te vea.
– Bueno... ¿Qué te parece?
– Muy elegante, Papá. Te va muy bien.

3 – ¡Iñigo! ¡No me digas que vas a llevar ese pantalón para salir!
– ¿Por qué no, Mamá?
– ¡Porque es horrible!
– Bueno, a mí me gusta.
– Y tiene que ser muy incómodo – es muy ajustado.
– No, ¡está muy bien!

4 – ¿Qué te parecen éstas?
– ¿Las zapatillas?
– Sí. ¿Te gustan?
– Sí. Son muy bonitas. ¿Te van bien?
– Sí, son muy cómodas.
– Cómpratelas, entonces... Son una ganga.

98 Hablar 7L6, 7S3

This worksheet supports students in practising and adapting a simple conversation. The items of clothing are in the singular: more able students could be encouraged to develop conversations which require more complex plural pronoun and adjectival agreement. Remind students before they start of the need for *lo/la*. They could write these into the appropriate box on the page where they will be needed (B will need them for *¿Puedo probármelo/la?*, *Me lo/la llevo.*)

99 Leer 7W2, 7S7

This worksheet focuses on expressions which refer to time and occasion. Students can work through the exercises at their own pace. In the first exercise, students read each text and underline the two expressions of time which are found in each. In the second exercise, they write the pairs of phrases which express a similar idea in different forms.

As a possible plenary, remind students that these can be used across a range of topics and ask them to suggest ideas: as an example, you could use *'El fin de semana en invierno me despierto tarde a las nueve; en verano, me levanto temprano'*. The **¡extra!** exercise could then be done for homework.

Answers

a Rafael – en el colegio, en invierno.
Nuria – en verano, para ir al instituto.
Gerardo – para salir con mis compañeros, los fines de semana.
Daniela – en mis vacaciones, cuando salgo con mis amigos.
Luis – los sábados y domingos, cuando hace frío.
b en invierno/cuando hace frío; en verano/en mis vacaciones; para ir al instituto/en el colegio; los sábados y domingos/los fines de semana.

100 Escribir 7S1, 7S3, 7T5

This worksheet helps students understand the word order in Spanish with items of clothing, adjectives and extra details. Prepare by brainstorming quickly adjectives of colour and others expressions with *de*, e.g. *de cuadros, de manga larga*. Showing students an exact translation often helps them grasp the word order, e.g. *una camiseta azul de manga corta* 'a T-shirt blue of/with sleeve short'. Ask them how this example could be adapted, e.g. *una camiseta verde de cuadros rojos*. Remind them that adjectives agree with the noun they describe – check they understand this also for

cuadros/lunares (mpl), flores/rayas (fpl). Students can now work through the exercises at their own pace. In the first, they compare the Spanish and English versions. In the second, they put the parts of each description in the correct order and, in the third, they adapt the descriptions by altering adjectives. Finally, they complete the description by inserting the nouns and their own choice of adjectival phrases which best match each picture.

Answers

1
1 a shirt white of sleeve short   **2** a shirt grey checked/of checks   **3** shoes brown of heel high   **4** jeans blue and a T-shirt red striped/of stripes white

2a
1 un pantalón blanco de rayas negras
2 una camisa roja de manga larga
3 una chaqueta negra de cuadros verdes   **4** zapatos negros de tacón alto
5 calcetines amarillos de flores rosa

101 ¡Así se hace! 7L3

This graded worksheet helps students listen more carefully for detail. Before listening to each section, ask students to anticipate what they might hear by feeding back any items of vocabulary suggested by the pictures: are there any words which sound similar? In exercise 1, students tick the item mentioned in each section of the recording. In exercise 2a, they identify which items are being described by writing the number of the appropriate recorded section beside the matching piece of artwork. Fast-finishers or more able students can note when the item is/was worn (ex. 2b – **¡extra!**).

Answers

1
1a **2**a **3**a **4**b **5**b
2a
a6 **b**4 **c**1 **d**3 **e**5 **f**2
2b
1 en verano **2** al colegio **3** el fin de semana **4** cuando hace frío **5** cuando salgo con mis amigos **6** durante las vacaciones

TRANSCRIPT

CD4, track 10

Exercise 1
1 – ¿Qué tipo de zapatos te gusta llevar?
– Prefiero zapatos planos.
2 – ¿Qué vas a llevar para la fiesta?
– Creo que voy a llevar mi falda azul de flores. ▶

3 – Uf, ¡qué calor hace! Voy a llevar un pantalón corto.

4 – Buenos días. ¿Qué desea?
– Quisiera una camiseta de manga larga.

5 – ¿Dónde están mis gafas de sol?
– ¿Tus gafas de sol? Allí en la mesa.

TRANSCRIPT

CD4, track 11

Exercise 2a

1 – ¿Qué ropa te gusta llevar?
– Depende. En verano, me gusta mucho mi camiseta de manga corta.
– ¿De qué color es?
– Es azul con rayas blancas. Es muy bonita.

2 – ¿Los profesores llevan algo formal o informal en el colegio?
– Más bien formal. Yo llevo un pantalón, con una camisa de rayas, por ejemplo.
– ¿Llevas una chaqueta?
– No. Llevo una camisa de manga larga. Es suficiente.

3 – Juan, ¿qué vas a llevar el fin de semana? ¿Qué pongo en la maleta?
– Mi camisa blanca. La de manga corta.
– Vale.

4 – Cuando hace frío, no llevo jerseys porque no me gustan.
– ¿No?
– No. Prefiero llevar camisetas de manga larga.

5 – Si salgo con mis amigos me gusta la ropa cómoda.
– ¿Vaqueros? ¿Jersey?
– Vaqueros, sí. Pero prefiero algo un poco más elegante – una camisa bonita, por ejemplo, de manga larga.

6 – No me interesa mucho la ropa.
– ¿No?
– No. Durante las vacaciones llevo pantalón corto, zapatillas de deporte, y una camiseta de manga corta. Y ya está.

102 Gramática 7W2, 7W4

This worksheet gives further graded practice in the agreement of colour adjectives. After students have read through the grammar reminder, in exercise 1 they choose the word which best fits each gap from the list of four given for each paragraph, and in 2 they choose the correct form of the adjective.

Answers

1 **1** azules **2** blanca **3** blancas **4** negro **5** negro **6** blanca **7** marrones **8** negros
2 negra, naranja, verdes, azul marino, amarillos, negro, azules, lila, blanca, rojas

103 ¡extra! 7W2, 7W4

This extension worksheet provides an opportunity for more able students to explore, step by step, the positioning of object pronouns in a sentence. In exercise 1, students write the correct object pronoun. In exercise 2a, students identify the object pronoun and the infinitive. In 2b, they rewrite the sentences from the previous exercise according to the model given. In exercise 3, students write two sentences for each item, with the object pronoun in each of its two possible positions. Remind students of the rule for stress in Spanish words, in explaining that *probármelo* needs to have an accent on the letter *a* (otherwise the stress would fall on the next to last syllable, giving *probar_me_lo*).

Answers

1
1 los **2** las **3** la **4** lo **5** las **6** lo

2a
1 El jersey rojo es muy bonito – **lo** quiero comprar. **2** Me gusta la camisa, Mamá. ¿**La** puedo comprar? **3** ¿Las zapatillas blancas de deporte? No, no **las** voy a llevar. **4** Quiero un vestido negro. ¿Dónde **lo** puedo comprar? **5** Los vaqueros son muy largos. No **los** quiero llevar.

2b
1 El jersey rojo es muy bonito – quiero comprarlo. **2** Me gusta la camisa, Mamá. ¿Puedo comprarla? **3** ¿Las zapatillas blancas de deporte? No, no voy a llevarlas. **4** Quiero un vestido negro. ¿Dónde puedo comprarlo? **5** Los vaqueros son muy largos. No quiero llevarlos.

3
1 La camiseta roja – ¿me la puedo probar?/¿puedo probármela? **2** Los zapatos marrones – ¿me los puedo probar?/¿puedo probármelos? **3** Las sandalias rojas – ¿me las puedo probar?/¿puedo probármelas? **4** El pantalón gris – ¿me lo puedo probar?/¿puedo probármelo? **5** La chaqueta negra – ¿me la puedo probar?/¿puedo probármela? **6** Los vaqueros azules – ¿me los puedo probar?/¿puedo probármelos?

Workbook A Unit 11
page 54 (*Section A*)

Answers

ex 2a:
1 rojo **2** azules **3** rosa **4** naranja **5** blancas **6** verde

ex 2b:
1 red **2** blue **3** pink **4** orange **5** white **6** green

page 55 (*Section B*)

ex 1a:
1a **2**h **3**g **4**j **5**i **6**d **7**e **8**c **9**b

ex 1b:
1 shoe style **2** sleeves **3** colour shade **4** material patterns

ex 2:
1 cuadros **2** manga larga **3** sin **4** planos **5** de **6** de manga

page 56 (*Section C*)

Answers

ex 1a:
– Buenos días. ¿**Qué** desea?
– Busco una **camiseta**.
– ¿De qué **talla**?
– Cuarenta.
– ¿De qué **color**?
– Amarilla.

ex 1b:
– ¿De qué color prefiere?
– ¿La tiene en verde?
– Sí, aquí tiene.
– ¿Me la puedo probar?
– Sí, claro.

ex 1c:
– ¿Cómo le queda?
– Está demasiado holgado. ¿Tiene la talla 38?
– Aquí tiene la talla 38.
– Sí, está bien. ¿Cuánto es?
– Diecinueve euros.
– Me la llevo.

ex 2:
1b **2**c **3**e **4**a **5**d

page 57 (*Section D*)

Answers

ex 1a:
light = ligero;
strong = resistente;
cheap = barato;
expensive = caro;
smooth = suave;
wide = ancho;
comfortable = cómodo.

ex 1c:
extraligera, superresistente, extrasuave, extraancho, supercómodos.

ex 2a:
¿Qué modelos tiene? Which models have you got? ¿Qué tiene de especial? What's special about it? ¿Cómo es la tabla? What is the board like? ¿De qué colores tiene? What colours have you got? ¿Cómo son las ruedas? What are the wheels like? ¿Cuánto cuesta? How much is it?

ex 2b:
Note: the above questions (2a) have been recorded on CD4, track 12, for pronunciation practice.

Workbook B Unit 11

page 54 (Section B)

Answers

ex 1b: vaqueros

¡**extra!** calcetines

ex 2:
1 Me gusta el vestido **rojo rosa naranja amarillo**.
2 Quiero comprar las zapatillas **azules amarillas grises negras naranja blancas**.
3 Me encanta la camiseta **rosa negra naranja verde**.
4 ¿Te gustan los calcetines **naranja azules grises**?

5 Voy a llevar las medias **blancas azules grises**.
6 ¿Dónde está la falda **verde negra rosa naranja**?

page 55 (Section B)

Answers

ex 1:
1a **2**c **3**j **4**i **5**h **6**k **7**e **8**g **9**b
10d **11**f

ex 2:
1 cuadros **2** oscuro **3** llevo, claro **4** vestido, mangas **5** zapatillas de rayas

ex 3:
1 llevé **2** llevaste **3** llevé **4** llevó **5** llevaste

page 56 (Section C)

Answers

ex 1a:
– Buenos días. ¿**Qué** desea?
– Busco una **camiseta**.
– Muy bien. ¿De qué **talla**?
– No **estoy** seguro. En inglés es treinta y seis.
– Pues, **cuarenta y dos**, creo.

ex 1b:
– ¿De qué color prefiere?
– ¿La tiene en verde claro?
– Sí, aquí tiene.
– ¿La puedo probar?

– Por supuesto. El probador está a la izquierda.

ex 1c:
– ¿Cómo le queda?
– Está demasiado holgado.
– Pues, aquí tiene en la talla cuarenta.
– A ver... sí, está bien. ¿Cuánto es?
– Diecinueve euros con noventa y cinco.
– Me la llevo.

ex 2:
1b **2**c **3**e **4**a **5**d

page 57 (Section D)

Answers

ex 2a:
¿Qué modelos tiene? Which models have you got? ¿Qué tiene de especial? What's special about it? ¿Cómo es el chasis? What is the board like? ¿Cómo es la tabla? What is the frame like? ¿De qué colores tiene? What colours have you got? ¿Cómo son las ruedas? What are the wheels like? ¿Cuánto cuesta? How much is it? ¿Qué me recomienda? What do you recommend?

ex 2b:
Note: the above questions (2a) have been recorded on CD4, track 13, for pronunciation practice.

Unidad 12 La paga	Topic/Language/Culture	Grammar and skills	National Criteria
12A ¿Cuánto dinero recibes? (pp.108–109) **Objectives** • talk about pocket money and jobs • learn how to build up longer sentences • learn how to say 'doing'	¿Cuánto dinero recibes a la semana? recibo... euros ¿Quién te da el dinero? mi (padre) me da... mis (abuelos) me dan... ¿Estás contento/a? sí, (no) estoy muy, bastante contento/a ¿Tienes un trabajo? trabajo de... a.... en una panadería, un bar, una tienda, el jardín, el garaje, una cafetería, en casa, vendiendo, ayudando, limpiando, sirviendo, estudiando, escribiendo	**Grammar** Gerunds **Skills** Learn how to build up longer sentences	**Attainment** AT1 Levels 2–3; AT2 Level 4; AT3 Level 3 **Framework Objectives** 7W1, 7W2, 7W3, 7W5, 7S2, 7S3, 7S6, 7T1, 7T3,7T5, 7L3, 7L6 **Programmes of Study** 1bc, 2acfhj, 3bcd, 5a **QCA Scheme of Work** Context: pocket money **Assessment for learning** Objectives, p.109 Ex2 & 3, Plenary
12B ¿En qué gastas el dinero? (pp.110–111) **Objectives** • say what you spend your money on • learn how to plan your writing	¿En qué gastas el dinero? gasto el dinero en... libros, revistas, tebeos, CDs, DVDs, regalos, caramelos, chocolate, bebidas, ropa, ahorros, juegos, tarjetas, meriendas, helados, recuerdos, bebidas salir al cine / a los conciertos / a las discotecas / a los partidos de fútbol ¿Cuánto gastas en ... a la semana? gasto .. en ... ¿Ahorras dinero? Sí, ahorro.. a la semana	**Skills** Use high frequency words (WS108 Leer)	**Attainment** AT1 Level 3; AT2 Level 3; AT3 Level 2 **Framework Objectives** 7W1, 7W2, 7S2, 7S3, 7S5, 7S6. 7T1, 7T2, 7T5, 7L3, 7L6, 7C2 **Programmes of Study** 1bc, 2abcfh, 3bcde, 5af **QCA Scheme of Work** Context: pocket money **Assessment for learning** Objectives, p.110 Ex 2, Plenary
12C ¿Para qué? (pp.112–113) **Objectives** • give reasons for doing things using para + infinitive • revise the pronunciation of r and ñ	trabajo, estudio, preparo, hago deporte, llamo a... paso la aspiradora, ahorro dinero para... ¿Para qué preparas las comidas? para ayudar a mi madre / mi abuela ¿Para qué trabajas? Para... comprar (una camiseta), ver (una película), tener (buenas notas, un dormitorio limpio), ganar dinero para los vacaciones, ayudar, organizar una fiesta, estar en forma	**Grammar** para + infinitive **Skills** Compound words ¡Así se hace! Connectives (WS112 ¡extra!) **Pronunciation** Revise r and ñ	**Attainment** AT1 Level 4; AT2 Levels 2–4; AT3 Level 2; AT4 Level 2 **Framework Objectives** 7W1, 7W2, 7W6, 7W7, 7S2, 7S3, 7S6 , 7T1, 7T2, 7T5, 7T6, 7T7, 7L3 **Programmes of Study** 1abc, 2abcefhj, 3abcde, 5acdf **QCA Scheme of Work** Context: pocket money **Assessment for learning** Objectives, p.113 Ex4 & 5, Plenary
12D Gastando dinero de vacaciones (pp.114–117) **Objectives** • say who you spend your money on holiday • learn how to write a structured text	compro... recuerdos, helados, bebidas en la playa, tebeos y revistas, tarjetas y sellos tomo meriendas voy al cine/a conciertos/ a fiestas	**Skills** Writing a structured text (¡Así se hace!) Listening for gist (WS106 Escuchar)	**Attainment** AT1 Level 3; AT2 Level 3; AT3 Levels 2–4; AT4 Levels 4–6 **Framework Objectives** 7W1, 7S2, 7T1, 7T2,7T3, 7T7T3, 7T4, 7T5, 7T6, 7L3, 7L6 **Programmes of Study** 1c, 2abfj, 3de, 5acdef **QCA Scheme of Work** Context: pocket money **Assessment for learning** Objectives, p.114 Ex 2 & 3, Plenary. All revision activities p.116

Other resources: ¡Ahora tú! pp.140–141   WS 104–112   OHTs 20–21   WBA & B pp.39–63   Assessment Units 11–12 (R & A file pp.136–139)   Just Click CD-Rom

168

12 La paga

12A ¿Cuánto dinero recibes?
pp. 108–109

> **Objectives:**
> - talk about pocket money and jobs
> - learn how to build up longer sentences
> - learn how to say 'doing'
>
> **Key Language:** see p.168 for full list
>
> **Grammar:**
> - learn how say 'doing' (gerund)
>
> **Skills:**
> - learn how to build up longer sentences
>
> **Resources:** OHT 20 (jobs); Worksheet 107 (Hablar – money), 111 (Gramática – gerund); CD4; Workbooks A and B p.59; *Just Click* CD-Rom.

Lesson starter 7W2, 7W3

Reinforce words for language learning. Put up the following headings on the board or OHT and check students know the English meanings, and elicit an example for each: *verbo (forma 'yo'), verbo (forma 'ellos/as'), verbo (infinitivo), sustantivo, pronombre, palabra conjunctiva*. Ask students to read through the speech bubbles for Carmen and Pablo and find at least two Spanish examples for each heading. When eliciting answers, highlight the use of *me*, meaning 'me/to me/for me'. Contrast this with the reflexive use: how can students tell when the *me* is reflexive and when it isn't? (Verb ending has to be in the *yo* form: will end in *-o* in the present tense.)

Alternative lesson starter *(for lessons starting part-way through the section)* 7W1

This exercise will help students learn the relevant infinitives which they will need later in their work on forming gerunds. As students come in, have the following up on the board or OHT: *tengo que... trabajar, ayudar, estudiar, limpiar, lavar, hacer, vender, servir, escribir*. Students' task is to check the meanings of any of the infinitives they don't know (see vocabulary section at the back of the Student's Book), and see how many they can complete with any suitable language within the time limit you've set, e.g. *Tengo que trabajar... mucho en casa*.

Working in a group of three or four, students then read out their sentences in tune to the rest of the group who give a version in English. As a whole class, one to two verbs can be checked for the variety of possible responses from the class.

1a 💿 Escucha (1–6). ¿Cuánto dinero reciben? AT1.3; 7L3

Students listen and note the total number of euros each of the six people receives.

> **Answers**
>
> 1 5€   2 10€   3 15€   4 25€   5 12 €   6 3€

> **TRANSCRIPT**   CD4, track 14
>
> **1** – ¿Cuánto dinero recibes a la semana?
> – Bueno, mis padres me dan 5€.
> – Gracias.   ▶

2 – ¿Cuánto dinero recibes a la semana?
– Normalmente recibo 10€.
– ¿Tus padres te dan el dinero?
– Bueno, mi madre me da el dinero.
3 – ¿Cuánto dinero recibes a la semana?
– Diez euros de mis padres y cinco de mis abuelos. 15€ en total.
4 – ¿Cuánto dinero recibes a la semana?
– Mi padre me da 25€.
– ¡Es mucho!
– Pero compro mi ropa.
– Ah, sí.
5 – ¿Cuánto dinero recibes a la semana?
– Mi madre me da 6€ y mi padre me da 6€.
– 12€. Está bien.
– Sí, es bastante.
6 – ¿Cuánto dinero recibes a la semana?
– Recibo 3€ de mi madre.
– Es poco, ¿no?
– Sí, es muy poco. Pero tengo muchos hermanos.

1b 💿 ¡extra! Escucha otra vez. ¿Quién les da el dinero? AT1.3; 7L3

Students note who gives each person their pocket money.

> **Answers**
>
> 1 padres   2 madre   3 padres + abuelos   4 padre   5 madre + padre   6 madre

1c 📖 Lee lo que dicen. Pon las personas en orden. AT3.3; 7T3

Students read the texts and write the names of the young people in order a) from those who receive most to those who receive least, and in b) from those who are happiest to those who are least happy. Remind students that they will not need to read all of the information in the speech bubbles. By scanning rapidly, how quickly can they locate the amount of money the young people receive, and what is the visible clue? (the euro symbol). What is the key word they need to scan for to answer part b)? (*Contento/a*). What are the modifiers which will give them the detailed information they need? (*no muy... muy, bastante*). Highlight the new phrases: *Es mucho/Tengo suficiente*. How can you make these negative?

> **Answers**
>
> a) Más dinero: Pablo, Agustín, Marina, Carmen, Esteban.
> b) Más contento: Agustín, Pablo, Esteban, Carmen, Marina.

1d 📖 ¡extra! There are three past tenses in the bubbles in 1c. Can you find them? 7W5

Students look for the three past tenses.

> **Answers**
>
> gané (Marina); fui (Marina); compré (Agustín).

2 ☑ 💬 **Habla con tu pareja. Imagina que eres una persona del ejercicio 1c. Cambia las palabras. AT2.4; 7L6**

Working in pairs, students base their dialogue on the content of the speech bubbles in exercise 1c. The partner asking the questions decides who their partner is going to be by beginning with the name, e.g. Agustín, Marina etc.

Support

Students will find this exercise easier if the information is written on the board or OHT in table form thus:

	Recibo...	Me lo da/n...	¿Contento?
Agustín	18€	padres, abuela	☺ ☺
Carmen	15€	padres	☹
Esteban	12€	madre, tíos	☺
Marina	16€	gano mi dinero	☹ ☹
Pablo	20€	padres	☺

3 ☑ 📖 **¿Tienes un trabajo? Une las frases y los dibujos. AT3.2; 7S2, 7T1**

Students match each sentence to the appropriate photo. You might like to present the language for jobs first using OHT 35. Ask students to translate as a whole class sentences 4 and 6 – highlight the presence of the personal *a*.

Answers

1A **2**C **3**D **4**A **5**E **6**B

Gramática: gerunds 7W5

Students look back at the sentences in 3 and answer the questions. **Answer 1** the *-ando* and *-iendo* correspond to 'ing' in English.

You might like to use Worksheet 111 (Gramática) at this point.

4 💿 **Escucha (1–7) y escoge la respuesta correcta. AT1.2; 7L3**

Students listen and choose the correct reply, noting the appropriate Spanish words.

Answers

1 los lunes y viernes **2** el coche **3** padre **4** jardín
5 limpiando **6** ocho **7** las camas

TRANSCRIPT
CD4, track 15

1 Trabajo en una panadería vendiendo pan y pasteles. Trabajo los lunes y viernes.
2 Trabajo ayudando a mis padres a lavar el coche.
3 Gano dinero ayudando a mi padre en casa.
4 Trabajo ayudando a mi madre en el jardín.
4 Trabajo en una cafetería limpiando las mesas.
5 Trabajo ocho horas en total.
6 Trabajo en casa haciendo las camas.

5 🖊 **Rellena las frases siguientes.**

Students now write a paragraph about the pocket money that they receive, what they buy with it, who gives it to them, what chores they do around the house in order to earn it. They can use the unfinished sentences as a template.

6 ¡Así se hace! **Building up answers**

Read through the sentences with students, looking at how they are extended each time.

Plenary 7S3, 7S6, 7T5

☑ Build on the *Así se hace* strategy. Give students a piece of paper and play a game similar to consequences. Ask students to write a single sentence about pocket money or jobs, then pass it on to their neighbour who adds another appropriate one. This in turn is passed to a third, fourth and fifth person who each writes another sentence, different to any which has yet appeared on the page. Put the following prompts on the board or OHT to remind students of the kinds of things they can include: 1 *Cantidad de dinero/euros* 2 *¿Cuándo? – ¿a la semana, al mes?* 3 *¿Quién? – ¿padre(s), abuelo(s)?* etc. 4 *¿Contento o no?* 5 *¿Tienes un trabajo? – ¿qué haces?* The information does not have to be written in this order – it will be more challenging and varied if it isn't. Ask a number of students to read aloud the final version they received while the rest of the class listen. Does it make sense? Are there any inconsistencies? Are all the topics covered?

Extension

Ask students to rewrite the version they ended up with, joining the sentences together as elegantly as possible using connectives. Refer them to Agustín's speech bubble on page 108 as a model.

Alternative plenary *(for lessons ending part-way through the section)* 7W2, 7W5

☑ Put up the following sentences on the board or OHT. Students' task is to answer the questions within a set time limit.
1 Mis padres me dan dinero. 2 Me levanto a las ocho. 3 Mi madre me compra mucha ropa. 4 Mi abuelo me da cinco euros a la semana. 5 Me lavo y me visto antes de desayunar. 6 Mis amigos me pagan la entrada al cine o a la discoteca. 7 Mi hermana me ayuda con los deberes.

Questions

A Which sentences contain a reflexive verb? How can you tell? **B** What does the *me* mean in the sentences which don't have a reflexive verb? **C** Write the Spanish words which convey who is doing the action in sentences without a reflexive verb.

Answers

A 2, 5 (both *me* and -o ending) **B** me/to me/for me
C padres, madre, abuelo, amigos, hermana

12B ¿En qué gastas el dinero?

pp. 110–111

Objectives:
• say what you spend your money on
• learn how to plan your writing
Key Language: see p.168 for full list
Resources: Visual 104 (items bought with pocket money); Worksheet 108 (Leer – high-frequency words); CD4; Workbooks A and B p.60; *Just Click* CD-Rom.

Lesson starter 7W1

Put up the list of verbs below on the board or OHT, and ask students to choose the most appropriate verb for each group of items listed below the pictures in exercise 1a. There will be one group of words left over. Set a tight time limit. Verbs: *comer/beber, no gastar, dar, llevar, leer, ver, escuchar, hacer.*

1a 📖 Lee la encuesta y contesta a las preguntas. AT3.2; 7S2, 7T1

Students read the survey and answer the questions in Spanish.

Answers

1 los CDs   **2** Más popular   **3** No   **4** Sí   **5** No

1b 💿 Escucha (1–6) y escribe en qué gastan su dinero. AT1.3; 7L3

Before tackling the listening, you might like to use OHT 36 for presenting or reinforcing the Spanish for items commonly bought with pocket money. Students listen and note what each person spends his or her money on. They can use the vocabulary from the list in 1a to help. Warn students there may be more than one thing to note in each section.

Answers

1 ropa   **2** libros + ahorros   **3** cine + revistas + ropa   **4** CDs (música)   **5** deporte   **6** DVDs + juegos de ordenador + tebeos

TRANSCRIPT   CD4, track 16

1 – ¿En qué gastas tu dinero?
  – Gasto mucho dinero en ropa. Me encanta la ropa.
  – ¿Qué compras?
  – Todo, pero sobre todo zapatos y camisas.
2 – ¿En qué gastas tu dinero?
  – Yo gasto mi dinero en libros. Leo mucho. También ahorro dinero para las vacaciones. Ahorro 5€ a la semana más o menos.
3 – ¿En qué gastas tu dinero?
  – Gasto mi dinero en ir al cine, en comprar revistas y ropa. Muchas cosas.
  – ¿Revistas de cine?
  – No, revistas de fútbol y deporte.
4 – ¿En qué gastas tu dinero?
  – En CDs. Me encanta la música.
  – ¿Música española?
  – Sí, e inglesa también.
5 – ¿En qué gastas tu dinero?
  – Gasto mi dinero en deporte. Voy a la piscina todos los días.
6 – ¿En qué gastas tu dinero?
  – En DVDs, juegos de ordenador y tebeos.
  – ¿Cuánto dinero gastas en tebeos?
  – 2 o 3€ a la semana.
  – ¿Y en DVDs?
  – 10€.

1c 💿 ¡extra! Escribe un detalle extra (o más) sobre las personas. AT1.3; 7L3

Students listen again and note an extra detail or two about how each person spends his or her money.

Answers

1 zapatos + camisas   **2** ahorra cinco euros a la semana
3 revistas de fútbol y deporte   **4** le encanta la música inglesa y española   **5** va a la piscina todos los días   **6** gasta dos o tres euros en tebeos + diez euros en DVDs.

2 ☑ 💬 Habla con tu pareja. Cambia las palabras. AT2.3; 7S3, 7L6

Students use the model given to answer questions about their own spending habits. Brainstorm with students the language they might use in the substitutions.

3 📖 Juego 7S2, 7T2

Students work in groups of four to play the game, using the moves at the top to guide them. Practise the pronunciation of these with students, and make it a rule that the person who lands on a square which contains writing in Spanish has to read it aloud to the rest of the group who translate it into English. Each group will need a dice and counters. You will need to explain the meaning of *recibiste* as students have not met the preterite tense of *-er/-ir* verbs, but they should be able to work out the meanings of *ganaste* and *compraste*: refer students back to the preterite tense of the verb *llevar* in Unit 11C.

Plenary 7S3, 7S6, 7T5

☑ Ask students to work in pairs to invent two more instructions for the board game, with scenarios which mean that players either miss a turn, go back three squares or move forward two – they can choose any two of these. Have students read out one of their scenarios for the rest of the class, but omitting the final instruction – other members of the class call out ¡*Avanza dos casillas!*, ¡*Retrocede tres casillas!* or ¡*Pierde un turno!* depending on their view of the content. Are they in agreement with the authors of the scenario?

Alternative plenary *(for lessons ending part-way through the section)* 7L3, 7L6

☑ Highlight the importance of listening for gist – getting an idea of what a sentence is about. Put up a list of topics which students have covered in recent units: *el dinero, el trabajo, la rutina, la comida, las bebidas, la ropa, en la oficina de turismo, en el pasado.* Call out a series of sentences as students listen for the gist and tell you the topic area to which it relates, e.g. T: *Fui a la playa con mi familia.* S: *En el pasado.*

Once students understand the exercise, they can look back through the Student's Book Units 10–12 and choose or adapt as many sentences as they can within your given time limit. They can either work in pairs or small groups to do the exercise as you have modelled it.

12C ¿Para qué?

pp. 112–113

Objectives:
- give reasons for doing things using *para* + infinitive
- revise the pronunciation of *r* and *ñ*

Key Language: see p.168 for full list

Grammar:
- using *para* + infinitive

Skills:
- revise the pronunciation of *r* and *ñ*

Resources: OHT 21 (reasons); Worksheets 110 (¡*Así se hace!* – answering questions), 109 (Escribir – assembling a text), 112 (¡**extra!** – connectives); CD4; Workbooks A and B p.61; *Just Click* CD-Rom.

Lesson starter 7W1

To prepare students for the texts in exercise 1, set them the following two-part puzzle. In **a)** students spot the odd one out, and in **b)** they take each word which they have identified as the odd one out and relocate it in the correct group 1–6.

1 dinero, caro, pagar, monopatín
2 isla, CDs, costa, montaña,
3 río, atletismo, deportista, juegos olímpicos,
4 moto, bicicleta, deportes acuáticos, coche
5 un ordenador, videojuegos, DVDs, día
6 verano, mes, euro, semana

Answers

a 1 monopatín **2** CDs **3** río **4** deportes acuáticos **5** día
6 euro
b 1 euro **2** río **3** deportes acuáticos **4** monopatín **5** CDs
6 día

Alternative lesson starter (for lessons starting part-way through the section) 7W1

Give students five minutes to write down as many relevant words which occur to them for two of the pictures 1–6 in exercise 4. These can include nouns, adjectives or verbs. Ask a number of students to read out the words on their list and the rest of the class tries to identify the picture. This could also be done in pairs or in small groups.

1 📖 Lee las cartas. ¿Quién escribe? AT3.4; 7T1, 7T6

Students read the texts and match each author of each of the letters to the appropriate picture.

Answers

1 Andrea **2** Jorge **3** Ángel **4** Marisol **5** Pili

Gramática: para + infinitive 7W1, 7W2

Read through the information with students on the use of para + infinitive. Ask students to reread the letters and list as many examples as they can find for each person. What does each infinitive mean?

Answers

Ángel – para jugar ('to play'), para ver ('to see'); Andrea – para ir ('to go'), para hacer ('to do'), para tener ('to have'); Pili – para pagar ('to pay for'); Marisol – para pagar ('to pay for'); Jorge – para comprarme ('to buy'), para salir ('to go out').

2 📖 Empareja las dos partes de cada frase. Hay varias posibilidades. 7S2

This could be done as an oral exercise initially. Model first, then students can do it in pairs or small groups. Combine two half phrases as suggested, and students have to tell you if it makes sense or is OK (Sí, está bien), or whether it doesn't make sense (no tiene sentido), e.g. T Voy a volver a casa a las diez para estar en forma. S ¡no tiene sentido! Students can subsequently write six sentences which do make sense.

Support

Some groups of students need more time to absorb meaning – have an OHT or sheet of paper prepared with half a dozen sentences already written down. Students can read them and 'mark' your work by giving each sentence a tick or a cross – they usually enjoy this!

3 💿 Escucha (1–5) ¿Qué hacen? AT3.3; 7L3

Students listen to the recording and note what each person is saving his/her money for. You might like to reproduce the following on an OHT or paper as an alternative listening exercise. Students complete the gaps with the correct Spanish word.

1 Ahorro dinero para comprar un ...... para mi hermano.
2 Trabajo para ...... a Méjico, donde voy a pasar un ......
3 Ahorro dinero para comprarme ...... especial. Quiero comprarme vaqueros y .....
4 Ahorro mi dinero para comprarme un ....., y para ..... videojuegos.
5 Trabajo para comprarme ...... para el Real Madrid. El problema es son ....

Answers

1 regalo **2** ir, mes **3** ropa, camiseta **4** ordenador, ver
5 entradas, caras

CD4, track 17

1 – ¿Qué haces con tu dinero?
– Lo ahorro.
– ¿Para qué?
– Para comprar un regalo para mi hermano. Es su cumpleaños.
– ¿Qué le vas a comprar?
– Un DVD del Señor de los Anillos.
– Muy bien.
2 – ¿Para qué trabajas?
– Trabajo para ganar suficiente dinero para viajar.
– ¿Adónde quieres ir?
– Quiero ir a Méjico en verano.
– ¿Necesitas mucho dinero para las vacaciones?
– Sí, claro. Quiero pasar un mes allí.
3 – ¿Ahorras tu dinero?
– Sí, bastante.
– ¿Para qué?
– Para comprarme ropa. Mis padres me dan bastante dinero y compran ropa de colegio pero yo me compro ropa especial.
– ¿Quieres algo especial?
– Quiero comprar unos vaqueros y una camiseta.
4 – ¿Gastas todo el dinero que recibes?
– No, ahorro casi todo.
– ¿Para qué?
– Quiero comprarme un ordenador. Hay un ordenador en casa pero me gustaría tener un ordenador en mi dormitorio para jugar a videojuegos.
5 – ¿Cómo ganas el dinero?
– Trabajo muchísimo, todas las tardes.
– ¿Quieres comprarte algo especial?
– Sí, trabajo para comprarme entradas para el Real Madrid. Soy hincha del Real Madrid.
– ¿Son caras?
– Sí, las entradas son caras.

4 ☑ ✍ Mira los dibujos y escribe unas frases. AT2.2; 7S3, 7T5

You might like to use the lower half of OHT 21 before students tackle this exercise. For each picture they write a sentence beginning Gano dinero... incorporating a gerund and para with an infinitive.

Answers

1 Gano dinero lavando coches para ir a un partido de fútbol.
2 Gano dinero trabajando en una tienda para comprar(me) ropa. **3** Gano dinero haciendo camas en casa para ir de vacaciones. **4** Gano dinero trabajando en una cafetería para ahorrar mucho dinero. **5** Gano dinero trabajando en un garaje para comprarme zapatillas de deporte (nuevas). **6** Gano dinero pasando la aspiradora para comprar un regalo para mi madre.

5 ☑ 🖊 ¿Qué haces? ¿Para qué? Escribe un párrafo... AT4.4; 7T7

Students now write a paragraph about their own reasons for working, earning or saving money. Students can then pass their first draft to their partner for checking. You might like to give them a list or work with the whole class to put together a list. Items which could be included are: legibility of handwriting, spelling, verb endings, adjectival endings.

💿 Pronunciación: revision of r and ñ. 7W6

Read the tongue twisters with students and encourage them to practise them in pairs. Check the meanings with them.

TRANSCRIPT   CD4, track 18

r
¿Para qué compra Patricia un parasol?
Para parar el sol. Es como un parachoques o un parabrisas.
Paran choques y brisas.
¿Y paramilitares paran militares?
No, claro. Y paranoia no para 'noia'.
ñ
Niños pequeños y niñas pequeñas van a las montañas.

---

6 💡 ¡extra! Compound words

Read through the explanation in English with students. The search for the meanings of the four compound words listed, could then be approached as a whole class activity, individually or in pairs.

Answers

abre/latas (opens/tins) tin opener
para/brisas (stops/breezes) windscreen
abre/cartas (opens/letters) letter opener
para/aguas (stops/water) umbrella

Plenary 7W7

☑ Give students a set time, and ask them to work in pairs and use the Resumen page to test each other on the phrases met so far in the unit. When the time is up, ask students to note down for homework what they had difficulty with and what they need to learn. This is then their personal target, which will be tested by their partner again at the start of the next lesson. Brainstorm useful ways of memorising language.

Alternative plenary (for lessons ending part-way through the section) 7W1

Students choose five of phrases 1–8 in exercise 2 and invent alternative endings using any language they know, e.g. *Voy a volver a casa a las diez para ir a la cama.* Students can work in pairs or small groups.

Extension

Ask students to extend their sentences by adding *porque* and a reason at the end, e.g. *Voy a volver a casa a las diez para ir a la cama porque estoy muy cansado.*

12D Gastando dinero de vacaciones
page 114

> **Objectives:**
> • say how you spend your money on holiday
> • learn how to write a structured text
> **Key language:**
> see p.168 for full list
> **Grammar:**
> • present tense (revision)
> **Skills:**
> • learn how to write a structured text
> **Resources:** Worksheet 106 (Escuchar – listening for gist); CD4; Workbooks A and B p.62; *Just Click* CD-Rom.

Lesson starter 7W1, 7T4

Write up the word *VACACIONES* in capital letters and ask students to devise a 'word comb', writing vertically those items or occasions on which they might spend money when on holiday, e.g. *patatas bra**V**as* for the letter *V*, *revist**A**s* for the letter *A* etc. They can use the dictionary if liked. Set a time limit then have students call out their different suggestions for each letter: which are the most interesting/unusual/least mentioned?

1 📖 Lee y pon las frases en orden de importancia para ti. AT3.2; 7S2.

Students say or write down which items they spend their pocket money on in order of preference.

2 ☑ 💿 Escucha (1–5) y escribe la(s) letra(s) del dibujo correcto. AT1.3; 7L3

Students listen to the recordings and choose the correct picture A–H for each of the five recordings. You will need to alert students to listen for two items in sections 4 and 5.

Answers

1G   **2**D   **3**H   **4**A + F   **5**C + B

TRANSCRIPT   CD4, track 19

1 – ¿Cómo gastas el dinero de vacaciones?
– Pues en tarjetas. Mando tarjetas a todos mis amigos en España y América del Sur.
– Gracias.
2 – ¿Cómo gastas el dinero de vacaciones?
– Bueno, mis padres compran la comida y no compro bebidas ni meriendas.
– Entonces, ¿en qué gastas el dinero?
– En salir. Voy al cine o a conciertos y saco las entradas con mi dinero.
– Gracias.
– De nada.
3 – ¿Cómo gastas el dinero de vacaciones?
– En fiestas. Me gusta organizar fiestas para mis amigos.
4 – ¿Cómo gastas el dinero de vacaciones?
– Bueno, compro recuerdos para mi familia, me gusta leer tebeos y tengo tiempo para leer tebeos en la playa. Sí, recuerdos y tebeos.
5 – ¿Cómo gastas el dinero de vacaciones?
– Si hace calor, compro muchas bebidas cuando tengo sed. También helados. Me encantan los helados: de chocolate, de fresa, de vainilla, de todo.

---

3 ☑ 💬 **Habla con tu pareja. AT2.3; 7L6**

Students use the examples in the speech bubbles to ask others what they spend their money on, on holidays.

Extension

Students could design a simply survey sheet and ask a number of students in the class, tabulating their results. In mixed gender classes, if they also noted whether each person was male or female, they could see whether there were any gender differences in the spending habits of teenage boys and girls on holiday.

4 📖 ¡Así se hace! **Writing a structured text AT3.4; 7T1, 7T2, 7T3**

Students use the information around the letter to examine how to write a structured text and include a wide variety of information and opinions. Work through each point with them, asking students to locate the relevant sections in the text and read them aloud.

Plenary 7W5, 7S7, 7T5, 7T6

☑ Use the sample letter in exercise 4 as a basis for the plenary. Ask students to work in pairs or small groups to draw up an outline plan for a similar letter. You could also highlight the presence of the preterite tenses *vi* and *gustó* and the future tense *vamos a ir*, reminding students that they can now include several time references in their writing and time phrases which indicate these, e.g. *el año pasado, en verano, en el mes de (julio)* etc. Elicit from them other verbs from Unit 10D which could be used here (*visité, jugué, navegué, compré, leí, escribí, escuché*). Give them the following headings for each paragraph, plus the examples (in italics) if liked, and ask them to produce something similar for three paragraphs. As content, they could include: amount of pocket money received, information on their part-time job, how they spend their money usually, what they spend their money on when on holiday.

Paragraph (1):
Content (which topic or aspect?): e.g. *How much pocket money I get – who from, when.*
Key sentence: e.g. *Voy a hablar un poco de mi dinero.*
Extra information: *Money I also get from working in bar on Saturdays – how much.*
Opinion: *Fairly happy, but my sister gets more and she does not help much at home.*

When the time limit is up, students pass their suggested outline to another group, who can check that it covers all the points and who can make further suggestions if necessary.

Resumen *(page 115)*

The Resumen page is a reference point for students at any time, and can be used by students working in pairs to revise vocabulary section by section.

Repaso *(page 116)*

☑ This page revises work from Units 11 and 12.

1 💿 **Escucha (1–4). Apunta 3 detalles para cada persona. AT3.4; 7L3**

Students listen to the four conversations and note down any three details about each.

Answers

Susana – 25€, tienda, ropa, le encantan zapatos.
Felipe – 35€, garaje, ir al cine.
Sofía – 15€, no trabaja: ayuda en casa, CDs y libros.
Miguel Ángel – 50€, tienda de ropa, camisas.

TRANSCRIPT CD4, track 20

1 – Buenos días. ¿Cómo te llamas?
– Buenos días. Soy Susana.
– ¿Cuánto dinero recibes a la semana?
– Recibo 25€. Trabajo en una tienda.
– ¿En qué gastas el dinero?
– En ropa sobre todo. Me encantan los zapatos.
– Gracias.
– De nada.

2 – Buenos días. ¿Tu nombre, por favor?
– ¡Hola! Soy Felipe.
– ¿Cuánto dinero recibes a la semana?
– 35€. Trabajo en un garaje.
– ¿En qué gastas el dinero?
– En salir. Me gusta mucho el cine.
– Gracias.
– De nada.

3 – Buenos días. ¿Cómo te llamas?
– Buenos días. Soy Sofía.
– ¿Cuánto dinero recibes a la semana.
– 15€.
– ¿Trabajas?
– No. No trabajo. Ayudo un poco en casa.
– ¿En qué gastas el dinero?
– En libros y CDs.
– Gracias.

4 – Buenos días. ¿Cómo te llamas?
– Buenos días. Me llamo Miguel Ángel.
– ¿Cuánto dinero recibes a la semana?
– Recibo 50€. Trabajo en una tienda de ropa.
– ¿En qué gastas el dinero?
– En ropa. Me gustan las camisas. Compro muchas camisas.
– Gracias.
– De nada.

2 💬 **Haz diálogos con tu pareja según los dibujos. AT2.4; 7L6**

Students use the picture prompts in the grid and the sample conversation to generate four conversations.

3 📖 **Mira los dibujos e identifica a las 4 mujeres. AT3.4; 7T1, 7T3**

Students read the descriptions and match each one to the appropriate picture. There will be two left over.

Answers

a2 **b**1 **c**4 **d**3

4 ✒ **Describe a las 2 otras mujeres. AT4.3; 7T5, 7T6**

Students write a description of the two people from exercise 3 whose descriptions did not feature there. They can use the texts in exercise 3 as a model for their own writing or lift and adapt the sentences as necessary.

Reading *(page 117)*

1 📖 **Lee la carta y contesta a las preguntas. AT3.4; 7T6**

This shows students how the reading strategies they have met in ¡Así!1 can help them to understand this longer text, *Querida tía Dolores.*

Answers

1e **2**c **3**f **4**a **5**b **6**d **7**g

¡Ahora, tú! (pp. 140–141)

Differentiated self-access reading and writing exercises: see page 37 for more information.

page 140

1 💿 **Look at the questionnaires and answer the questions.**

Answers

1 Adriana **2** Bea **3** Andrés **4** Bea **5** Andrés **6** Andrés **7** Bea **8** Adriana **9** Bea

2 📖 **Put the words in order to make sentences.**

Possible answers

1 Gasto mi dinero en chocolate y bebidas. **2** Mis padres me dan quince euros y mi abuelo me da cinco euros. **3** Mis padres me compran ropa. **4** Recibo veinte euros a la semana. **5** Preparo el desayuno y hago las camas. **6** No trabajo pero ayudo a mis padres en casa./No ayudo a mis padres en casa pero trabajo. **7** Ahorro cinco euros a la semana. **8** Ahorro mucho para ir de vacaciones.

3 ✏️ **You have won the lottery...**

An open-ended writing exercise asking students to describe an imaginary week showing what they would spend their money on each day if they were to win the lottery. Encourage them to use the prompts given and add as much extra detail as possible.

page 141

4 📖 **Do the quiz from a Spanish magazine.**

A multiple-choice questionnaire based around earning and spending money, revising language from the unit.

Students write their own answers here.

Worksheets Unit 12

104 **¿En qué lo gastas?**
AT3.1; 7W1

Visuals: items to spend money on from Section B.

105 **Resumen AT3.1; 7W1**

List of key language from the unit.

106 **Escuchar 7L3**

This worksheet focuses on listening for gist and helps students learn micro-skills which will be useful in other topic areas.

1 Play the first section of the recording and instruct students to jot down any nouns and verbs they hear – write these up on the board or OHT and help students work out with which of the topics suggested they most closely fit. Play the rest of the recordings as students work individually.

Answers

1 1c **2**f **3**d **4**a **5**e

CD4, track 21

1 – ¿Qué quieres comer?
– No sé... Algo caliente. Calamares con patatas fritas. ¿Y tú?
– Aceitunas y pan, creo.
2 – Mis padres están separados, y vivo con mi madre.
– ¿Tienes hermanos?
– Sí, un hermano mayor y una hermana.
3 – No sé que llevar a la fiesta de Marisol. ¿Llevas algo formal?
– No. Voy a llevar mi pantalón negro y una camiseta de manga larga.
4 – ¿Es grande?
– No. Tiene dos dormitorios, una cocina, un salón-comedor y un cuarto de baño. Es bastante pequeña. ▶

5 – Ayudo a mi padre – lavando el coche y trabajando en el jardín los sábados. Gano ocho euros por semana.
– ¿Ocho euros por todo eso? ¡No es mucho!

2 In the second section, instruct students to work together to do the two exercises suggested in the bullet points, and elicit their replies. Words common to all three themes might be: numbers, the words *dinero, euros, a la semana, estoy contento/a, (no) me gusta...* Useful words specific to each topic might be:
A *recibo, me da/n, padre, madre, padres, abuelo* etc.
B *trabajo, ayudo, lavando, vendiendo, clientes, cafetería, garaje* etc.
C *tebeos, revistas, ropa, DVDs, CDs, salir, cine, discoteca* etc.

Answers

2 **A** 3, 4 **B** 1 **C** 2, 5

CD4, track 22

1 – Trabajo siete horas los sábados sirviendo a los clientes en la cafetería de mis tíos.
2 – Depende. A veces en regalos para mis amigos o para miembros de la familia, pero normalmente en CDs, ropa o caramelos.
3 – Me lo dan mis padres. A veces me da algo mi hermano mayor también si gana mucho esa semana.
4 – Recibo diez euros a la semana. Mis amigos dicen que es poco, pero para mí es suficiente. Mi madre no gana mucho. ▶

5 – Me encanta salir, así que lo necesito para comprar entradas para el cine o la discoteca, o para ir a los partidos de fútbol.

3 In section 3, students will still need their listening-for-gist skills though the differences in shades of meaning are finer here. They write down the number of the recorded reply which matches each question **a–f** most closely. There is a distractor.

Answers

3 **a**4 **b**2 **c**5 **d**1 (**e** – distractor) **f**3

CD4, track 23

1 – Casi nada. No me gusta mucho leer. A veces, compro revistas o tebeos pero en general, no mucho.
2 – Sí, ayudo a mi madre los sábados en su oficina, enviando correos electrónicos.
3 – Para gastar en las vacaciones, para comprar recuerdos o helados, y para ir de compras en el centro.
4 – Unos veinte euros a la semana. Me los dan mis padres.
5 – En ropa generalmente, o en salir. Vivo lejos del centro, entonces gasto mucho en billetes de autobús también.

107 **Hablar 7S3, 7L6**

This worksheet provides practice of the vocabulary and structures in Unit 12A. It encourages students to prepare for conversation work, focusing on the elements they need to have in their minds in order to give themselves the best chance of success. More able students can be encouraged to add the use of the gerund.

108 Leer 7W2, 7S5

In preparation for the reading exercise, students revisit high-frequency words and negatives which matter when reading for detail. They put the phrases into order from the biggest spender to the one who spends least.

Answers

Gasto todo. Gasto mucho. Gasto bastante. Gasto poco. Gasto casi nada. No gasto nada.

a Students read the sections of text and complete the graph.

Answers

30E						
25E						
20E						
15E						
10E						
5E						
	JULIO	ELENA	FEDE	LUIS	ANA	PILAR

b Students choose the correct response for each person:
Julio **A**   Elena **B**   Fede **A**   Luis **A**
Ana **C**   Pilar **B**

109 Escribir 7S3, 7T5

This worksheet supports students in writing short sentences which contain a summary of the language of the unit. Students use the pictures to help them complete the gaps, and the prompts at the bottom give them an idea of the kind of language needed.

More able students could be encouraged to give additional information (and connectives) to create a fuller account.

Suggested answers

1 treinta **2** mi padre **3** muy **4** en una cafetería **5** cinco **6** trabajando **7** CDs, revistas **8** comprarme una bicicleta **9** postales, regalos

110 ¡Así se hace! 7T1

This worksheet gives students practice in answering questions in Spanish. As the answers use the first person, students will be able to select words from the text without needing to make any grammatical alterations. It reminds

them of the need to pay attention to high-frequency words like *en*.

Students who need support could be asked initially to read through the text and use different markings (solid lines, dotted lines, wavy lines, circling words) or colours to locate where Iñigo talks about **a)** his work, **b)** the money he earns/gets, **c)** going out, **d)** holidays – where and what he does, **e)** savings. This will help them locate the answers more quickly. For some students, you might like to make this a reading exercise by giving them the underlined parts of the answers below in a jumbled and numbered list, and they simply have to select the correct answer or copy it into place.

Answers

1 en Málaga **2** cerca de casa
3 periódicos, revistas y tebeos **4** mi tío
5 mis padres **6** ayudar en casa **7** salir
8 vacaciones **9** agosto **10** al parque de atracciones

111 Gramática 7W5

This grammar worksheet gives further revision and practice of the gerund. The first exercise requires students to complete the grid explaining the formation of the gerund; the second asks students to choose the correct gerund for each gap, and the final exercise needs students to actively form the gerund from verbs they already know. It contains some examples of the gerund with the verb *estar* – with more able groups you might like to revise all parts of *estar* and use this an opportunity for teaching the present continuous.

Answers

1

Verbs ends in...	-AR	-ER	-IR
Take off...	-ar	-er	-ir
Add...	-ando	-iendo	-iendo

2 1 trabajando **2** lavando
3 limpiando **4** vendiendo
5 escribiendo **6** saliendo
3 1 haciendo **2** ayudando **3** jugando
4 estudiando **5** limpiando
6 preparando **7** viendo
8 recibiendo **9** volviendo

112 ¡extra! 7W2, 7S6

This worksheet reinforces connectives met in this unit and expands them to give more able students a wider range. In the first section, they complete the list with the correct English equivalent and, in the second, they select the correct connective. Finally, they rewrite

the paragraph, using as many connectives as they can and as are appropriate.

Answers

1 entonces – then, porque – because, para – in order to, pero – but.
2 1 también **2** pero **3** entonces
4 por eso **5** como **6** así que
7 porque **8** para

Pruebas Unidades 11 y 12

R and A File pp.136–139

Prueba: Escuchar *(page 136)*

ex 1: AT1.5

Answers

Example **1** Julia **2** Mariana **3** Julia
4 Ernesto **5** Julia **6** Ernesto **7** Julia
8 Mariana **9** Ernesto
Mark scheme: 1 mark for each correct answer.
Total: 8.   6+ shows evidence of performance at Level 5 .

TRANSCRIPT

CD4, track 40
– Oye, este fin de semana voy a comprar un nuevo par de zapatos. No me gustan las botas, no las llevo nunca. ¿Te interesa la moda Ernesto?

– En general sí. Yo también voy de compras. Voy a comprarme un nuevo bañador para practicar la natación y unos vaqueros porque los llevo todos los días. Y tú Mariana, ¿Te gustan los vaqueros?

– Yo prefiero los vestidos bonitos. Tengo vestidos de todos los colores, pero mi favorito es azul de rayas amarillas. A veces lo llevo para el colegio porque no tenemos uniforme y puedo elegir mi ropa. Tú no ¿Julia?

– ¡No! Yo tengo que llevar un uniforme gris horrible con medias que detesto. Pero los fines de semana, llevo mi jersey favorito que es lila. También puedo llevar zapatos de tacón alto y no los planos del uniforme.

ex 2: AT1.5

Answers

Example **1**V **2**M **3**V **4**V **5**V **6**M **7**M
8V **9**M **10**M
Mark scheme: 1 mark for each correct answer.
Total: 9: 6+ shows evidence of performance at Level 5 .

TRANSCRIPT
CD4, track 41

- Sí señor, ¿en qué puedo ayudarle?
- Quiero un par de zapatos cómodos. ¿Qué me aconseja?
- Éstos son muy populares.
- Sí, me gustan. ¿Los tiene en el cuarenta y dos?
- ¿Qué color quiere, señor?
- Los negros.
- Muy bien.
- ¿Puedo probármelos?
- Claro señor.
- ¿Cómo le quedan?
- Son un poco pequeños. ¿Los tiene en el cuarenta y cuatro?
- Lo siento, señor, sólo en marrón. Pero son €100, ¡son menos caros!
- No, el color no me gusta. No los compro. Gracias, adiós.
- De nada, señor. Adiós.

ex 3: AT1.6

Answers

example: spends – the holidays – cars – record shop – CDs – more – save – next year – his cousin
Mark scheme: 1 mark for each correct answer.
Total: 8. 6+ shows evidence of performance at Level 6 .

¡extra! 1 mark for each additional piece of information which can include: He quite liked working in the garage. It wasn't very interesting. The music shop is small. He works on Saturday and Sunday mornings. He really enjoys it. He likes the kind of music they have. Last year he earned 18€. This year he earns 20€. He buys things for his mountain bike. He'll go to France in the summer.

TRANSCRIPT
CD4, track 42

¡Hola! soy Eduardo y voy a hablar de cómo gano y gasto mi dinero. Yo trabajo para ganar dinero. Durante las vacaciones trabajé en un garaje, lavando coches y haciendo el café. Me gustó bastante pero no es un trabajo muy interesante. De momento, trabajo en una pequeña tienda de música los sábados y los domingos por la mañana. Me encanta porque me gusta el tipo de música que tenemos y además ime dan un descuento cuando quiero comprar un CD! Gano €18... no, no.. eso lo gané el año pasado. Este año recibo €20. Ahorro un poco y todavía tengo suficiente para comprar cosas para mi bicicleta de montaña. Estoy bastante contento pero el año que viene, tengo la intención de ir a trabajar en Francia porque mi primo vive allí y puedo vivir con su familia durante el verano.

Prueba: Hablar *(page 137)*
ex 1: AT2.4

Mark scheme: 2 marks for each sentence which would be understood by a sympathetic native speaker. 1 mark for the first two elements plus 1 for the third OR 1 mark for the first element plus another for the second two.
Total: 10. 6+ shows evidence of performance at Level 4.

ex 2: AT2.5

Mark scheme: 1 mark for each sentence which would be understood by a sympathetic native speaker. Any reasonable information which makes sense in context is acceptable.
Total: 5. 3+ shows evidence of performance at Level 5 .

ex 3: AT2.6

Mark scheme: 2 marks for each sentence (minimum 5) which would be understood by a sympathetic native speaker. Any reasonable information which makes sense in context is acceptable.
Total: 10. 7+ shows evidence of performance at Level 6.
2 marks each for each extra piece of information in a similar format.

Prueba: Leer *(page 138)*
ex 1: AT3.4

Answers

1 no (le) gusta
2 comprar revistas de coches
3 tienda
4 ies genial!
5 los sábados
6 20€
7 música/caramelos
Mark scheme: 1 mark for each correct answer.
Total: 7. 4+ shows evidence of performance at Level 4.

ex 2: AT3.5

Answers

Example **1**c **2**e **3**b **4**d **5**f **6**a
Mark scheme: 2 marks for each correct answer.
Total: 10. 7+ shows evidence of performance at Level 5.

ex 3: AT4.6

Answers

1c **2**d **3**a **4**b
Mark scheme: 2 marks for each correct answer.

Total: 8. 6+ shows evidence of performance at Level 6.

Prueba: Escribir *(page 139)*
ex 1: AT4.4

Mark scheme: The words need not necessarily be absolutely correct but should be easily understood by a sympathetic native speaker.
Total: 5. (no half marks, round up). 3+ shows evidence of performance at Level 4.

¡extra! 1 mark for each additional piece of information in a similar format.

ex 2: AT4.5

Mark scheme: 2 marks for each correct answer to the five questions in the letter. Any reasonable information which makes sense in context is acceptable. The words need not necessarily be absolutely correct but should be easily understood by a sympathetic native speaker.
Total: 10. 7+ shows evidence of performance at Level 5.

¡extra! 2 marks for each additional piece of information in a similar format.

ex 3: AT4.6

Mark scheme: 2.5 marks for each correct answer. Any reasonable information which makes sense in context is acceptable. The words need not necessarily be absolutely correct but should be easily understood by a sympathetic native speaker.
Total: 10. 7+ shows evidence of performance at Level 6.

¡extra! 2 marks for each additional piece of information in a similar format.

Pruebas: Fin de año

R and A File pp.140–143

Prueba: Escuchar *(page 140)*
ex 1: AT1.2–3

Answers

Example **1**: 13 **2** española **3** Francia **4** 19 noviembre **5** any of: padres, 2 hermanas, hermanas gemelas **6** (salir con) amigos/playa **7** 15 **8** mejicano **9** España/Barcelona **10** 24 julio **11** any of: padre, madrastra, hermano mayor **12** (ir al) cine
Mark scheme: 1 mark for each correct answer.

Total: 10. 6+ shows evidence of performance at Level 2.
8+ shows evidence of performance at Level 3.

¡extra! information may include any of the above not already awarded a mark.

In addition, for Pablo: Padre trabaja en Barcelona/España – Cuatro en la familia – Hermano no vive con la familia – No tiene muchos pasatiempos.

TRANSCRIPT
CD4, track 43

– ¡Hola! me llamo Ana y tengo trece años. Soy española pero vivo en Francia con mi familia. Mi cumpleaños es el diecinueve de noviembre. Somos cinco en mi familia: mis padres, mis dos hermanas gemelas y yo. En mi tiempo libre, me encanta salir con mis amigos o ir a la playa.
– ¡Hola! soy Pablo. De nacionalidad, soy mejicano, pero ahora vivo en Barcelona en España porque mi padre trabaja aquí. Tengo quince años y celebro mi cumpleaños el veinticuatro de julio. Somos cuatro en mi familia, mi padre, mi madrastra y mi hermano mayor que no vive con nosotros. No tengo muchos pasatiempos pero me gusta ir al cine los fines de semana.

ex 2: AT1.4

Answers

Example **1**: el museo **2** en coche **3** lejos **4** 10 **5** a la derecha **6** el puente **7** a la izquierda **8** llueve
Mark scheme: 1 mark for each correct answer.
Total: 7. 5+ shows evidence of performance at Level 4 .

TRANSCRIPT
CD4, track 44

– Perdone, señora, ¿Por dónde se va al museo?
– ¿Al museo? Vamos a ver... usted va a pie?
– No, en coche.
– Menos mal porque está bastante lejos pero sólo a diez minutos en coche.
– Muy bien.
– Baje esta calle, tome la segunda calle a la derecha y siga hasta el puente. Cruce el puente, siga todo recto recto recto y el museo está a mano izquierda.
– Muy bien. Gracias.
– De nada. Pero dése prisa porque empieza a llover – ¡ah sí! Llueve ahora. Adiós.
– Adiós.

ex 3: AT1.5–6

Answers any 8 of the following; answers must cover all three tense boxes.

PASADO	PRESENTE	FUTURO
Moved here last year	Lives in a small semi	Big new flat in town centre
Lived in the west	Loves basketball	Go to the sports centre every day
Didn't work at school last year	Plays basketball 2/3 times a week	Going camping with friends in the summer
Got bad marks	Likes school	Starting a new job next week
Music centre broke last weekend	Teachers are nice	Will buy a new music system
	Teachers make him work hard	

Mark scheme: 1 mark for each correct answer.
Total: 8. 5+ shows evidence of performance at Level 5.
7+ shows evidence of performance at Level 6.
1 mark for each additional piece of information from the above which has not already been awarded a mark.

TRANSCRIPT
CD4, track 45

– Soy Antonio y contesto a tus preguntas:
– De momento, vivo en Burgos, nos trasladamos aquí hace un año porque antes viví en el oeste. Ahora vivimos en una pequeña casa adosada, pero mi padre dice que el año que viene vamos a tener un gran piso nuevo en el centro. Entonces, voy a ir al polideportivo todos los días porque, ya sabes, me encanta el baloncesto y juego dos o tres veces a la semana.
– En cuanto al colegio, me gusta bastante ahora – los profesores son simpáticos, aunque me hacen trabajar mucho. El año pasado, no hice mucho en el colegio y saqué malas notas. En verano, si saco buenas notas, voy a hacer camping con mis compañeros de clase. ¡Lo vamos a pasar bomba!
– Otras noticias... la semana que viene voy a empezar a trabajar en un supermercado. Voy a ganar bastante dinero para comprarme un nuevo equipo de música. El mío se rompió el fin de semana pasado.
– Eso es todo, espero tus noticias. ¡Hasta luego!

Prueba: Hablar (page 141)
ex 1: AT2.2

Mark scheme: 1 mark for each sentence which would be understood by a sympathetic native speaker. Any reasonable information which makes sense in context is acceptable.

Total: 5. 3+ shows evidence of performance at Level 2 .

¡extra! 1 mark for each additional piece of information.

ex 2: AT2.3–4

Mark scheme: 1 mark for each sentence which would be understood b a sympathetic native speaker.
Any reasonable information which makes sense in context is acceptable.
Total: 8. 4+ shows evidence of performance at Level 3.
6+ shows evidence of performance at Level 4.

ex 3: AT2.5–6

Mark scheme: 1 mark for each sentence which would be willingly understood by a sympathetic native speaker. Any reasonable information which makes sense in context is acceptable.
Total: 12. 8+ shows evidence of performance at Level 5.
10+ shows evidence of performance a Level 6.

¡extra! 1 mark for each additional piece of information.

Prueba: Leer (page 142)
ex 1: AT3.2–6

Answers

Example: Patricia **1** 13 **2** Santander/Spain **3** small town/villag **4** bus **5** 20 **6** 2000 (+) **7** 30 **8/9** two of : maths/Spanish/sport **10/11** history/chemistry **12–14** won basketball cup – did an hour's swimming practice every day – did a project in class on keeping the school environment clean **15** her chemistry teacher **16–20** teacher says she doesn work hard enough, she talks too much, she isn't interested, she was given mor homework than the others last week, she's asked more difficult questions than the others **21** poor **22** she'll enc up hating science **23** not interested

24 to say she's exaggerating 25 very sad
Mark scheme: 1 mark for each correct answer. The level of difficulty increases as the students work through the text. Not all students will complete the reading or answering of questions. This is reflected in the National Curriculum related levels.
Total: 25. 5 marks or more shows evidence of performance at Level 2. 9 marks or more shows evidence of performance at Level 4. 20 marks or more shows evidence of performance at Level 6.

Prueba: Escribir *(page 143)*

ex 1: AT4.2

The words need not necessarily be absolutely correct but should be easily understood by a sympathetic native speaker. Any reasonable information which makes sense in context is acceptable.
Mark scheme: 1 mark for each correct answer.
Total: 7. 4+ shows evidence of performance at Level 2.

¡extra! 1 mark for each additional piece of information in a similar format.

ex 2: AT4.4

The words need not necessarily be absolutely correct but should be easily understood by a sympathetic native speaker. Any reasonable information which makes sense in context is acceptable.
Mark scheme: 1 mark for each correct answer.
Total: 8. 6+ shows evidence of performance at Level 4 .

¡extra! 1 mark for each additional piece of information in a similar format.

ex 3: AT4.5–6

The words need not necessarily be absolutely correct but should be easily understood by a sympathetic native speaker. Any reasonable information which makes sense in context is acceptable.
Mark scheme: 2 marks for each correct answer.
Total: 10. 6+ shows evidence of performance at Level 5 . 8+ shows evidence of performance at Level 6.

¡extra! 2 marks for each additional piece of information in a similar format; students should cover past, present and future for the higher levels in their additional information.

Workbook A Unit 12

page 59 *(Section A)*

Answers

ex 1a:
vender – vendiendo; lavar – lavando; hacer – haciendo; ayudar – ayudando; preparar – preparando.

ex 1b:
1 Gano 12 euros **trabajando** en el jardín.
2 Gano 7 euros **lavando** el coche.
3 Gano 15 euros **preparando** la comida.
4 Gano 25 euros **vendiendo** revistas.
5 **Gano** 9 euros **ayudando** a mi madre en casa.
6 **Gano** 17 euros **haciendo** las camas en un hotel.

ex 2:
a ¿Cuánto dinero recibes a la semana?   4, 7
b ¿Tus padres te dan el dinero?   2, 5
c ¿Estás contento/a   3, 6
d ¿Cómo ganas más dinero?   1, 8

page 60 *(Section B)*

Answers

ex 1:
1 No **ahorro**, me gusta gastar mi dinero. **2** Gasto diez euros al mes en **revistas**. **3** **Gasto** mucho en caramelos a la semana. **4** Compro **ropa** y tebeos. **5** Ahorro mi **dinero** para comprar juegos de ordenador. **6** **Gasto** mi dinero en DVDs. **7** Gasto cinco euros a la semana en **regalos** para mis amigos. **8** Gasto mucho en ir al cine o **en** conciertos.

page 61 *(Section C)*

Answers

ex 1a:
1b (comprar una camiseta de mi equipo de fútbol);
2f (comprar CDs);
3e (ir al cine);
4c (salir con mis amigos);
5a (comprar zapatillas de deporte);
6d (comprar una bicicleta de montaña).

ex 1b:
1 Ahorro dinero para comprar CDs.
2 Ahorro dinero para comprar zapatillas de deporte. **3** Ahorro dinero para salir con mis amigos. **4** Ahorro dinero para ir al cine. **5** Ahorro dinero para comprar una bicicleta de montaña.
6 Ahorro dinero para comprar una camiseta de mi equipo de fútbol.

ex 2:
1b **2**d **3**c **4**e **5**a

page 62 *(Section D)*

Answers

ex 1b:
'tebeos' occurs twice

¡extra! the grey squares make up the word 'compro'

ex 1c:

Plural nouns	Verbs
helados recuerdos sellos tebeos bebidas fiestas meriendas tarjetas	gasto voy tomo

Word left over is 'dinero'.

Workbook B Unit 12

page 59 *(Section A)*

Answers

ex 1a:
lavando, ayudando, haciendo, preparando, vendiendo, sirviendo

ex 1b:
1 Gano doce euros trabajando en el jardín.
2 Gano siete euros con cincuenta lavando el coche.
3 Gano veinte euros sirviendo bebidas.
4 Gano quince euros preparando la comida.
5 Gano veinticinco euros vendiendo revistas.
6 Gano nueve euros ayudando en casa.
7 Gano diecisiete euros haciendo las compras.

page 60 *(Section B)*

Answers

ex 1:
1 No **ahorro** nada, me gusta gastar mi dinero. I don't save anything. I **like** spending my money. **2** Gasto diez euros al mes en **revistas**. I **spend** ten euros a month on magazines. **3** **Gasto** mucho en caramelos a la semana. I spend a lot on sweets per **week**.
4 Compro **ropa** y tebeos. I buy clothes and **comics**. **5** Ahorro mi **dinero** para comprar juegos de ordenador. I save up my money to buy **computer** games. **6** Me gusta **gastar** mi dinero en DVDs. I like spending my **money** on DVDs. **7** Gasto cinco euros a la semana en **regalos** para mis amigos. I spend five euros a week on gifts for my **friends**. **8** Gasto mucho en ir al cine o **en** conciertos. I spend a **lot** on going to the cinema or on concerts.

Page 61 (Section C)

Answers

ex 1:
1b 2d 3c 4a 5e

ex 2:
a abre/cartas (opens/letters)
b abre/latas (opens/tins)
c busca/palabras (searches for/words)
d lava/coches (washes/cars)
e lava/manos (washes/hands)
f lava/platos (washes/dishes)
g para/brisas (stops/breezes)
h para/caídas (stops/falls)
i para/choques (stops/shocks)

1 car wash, dishwasher
2 wordsearch
3 parachute
4 windscreen, bumper
5 letter-opener, tin-opener
6 car wash

page 62 (Section D)

Answers

ex 1b:
'tebeos' occurs twice

ex 1c:
the grey squares make up the word
'compro'

ex 1d:

Nouns, masculine plural	Nouns, feminine plural	Verbs (in their first person form)
helados recuerdos sellos tebeos	bebidas fiestas meriendas tarjetas	gasto voy tomo

Word left over is 'dinero'.

National Curriculum levels

Attainment Target 1: 💿 Listening and responding

Level 1	I can understand some simple classroom instructions, short phrases and questions.
Level 2	I can understand a lot of classroom instructions, phrases, questions and statements.
Level 3	I can understand short messages and conversations that use words I have met before and can pick out the main points, including some opinions.
Level 4	I can understand the main points and some details of longer messages and conversations.
Level 5	I can understand the main points and specific details of longer passages from several topics I have studied. I can recognise if people are talking about present and past **OR** future events, and if they are giving opinions.
Level 6	I can understand the main points and specific details of longer passages from several topics, even for topics I haven't studied before. I can recognise if people are talking about present, past **AND** future events, and if they are giving opinions.

Attainment Target 2: 💬 Speaking

Level 1	I can say single words or short phrases.
Level 2	I can say a lot of short phrases.
Level 3	I can take part in very short conversations (2 or 3 sentences) and give some opinions.
Level 4	I can take part in short conversations (3 or 4 sentences). I can change phrases and use words I know to say something new.
Level 5	I can take part in short conversations asking questions, giving information and opinions. I can talk about present and past **OR** future events.
Level 6	I can take part in conversations asking questions, giving information and opinions. I can talk about present, past **AND** future events. I can use words and phrases I have learnt in new topics.

Attainment Target 3: 📖 Reading and responding

Level 1	I can understand single words.
Level 2	I can understand short phrases in topics I have studied. I can use a glossary or book to find out the meaning of new words.
Level 3	I can understand short texts in topics I have studied and can pick out the main points, including some opinions. I can use a dictionary or glossary to look up new words.
Level 4	I can understand longer texts and pick out the main points and some details. I can work out the meaning of words without having to use a glossary or dictionary.
Level 5	I can understand different types of texts from various topics I have studied and recognise if they are about the present and past **OR** future events. I can pick out main points and specific details, including opinions.
Level 6	I can understand different types of text from various topics, even for topics I haven't studied before. I can recognise if they are about the present, past **AND** future events. I can pick out main points and specific details, including opinions.

Attainment Target 4: ✏️ Writing

Level 1	I can copy correctly or select single words I have met before.
Level 2	I can copy correctly or write short phrases I have met before and can write single words from memory.
Level 3	I can write 2 or 3 short sentences on topics I have studied from memory or with help. I can give opinions.
Level 4	I can write short paragraphs of 3 or 4 sentences from memory. I can change phrases and use words I know to say something new.
Level 5	I can write longer paragraphs asking questions, giving information and opinions. I can write about present and past **OR** future events.
Level 6	I can write several paragraphs and can use words and phrases I have learnt in new topics. I can write about present, past **AND** future events.

Acknowledgements

The authors and publisher would like to thank the following people, without whose support they could not have created *¡Así! 1*:

Helen Redford and Ian Blair for their detailed advice throughout the writing
Michael Janes for editing the materials.

Transcript recorded at Air Edel, London with
Azucena Durán, Javier Fernández-Peña, Javier Alcina,
Sergio Martínez-Burgos, Melisa Martínez, Jorge Peris Diaz-Noriega,
Lidia Sarabía, Gonzalo Perez and Cayetana Fernandez;
produced by Colette Thomson, Footstep Productions.

Front cover photograph: Terra Mitica Theme Park,

Benidorm, Spain by Enrique Algarra/Powerstock Zefa